Histories for the Subordinated

Histories for the Subordinated

DAVID HARDIMAN

Seagull
BOOKS
london new york calcutta

Seagull Books
Editorial Offices
1st Floor, Angel Court, 81 St Clements Street
Oxford OX4 1AW, UK

1 Washington Square Village, Apt 1U
New York, NY 100012, USA

26 Circus Avenue, Calcutta 700017, India

Seagull Books 2007

Published by arrangement with Permament Black, India

ISBN 1 9054 2 238 5

British Library Cataloguing-in-Publication Data
A Catalogue of this book is available from the British Library

Typeset by Guru Typograph Technology, Dwarka, New Delhi 110045
Printed and bound by Biddles Ltd, King's Lynn, UK

Contents

Acknowledgements

I compiled this selection of my writings at Rukun Advani's suggestion, and it has provided me with an opportunity to reflect on my work in an introduction, which I have written especially for this collection. As my editor at Oxford University Press, and then as my publisher at his own Permanent Black, Rukun has given me consistent encouragement and support over these years. My first thanks are to him, and also to Anuradha Roy, who has edited the volume.

I would like also to thank Anthony Low and Ranajit Guha, my early mentors at Sussex University and the Australian National University, as well as all of my colleagues in the Subaltern Studies group. During the 1980s I was based at the Centre for Social Studies in Surat, and I remember with appreciation the support and inspiration I received from its founder and original director, the late I.P. Desai. Two others who meant a lot to me and are also, sadly, no more were A.R. Desai, in Bombay, and Komal Kothari, in Jodhpur. Other colleagues and friends who I would like to single out for particular mention and thanks are Shahid Amin, David Arnold, Gautam Bhadra, Jan Breman, Dipesh Chakrabarty, Partha Chatterjee, Richard Grove, Ramachandra Guha, Rajkumar Hans, Douglas Haynes, Satyakam Joshi, Lancy Lobo, Kashyap Mankodi, Makrand Mehta, Shirin Mehta, Gyan Pandey, Mahesh Rangarajan, Mario Rutten, Sumit Sarkar, Tanika Sarkar, Ghanshyam Shah, Ajay Skaria, and Achyut Yagnik. A special word is due for Kanu Bhavsar, who has travelled extensively with me on almost all my research projects, providing companionship and help with great commitment.

I met Parita Mukta, my partner, while I was in Surat, and during those years we travelled extensively in India, enriching our lives together in so many ways. She encouraged me to re-examine many of my strongly held beliefs, in the process opening up whole new paths of emotional understanding. The photograph that I have used for the jacket of this book was taken in Okha, in Saurashtra, when I was accompanying Parita for her research on Mirabai. It is of Dosabhai Kalyanji, who had migrated from his village at a time of drought to stay with his daughter and son-in-law, also shown in the picture. The family looked after us with great generosity at a time of hardship. This was a period when we were taking part in many all-night *bhajan* gatherings, engaging closely with a strong and vibrant people's culture. This experience is reflected most eloquently in Parita's *Upholding the Common Life: The Community of Mirabai* (OUP, New Delhi 1994), but it left a strong mark on me also, as I hope is reflected in some of the essays in this collection.

I hope that this book will serve as a tribute for the poor and marginalized in their lives of adversity, and hence the title *Histories for the Subordinated.* I do not, of course, advance any claim to speak for them, this they do for themselves. In providing an example of how such histories may be written, I would like it to be of some value for people who have shown so much resilience in the face of continuing oppression.

Introduction

The essays in this collection represent a selection of my writings that have been published from 1984 onwards, with the exception of one, the first, which has not been published previously.[1] They have been chosen so as to provide an introduction to a variety of issues that I have researched and written on during these two decades. As the title to the collection indicates, they are rooted in my strong involvement in the *Subaltern Studies* project from the late 1970s onwards, but also reflect my ongoing engagement with other areas of Indian historical enquiry. My initial work in the 1970s was in the study of Indian nationalism, and I have continually engaged with this issue over the years, teaching it in university courses and—more recently—writing a book on Gandhi. Indeed, my 'subaltern' writing has frequently sought to grasp the ways in which subordinate groups have shaped the construction of 'the Indian nation' as we know it. I have also engaged with the debate on the transition to capitalism in India and changes to rural class structures. During the 1990s a significant part of my work was in the field of Indian environmental history, in which I looked in particular at popular uses of forests and water resources.

Much of my writing has focused on particular communities, for whom I have sought to construct a history. These have been 'a people without history', by which is meant those whose history has been marginalized in conventional historical scholarship. In fact, they have their own histories, but these are often retained in an oral rather than written form. Because of this, my work has involved considerable use of oral testimony, collected in extensive travels in western India. I am not however an 'oral historian' in the strict sense of the term, as my writing has not depended primarily on the analysis of oral testimonies that exist as a self-constructed archive of tapes. Indeed, until recently I never used a tape recorder, but took only notes as I listened. Rather, I see myself as a historian whose interpretation of the archive is rooted in interactions with contemporary representatives of the people I have written about. This, I believe, makes for a more engaged form of writing that, I hope, will speak to and mean something to these groups.

In focusing on specific communities, I have tried always to present a rounded, sympathetic, but—if necessary—critical understanding of their history. It does them no service, in my opinion, if we inflate their virtues and ignore their blemishes. This is often done with good intention as a means to combat a prevailing derogation of the group in question, but it creates an unrealistically positive identity and has to be seen as a form of myth-making rather than historical investigation. As a corollary, such writing tends to be wholly negative about those who dominate the community in question. Although this may be understandable, it does not in my opinion justify the creation of histories that ignore either the faults of the powerless or the possibility of virtue among the powerful.

My initial research and writing during the 1970s was on the nationalist movement amongst the peasants of central Gujarat. I became involved in what was to become the *Subaltern Studies* project in 1977, when Ranajit Guha asked Gyanendra Pandey and myself to meet up and discuss new approaches to the study of Indian nationalism.[2] The group expanded over the next two years to include David Arnold, Shahid Amin, and Partha Chatterjee. In a series of intense and frequent discussions in Sussex, London, and Oxford, we thrashed out our core themes. We argued that in colonial India there were two interrelated but separate domains of politics—the elite and the subaltern. Whereas the elite domain was characterized by its engagement with the structures of power established by the colonial state in terms that were understood by colonial administrators as 'political', radically different forms of encounter marked the subaltern domain. We sought to analyse and define this latter domain of power. We saw within it, for example, a constant interplay between subordination and resistance, as well as solidarities rooted in notions of community. It was generally suffused with a religiosity that forged a powerful commonality, despite the self-alienation that religious belief (so we then argued) entailed. In maintaining that the subaltern sphere was also political—though structured very differently—we distanced ourselves from the prevailing opinion that most popular action in India had been pre-political in its form.[3] We took issue with Marxian historians whose understanding of popular consciousness was, we held, both highly economistic and rooted in a teleology of evolutionary stages. We held that the nationalist movement in its mature Gandhian phase had a strong subaltern dimension that took it often in directions that were far more radical than intended by its predominantly elite leadership. The history of Indian nationalism was thus one of subaltern militancy being held on a constant leash. In revealing the extent of subaltern involvement, we also took issue with a school of historians based in Cambridge who sought to depict Indian nationalism as the venture of a self-interested elite who had manipulated the masses for self-seeking ends.

My book *Peasant Nationalists of Gujarat: Kheda District 1917–1934* was published in 1981—just before the first volume of *Subaltern Studies*—and bore the imprint of this new approach. In it I studied a relatively prosperous community—the Patidars of Gujarat—who had played a leading role in the Gandhian phase of the struggle after 1917. I argued that although they were a dominant caste that exploited the poor and landless peasantry, often very ruthlessly, their politics differed structurally from that of the local elite. Whereas the elite either collaborated with colonial rule or sought through the politics of constitutional lobbying to gain greater power for themselves in local government bodies that had been granted on a limited scale by the British, the mass of the Patidars sought to change local power relationships more radically through the politics of protest—seen most typically in no-tax campaigns. These were characterized by a caste-based solidarity. By championing their protests, Gandhi and the Congress won the allegiance of this peasantry. I sought to show how, time and time again, the Patidars had participated in the movement on their own terms, making it a vehicle for their political self-assertion against local representatives of the colonial bureaucracy. I argued that there was no obvious correlation between their short-term economic grievances and demands, and their participation in the larger movement. As there was relatively little religious content to their involvement, I discounted this as a major mobilizing force and argued that this was a community—rather than class in the strict sense of the term—whose participation was informed by a high degree of political self-consciousness, albeit that of a rurally dominant group.

Chapter 4 of the present book, 'The Quit India Movement in Gujarat', stems essentially from this period of my research and writing, though due to the vagaries of publishing it did not appear in print until 1988. It was written as a contribution to a collection of essays, edited by Gyanendra Pandey, on the Quit India Movement of 1942 in different regions of India. My essay seeks to provide an overview of this protest in its various dimensions in Gujarat. Much of it concerns the middle-class and higher-caste nationalists of the cities—such as the Brahmans, Baniyas, and Brahmo-Kshatriyas of the walled city locality of Ahmedabad, and the Patidars residents of Raopura in Baroda—and the dominant-caste Patidar and Anavil Brahmans of the rural areas of mainland Gujarat, all of whom provided the backbone of this strongly organized and powerful movement. It reveals that lower-class participation was at best patchy—limited to the non-Muslim working class for a limited time in the cities and, in rural areas, to some adivasis of South Gujarat and the Panchmahals. Most notably, the Muslim millworkers of Ahmedabad, whose loyalties lay with Jinnah's Muslim League, were largely indifferent to the movement, as were the lower-caste Baraiyas of central Gujarat, who saw it as a protest that was primarily in the interests of their oppressors, the Patidars. In all, the movement was not, I conclude, characterised by much social radicalism.

The essay demonstrates how nationalist leaders built coalitions of disparate groups and interests under their overall hegemony. In 1942, unlike in 1920–2 and 1930–1, Gandhi and his more fervent followers were not at the forefront, and this led to a different quality to this particular movement. In contrast to earlier nationalist protests in the province, 1942 was notable for its considerable violence, with riotous demonstrations, the bombing of government and other property, and raids on police stations by nationalistic dacoits. Although the president of the Gujarat Provincial Congress Committee, Vallabhbhai Patel, had advocated peaceful protest in speeches in the days leading up to the launch of the movement, evidence is provided to suggest that he secretly encouraged acts of sabotage and other violent attempts to disrupt the British war effort. In this he gave an opening for many young left-leaning nationalists to come to the fore once he and the other top leaders had been jailed. It was they above all who had the organization, discipline and will to carry through such a programme. Some of the Gandhian leaders, such as Morarji Desai, were critical of Patel in this respect, as they feared that this would bring a lurch to the left in the politics of Gujarat. As it was, the pro-capitalist wing of the Gujarat Congress remained firmly in control once the movement had ended, and in fact they gained most from its legacy.

With the benefit of hindsight, this may lead us to ask to what extent Patel—the 'iron man' of Gujarat at that time—fostered a climate of violence that has bred a monster in present times, for these same areas of Gujarat have recently witnessed some most ugly pogroms of Muslims and Christian minorities in the name of 'popular outrage'. Patel is, moreover, celebrated today by the Hindu right as a no-nonsense politician who had little time for the supposedly woolly idealism of Gandhi's pacifism and nonviolence. The evidence does not, in my view, support such an argument. Gujarat had witnessed considerable turbulence and violence by the people of Ahmedabad and central Gujarat during the Rowlatt Satyagraha of 1919, at a time when Gandhi rather than Patel was the dominant figure in local nationalist politics. There was therefore nothing particularly novel about violence *per se*, and unlike in 1919 the violence of 1942 was directed and kept under strict control. The attacks were largely on the police or against property. There were not at that time any attacks on Muslims, even though they on the whole refused to support the movement. The violence, in other words, lacked the vicious quality seen in the ruthless and murderous scapegoating of entire minority communities in Gujarat in recent years.

After concentrating during the 1970s on mainstream nationalism in Gujarat, I turned my attention in the early 1980s to a more unambiguously 'subaltern' phenomenon, a highly 'religious' movement of 1922–3, when large numbers of adivasis in southern Gujarat reformed their whole way of life under the influence of a goddess—or Devi—called Salabai. Chapter 2 of the present book, 'Adivasi Assertion in South Gujarat: The Devi Movement of 1922–3' was my initial essay on the topic—later written up in full as a book of 1987 called *The Coming of the Devi: Adivasi Assertion in Western India*. It was an important essay for me as the process of writing involved an extremely fruitful dialogue with others in the Subaltern Studies group that helped me clarify and enrich the analysis of my material. It was published as a contribution to *Subaltern Studies III*—the volume that, more than any other, brought the project to an international audience, with recognition that this was a major intellectual departure.[4]

The essay focuses on the issue of how we should understand and interpret this remarkable movement. Many nationalist leaders took it as evidence of the 'backwardness' and lack of education of adivasis, though they saw it also as an opportunity to 'uplift' them by encouraging them to follow a more Gandhian way of life. As the movement had involved the renunciation of liquor, meat and fish, and had encouraged regular daily washing of the body, it was possible to turn the movement in such a direction. I argued that it had, however, other dimensions; most notably that of resistance to a particularly oppressive local elite—Parsi liquor dealers and landlords. Besides encouraging the giving up of the liquor that such people supplied on highly exploitative terms, the movement also involved a labour boycott of Parsis. Nationalist leaders were far less comfortable with this aspect of the movement, and they encouraged adivasis to go back to work for the Parsis. They thus sought to emphasize the moralistic aspects of it, while trying to smother the social conflict that it had also generated.

I argued that various interpretations of such movements put forward hitherto by social scientists and historians were inadequate. It was not, for example, a messianic movement, as there were no messianic figures associated with it. The most popular sociological theory for such phenomena was that of 'Sanskritization'. This sought to explain mobility within the Indian caste system by arguing that upwardly mobile fractions of particular castes often reformed their way of life to accord with notions of orthodox Hindu 'purity'. In doing so, they made a claim for higher status without challenging the hierarchical social system as such. I argued that in practice such claims were normally resisted by the high castes, so that such movements often led to sharp social conflict. This was, in other words, a form of self-assertion that had the potential to fracture local caste hierarchies, for, when the high castes were forced to concede such demands, their control could no longer rest on the policing of strict standards of purity and pollution. In the case of the Devi Movement, adivasis did not claim any caste status; rather, they demanded that they be accorded a respected position in society on their own terms. I argued, furthermore, that such theories lacked a historical dimension, and I sought to situate such movements at a very particular historical juncture—that of the subjugation and exploitation of certain subaltern communities under colonial rule and a challenge to older structures of power by an emerging popular-nationalist leadership. One important implication of my argument, so far as I was concerned, was that such 'religiosity' did not represent a form of self-alienation. Nor was it helpful to see it as a form of 'false consciousness'. It was, I believed, informed by a clear understanding of social, political, and moral interests, and it brought a definite improvement in the lives of these particular adivasis.

The first chapter here, on Motilal Tejawat's movement amongst the Bhils of northern Gujarat and southern Rajasthan, develops the theme of adivasi assertion and nationalist reaction in a very different social context—one dominated by Rajput landlords who were feudatories of the great Rajput maharajas of that region. The Bhils—in marked contrast to the other adivasi communities found in southern Gujarat—had a long history of violent insurrection against their overlords as well as blood feuds amongst themselves. When they rebelled in 1921 under the leadership of Motilal Tejawat, a sympathetic local Baniya, they managed to both unite amongst themselves and to carry on their struggle against the landlords in a remarkably non-violent manner. Motilal Tejawat was an admirer of Gandhi, and he believed that his movement was a part of the Non-Cooperation Movement being waged at that time by Gandhi. He was soon disabused of this by Gandhi, who on the one hand refused to support a struggle against other Indians—namely landlords and maharajas—and on the other condemned the Bhils for carrying bows and arrows and other weapons. When the British eventually sent troops to crush the movement in a murderous manner in early 1922, the Congress leadership remained largely silent. The movement was as a result marginalized in nationalist historiography. Whereas the massacre at Amritsar in 1919 became a major event in this history, this other massacre in a remote hill tract was forgotten.

This essay on the Tejawat-led movement was written originally in response to a campaign initiated in 1997 by some local politicians to remember these adivasi 'freedom fighters'. They had taken up the issue after hearing harrowing oral accounts by old Bhils of the carnage inflicted in 1922. I had not hitherto heard of this massacre—together, the British and the nationalists had succeeded only too well in covering it up—and I had never carried out on-the-spot investigations of the movement. Some years before, I had read an account of the event in the National Archives in Delhi but had failed to appreciate the significance of something that was made light of in this colonial source. I made good this lack by travelling to the area in late 1997 to interview the old Bhils myself. I wrote the essay initially in early 1998, though I did not publish it at the time as I wanted to carry out more research on the topic. This I did at a later date, but then decided to give a very different emphasis to my research on the Bhils of this region as a result of my discovery of extensive archival records by Christian missionaries who were carrying out medical and educational work amongst them at that time. I have therefore added some extra material and written a postscript to the essay which updates the account of recent initiatives to commemorate the massacre. I decided to start the present volume with this essay as the theme of forgetting and remembering is central to the study of subaltern history.

Chapter 5 of the present book, on the history of drink and drinking in South Gujarat, flowed from my work on the Devi Movement. With liquor so central to this movement, it became necessary to carry out a careful investigation of this history. I found here a little recorded but harrowing tale of a growing commercialization of everyday life that was forced on the poor by a callous and insensitive colonial state. Laws and controls were implemented that were designed to make liquor and toddy into purely marketed commodities that paid high rates of tax. In the process, the wide-scale, popular traditions of distillation of country liquor and tapping of toddy trees were made into crimes. The profoundly impoverishing implications of this measure for large numbers of peasants had parallels with colonial initiatives that are studied in other chapters in this collection, such as the laws relating to credit and debt, forests and water. Disturbingly, many amongst the Indian elites supported such measures, either through self-interest and callousness, or for moralistic reasons—as was the case with liquor. The poor found only a few champions, notably some paternalistic colonial officials as well as certain nationalists.

This and the other essays on the social and economic effects of colonial policies examine a rich tapestry of classes, professions, castes, and communities—from colonial officials, to Indian princes, landlords, merchants, usurers, liquor dealers, forest contractors, middle-class nationalists, rich peasants, adivasis, the poor and the landless. Their fortunes can be seen to both intertwine and conflict in highly complex ways, with fractions within these groups often diverging. For example, in the case of the liquor laws, ruthlessly Social Darwinist colonial modernizers came into sharp dispute with neo-conservative paternalistic officials. Similar tendencies were seen in the debate on the laws on moneylending and forest reservation. Likewise, many faultlines are exposed amongst the peasantry, with some benefiting from and supporting colonial initiatives, others opposing them. All of this, I believe, provides a counter to a frequently-heard criticism of *Subaltern Studies*, namely that in focusing on conflict between supposedly undifferentiated elites and subalterns it ignores the complex and multifaceted intertwining of social and productive layers that are so strong a feature of Indian society.[5]

Ranajit Guha has argued in an essay in *Subaltern Studies VI* that subordination involves a constant interplay between collaboration and resistance. In general, the subaltern are compelled through a wide variety of coercive and cultural mechanisms to accept their subordinate position; only occasionally and in exceptional circumstances do they resist in an outright manner. In cases in which persuasion can be seen to predominate, the elites can be considered to have maintained an ideological 'hegemony'.[6] In my work on the Devi Movement, I found that in the case of Parsi liquor dealers, coercion tended to outweigh persuasion, and that their hegemony was in consequence weak.

This was in striking contrast to the control exercised over adivasis by Baniya usurers. Though highly exploitative, they were able to dominate the adivasis with hardly any coercion, with their power being unchallenged, even during the most radical phase of the movement. This phenomenon was repeated throughout western India—Baniya usurers were generally considered respectable people with a right to take a certain amount of produce from the peasantry in return for annual advances of cash and goods in kind. In only a few isolated cases were there any revolts against them during the colonial period. The question that then posed itself to me was how they had maintained their sway in this respect so extensively over time.

This led me on to my next major project, which was to write a history of Baniya usury in western India from medieval to postcolonial times. Two of the chapters in this collection relate to that project. The findings as a whole appeared as a monograph of 1996 titled *Feeding the Baniya: Peasants and Usurers in Western India.* The chapter in the present collection, 'Usury, Dearth and Famine in Western India', argues that usurers who operated in alliance with succeeding rulers in ever-evolving ways managed to appropriate the peasant's surplus in a particularly adroit manner. Whereas in Islamic western Asia and in Europe the profession of moneylending was stigmatized, in India it was considered a most respectable occupation. I examine the practices and beliefs surrounding an institution that had strong economic, political, moral, and sacred underpinnings. I then go on to examine how the system operated during famines, when the credit supplied by usurers tended to dry up. This created tension, and in some cases revolt, the pattern of which is observed as a means to understand the system in general.

Chapter 3, 'Community, Patriarchy, Honour: Raghu Bhangare's Revolt,' also arose out of this project, as my research in the archives in Bombay revealed a long and rather exceptional history of social banditry against Baniya usurers within the Mahadev Koli community of the ghat region to the north-east of Bombay city. This drew me into a study of this community and its traditions and led to the writing of this essay in the early 1990s. My starting point was a number of popular legends of the Mahadev Kolis that valorized such outlaws. These, it appears, strengthened their community identity. It defined them as a group with interests in common against outsiders, whether these were usurers, policemen, or white colonial officials—the *gora* sahibs. Also, it established their ideals for honourable behaviour within the community, setting out the ways in which family patriarchs, mothers, and their sons were expected to behave. It helped to reveal community solidarity and its limits. There was here a whole politics of honour and shame, involving feuds and vendettas, both within and outside the community. The essay is thus a study of feudal–patriarchal politics in which the male subaltern often followed the violent ways of his superiors, through, for example, looting, enforced tax demands, punishment, mutilations, and murder. It could involve sexual aggression and rape, though this was a matter of controversy within the community, being generally considered immoral.

In examining such issues I was sensitive to the charge that Subaltern Studies had largely ignored issues of gender. Gayatri Chakravorty Spivak had, notably, argued in what was otherwise a largely sympathetic review of the project published in *Subaltern Studies IV*, that the people and communities who were the subject of the project were implicitly male and that women with their particular experiences were silenced. She pointed out that this was the case with my own study of the Patidar community of Gujarat.[7] This point was well taken; I had failed to bring out the history of the engagement of Patidar women in the movement, and it was one that had deserved attention.[8] Alive to this issue when I examined the history and legend of Raghu Bhangare, I maintain in my essay that the popular memory of his escapades celebrates a violence that brought profound suffering for the women of the community, who—left isolated at such times—became the target for reprisals by the police and other enemies of their erstwhile male 'protectors'. They faced starvation, imprisonment, rape, and even death in 'honour' reprisals. There can be no unproblematic celebration of a subaltern politics of honour when we view the matter from such a perspective.

I also argue in this essay that the period from around 1830 to 1850 saw a transition from an older politics in which Mahadev Koli chiefs aligned themselves with different factions of the ruling class, often coming into mutual conflict, to a politics in which the community as a whole generally acted in solidarity against outsiders—in particular the Baniya usurers who, supported by the colonial state, were usurping their power. The noted outlaw Raghu Bhangare was the single most important figure associated with this change, and—significantly—he is the only nineteenth-century hero who is remembered to this day in the region. Such banditry aimed against usurers continued till well after Indian independence, but it has largely died away today.

The politics of patriarchal honour and shame, involving simmering feuds and bloodthirsty attacks on those singled out as enemies, was in twentieth-century India replaced increasingly by other forms of resistance, such as satyagraha—a non-violent and largely legal form of protest involving disobedience of selected laws. Both the Motilal Tejawat and Devi movements saw a transition to this style of politics. There was also the terrorist campaign, involving sabotage and assassination, which was seen to some extent in the Quit India Movement. In such resistance, older notions of patriarchal honour were replaced with new notions of community or national honour that were gendered in different ways. Gandhi, for example, celebrated the 'feminine' quality of satyagraha, and sought to build a force of androgynous moral crusaders in ways that raised as many questions about gender roles as it resolved.[9]

My research and writing on adivasis led me next into the field of environmental history. Many adivasis in western India lived in areas that were designated during the colonial period as reserved and protected forests, and along with large numbers of forest dwellers in other parts of India they found themselves dispossessed of their chief resource base. This caused great suffering and led in some cases to revolt. Ramachandra Guha took up this important but largely ignored history in a central way in the 1980s in the context of the Uttaranchal region of the Himalaya. One of his first essays on this topic was published in *Subaltern Studies IV* in 1985, and an important book of 1987 soon followed.[10] At the same time, the resurgence of the environmental movement in India created a new mythology about the harmonious and eco-friendly lifestyle of original forest-dwellers that had been shattered by colonial and postcolonial forest policies. In 1989 I examined this issue in the context of one forest region of western India, the Dangs. My conclusion, published five years later, was that such arguments were informed by a modern environmentalist consciousness alien to forest-dwellers of pre-colonial and colonial times. There was, for example, no awareness that such vast tracts of deep forest could be destroyed by human agency. Access to forest resources had, moreover, always been contested, with unequal relationships of power determining who benefited most. My essay therefore focussed on changes in structures of power within the forests, which saw shifts over time that were of advantage to certain groups but of great disadvantage to others.[11]

These various studies led me to demarcate a number of *domains of power* that were realms of both *collaboration/hegemony* as well as of *resistance.* Writing in 1992, I listed the most important ones for the Indian peasantry of the period 1858–1914 as the domains of (1) European planters, (2) indigenous landlords, (3) usurers, (4) the colonial land-tax bureaucracy, and (5) colonial forest officials. There were others, such as those that lay between liquor dealers and peasants.[12] These domains could each be analysed individually. Most had long histories that, in some cases, preceded colonial rule and in others stretched beyond it into postcolonial times. In my own research and writing I focussed, for example, on the relationship between the Patidars of Gujarat and the land-tax bureaucracy, the adivasis of southern Gujarat and liquor dealers and forest officials, the Bhils of the Rajasthan–Gujarat border region and indigenous landlords, and the peasants of western India in general against usurers. In each case, I examined how each relationship evolved over time, involving a constant interplay between collaboration/hegemony and resistance. In practice, several domains might be braided together, which made for an often complex mix. I found, however, that it was valuable for heuristic purposes to demarcate domains, as each had its own unique hegemonic elements and modes of resistance that were in a state of constant flux.

Chapter 9 herein, 'Farming in the Forest: The Dangs 1830–1992', flowed from a movement that was launched in 1990 when some adivasis decided to occupy areas of reserved forest that they claimed had been taken from them by the colonial forest department in the nineteenth century. They saw themselves as re-establishing their old rights to farm in the forest. In doing so, they broke the forest laws. The essay was written after I had studied this movement on a research trip to the Dangs in 1992. In it, I deploy some of the material that I had used in the *Subaltern Studies VIII* essay in a summarized form, but carry the analysis through beyond the 1940s to 1992 in the light of the recent movement. In it I seek to show that postcolonial forest policy was not only a continuation of colonial forest policy, but that it was deployed in often more appropriative and exploitative ways. Since Indian independence in 1947 the area that the local people were forbidden to farm had regularly expanded, while they were provided with no alternative forms of employment. The relationship between the people of the Dangs and the Forest Department continued to be one that was characterized by antagonism rather than co-operation. These pressures led to the movement of 1990.

A postscript is required to this essay. Since it was published in 1996, the Dangs have become well known both nationally and internationally as a result of a wave of attacks on Christians in the area. During the 1980s and 1990s evangelical Christian missionaries, originating in most cases from Tamilnadu, managed to convert around a tenth of the population of the Dangs to Christianity (representing a total of between 15,000 and 20,000 converts). This was made an issue by the Hindu right, which was seeking to extend its power into adivasi areas that had been controlled hitherto by Congress Party politicians. Fundamentalist sadhus were encouraged to work in the Dangs to win its inhabitants over to that homogenized form of belief and worship that Romila Thapar has characterised as 'syndicated Hinduism'.[13] As conversion to Christianity often caused disruption within families and villages—for the converts refused to participate in community rituals and social ceremonies—the Hindu right was able to tap a source of discontent. Also, some ambitious young Dangis who were excluded from leadership within the Congress Party saw this as providing a means to win popularity and possible votes. They therefore joined the Bharatiya Janata Party (BJP) and, with the connivance of fundamentalist sadhus, launched a series of attacks on Christians from late 1998 onwards. In this way, older grievances revolving around the loss of resources, minimal developmental investment, and a corresponding lack of employment were submerged in a strongly manipulated sense of outrage against supposedly 'anti-national' missionaries who were depicted as agents of foreign powers. Christians were beaten up, churches were burnt down, and many were rounded up and taken in buses and trucks to a Hindu pilgrimage place on the border of the Dangs to be 'reconverted' to Hinduism through ritual purification (shuddhi).[14] A new and very ominous politics has thus emerged, which I continue to monitor and intend to engage with in my writing in future.

My engagement with environmental history from 1989 onwards led to a paper at a conference on 'South Asia's Changing Environment' at Bellagio in Italy in 1992. Chapter 7, here, 'Small-Dam Systems of the Sahyadris', was the outcome. It was published in 1995 in a selection of papers from this conference. In this I shift my focus from forests to water resources, examining the history of an extensive system of small-scale irrigation works in the valleys of the Sahyadri mountain range of western India. This was an area with which I was familiar from my research on the Devi Movement, and while travelling in these mountains I had noticed these systems and kept them in mind as a possible future topic of research. The controversy over large dams that was raging at that time in the context of the powerful movement against the Narmada Dam provided the incentive for me to focus on this history.

Much of the historical writing on irrigation systems had stressed their organisation from top down—by rulers or by local gentry. Here, I argue that although this was no doubt important, such systems often relied on much locally organized work and skill, as well as initiative. They arose and were operated, in other words, through co-operation between rulers and peasants. The small-dam systems of the Sahyadris had been developed many centuries before colonial rule and they continued to thrive until the British conquest of this region in the early nineteenth century. Thereafter they declined, so that what is seen today is merely a pale remnant of what was once an extensive system. I examine the reasons why colonial rule proved to be so detrimental to such a form of irrigation.

Whereas small-dam systems were found mainly in a comparatively limited number of suitable piedmont areas, wells had historically provided by far the most important form of irrigation for peasants in India. This situation changed during the colonial period, as canal systems were developed in many riverain areas. In Gujarat, on the other hand, wells continued to prevail throughout the nineteenth and twentieth centuries. Today, however, such irrigation is in a state of crisis due to the insatiable demand for water in 'green revolution' agriculture and advances in boring and pumping technology that enable deeper and deeper supplies of subsoil water to be tapped. Many wells have as a result gone dry, and only those farmers who have the resources to drill the deepest wells are able to maintain a supply, which they then sell to other peasants for profit. This is widely seen as a major environmental problem, and has formed the subject of much discussion. In my essay 'Well Irrigation in Gujarat: Systems of Use, Hierarchies of Control,' published here as Chapter 8, I look at some of the arguments advanced about the causes of this state of affairs, and, based on my reading of the irrigation history of Gujarat, give my own opinions on the long-term causes of this crisis. In this, I was able to benefit from research that I had carried out in 1976 on village society and economy in central Gujarat that I had not hitherto made use of in my writing. This allowed me to argue that the supposedly 'free' market in water in Gujarat is in fact regulated very strongly by considerations of caste and community, with the dominant caste peasants, who tend to own the more productive wells, favouring members of their own caste first and foremost.[15] Although there is a general crisis of water availability, it is not one that affects well-off farmers who can afford to bore deep tubewells, along with fellow members of their caste, but only those of poor subordinate castes whose wells have gone dry and who have to depend on the largesse of well owners to obtain water for agriculture. As in the past, a dominant group exerts power in rural society, though the structure of domination has changed significantly. Whereas formerly an elite ruled through a combination of brute force and cultural hegemony, the new and much broader class of prosperous farmers maintains its power through a mix of financial power and dominant caste solidarity.

My practice as a historian of the subordinated has been to work at two levels; first, as a person concerned with the many injustices suffered by the exploited and oppressed sections of society in the here and now; second, as a historian who endeavours to examine evidence from the past in as scrupulous a manner as possible. My aim has been to establish a sympathetic rapport with subalterns in their lives and struggles—both past and present. From this has emerged, I hope, a history that brings out some of the complexities, contradictions, triumphs as well as tragedies of the past.

In this I have sought to be as open as I can to new ways of understanding and presenting my research. In *Subaltern Studies*, I have been fortunate to work with a group of scholars who have sought constantly to ask new questions and open themselves to new answers, even when it means abandoning old orthodoxies and positions. This method was incorporated within the project from the start, in that it set out a series of hypotheses that were to be tested through a series of concrete historical studies. It was always open to the possibility—indeed likelihood—that the theories would have to be modified and even in some cases abandoned if the exercise revealed that need. Because of this the project has shifted and changed considerably over time, in a way that can be unsettling for critics who like to set out a supposed subalternist position and then either commend or contest it. The process has been for me—I must admit—often challenging and unsettling, and I have not always agreed with the directions that some members of the group have taken. In this section of the Introduction I shall examine what has often been described as the 'postructuralist' or 'linguistic' turn in *Subaltern Studies* and say something about my feelings on this contentious matter.[16]

In its early years, *Subaltern Studies* had, following Marx and Gramsci, been informed by a certain optimism about the historical role of the subaltern, who was seen as the force for a socialist future. The peasants of Vietnam had recently defeated the armed might of the USA, and even India had its peasant revolutionaries in the Naxalites. The most influential challenge to this worldview, so far as the left was concerned, came from Michel Foucault. He rejected the socialist faith that the global rule of the bourgeoisie would unleash forces that would inaugurate a new socialist order, arguing that bourgeois modernity had created a disciplinary structure of power that had been so internalized by the people that they were no longer were able to resist it in any fundamental ways. Residing at the very heart of the institutions of bourgeois governance, this was a more insidious form of subjugation than the more obviously coercive and arbitrary form of power associated with the previous feudal order. The belief of socialist intellectuals that the masses would in time become aware of their true class interests and overthrow the bourgeoisie through an act of revolutionary violence was not only misguided but potentially disastrous for all those who might be guided by it. In the changing climate of the 1980s—as states that claimed allegiance to Marxism succumbed to the forces of global capitalism—Foucault's pessimism seemed for increasing numbers on the left to be more in touch with the realities of the time.

The first substantial critique of *Subaltern Studies* from such a perspective appeared in 1985 in its own pages. Writing in Volume 4, Gayatri Spivak expressed her reservations about a notion of 'subaltern consciousness' found in *Subaltern Studies* that assumed that a popular collective—or class—consciousness was in itself an agent of radical change. Following Barthes and Foucault, she criticized this as a form of humanism that supposed the gendered individual to be master of his own destiny.[17] Rosalind O'Hanlon made a similar point in 1988.[18] The implication was that *Subaltern Studies* had been falsely optimistic about the radical potential of popular action. In another article produced around this time, Spivak raised the question as to what extent, if any, the outside observer can represent the subaltern. Given the chasm that exists between those who inhabit a space of privilege and those who do not, any representation runs the risk of being an exercise in bad faith. Too often, the outsider inflicts her or his beliefs on the subaltern, whether these are of a conservative, nationalist, Marxian, socialist, feminist, environmentalist, or any other bent. In such a situation, she felt, 'the subaltern cannot speak'.[19]

Another respect in which *Subaltern Studies* was open to criticism lay in its use of structuralist analysis, as in Ranajit Guha's investigation of the 'elementary aspects of peasant insurgency' or Partha Chatterjee's examination of the structure of subaltern community consciousness.[20] Structuralism was coming under increasing attack at that time—most notably by Jacques Derrida in *Of Grammatology*, published originally in French in 1967. Gayatri Spivak had brought this work to the notice of the English-reading public in her translation of 1976, for which she had provided a long and erudite introduction.[21] Using his method of linguistic 'deconstruction', Derrida subjected a number of post-Enlightenment thinkers to a rigorous examination of the way they deployed language to create particular effects that they claimed—misguidedly—to be statements of the 'truth'. In seeking to reduce all human experience to certain structural 'essentials', he found them guilty of a logocentrism that was both ethnocentric and metaphysical.[22] Even Claude Lévi-Strauss, a structural anthropologist who saw himself as being in strong sympathy with his subject—the native inhabitants of the Brazilian rain forests—and who claimed to be profoundly anti-ethnocentric in his politics, in fact thought and wrote in deeply ethnocentric ways.[23] All such exercises had, by their nature, to ignore or marginalize the many examples that defied their structures. Derrida's task, as he saw it, was to reveal the silences by deconstructing the texts. This brought out what he called the 'pluri-dimensional' nature of human thought and action.[24]

Derrida claimed that Lévi-Strauss, following in the tradition of Rousseau, constructed a critique of a debased 'Self' by romanticizing a remote 'Other'.

> Non-European people were not only studied as the index to a hidden good Nature, as a native soil recovered, of a "zero degree" with reference to which one could outline the structure, the growth, and above all the degradation of our society and our culture. As always, this archaeology is also a teleology and an eschatology; the dream of a full and immediate presence closing history, the transparence and indivision of a parousia, the suppression of contradiction and difference. The anthropologist's mission, as Rousseau would have assigned it, is to work toward such an end.[25]

Such exercises could only work by essentializing both 'Self' and 'Other'. In fact, there is a process of constant oscillation between such poles—what Derrida labels as '*differance*' (to distinguish it from 'difference').

At the Subaltern Studies conference that was held in Calcutta in 1986, Gayatri Spivak—who was now becoming an important participant in the project—argued very strongly that we needed to devote much more attention to the ways in which subalterns have been understood by elites in their texts. She argued that although a start had been made in this latter respect, much greater theoretical sophistication was required. In particular, she believed that the deconstructive method deployed by Derrida would be particularly pertinent. She provided an example of this in her own paper at this conference which analysed Mahasweta Devi's Bengali short story 'Stanadayini' from a variety of ideological positions.[26] For some in the audience, this appeared to valorize a relativistic approach to social issues that served to depoliticize rather than radicalize.[27]

At that time, I had many misgivings on these matters. I felt that the focus on textual analysis from a poststructuralist perspective would lead to a neglect of the study of the subaltern, as well as political quiescence.[28] The debate forced me, nevertheless, to read poststructuralist writings and develop my views in relationship to them. As I saw it, a central concern of my work was the one that Dipesh Chakrabarty had identified as a crucial element in the Subaltern Studies project, namely 'to understand the consciousness that informed and still informs political actions taken by the subaltern classes on their own, independent of any elite initiative.'[29] If, I felt, we took to heart Gayatri Spivak's argument that our efforts to understand subaltern consciousness would be blocked always by our own beliefs and agendas, then such an exercise was deeply flawed. We would never be able to hear 'the voice of the subaltern' in any meaningful way.

I refused to accept this. As I saw it, the argument was based in part on a truism that the complexities of the consciousness of any person are so great that our understanding can never be entirely full and complete. At best, we can reach only for an approximate and perhaps hypothetical understanding. However, we spend our lives doing this, and it is hard to see how we can live otherwise. More substantially, I felt that the argument posed a radical binary divide between the authorial 'Self' and the subaltern 'Other'. Dipesh Chakrabarty's statement, quoted above, tends in this direction, for it emphasizes a notion that subaltern consciousness is informed through *independent* political action. Obviously, if there are two wholly autonomous spheres of life, there will indeed be little meaningful communication, and misunderstanding will inevitably outweigh even an approximation of understanding. It would be better, rather, to follow Derrida and reject such extreme dichotomies. We needed to emphasize the fact that Subaltern Studies focuses on the *relationship* between elite and subaltern as a historical process. On the one hand the fact of subordination generates particular forms of consciousness and political action. On the other, the bonds between the dominant and the subordinate are always strong, and often mirror each other. Though to a certain extent alien to each other, they also have much in common. Boundaries are by no means clear-cut, they are always shifting. Their relationship is being ever modified through an ongoing process of mutual dialogue. Indeed, speaking across the divide and hearing/interpreting what is said is not just possible: it is, I would argue, constitutive of this relationship for both parties.

As it is, Gayatri Spivak has provided a more nuanced approach to this issue in her subsequent book, *A Critique of Postcolonial Reason*. Here she accepts that the intellectual with a moral commitment to the poor and oppressed may communicate across this supposed divide, so long as she or he steers clear of all 'missionary claims'—that is, avoids any assertion that the subaltern is endorsing any preconceived ideological position.[30] What is required above all is moral sympathy and empathy. I would endorse this wholeheartedly, as my whole method has always revolved around developing a rapport with present-day descendents of the subjects of my histories, as I said earlier in this Introduction.

Poststructuralists commonly hold that identities are created in language and have no existence outside discourse. Marxists are criticized for seeing class identities as objective realities that people become conscious of through their experience of everyday life, rather than the linguistic constructs that they in fact are.[31] Against this, Marc Steinberg has pointed out how many poststructuralists go to the opposite extreme, reifying language as the only reality. He argues that E.P. Thompson and his followers were well aware of the power of language in history, and they sought to bring out the connection between the discursive and the material.[32] By so doing, they avoided making a fetish of the text. Thompson had always stressed that class is above all a historical process:

> people find themselves in a society structured in determined ways (crucially, but not exclusively, in productive relations), they experience exploitation (or the need to maintain power over those whom they exploit), they identify points of antagonistic interest, they commence to struggle around these issues and in the process of struggling they discover themselves as classes, they come to know this discovery as class-consciousness.[33]

From such a perspective, classes and other groups with a sense of self-identity could never be seen as static or 'natural' collectivities that existed in an unchanging state over time. They were, rather, fluid groups that emerged and dissolved through interaction and struggle. *Subaltern Studies* had in a similar manner been aware from the start of the constructed nature of identities. Applied to my own writing, my examination of the category of 'tribal' or 'adivasi' in *The Coming of the Devi* adopted such an approach. I sought, in effect, to deconstruct terms that were generally applied in a very positivistic and ahistorical way and situate their use within a clear historical context.[34] In this, neither class nor language was reified.

Some of the other points made in this debate were well taken. Our work had certainly been informed by a teleology that could in some cases give it an optimism that was hardly warranted. No historical process is 'inevitable', and the struggles of the subordinated will not necessarily give birth to a more democratic society. Nevertheless, we should acknowledge that many people will, with reason, regard certain developments as 'progress'. Certain principles that were valorized during the Enlightenment thus had the potential to liberate the subaltern to an important degree. Amongst these were the liberal economics that made labour contractual and based on merit rather than being bound by feudal ties; a valorization of the individual over and above the tyranny of the community; the programme for a rule of law that established human rights and provided for the poor an alternative power of appeal; the notion that all humans were equal before the law regardless of class, caste, religion, or gender, and so on. Following the long tradition of critical analysis of bourgeois society, we cannot but be aware of the profound limits to such rights and freedoms—particularly when we are dealing with a colonial territory such as that of India. Nonetheless, for increasing numbers of the subordinated of India and elsewhere, these values and practices have been perceived—to a greater or lesser degree in each case—as an advance on what had gone before. The process opened them to an understanding that they could both liberate themselves to a meaningful degree in the here and now and anticipate a still greater liberation in the future. In this, there was a meaningful sense of historical 'progress'.

As it is, those who have rejected the teleology of progress have sometimes produced surrogates of their own. For example, followers of Foucault might deploy the concept of discipline in such a manner. As Martin Dinges argues: 'Theoretically, the concept of a disciplinarian society implies a teleological view of history, one that sees it as a process of increasing discipline. Opposing tendencies are interpreted only as setbacks, which demonstrates the ideological character of the concept . . . the concept tends to lead to the reification of discipline.'[35] Dinges also notes that Foucault fails to address the issue of power emanating from non-elite sources and its relationship to the history of discipline. He sees this as 'a serious barrier' to accepting Foucault's approach.[36] Whereas Gramsci always understood that hegemony of any sort invites resistance that has the potential to change existing power constructs, Foucault—in his earlier work at least—discounted any such possibility due to the supposed ubiquity of bourgeois power.[37]

The critique of structuralism was also well taken; indeed at the Calcutta Subaltern Studies conference in 1986 I had raised this point in the debate, arguing that an undue focus on structures had in some cases led to a neglect of the analysis of historical change. Derrida's writings helped me clarify my argument in this respect. Nonetheless, I was emphatic that the structural analysis carried out by Ranajit Guha of peasant insurgency, and by Partha Chatterjee of peasant community consciousness, had provided remarkable insights that had greatly extended our understanding of popular resistance in colonial India. Their investigations had, I felt, great heuristic value. What we must, however, bear in mind is that each such 'structure' incorporates its own *differance*, and it was through the play of such *differance* that historical change occurred. Good historical writing should, I believe, be able to incorporate both an awareness of structure for heuristic purposes while situating it within an overall narrative of change.

One major problem with much postructuralist and discourse analysis—so far as I saw it—was that it tended to be rooted in logical enquiry rather than a dialectical engagement with the human life-world. Its method was to examine literary, philosophical, and historical writings with the intention of laying bare their hidden ideological and metaphysical presumptions. Concentrating as they did on textual analysis, there was a tendency for the human subject to be displaced. Too easily, all social conflict came to be seen as a type of linguistic game.[38] We could not, I believed, turn our backs so lightly on the revolutionary principle developed by Marx that philosophy was only meaningful as a form of dialogue with the oppressed. Whereas idealist philosophers formulated their theories through abstract reasoning, Marx had sought to create a materialist theory that engaged with subaltern life as a continuing 'practical-critical activity'.[39] His analysis of the capitalist system arose from insights that he had gained from his involvement in socialist politics and from his strong empathy with the suffering of the contemporary working class and peasantry of Germany, France, and Britain.

To end this discussion on a note of speculation, I feel that the debate has become trapped within a certain dialectic that may perhaps be superseded through an acknowledgement of the validity of beliefs that cannot be valorized through logical reasoning as such. In *Dialectic of Enlightenment*, Adorno and Horkheimer claimed that a central consequence of the Enlightenment was that 'every specific theoretic belief succumbs to the destructive criticism that it is only a belief—until even the very notions of spirit, truth and, indeed, enlightenment itself, have become animistic magic.'[40] In this, they recognized the nihilistic directions in which theory was already going and predicted the eventual philosophical consequences. The Enlightenment had sought to dispel the fear of the spirit world by providing knowledge in its place. Through knowledge, nature would be subject to the control of human beings. The knowledge of the Enlightenment was, however, rooted in a positivist science that was unable to recognize any reality beyond what could observed, measured, classified, and manipulated. Rather than conquering fear, science merely created vast areas of ignorance and thus uncertainty. In this respect: 'Enlightenment is mythic fear turned radical.'[41] Poststructuralism is itself trapped within this dialectic—it seeks understanding but its own terms prevent any knowing. It can only unsettle and disturb, not create.

Adorno and Horkheimer argue that 'myth is already enlightenment; and enlightenment reverts to mythology.'[42] They themselves provide no particular answer to the dilemma they pose, ending by falling back on a demand for greater enlightenment—which was wholly understandable at the time they wrote—in 1944—when Hitler had yet to be defeated. Let us however pursue the idea that we can never escape what Adorno and Horkheimer describe as 'myth'—that is a belief or faith that stems from feelings that cannot be formerly proved or disproved—and ask whether this might be empowering rather than disabling. For example, Marx and his successors were driven by a moral belief—that of commitment to the poor and oppressed—that went beyond logic *per se.* We can describe it as a 'passion' that sustained their life's work. Gramsci was conscious of this when he stressed the need for such a moral quality: 'Only passion sharpens the intellect and co-operates to render intuition clearer.'[43] It provided the base to built the political organization for the ongoing struggle.[44] Sartre, likewise, stressed that such a passion involved a continuing struggle: 'one must live it, one must oppose other passions to it, one must combat it tenaciously, in short one must work oneself over.'[45]

A passion of this sort is metaphysical in as much as it is informed by a moral consciousness—or faith—that is taken as a given and which cannot ultimately be proved or disproved through processes of logical reasoning. This faith exists in a dialogical relationship with our experience in the world and our logical understanding of it. It accords—I would hold—with Gandhi's notion of a 'truth' that is reached through a complex dialogue, in which reasoned argument is reinforced with gut feeling and political contingency. Gandhi knew that reason by itself rarely persuaded, for people tend to be guided as much by emotion as by rational argument.[46] In this, Gandhi showed much greater self-awareness than the activist who tries to portray his or her metaphysics as a form of objective rationality. This necessarily gives an opening to an acceptance of the validity of belief in the divine, by which I mean the psychic experience of an essence that cannot be confirmed through materialist observation. Such an experience is for large numbers a deeply empowering passion, and it cannot—I would argue—be seen in itself as self-delusion or self-alienation. What matters are the actions and politics that faith gives rise to. While it is pointless to question any faith—whether it is secular or religious—we can certainly engage in debate with its manifestations. This, I contend, provides some of the grounds for a more fruitful engagement with the world of the subordinated.

Notes

1. A full list of my writings can be found at the end of this book. This can be used to trace the original date and place of publication of the chapters included in this collection, as well as to obtain details of other of my writings that I shall refer to in this introduction.

2. Ranajit Guha was at that time teaching at Sussex University, where I had completed my Ph.D. in 1975 under the supervision of D.A. Low. I had first met Ranajit in Delhi in 1971, and have been inspired by him ever since. He was very much the mentor for us younger members of the Subaltern Studies group in the late 1970s and early 1980s.
3. Dipesh Chakrabarty, in a review of *Subaltern Studies*, highlights this as one of the most important breakthroughs of the project. Dipesh Chakrabarty, *Habitations of Modernity: Essays in the Wake of Subaltern Studies* (New Delhi, 2002), pp. 8–11.
4. It was after this that leading postcolonial theorists in the United States—notably Edward Said and Gayatri Spivak—began to champion the project. See their contributions in Ranajit Guha and Gayatri Chakravorty Spivak, *Selected Subaltern Studies* (New York, 1988).
5. David Ludden has, for example, argued that 'Subaltern Studies covertly jettisoned modes of agrarian studies that focused on the complexities of production and class.' David Ludden, 'Subalterns and Others in the Agrarian History of South Asia,' in James C. Scott and Nina Bhatt (eds), *Agrarian Studies: Synthetic Work at the Cutting Edge* (New Haven, 2001), p. 209.
6. Ranajit Guha, 'Dominance without Hegemony and its Historiography,' in Ranajit Guha (ed.), *Subaltern Studies VI* (New Delhi, 1989), pp. 229–31.
7. Spivak, 'Subaltern Studies: Deconstructing Historiography', *Subaltern Studies IV* (New Delhi, 1985), pp. 356–61.
8. I have examined this problem, and one reason for my failure in this respect, in *Gandhi in His Time and Ours* (New Delhi, 2003), p. 119.
9. I have discussed these issues in *Gandhi in His Time and Ours*, chapters 3 and 5.
10. Ramachandra Guha, 'Forestry and Social Protest in British Kumaun, *c.*1893–1921', in Ranajit Guha (ed.), *Subaltern Studies IV* (New Delhi, 1985); Ramachandra Guha, *The Unquiet Woods: Ecological Change and Peasant Resistance in the Himalaya* (New Delhi, 1987).
11. David Hardiman, 'Power in the Forest: The Dangs, 1820–1940', in David Arnold and David Hardiman (eds), *Subaltern Studies VIII* (New Delhi, 1994).
12. David Hardiman, 'Introduction', in David Hardiman (ed.), *Peasant Resistance in India 1858–1914* (New Delhi, 1992), p. 11.
13. Romila Thapar, 'Syndicated Moksha?', *Seminar*, 313, September 1985.
14. Satyakam Joshi, 'Tribals, Missionaries and Sadhus: Understanding the Violence in the Dangs', *Economic and Political Weekly*, vol. 34, no. 37, 1999; William Dalrymple, 'Baptism by Fire', *The Guardian Weekend*, 20 March 1999.

15. This finding has been reinforced subsequently by the conclusions of a painstaking study of well irrigation in northern Gujarat. Navroz K. Dubash, *Tubewell Capitalism: Groundwater Development and Agrarian Change in Gujarat* (New Delhi, 2002). For some of my further reflection on this topic, see David Hardiman, 'The Politics of Water Scarcity in Gujarat', in Amita Baviskar (ed.), *Waterscapes: The Cultural Politics of a Natural Resource*, Permanent Black, forthcoming.
16. Sumit Sarkar—once a member of the group—has, for example, argued that this move 'has been debilitating in both academic and political terms'. Sumit Sarkar, 'The Decline of the Subaltern in *Subaltern Studies*', in Sumit Sarkar, *Writing Social History* (New Delhi, 1997), p. 85.
17. Gayatri Chakravorty Spivak, 'Subaltern Studies: Deconstructing Historiography', in Ranajit Guha (ed.), *Subaltern Studies IV* (New Delhi, 1985), pp. 335–7.
18. Rosalind O'Hanlon, 'Recovering the Subject: Subaltern Studies and Histories of Resistance in Colonial South Asia', *Modern Asian Studies*, 22: 1, February 1988.
19. Gayatri Chakravorty Spivak, 'Can the Subaltern Speak?' in Cary Nelson and Lawrence Grossberg, *Marxism and the Interpretation of Culture* (Basingstoke, 1988).
20. Ranajit Guha, *Elementary Aspects of Peasant Insurgency in Colonial India*, New Delhi 1983; Partha Chatterjee, 'Agrarian Relations and Communalism in Bengal, 1926–1935,' in R. Guha (ed.), *Subaltern Studies I* (New Delhi, 1982).
21. Jacques Derrida, *Of Grammatology*, translated by Gayatri Chakravorty Spivak (Baltimore, 1976).
22. Ibid., p. 79.
23. Ibid., p. 120.
24. Ibid., p. 86.
25. Ibid., pp. 114–15.
26. This paper was published subsequently in a revised form as Gayatri Chakravorty Spivak, 'A Literary Representation of the Subaltern: Mahasweta Devi's "Stanadayini," ' in Ranajit Guha (ed.), *Subaltern Studies V* (New Delhi, 1987).
27. See my report on the conference: David Hardiman, 'Subaltern Studies at Crossroads', *Economic and Political Weekly*, 15 February 1986.
28. Ibid., p. 290.
29. Dipesh Chakrabarty, 'Invitation to a Dialogue', in R.Guha (ed.), *Subaltern Studies IV* (New Delhi, 1985), p. 374.
30. Gayatri Chakravorty Spivak, *A Critique of Postcolonial Reason: Toward a History of the Vanishing Present* (Cambridge, Mass., 1999), p. 310.

31. Gareth Stedman Jones, *Languages of Class: Studies in English Working-Class History* (Cambridge, 1983), provided one of the first important critiques of Marxian social history from such a perspective.
32. Marc W. Steinberg, 'Culturally Speaking: Finding a Commons between Post-structuralism and the Thompsonian Perspective', *Social History*, 21:2, May 1996, p. 193.
33. E.P. Thompson, 'Eighteenth-Century English Society: Class Struggle without Class?' *Social History*, 3:2, May 1978, p. 149.
34. *The Coming of the Devi*, pp. 11–17.
35. Martin Dinges, 'Michel Foucault's Impact on the German Historiography of Criminal Justice, Social Discipline, and Medicalization', in Norbert Finzsch and Robert Jütte, *Institutions of Confinement: Hospitals, Asylums, and Prisons in Western Europe and North America, 1500–1950* (Washington, 1996), p. 168.
36. Ibid., p. 172.
37. In his later work, Foucault argued that due to the dispersed nature of the disciplinary power of the bourgeois order, resistance would have to be similarly diversified, taking place within a number of spheres of life. See the discussions in Graham Burchell, Colin Gordon and Peter Miller (eds), *The Foucault Effect: Studies in Governmentality* (Hemel Hempstead, 1991). I am fully in accord with this, for, as already stated, my work has often analysed the interaction of domination and resistance within certain defined hegemonic spheres.
38. For an elaboration of this sort of argument, see Peter Dews, 'Editor's Introduction', to J. Habermas, *Autonomy and Solidarity* (London, 1986), p. 24.
39. Karl Marx, 'First Thesis on Feuerbach', in K. Marx and F. Engels, *Collected Works*, vol. 5 (Moscow, 1976), p. 6.
40. T. Adorno and M. Horkheimer, *Dialectic of Enlightenment*, translated by John Cumming (London, 1979), p. 11.
41. Ibid., p. 16.
42. Ibid., p. xvi.
43. Quoted in John M. Cammett, *Antonio Gramsci and the Origins of Italian Communism* (Stanford, 1967), p. 197.
44. Antonio Gramsci, *Selections from the Prison Notebooks* (London, 1917), pp. 139 and 349.
45. J.P. Sartre, *The Problem of Method* (London, 1971), p. 12.
46. On this, see my *Gandhi in His Time and Ours*, pp. 51–2.

CHAPTER 1

A Forgotten Massacre

Motilal Tejawat and his Movement amongst the Bhils 1921–2

In its English edition of 1 September 1997, *India Today* published an article titled 'The Other Jallianwala'. This told the story of a massacre carried out in March 1922 on the border between Gujarat and Rajasthan by Indian troops under the command of a British officer, Major H.G. Sutton. About 1,200 'tribals'—'more than three times the number at Jallianwala Bagh'—were believed to have been killed. The report noted that the British appeared to have suppressed all information about this event, so that knowledge about it today rests almost entirely on oral accounts by survivors and people who live close to where the firing took place. The *India Today* article was based largely on such oral accounts, collected by its reporter in Gujarat, Uday Mahurkar.

According to Mahurkar, the massacre occurred when Sutton and his troops of the Mewar Bhil Corps moved in to suppress a powerful protest movement led by Motilal Tejawat, 'a renowned Rajasthani freedom fighter of Mewar'. Tejawat had come to the area 'with two thousand agitating tribals'. He held a meeting attended by an additional three thousand. At this meeting Tejawat demanded, amongst other things, a lowering of taxes levied by 'local rulers'. When Sutton's troops appeared, the crowd began shouting slogans at them, and a shot was even fired in the air by one 'tribal'. Sutton ordered his men to open fire. According to Koyaji Patel, aged ninety (and thus fifteen at the time): 'As the firing began and people started running helter-skelter, I hid myself behind a farm fence. What I then saw was simply unbelievable. People were literally falling like ninepins to the bullets. The sepoys were killing people for their silver ornaments.' According to Koyaji Patel and other informants, the corpses were carried to a nearby well and dumped in until it was full to the brim. The article carried a photograph of this well—a large stone-lined structure, about six metres across.

Mahurkar interviewed the historian L.P. Mathur, now retired from the Department of History of Udaipur University. Mathur—'an expert on reforms and movements among the Bhils'—is quoted as saying that evidence of the massacre was 'completely suppressed'. Quoted also was the director of the Tribal Research Institute of the Gujarat Vidyapith, Ahmedabad, Siddharaj Solanki, who endorsed the idea of a cover-up, although he did note that a couple of newspapers carried accounts of the killing a few months after it happened.

Mahurkar concluded that 'comparisons with Jallianwala Bagh are inevitable,' yet felt that some sort of harder evidence was needed to establish the facts of the case. He suggested that excavations could perhaps be carried out to find skeletons of those buried or thrown into the well. He noted also that: 'Former Gujarat chief minister Amarsinh Chaudhary, himself a tribal and an MLA from the area, is now trying to get a memorial erected there.'

A slightly longer version of the same article appeared in the Gujarati edition of *India Today* of 5 September 1997, with some differences in the photos. The title was '*Gujaratno Jaliyanvala Bag*', or 'Gujarat's Jallianwala Bagh'. The photograph of the well into which the bodies were allegedly thrown was replaced with a picture of about a dozen middle-aged men standing on the sides of a hillock, some dressed in white kurta-pyjama, others in shirt and trousers, gesturing to the camera. This, according to the caption, showed the site of the well—now covered and with a tree growing on top—into which the bodies had been dumped. Although the caption does not state it, one of those dressed in white kurta-pyjama is no less a person than ex-chief minister Amarsinh Chaudhary. Another, in similar political uniform, is Lakshman Kothval, the former Taluka Panchayat Pramukh. Both are members of the Congress Party.

Amarsinh Chaudhary, although an MLA for the area (Sabarkantha district), is in fact from a very distant part of Gujarat: Vyara taluka of Surat district. He is a member of the Chaudhary community of South

Gujarat, listed as a scheduled tribe. He is known as a 'modernizer' amongst the adivasis of Gujarat, eager to bring them into the mainstream. He heard about the massacre while carrying out his constituency duties in the area. He brought up the issue with *India Today*, and accompanied their reporter to the scene of the event, in a visit calculated to coincide with the celebrations of the fiftieth anniversary of Indian independence. In his view, historians had neglected the role of adivasis in the freedom struggle, and he was seeking to correct this bias. He intended to prepare a book about the massacre.[1]

This initiative in bringing to light a forgotten massacre was in certain respects an admirable one. Clearly, there had been a carnage that had been ignored in the histories of the nationalist movement of India. Interviews with survivors were used to good effect to piece together a powerful history of the event. My first reaction on reading the piece was one of praise for an excellent piece of oral history. Also, I was somewhat dismayed by my ignorance of the event, for although I have studied the history of the adivasis of Gujarat during the colonial period in some detail,[2] and knew that there were some clashes between the Bhils and the British in 1922, I was not aware of killings on such a scale.

I knew of these clashes from a file in the National Archives in New Delhi on Motilal Tejawat's movement which I had read through about ten years before.[3] The *India Today* article prompted me to return to the notes I had taken at that time. Turning to the entries for March 1922, I found that there was in fact a record of the event. On 10 March 1922, three days after the firing, the Government of India had put out a press communiqué that stated that a party of 2,000 Bhils under Motilal Tejawat had clashed with the Mewar Bhil Corps under Major Sutton. 'Motilal opened fire and the Bhil Corps replied with the result that 22 of Motilal's party were killed and 29 wounded.' The communiqué concluded by stating that Motilal himself had fled towards Idar. There were five other reports in the file, of varying length, describing the firing. There was among them a fortnightly report of 31 March 1922 by the Political Agent in Rajputana that stated that the casualties had been widely exaggerated, with rumours afloat of hundreds and even thousands of deaths. I also came across a note I had taken from the *Bombay Chronicle* of 13 March 1922, which repeated the press communiqué almost verbatim. From what I could see, the matter had entered the public domain, but very little had been made of it. Why was this so?

In December 1997, I took advantage of a visit to Gujarat to travel to the area in which the massacre had taken place and carry out some investigations of my own. At the site of the massacre at Dadhvav, I found that a black flag had been erected on a pole over what was claimed to be the well in which the bodies were buried. I was told that this flag had been raised after the article in *India Today*. I, too, interviewed some survivors of the massacre, and others with knowledge of the events.[4] I visited Udaipur as well, to meet scholars who had studied the Bhils of the region, and to collect secondary literature on the subject. There, I met L.P. Mathur, the historian interviewed by *India Today*, who has written two books on protest movements amongst the Bhils.[5] As might be expected, he was well aware of the file in the National Archives on Motilal Tejawat's movement. He told me he had informed the *India Today* reporter about this file, and stated the number killed according to the government report—namely twenty-two. This piece of information is however noticeably absent from the *India Today* article. Clearly, the comparison sought to be made with Jallianwala Bagh would have lacked much of its force if this information had been included.

However, even twenty-two deaths are twenty-two too many, and there is every indication that far more died on that day, shot down on the order of a British officer. The importance of the topic does not lie in quibbles over casualty numbers, but rather how we insert this event within the history of India and the history of Indian nationalism, of which it clearly was a part. The *India Today* article is somewhat ambivalent in this respect. At one level, the article creates the impression that the movement was within the mainstream of the Indian nationalist movement. Motilal Tejawat is described, unproblematically, as a 'renowned . . . freedom fighter'. In such a light, the nationalist leaders would have taken the matter up and made it a major issue had they not been denied knowledge of the massacre by the British cover-up. At another level, there is a more subalternist thrust to the argument. A nationalist of Mewar, Balwant Singh Mehta, now ninety-eight years old, is quoted as stating that the massacre was forgotten because 'unlike Jallianwala Bagh . . . those killed were poor, illiterate tribals.' This is also Amarsinh Chaudhary's position—that due to their elitist bias, historians have ignored the role of adivasis in the nationalist movement. In this article I shall seek to show that the massacre was ignored in part because Motilal Tejawat's movement did not conform to Gandhian precepts, and in part because it occurred at a particular juncture in the history of the nationalist movement. Publicity about the massacre did not at that moment accord with the overall political agenda of the nationalist leadership. This above all—and not a count of the number of casualties as such—set apart the carnage inflicted in March 1922 in an obscure village on the frontier between Gujarat and Rajasthan.

II

L.P. Mathur is not the only scholar who has written about Motilal Tejawat's movement of 1921–2; in recent years, Premsinh Kanthariya, P.C. Jain, Hari Sen and Denis Vidal have also done so.[6] Their work shows that Motilal Tejawat (1885–1963) was an Oswal Jain Baniya of Koliyari, near Udaipur. After education to fifth standard he was employed, in 1912, as a storekeeper at Jharol, a landlord (*thakor*) estate south-west of Udaipur. This was in a predominantly Bhil region, and Motilal was witness to the way in which his employer, the Rajput thakor, and his henchmen, maltreated the people. They were forced into free labour, and beaten and tortured if they failed to satisfy the demands of their overlords. Poor women were often abducted and raped. Motilal recorded these abuses in his diary, now held by his son Manilal in Udaipur, and consulted by several of these historians. Disgusted by what he saw, he resigned his position in 1920 and went to work for a Baniya shopkeeper in Udaipur city.

Soon afterwards, however, the shopkeeper sent Motilal to Jharol on business. While he was there, the thakor ordered him to hand over some building materials belonging to Motilal's new employer. When Motilal protested, he was arrested, imprisoned, beaten up and made to eat dirt. His employer, an influential man in Udaipur, managed to have him released soon after. The experience proved a formative one, for Motilal then gave up his job in Udaipur and devoted himself to full-time political activity, his mission being to carry out social reform amongst the Bhils and to champion their demands against the oppressive landlords.

Motilal was inspired in part by a powerful movement that had been continuing in Bijolia—also in Mewar state—since 1897. This was another estate under an autocratic thakor, and the movement was against high taxes and arbitrary charges. The movement took a new turn in 1916 under the inspired leadership of the radical nationalist V.S. Pathik. He organized an alternative system of government under the control of local people. The agitation had entered a particularly intense phase in 1920–1.[7] Motilal had an anti-landlord pamphlet from this movement copied and circulated in the Jharol area. He got a good response from the people, who respected him for the stand he had taken against the thakor, and they formed an *eki*, or unity, league. He and some leading villagers of the estate put together a list of demands against the thakor, which they took in June 1921 to Udaipur to present to the Maharana, Fateh Singh. The ruler appointed a committee to examine their grievances, and announced that some concessions would be granted. These were, however, too minor to satisfy the peasants. Motilal told the peasants to boycott the thakors and their officials, to refuse taxes, and to establish their own councils to settle disputes. They were told to join the eki, swearing an oath of loyalty on an unsheathed sword.

Motilal was a religious man who believed that his actions enjoyed divine support. Besides championing the grievances of the predominantly Bhil peasantry against the landlords, he also felt he had a religious duty to persuade them to give up drinking liquor, to stop killing animals, and to refrain from stealing. Some other Baniyas of the region joined him in this activity. In this, they were linking up with a longstanding religious reform movement of the region, known as the Bhagat movement. This involved Bhils taking an oath to abstain from all crimes and acts of violence against other humans as well as animals, to abjure liquor, and take a daily bath. They were to earn their livelihood through agriculture.[8]

Motilal saw his protest as being a part of the wider movement for independence led by Gandhi, then at its height during the noncooperation movement. In speeches he stated that once 'Gandhi raj' was established they would only have to pay one anna in the rupee to the state. Some of his followers took to wearing white caps. He clearly believed that in trying to wean the Bhils away from violence he was following the programme of the Gandhian movement closely. As yet, however, Gandhi knew nothing of him or his movement.

In August 1921, Motilal was arrested by the thakor of Jharol. Six to seven thousand Bhils from 65 villages gathered together, marched into Jharol and forced his release. Thousands more Bhils then came forward to take the oath of eki. Bhils who refused to do so found themselves subjected to social boycott. They came not only from Mewar, but also from the adjoining states of Sirohi, Idar, Danta and Pol. In early 1922, Motilal began touring this area, accompanied always by several thousand Bhils armed with bows and arrows, demanding reform from the local thakors and ruling princes. There were some minor clashes, with aggressive state policemen and officials being beaten. There is no record of anyone being killed by the Bhils—by their standards they were protesting in a remarkably non-violent manner.

III

This was not however how Gandhi saw it when his attention was drawn to the matter in early 1922. In the 2 February issue of *Young India* he commented:

> I hear that a gentleman by name Motilal Puncholi hailing from Udaipur claims to be my disciple and to preach temperance and what not among the rustics of the Rajputana States. He is reported to be surrounded by an armed crowd of admirers and establishing his kingdom or some other-dom wherever he goes. He claims, too, miraculous powers. He or his admirers are reported also to have done some destructive work. I wish that people will once for all understand that I have no disciples . . . None works in my name; none has authority to use my name save under my own writing . . . nobody has any authority from me to use any arms, even sticks, against any person.
>
> I understand that these brave but simple rustics have been induced to refuse payment of taxes due to the State to which they belong. They are even told that I have asked the tax-payers belonging to the Sirohi State not to pay more than Rs. 1˘ each. Now I know nothing of all this. No one has consulted me about the matter. Pandit Ramakant Malaviya, Chief Minister of the State, has kindly brought the matter to my notice and he tells me that great mischief is being done in my name. If my writing reaches these

> countrymen at all, I would like to tell them that they should lay all their grievances before the State authorities and never resort to arms. If they wish to withhold payment of tax which they consider excessive, it is their right. But it is a right never to be exercised lightly. They must cultivate public opinion and let the case see the light of day. If they do not take these precautions they will find everything and everybody arrayed against them and they will find themselves heavy losers in the end.

The statement was published under the heading 'Danger of Mass Movement', and it was made at a time when Gandhi was developing severe doubts about the massive movement of protest against the colonial state that he had launched in India just over a year before. There had been many instances in which supporters of the struggle had failed to heed his plea for complete non-violence, and he had doubts whether the Indian people were ready for such an experiment. Then, only two days after the above statement was published, nationalists in Gorakhpur district attacked and killed twenty-three policemen at Chauri-Chaura.[9] Horrified by the carnage inflicted in his name, Gandhi advised the immediate suspension of civil disobedience all over India. The Congress Working Committee agreed to this on 12 February.

Gandhi's unsympathetic reaction to Motilal Tejawat's movement can be explained in part by such misgivings. But probably more important was the fact that he had learnt about it from the chief minister of Sirohi state, Ramakant Malaviya, and this had without doubt coloured his views adversely. Malaviya was a son of the leading UP nationalist, Madan Mohan Malaviya. The Rao of Sirohi had appointed Ramakant as chief minister in October 1921 in the hope that he would deflect possible nationalist protest against the state.[10] In late 1921 Malaviya had joined with the Agent in Rajputana, R.E. Holland, in negotiating with the leader of the Bijolia movement, V.S. Pathik. Because the terms he negotiated for the suspension of that movement were advantageous to the Mewar peasantry, he was seen in a positive light at that juncture in nationalist circles. As is clear from an article in *Young India* of 12 January 1922, Gandhi had great affection for the Malaviya family; in this article he lauded another son of Malaviya's, Govind, who had been imprisoned for his nationalist activities. When Ramakant wrote to Gandhi, pointing out to him that Bhils and Girasias wielding bows and arrows and spears were refusing, in Gandhi's name, to pay their taxes to an Indian prince, his immediate reaction was to condemn the protest as transgressing his code of non-violence.

As Denis Vidal has pointed out, this reaction and the subsequent position taken by the nationalist leadership in relation to the eki movement has to be seen in the context of the internal politics of the Indian National Congress at the time.[11] M.M. Malaviya was on the right wing of the Congress, in later years being the leader of the Hindu Mahasabha. He was on good terms with Rajput rulers in Rajasthan, notably the Rana of Mewar, and believed in the intrinsic benevolence of—as he saw it—these Hindu rulers. These considerations were important in the choice of his son as chief minister of Sirohi. Gandhi himself had much sympathy at that time for Malaviya's position on the Indian princes, believing that they could be persuaded to reform their societies in more benevolent directions, and that they were not a legitimate target for nationalist attack. In Gujarat, however, some of his leading supporters had a far less rosy view about the princes. One such person was Manilal Kothari, a lawyer of Limbdi state in Saurashtra and a fervent Gandhian, who had been prominent in nationalist agitations in British Gujarat since 1917. In late 1921 he was sent by Gandhi to the border region between Gujarat and Rajasthan to carry out social work amongst the Bhils. In early 1922 he organized a protest against the Governor of Bombay Sir George Lloyd when the latter was visiting Rajkot State, which led to Kothari's expulsion from Saurashtra by an order of the Bombay government of 1 February 1922. He returned to Ahmedabad just when Gandhi was considering how to respond to Motilal Tejawat's movement; Gandhi thereupon decided to depute him to go and investigate in person.

At this juncture, Motilal and his followers were still in Sirohi State, but close to the border with Gujarat. Manilal Kothari met up with them in Sirohi. He advised Motilal to keep the movement strictly non-violent, for any '*zulum*' on their part—he warned—would invite severe reprisal from the British: they would 'all be slaughtered like dogs.'[12] Next day, V.S. Pathik arrived in Motilal's camp. Pathik had been in contact with Gandhi since 1918, and enjoyed his support for the Bijolia movement on condition that he did not try to link it up with the wider nationalist struggle. Pathik gave Motilal advice similar to that of Manilal Kothari. Motilal replied that he would not act in a way that would cause any trouble.

On the following day, they all moved towards Abu Road, a town on the railway line between Ahmedabad and Delhi. There they came face to face with Sirohi state troops with Ramakant Malaviya at their head. Kothari and Pathik went out to meet Malaviya, and an agreement was reached that Motilal and his Bhils would leave the state. This they did on 7 February, returning to Gujarat, to the princely states of Palanpur and Danta.

There, Bhils continued to flock to Motilal's camp, offering their unwavering support. On 10 February, the British Political Agent in charge of this area reported that roads were being blockaded and people were refusing to pay their taxes, but so far there had been no acts of violence. V.S. Pathik was still with Motilal urging him to maintain non-violence. By now, he had become doubtful about Motilal's ability to control the movement. He saw that the Bhils were a law to themselves, not following Motilal's advice when it conflicted with their agenda. For example, it was beyond Motilal's power to persuade them to stop carrying weapons—a Bhil or Girasia male would have felt naked going out without his bow and arrow or some other weapon.[13] In Bijolia, Pathik had maintained a tight control over the movement, it had been free of violence, and the moral pressure thus maintained had—he believed—brought highly positive results. Seeing the Bhils *en masse*—armed with their traditional weapons—Pathik believed that violence could easily be triggered, providing an excuse for the British to crush the movement ruthlessly. As Motilal was linked in the popular mind with Gandhi, such violence could discredit the nationalist movement as a whole, as had been the case with the Chauri-Chaura debacle.[14]

Manilal Kothari was however more sympathetic towards Motilal and the Bhils. He sent a telegram to Gandhi: 'Five days in hills, met Moti Lal hundreds of Bhils in Danta Forest; your message duly communicated, much appreciated.'[15] On 11 February, Motilal forwarded a letter to Gandhi through Kothari:

> In whichever place I work, I work for satyagraha. I do not work for any other thing. The fact is that the Bhils and Girasias follow me in the same way as the whole of India is following you. They have bows and arrows and swords. These are their traditional weapons. They are farmers in the hilly tracts and are peaceful. They are truthful and righteous people. They are perfectly innocent and are lovers of religion (dharma). When I started

> satyagraha, these people gave me full cooperation with good faith. The same thing has displeased the officials. They want to suppress the Bhils by beating them and making them give bribes. But the Bhils are steadfast and intelligent. They know their self-interest. Now, neither the states nor the English are listening to my petitions. You are my only helper. Help me. I am ready to die for these poor people. Send somebody who can provide publicity for our cause. These people are ignorant and very simple. Manilal Kothari knows this fact very well. Do pay attention to my request.[16]

It is known that Motilal had been both upset and disheartened when he had learnt of Gandhi's disavowal of his activities in the *Young India* article of 2 February, for—as is apparent from this letter—he saw himself as a faithful follower of Gandhi. It is however clear from this letter that he knew he could not prevent his own followers from carrying arms—with all the possible dangers which that entailed. He argued that despite this, Gandhi should view them favourably as an intrinsically peaceful and religious-minded people who were suffering from the oppression of autocratic and corrupt state officials.

Gandhi gave his response in *Navajivan*, published on 26 February in Gujarati:

> In order to look into this matter, Shri Manilal Kothari went at my request to Shirohi and other places. It seems from the reports received from him that Shri Motilal Tejavat has been working mainly to persuade the *Bhils* to give up drinking and flesh-eating. It is beyond doubt that his activities have brought about an awakening among the *Bhils*. There would have been no ground for criticism if he had stayed at one place so that the *Bhils* could meet him, instead of roaming around accompanied by groups of them. I reproduce below the letter he has sent me through Shri Manilal.

[Motilal Tejawat's letter of 11 February, quoted above, was reproduced in Gujarati script, though the original was in Devanagari script.]

> This letter betrays ignorance about some matters. The British have nothing to do with the issue and the matter ought to have been brought to the notice of the States concerned in a proper manner. Shri Manilal says that in Palanpur, Danta and Shirohi States, he, Manilal, had received full co-operation from the authorities. Shri Motilal and the *Bhils* also listened to him and he was sure that they wished to carry on their work in a wholly peaceful manner. I hope that the *Bhils* will be satisfied if the States listen to their complaints and redress their grievances. Assuming that Shri Motilal has

> been at fault in some matters, both the Rulers and the subjects are likely to benefit if this is overlooked and the States take advantage of the good effects of his work among the *Bhils* and pay attention to improving their condition.

Gandhi's reaction, though more sympathetic in tone than his earlier article in *Young India*, was still not very welcoming towards his self-avowed disciple, Motilal Tejawat. He criticized him for 'roaming about'—somewhat hypocritically, seeing that he himself was constantly on the move at this time organizing his followers all over India. His argument that the princes and their officials would respond positively if the grievances of their subjects were stated in a clear and non-threatening manner, was also questionable. There was no evidence that the Sirohi officials were prepared to tackle the complaints of the Bhils and Girasias in a serious manner; Gandhi was placing great faith in the goodwill of Ramakant Malaviya—a faith which was to prove misplaced in the light of the subsequent brutal repression of Motilal's movement by the government headed by this man. The Mewar state had, it was true, sought to remedy the grievances of the peasants of Bijolia, but only after the British had intervened by forcing the abdication of the Maharana in mid-1921 and having his more amenable son put on the throne. Also, Holland, the Political Agent in Rajputana, had personally negotiated this settlement. All of this brings out another serious flaw in Gandhi's argument—that the British had 'nothing to do with the issue'. It is quite clear that nothing of any consequence could happen in these princely states without the involvement of British political agents, who were in direct touch with and were controlled by the Government of India in Delhi. It is to the role of the British in this affair that we shall now turn.

IV

The man who was in overall control of the affairs of the princely states of Rajasthan was the Agent to the Governor-General, Robert Erskine Holland. In contrast to many of his subordinates in the political department, he had a good grasp of the political realities of the situation and was a political operator of some subtlety. He understood that it was hard to defend the ways of the local Rajput thakors and their henchmen and that the villagers of Rajasthan had much justification for their protests. It was for this reason that he had in the previous two years engineered the abdication of the rulers of both Sirohi and Mewar states, with a view to establishing more 'modern' polities. During the Bijolia movement, he had personally negotiated a settlement that ran counter to the wishes of the local thakor.

Hence, when faced with the movement amongst the Bhils led by Motilal Tejawat, he realized he had a difficult situation on his hands. He knew that the grievances of the Bhils were warranted, and he knew also that the local rulers and thakors would repress their protest savagely if they had the power to do so, and that they could only have such a power if they were backed by British troops. The fate of the movement thus rested in British hands. Neither Holland nor his superiors in Delhi wanted a violent confrontation with the Bhils, for this was a time when the Government of India still thought it might be able to defuse the non-cooperation movement through negotiation. Holland decided to bide his time, while working behind the scenes trying to persuade the local rulers and thakor to agree to some concessions so as to defuse the movement. Hoping the movement would remain non-violent, he gave orders to his subordinates 'to avoid a conflict if possible.'[17]

Because of this, the movement was able to gather steam over the winter of 1921–2 without any significant confrontation. Then, on 16 February 1922, Motilal wrote to the British—his first direct communication with them—stating that his actions had not infringed the policy of the Congress. On 21 February, Holland wrote to his superiors in Delhi:

> Moti Lal has been disowned by Gandhi. I hear that he is nervous about his own safety, and now wishes to be allowed to quit Bhil country and settle near Ahmedabad. He undertakes not to interfere any further with Bhil affairs. Since Moti Lal has not committed any very serious offence in their territories Sirohi and Mewar Darbars would have no objection to this course . . .[18]

By this, Holland meant that he supported such a course of action, and that the states concerned would follow his advice. His strategy—to offer a safe pass to Motilal should he choose to leave the Bhils and go into exile in British Gujarat—was an astute one. Motilal was in fact under pressure from his Gandhian contacts to do this so that he could receive instruction in the techniques of satyagraha direct from the hands of Gandhi at his ashram in Ahmedabad. Motilal, seeing himself as a disciple of Gandhi, was strongly tempted to adopt this course.

This strategy was not however acceptable to the government of Bombay Presidency. The governor, Sir George Lloyd, informed the Government of India in Delhi that he did not want the agitator in his territory, and that he deserved to be punished harshly. He urged 'that in the interest of the Bhils this course will be the best.'[19] This argument was based on Lloyd's belief that subaltern action of the sort seen amongst the Bhils was engineered by extremist agitators who were manipulating poor and ignorant rustics to further their own nefarious designs. Holland knew that the truth was more complex, but it was the Governor of Bombay who was to prove to have the ear of the Viceroy, Lord Reading, in this matter.

On 2 March, Lloyd wrote to Lord Reading that he had proof that Gandhi was in direct contact with Motilal through 'an extremist' (namely Manilal Kothari). Barely a month before, Kothari had caused great offence to the governor when he led protests against him on an official visit to Rajkot, so that there was a personal tinge to his comment. Lloyd concluded:

> From this it is apparent that Gandhi is not entirely unconnected with the Bhil affair and confirms me in my view that no compromises should be made with Moti Lal who should be severely punished even if he surrenders.[20]

Reading replied to Lloyd that he agreed entirely with him, and that:

> We have instructed Holland to demand unconditional surrender of Moti Lal and troops are in readiness to act in support of the demand when called on by local authorities.[21]

This hardening in the position of the Government of India came at a time when it became apparent that the nationalist agitation was flagging following Gandhi's withdrawal of civil disobedience after Chauri-Chaura. Lord Reading now believed he could move in on the nationalists, arrest their leaders and crush their resistance without suffering any very grave political consequences. A political phase that had lasted nearly two years—a period when the British had been put on the defensive after their excesses in Amritsar in 1919—was seen, in other words, to be at an end. Once more, nationalists were to be disciplined, if need be, through brute force.

It was at this fateful juncture that news came that Motilal and his followers had decided to return to Mewar to once more put their grievances to the Rana. The Mewar Bhil Corps, stationed close to the border between Gujarat and Rajasthan, and under the command of Major H.G. Sutton, was ordered to proceed immediately to intercept Motilal. The stage was thus set for the massacre of 7 March.

V

On 6 March, Motilal and about two thousand Bhils reached the territory of the Thakor of Pal. This Rajput estate, which came under Idar state, consisted of forty-two villages lying on the border between Gujarat and Rajasthan. They camped on the banks of the River Hera, close to a village called Dadhvav. Messages were passed from village to village that 'Motilal Vaniyo', and in some cases 'Motilal Gandhi' or just 'Gandhi,' had come and that they should gather for his darshan. He was, it was said, telling the people to protest against *veth* and *vero* (free labour demands and taxes), and that if they did this they would be free. People set out, reaching Dadhvav by the morning of 7 March, many carrying coconuts and coins, which they presented to Motilal after touching his feet. Several thousands came, swelling the numbers to three to four thousand in all. Around midday news came that a *paltan* [platoon] of the '*embeesee*' (MBC, or Mewar Bhil Corps) was approaching from Baleta village, led by a *gora saheb*—by name *sataan*—armed with '*three-nort-three banduk*', that is, 303 rifles known for their deadly and accurate fire-power compared with the old muskets used normally by the Bhils.[22]

Amongst Motilal's followers there was a spy planted by the Mewar police in mid-February, a Brahman beggar named Tek Chand of Motilal's home town of Koliyari. About two weeks later he gave a full statement to the British which provides us with the most detailed contemporary account of the events of that afternoon:

> . . . after we had taken our meals, one of Moti Lal's chowkidars came in with news that the paltan was coming. Moti Lal then asked the Bhils to take to their arms with instructions not to use them first and stood amongst a

> party of 100–200 Bhils near mango trees away from his seat. The Pal Bhils who were around Moti Lal said that among the paltan—Mewar Bhil Corps—were his brethren who would not kill them and that there was no reason for fear adding that they would join their *aiki* [union].
>
> One fat sadhu named Gyanji who was standing by Moti Lal stepped forward a little to ascertain whether the sepoys were in aiki and turning round indicated by a motion of his hand that they should oppose the Corps as the sepoys of the Corps were not in aiki.
>
> Immediately two or three men drawing out their swords and uttering the word *phoire, phoire* [a word to encourage men to fight] asked 200–300 Bhils to run [take] away Moti Lal and the remainder to string arrows. All the Bhils at once took up their bows and arrows, commenced firing and stepped forward with the shouts of 'phoire, phoire'. Some two or three men from amongst the gathering tried to stop this but in vain. The political Superintendent, Kherwara [Sutton], shouted out through Megaphone that they should have patience and stop their action but they did not listen and stepped on and on continuing their action. Four shots of muzzle loading guns were fired at the Political Superintendent. Dhanna Damor shouted out that the Political Superintendent had led the force and that they should therefore shoot him first, adding that they would then easily manage to bring the corps to their side. Dhanna Damor himself fired at the Political Superintendent two shots from a rifle which he had seized from Jharol, simultaneously encouraging other Bhils, whereupon the Political Superintendent asked them to stop shooting arrows and guns. Despite this they shouted out 'Moti Lal ki jai' 'Eklingji ki jai' and came on and on. When they came up too close to the Mewar Bhil Corps the Mewar Bhil Corps began firing. As soon as Moti Lal saw the regiment he made his way towards the Mohewa ki nal accompanied by Dhanna Damor and Kesa Gameti. After this occurrence, I, in order to save my life, ran away to my village Koliari. . .[23]

The impression conveyed by Tek Chand is one of aggression on the part of Motilal and the Bhils and forbearance by Sutton and his platoon until forced to fire in self-defence. The Bhils of the Mewar Bhil Corps are depicted as being unshakeable in their loyalty to the British, even though Motilal's followers believed that they might desert to their side. No doubt, the statement was tailored rather carefully to accord with the version of the events favoured by Sutton and the British.[24] The only other eyewitness account in the records is by Sutton himself, written on 7 March and stating merely that he had reached Pal at midday, that Motilal was there with about two thousand men, that he shouted through a megaphone from a distance of 200 yards that he wanted to talk with them, that Motilal had sent his Bhils to attack them before fleeing from the scene on a camel, and that he had had to order 'defensive firing', killing twenty-two and wounding twenty-nine.[25]

For other accounts of the massacre we have to rely on interviews with the people of the area conducted seventy-five years after the event. Memories, however, remain vivid, providing us with a powerful counter-narrative. In this account, Motilal, sitting beneath a mango tree, was holding a large and peaceful meeting on the banks of the River Hera outside Dadhvav village. This was a mixed-caste village with Kalals, Darjis, Bhils and Chamars and Dangi Patels, who were the chief cultivators. Others, accordingly, attended the meeting besides Bhils. There were many women. When news came of the approach of the paltan, Motilal told his followers that they would not be harmed, as the paltan's bullets would turn to water. The troops took up their position on a small hill overlooking the meeting-place. The crowd below began taunting them and shouting slogans. One Bhil fired a shot in the air. Sutton immediately ordered his bugler to give the signal to fire. There was a volley of shots—and men and women began falling to the ground. There was pandemonium as everyone tried to scramble to safety—many finding refuge in the nearby *Chamarvas* (Chamar quarters), situated outside Dadhvav and close to the meeting-place. Many fled with blood pouring from wounds, some dying on the way, others after they had reached their homes. The soldiers then searched the bodies, taking whatever valuables they could find.

About 1,200 to 1,500 lay dead, of whom about a third were women. Surveying the scene, Sutton decided that the first priority was to dispose of the bodies. People were allowed to come forward to drag away the bodies of their relatives and fellow-villagers. Many of the dead were however from distant parts. The Thakor of Pal, Pritvisingh, then appeared on the scene, and suggested that the unclaimed bodies be dumped in a nearby well. This well, known as Dekaria *kuvo*, was a large one, about fourteen metres deep and five metres across. It was owned by a Brahman, who had been given it in gift (*daan*) by the Thakor. Chamars from the adjoining *Chamarvas* were ordered to carry out the gruesome task. When full, the well was covered over. Some of the wounded were taken to the Christian mission at Biladiya, a nearby village, where the padre, Lea Saheb, treated them. As he treated the injured, Lea was visited by Pritvisingh, who told him that he was doing good work. Soon afterwards, police reinforcements came in motorized vehicles from the Gujarat side, sent by the Mahikantha political agent.[26]

In accounts found in the British records, the impression was given that the protesters were all male Bhils, armed to the teeth and spoiling for a fight. In the popular counter-history, the crowd consisted of men and women, mainly Bhils—for they made up the bulk of the population in the region—but with other castes represented. They had gathered with peaceful intentions, and did not initiate the violence in any serious respect. The firing was virtually unprovoked, and took the crowd by surprise. In this account, the local detail is much richer, the event being fitted into a local geography and sociology. The area, with its Brahmans, Patel cultivators, Chamars and other castes living amongst the Bhils, and with its British missionary and mission school,[27] appears less detached from the plains areas of Gujarat than is assumed in most accounts. Similarly, there is a local politics, revolving around the figure of the Rajput thakor, who puts in his appearance here on the side of the British.

VI

The most glaring discrepancy between the two accounts relates to the number of casualties—on the one side twenty-two, on the other 1,200 (according to those interviewed by *India Today*) or 1,500 (according to those who were prepared to venture a figure during my interviews). It is almost certainly the case that Sutton's figure of 22 was an understatement, and probably a large one at that. The local missionary, Lea, who treated the wounded later stated that 'there were a hundred casualties; dead and wounded were lying all around, some with fearful wounds. Our little hospital was filled and we were bringing in stretcher cases until 10 p.m.'[28] Twenty-two was for Sutton a politic figure—not representing a denial that a serious incident had occurred, but not an indicator, either, that the carnage had been out of all proportion to the seriousness of the situation. Sutton's superiors took up the cue, repeating his brief and laconic report of the massacre in their press communiqué of 10 March in a way that suggested that there were no apologies to be made. In such a light, the Bhils—believed by the British to be turbulent by nature—had opened fire; Sutton had to defend himself. As one such apologist, G.D. Ogilvie, stated a few days later, little more could be expected in a case involving a '. . . people little removed from savagery . . . childishly ignorant and inflammable . . .'[29]

The nationalist press, when it took any notice at all,[30] satisfied itself by merely regurgitating the government communiqué. For example, the report in *The Bombay Chronicle* of 13 March repeated the statement verbatim, though rather remarkably it put the number of dead at two hundred. Did this represent some sort of response to popular rumours about the event? As this newspaper made no further investigation of the matter, a misprint would seem to be the most likely explanation. The Gujarati weekly *Saurashtra*, which covered nationalist agitations in the princely states of Gujarat, had a report in its edition of 25 March which stated merely that: '. . . they had an encounter with Major Sutton and his party and there was a shooting. 20 died and 29 were injured. Motilal ran away towards Idar side. State officials are taking steps to solve the dissatisfaction and things are calming down.'[31] There is no suggestion in this report that the shooting might have been in any way out of order. Even the most obvious questions were not posed; for example, if the Bhils had, as alleged, made a violent attack, why had Sutton and his men suffered not a single casualty or even injury?

The nationalists on the Rajasthan side were less complacent in this respect. V.S. Pathik wrote to Holland on 26 March condemning the British action against Motilal:

> The communiqués further say that the firing by Government troops was in self-protection against the attack by Moti Lal's party. But so far as my information goes, scarcely a Bhil used his weapon. This is amply borne out even by the Government communiqué which mentions no casualty—not a single one—in the Government forces. Moreover, while the Government publishes only 22 as the number of Bhils killed, the reports which I have received through sources the reliability of which I have little reason to doubt, say that the number of casualties is above thousand. Thus the absence of a single casualty on one side, and the number rising to thousand on the other show that either the public remained wholly non-violent, resolutely facing the volley of bullets, or that the poor people were taken unawares and massacred in an unprovoked state. The attempt, after so

> much carnage, to keep the world in darkness about the happenings by closing all communications from or to the spot is a fact which leaves no room for any other conclusion than that I have come to. Again, the alarming rumours, daily increasing in velocity and spreading like wild fire, go a great way in strengthening the above view.
>
> . . . The situation is thus getting graver day by day, and still reports are pouring in to the effect that Government forces, instead of being withdrawn, are being reinforced. These reports are beginning to convince the public that the only object of the Government in spilling so much blood is to crush innocent hearts, and to satisfy its blood-thirsty propensities.[32]

According to Pathik, attempts to investigate the matter were being thwarted by the British, by 'closing all communications from or to the spot'. In the princely states it was comparatively easy to prevent investigations and other activities by nationalists—they could be arrested and expelled from the state, or even imprisoned, in wholly arbitrary ways. It appears that this sort of clamp-down, preventing any investigation, was operating in this case.

It is possible that the local authorities destroyed documents relating to the shooting. This is a claim made by the historian L.P. Mathur, who searched the local archives and the archives of the Rajputana Political Agency, now held in Bikaner, without, he says, finding a single reference to the event.[33] It appears, however, that he failed to find three important files on the subject in the Bikaner archive that are catalogued as records for Dungarpur and Marwar states. Most of the material in these files relates to Tejawat's movement in Mewar and adjoining states other than Dungarpur and Marwar, and this raises the possibility that the records were deliberately miscatalogued.[34]

Despite claims by the authorities that the firing had had a salutary effect on the Bhils of the region, the situation remained tense. In late March, the Bhils of three estates besieged their thakors in their mansions, the sieges being lifted only after the appearance of Mewar State soldiers under the command of a British officer. The troops then marched through the region to impress on the Bhils the power of the state.[35] Motilal himself had fled back towards the Sirohi side, where he remained in hiding.[36] In Sirohi state, the movement escalated, with widespread refusal by Bhils and Girasias to pay their taxes. Troops were mobilized under the command of Major Pritchard and punitive raids were carried out on several rebellious villages, with houses being burnt and stocks of grain destroyed. According to British records, three Girasias were killed in one such operation against Siawa village on 12 April 1922, which had involved, amongst other things, shelling the village with a twelve-pounder gun mounted on an armoured train. On 5 May the village of Valoria was machine-gunned, and according to Pritchard eleven Bhils and Girasias were killed. The people themselves claimed that twenty-seven had died. The headmen of these and other villagers were forced by Pritchard to break their eki oath before him in public.[37]

Unlike other princely states, the Sirohi authorities did not altogether prevent nationalists from coming to investigate what had happened. It appears that Ramakant Malaviya believed that he could get them to accept his version of the events.[38] His optimism in this respect proved misplaced, for their subsequent writings maligned the Sirohi authorities. Their report in *Tarun Rajasthan*, a nationalist paper published from Ajmer, was titled 'Assassination of Bhils in Rajasthan'. It alleged that 'scores of cows and buffaloes were shot down' and 'a pregnant woman was burnt alive.' Pritchard was described as a coward, and Malaviya was said to have broken his promises to the Girasias. They also published a pamphlet titled 'The Second Bhil Tragedy in Sirohi'. This reproduced long statements by Bhils whose villages had been attacked and destroyed by troops. At Balolia, they alleged, three Bhils had been shot dead, a sixty-year-old widow wounded, and a seventy-five-year-old widow stripped naked by the soldiers. When Pritchard had entered the village after the shootings, they claimed to have heard him say: 'We have killed fifty of you and wounded 150 and if you are not straight still we would kill more.' At Bhula, they stated, the troops burnt alive a ten-year-old boy.[39]

Even these investigations were partial, for officials were unwilling to allow the nationalist investigators to move freely in the Bhil and Girasia villages. As they stated:

> . . . we found at Keshabganj Railway Station and on our way back at Rohera and Pindwara that the State had deputed special men to enquire of all outsiders who alighted at the station and to turn them back if they intended to go among the Bheels.[40]

The publicity was, however, sufficient to put the Sirohi authorities on the defensive. Soon after, Ramakant Malaviya resigned his position as Chief Minister.

No such pressures were brought to bear on those responsible for the massacre at Dadhvav, the worst of all of these atrocities. This was because the nationalists of Gujarat made no attempt to make an issue of the matter. One important reason was that they were in disarray after Gandhi's arrest on 10 March—only three days after the shooting—and subsequent sentence to six years in jail on 18 March. But more important still was that they had no particular interest in taking it up. Motilal's movement was peripheral to their concerns, which were centred on the British-ruled areas of Gujarat. The grievances of subjects of princely states against their rulers were not at that time on their agenda. Gandhi had taken some interest in the movement during February and early March as it had, as he saw it, a violent potential that could reflect badly on the Congress. He had therefore sent Manilal Kothari to wean Motilal away from a looming disaster. This strategy nearly succeeded with Holland's attempt to gain permission for Motilal to leave his followers and join Gandhi in his ashram in Ahmedabad. After this initiative failed, and the disaster occurred, little could be done, so far as the Congress in Gujarat was concerned. There seemed little point in even sending a team to carry out an investigation on the spot, seeing that they would have been hindered at every turn by the local rulers and thakors.

The events that occurred at Dadhvav on 7 March 1922 therefore went unprobed at that time. Today, many years later, we are carrying out our investigations, but they are inevitably very inadequate compared to what might have been revealed had a full enquiry been carried out immediately afterwards. One thing is however clear. The authorities tried to pin all of the blame for what had happened on Motilal and his followers. As the political agent of the Mahikantha agency wrote three years after the massacre, Motilal 'has been the direct cause of great loss of life.'[41] Yet there is no evidence in any of the records that a single person was killed by any of his followers in 1921–2. The violence came from elsewhere. In early 1922 the British had a choice: either to force the local princes and thakors to change their ways profoundly and remedy the grievances of the people, or to suppress a largely peaceful and morally justified protest by the use of force. They chose the second course, and the violence, when it came, was vengefully one-sided.

VII

Amarsinh Chaudhary's initiative in publicising the massacre, which led to the article in *India Today* in 1997, soon petered out. When I visited Dadhvav on a subsequent occasion in late 2001, I saw that the black flag that had been erected in 1997 had vanished along with its pole, leaving nothing to commemorate the site. On the same visit, I met B.D. Damor, a medically-qualified Bhil who ran an impressive hospital at Shamlaji. He was very enthusiastic about my interest in Motilal Tejawat and his movement, saying he had tried to persuade the government to erect a memorial to the massacre; but officials in Gandhinagar had, he said, demanded documentary proof that such an event had occurred. He had not been able to provide such evidence at the time. He felt that my evidence could be critical, and I gave him copies of some of my material. Later, I found out to my dismay that he was involved in local politics, and a member of the BJP—a party I abhor. The BJP government subsequently sanctioned the erection of a memorial at Dadhvav, and it was completed in June 2003. Amarsinh Chaudhary, upset that he had lost the initiative, asserted that the monument had been built a kilometre away from the correct spot. Ramilaben Bara, the BJP candidate who lost to Chaudhary in the December 2003 election, countered that they knew that this was the case, but that the owners of the land on which the well stood had refused permission for them to erect it there. She went on: 'The Congress ruled Gujarat for decades, and Amarsinh Chaudhary was chief minister for years, but still they did not recognise the sacrifice.'[42]

Chaudhary's rejoinder, announced jointly with the Congress MP for the area, Madhusudhan Mistri, was that they had met the people of Dadhvav who had agreed to raise funds to build a memorial at the correct spot. According to Mistri: 'The BJP isn't serious about the monument, which was put up only with an eye on the next Lok Sabha election. The tribals never voted for them. How can the state commit such a blunder?'[43] He said that if the government were sincere in the matter, it would provide pensions to relatives of the survivors, on a par with the pensions that the government pays to old freedom fighters. The seven people who jointly owned the land in question had now agreed to provide a plot for the memorial. One of the owners, Chandubhai Damor, was quoted as saying that he was happy to do this, as the gesture would make him famous. In other words, he saw this as a way of taking his own place within the annals of what had now—somewhat abruptly—been accepted as Indian National History.

At the time—in 1922—the politics of the day had ensured that this history be marginalized. The massacre had occurred in a remote tract on the border of a princely state whose people were not as yet granted by Gandhi and his followers any legitimate role within the nationalist movement against British rule. Lacking any perceived place within nationalist history, the protest by these people, predominantly Bhils, was to find no place within subsequent written histories of either the colonial rulers or their nationalist successors. For half a century after Indian independence in 1947, the Congress Party dominated the politics of this area, with no other party providing any serious challenge to them in elections. In 1995 the BJP came to power in Gujarat and began to woo the so-called 'tribal vote' with increasing success. Although the Congress was still able to hang on to its seats in Sabarkantha district, it felt under increasing threat. It was in this climate that in 1997 Amarsinh Chaudhary took up the issue of the massacre at Dadhvav. He no doubt foresaw that the Hindu right might seek to curry support amongst the Bhils by according them an honoured place within the fold of Hindutva—as both Hindus and ideal 'freedom fighters'—and realized that he needed to take the initiative to deny them the advantage in this instance. He failed, however, to follow it through, so that the BJP was able to move in and claim the matter as its own. In this manner, partisan politicians have sought, crudely and manipulatively, to incorporate the Bhils within the History of the Nation State. We may leave the last word to Pahadji Damor, a survivor of the massacre, who told reporters in 2003 that so far as he was concerned, he did not care where they placed their memorial. What mattered to him was that the events of that terrible day should never be forgotten.[44]

Notes

1. Interview with Amarsinh Chaudhary, Gandhinagar, 20 December 1997.
2. See David Hardiman, *The Coming of the Devi: Adivasi Assertion in Western India* (New Delhi, 1987), and my writings in volumes III, IV, V and VIII of *Subaltern Studies* (New Delhi).
3. National Archives of India, Foreign and Political Department of Government of India (F. & P., GOI), 428-P (Secret-Printed) of 1922–3. (Hereafter 'NAI file on Motilal Tejawat'.)
4. I am grateful to Kasanbahi Parmar, a local social worker, for accompanying me on this trip and introducing me to several informants.
5. L.P. Mathur, *Resistance Movement of Tribals of India: A Case Study of the Bhils of Rajasthan in the Nineteenth Century* (Udaipur, 1988); L.P. Mathur, *Movements of Tribals During the Colonial Rule: Role of Ideologies* (New Delhi, 1995). The latter book has a whole chapter on the Motilal Tejawat movement amongst the Bhils that makes use of the file in the National Archives.
6. Premsinh Kankariya (in Hindi), *Bhil Kranti ke Praneta: Motilal Tejavat* (Udaipur: Rajasthan Sahitya Academy, 1985); Prakash Chandra Jain, *Tribal Agrarian Movement: A Case Study of the Bhil Movement of Rajasthan* (Udaipur, 1989), chapters 3 and 4; Hari Sen, 'Popular Protest in Mewar in the Late-Nineteenth and early Twentieth Centuries', unpublished Ph.D. thesis, University of Delhi, 1996, chapter 6; Denis Vidal, *Violence and Truth: A Rajasthani Kingdom Confronts Colonial Authority* (New Delhi, 1997), chapter 5.
7. Pushpendra Surana, *Social Movements and Social Structure: A Study in the Princely State of Mewar* (New Delhi, 1983); Ghanshyam Shalabha, *Kranticheta Vijay Singh Pathik* (Udaipur, 1990) (in Hindi).
8. Hari Sen, 'Popular Protest in Mewar,' p.192, mentions the movement to this effect led by the Bhil reformer Surmaldas of the 1870s. But the origins of this movement, associated with the shift of Bhils from a predominantly non-agricultural to agricultural way of life, would appear to go back even further. I have examined this movement in 'Assertion, Conversion and Indian Nationalism: Govind's Movement amongst the Bhils', in Rowena Robinson and Sathianathan Clarke (eds), *Religious Conversion in India: Modes, Motivations, and Meanings* (New Delhi, 2003).
9. See Shahid Amin, *Event, Metaphor, Memory: Chauri Chaura 1922–1992* (New Delhi, 1995).
10. R.E. Holland, Agent in Rajputana, to Foreign and Political Department, 30 September 1922, NAI file on Motilal Tejawat.
11. Vidal, *Violence and Truth*, pp. 145–55.

12. R.E. Holland to J.P. Thompson, 28 March 1922, NAI file on Motilal Tejawat.
13. Interview with Roop Singh Bhil, Udaipur, 18 December 1997. As a report on a gathering of Bhils at a fair in this area had earlier noted: 'Every man and boy was armed with the unfailing bow and arrows, and I specially noticed that the bow was invariably carried strung, while besides a couple of dozen arrows fastened in the waist cloth, four or five were held loose in the hand to be ready at a moment's notice.' Major W.A. Salmon, Acting Political Agent, Mahi Kantha, to Government of Bombay, Ahmedabad, 26 July 1881, in *Mahi Kantha Annual Administration Report 1883–84*, Oriental and India Office Collection, V/10/1542, p. 9.
14. For Pathik's views on Motilal's political acumen, and doubts about his ability to control his followers, see Pathik to Holland, 26 March 1922, NAI file on Motilal Tejawat.
15. Sir George Llyod to Lord Reading, 2 March 1922, NAI file on Motilal Tejawat.
16. Motilal Tejawat to Gandhi, 11 February 1922, *Navajivan*, 26 February 1922, p. 203.
17. Holland to Sir John Wood, Pol. Sec., F. & P., GOI, 29 September 1921; Fortnightly Report for Rajputana ending 31 December 1921; Holland to GOI, 3 January 1922, NAI file on Motilal Tejawat.
18. Holland to F. & D., GOI, 21 February 1922, NAI file on Motilal Tejawat.
19. Pol. Sec. to F. & D., GOI, to Holland, 26 February 1922, NAI file on Motilal Tejawat.
20. Lloyd to Reading, 2 March 1922, NAI file on Motilal Tejawat.
21. Reading to Lloyd, 3 March 1922, NAI file on Motilal Tejawat.
22. Interview with Peter Galji Bhanat, Samaiya village, Vijaynagar Taluka, Sabarkantha District, December 1997. Peter, a Christian convert, was nine at the time, and attending the mission school at Biladiya village. Interview with Sankaben Kamjibhai Balat, Biladiya village, Vijaynagar Taluka, Sabarkantha District, December 1997. Sankaben, a Bhil woman, was aged fifteen in 1922, and she went from her natal village of Pal to have the 'darshan' of 'Gandhi' at Dadhvav on 7 March.
23. 'Statement of Tek Chand, son of Ratan Lal Brahman, resident of Baroti under Para, at present residing in Koliari, Mewar, aged forty years, occupation beggar'. Reproduced in Holland to J.P. Thompson, 28 March 1922, NAI file on Motilal Tejawat.
24. As Shahid Amin has shown so succinctly, we need to read such statements—which may potentially be used in court or in an official enquiry—in terms of required rules of evidence needed to either convict or absolve accused people. Statements are generally tailored by the authorities so as to be as effective as possible in such a context. S. Amin, 'Approver's Testimony,

Judicial Discourse: The Case of Chauri-Chaura', in Ranajit Guha (ed.), *Subaltern Studies V* (New Delhi, 1987). Tek Chand, as a planted spy and eyewitness to a controversial event, knew that he was walking a tightrope in this respect. As he stated in his deposition, after fleeing the scene of the firing: '. . . [I] reported the fact to the Raj authorities and expressed my willingness to come to the Political Superintendent but they (Raj authorities) did not allow me to do so saying that I would be killed some where in these days. They afterwards informed the police officer at Udaipur. I was then sent to Captain Hornsby in Jharol who sent me here *via* Som.' By providing satisfactory evidence, it seems that Tek Chand saved his skin, for the time being at least (we do not know what happened to him thereafter).

25. Major H.G. Sutton to Political Agent, Mahikantha Agency, 7 March 1922, NAI file on Motilal Tejawat.
26. Interviews with Sankaben Balat in Biladiya; Peter Bhanat in Samaiya; Galjibhai Badaji Solanki in Dadhvav (a Chamar of the *Chamarvas* who was born in 1922, but was told by his parents all the details of the massacre); Damaji Panaji Gameti in Baleta (a Bhil aged ten in 1922) in December 1997. I have also utilised the interviews in the *India Today* article with Sukha Bodas of Chithoda village (age 85), whose father died in the firing; Kala Ramji Gameti of Baleta village (age 67), whose grandmother Somiben died; Koyaji Dhulaji Patel (age 90), who narrowly escaped death at the time; Surma Dholaji Ninama of Dadhvav (age 83), who was grazing his cattle nearby at the time and saw people fleeing with blood flowing from bullet-wounds; Thavaraji Surji Sadaat of Dantoli (age 84), whose elder brother Hirabhai died; Kurabhai Patel of Dantoli (age 60), whose uncle Koyabhai was wounded, and, according to his aunt, now deceased, managed to reach their home before collapsing and dying at the entrance; Jivabhai Kalabhai Asari of Dantoli (age 49), whose grandfather was killed.
27. A Church Missionary Society outstation had been established at Biladiya in 1888. It was upgraded to a full station in 1901, with a resident white missionary. See Anonymous (in fact R. Carter), *Battling and Building amongst the Bhils* (London, 1914), p. 60.
28. Reverend J. Irwin Lea, *Report of the Church Missionary Society Western India Mission 1922* (Madras, 1923), p. 44.
29. Quoted in a memo. from F. & P. Dept. to India Office, 15 March 1923, NAI file on Motilal Tejawat.
30. No mention of the massacre was made in either of Gandhi's weeklies *Young India* or *Navajivan*.
31. Translated from the Gujarati. Old files of *Saurashtra* can be found in the Gandhi Smriti Library, Bhavnagar.
32. B.S. Pathik to Holland, 26 March 1926, NAI file on Motilal Tejawat.
33. Interview with L.P. Mathur, Udaipur, December 1997.

34. These are Dungarpur, Register 9/2519/file 15 (1923); Marwar State, Mahekma Khas, file 106-A Police 1922. I am grateful to Ajay Skaria for bringing these files to my attention and providing a photocopy of the contents for me.
35. Fortnightly Report, Rajputana, 31 March 1922, NAI file on Motilal Tejawat.
36. He remained free until 1929, when he was arrested and sent to Mewar, where he was jailed until 1936. Subsequently he became a leading figure in the Mewar Praja Mandal, being jailed again from 1942 to 1945. He continued with his political and social work amongst the Bhils till his death in 1963.
37. Pol. Sec. F.& P., GOI, to Private Sec. to Viceroy, 13 April 1922; report by H.R.N. Pritchard, 14 April 1922; press communiqué from F. & P., GOI, 7 May 1922; report by H.R.N. Pritchard, 13 May 1922, NAI file on Motilal Tejawat.
38. Denis Vidal, *Violence and Truth*, pp. 148–9.
39. Report quoted in Vidal, *Violence and Truth*, p. 149. The pamphlet is reproduced in full in Kankaria, *Bhil Kranti ke Praneta: Motilal Tejavat*. See in particular pp. 119, 122, 124.
40. Ibid., p. 128.
41. Quoted in Chief Sec. to Pol. Dept., Govt. of Bombay to Agent in Rajputana, 7 April 1925, NAI file on Motilal Tejawat.
42. Milind Ghatwai, '1,200 Gujarat tribals killed by British at a different spot, says Congress: Tale of a memorial: Now here, nowhere', *Indian Express*, 29 July 2003.
43. Loc. cit.
44. Loc. cit.

CHAPTER 2

Adivasi Assertion in South Gujarat

The Devi Movement of 1922–3

I

In early November 1922 large numbers of adivasi—or tribal—peasants began to gather together in South Gujarat to listen to the teachings of a goddess (*mata* or *devi*) known as Salahbai. The Devi, who was not generally represented by any image, was supposed to have come out of the mountains to the east and expressed her demands through spirit mediums. The adivasis of several villages met together at a central place and listened while a number of them went into a state of trance. These men would shake their heads violently and begin to utter what were believed to be the Devi's commands. The principal commands were to abstain from eating flesh or drinking liquor or toddy, to take a bath daily, to use water rather than a leaf to clean up after defecation, to keep houses clean, to release or sell goats and chickens (which were kept for eating or sacrifice), and to boycott Parsi liquor dealers and landlords. It was believed that those who failed to obey these divine orders would suffer misfortune at the very least, and perhaps even go mad or die. The meetings normally went on for several days, after which the Devi moved on to another group of villages where the process was repeated.

This wave of possession by the Devi spread rapidly. Starting in the Baroda sub-divisions of Songadh and Vyara, it had by mid-November 1922 affected the whole of the British sub-division of Valod.[1] No adivasi village in this extensive tract was left untouched. By late November it had spread to Bardoli and Mandvi talukas, by 2 December it had reached Jalalpor taluka and by 14 December Surat city and the coastal areas. In December some new commands of the Devi began to be heard. Salahbai was telling the adivasis to take vows in Gandhi's name,

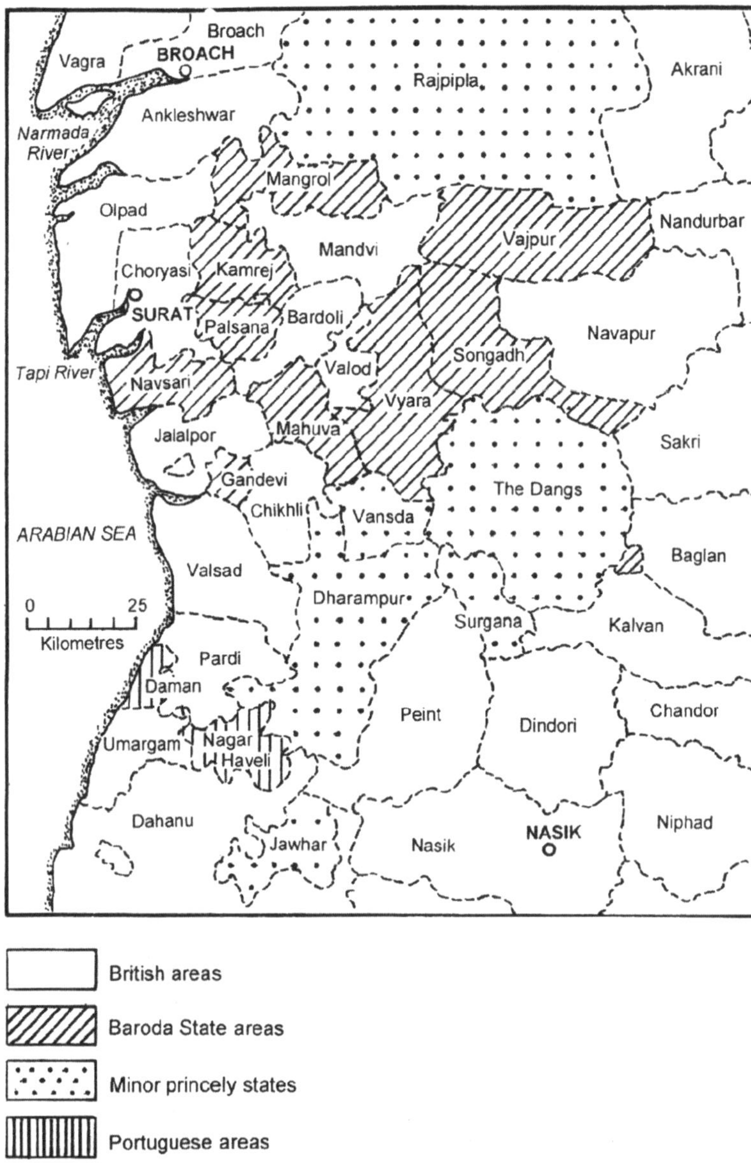

Map 1: Administrative Divisions of South Gujarat and Adjoining Regions during the Colonial Period

to wear khadi cloth and to attend nationalist schools. Rumours were heard that spiders were writing Gandhi's name in cobwebs. It was said that Gandhi had fled from jail and could be seen sitting in a well side by side with Salahbai, spinning his *charkha*.[2]

Government officials expected the movement to be a passing affair. The Mamlatdar of Bardoli commented: 'This is the tenth time within my knowledge that such rumours to stop drink are spread among Kaliparaj.[3] Such rumours spread rapidly but the effect has always been temporary.'[4] The mamlatdar's expectations were however to be proved wrong, for the Devi movement was to have a lasting effect on the area. In his annual report for 1922–3 the Collector of Surat district, A.M. Macmillan, noted that the impact of the Devi continued—particularly in the area in which the Chodhri tribe predominated. In this area liquor and toddy drinking had to a large extent stopped, and there was a marked improvement in the material condition of the adivasis. In response to popular demand Macmillan closed thirteen liquor shops in Mandvi taluka, one in Bardoli taluka and one in Valod Mahal.[5] In the following year Macmillan reported:

> The beneficial effects in the Chowdra areas of Mandvi where the effects of the movement persisted were obvious. The people did not require to borrow from sawkars to pay their land revenue instalments, as they had always previously done whether seasons were good or bad. They reduced their ceremonial expenses and so did not need to resort to the sawkars for advances for this purpose. Their general appearance, and the appearance of their houses and villages is noticeably improved, and they are able to afford to use brass cooking vessels and to buy better clothes and ornaments for their wives.[6]

The Devi movement of South Gujarat had many features in common with tribal movements in other parts of India during the late nineteenth and early twentieth centuries. These movements have not on the whole received much attention from scholars. The chief exception to this is the Tana Bhagat movement of 1914 among the Oraons of Chhotanagpur in Bihar, which shows many striking similarities to the Devi movement.[7] Other such movements have been reported in a summary form from tribal regions all over India. There are cases of such movements among the Bhils of east and north-east Gujarat,[8] among the Bhils of north-west Maharashtra,[9] among the Gonds of Madhya Pradesh and UP,[10] among the Oraons, Santals and Bhumij of Bihar,[11] and among the Khonds of Orissa.[12] In these areas movements with similar programmes swept through the tribal villages with surprising speed and force. They were relatively peaceful and often had a lasting effect. There were in addition many more violent movements involving adivasis, such as that of Birsa Munda,[13] which incorporated programmes of social reform.

In this essay I shall discuss the Devi movement in some detail in an attempt to gain a greater understanding of such movements in general. The themes which will be taken up concern the social, economic and political background, the actual history of the movement, and the meaning and significance of the reform programme adopted by the adivasis.

II

The adivasis who form the subject of this paper lived for the most part in a region known as the Ranimahals, or forest tract, of South Gujarat. This region is demarcated on the map. The Ranimahals are relatively flat; the precipitous mountains of the Sahyadri ranges appear only on their eastern borders. In the early nineteenth century the Ranimahals were covered largely by forest; during the course of the century the area was cleared of trees and fields were carved out. By 1920 the only extensive forests left were those in the northern and north-eastern portions. The soil of the Ranimahals was fertile and the rainfall plentiful, so that once the land was brought under the plough good harvests could be obtained from year to year from the same plot of land.

The chief tribes known as the Kaliparaj were the Chodhris, Gamits, Dhodiyas and Konkanis. There were also some smaller tribes such as the Naikas, Kotvaliyas and Kathodiyas. The parts of the Ranimahals inhabited by the four main tribes were adjacent to each other with borders overlapping to a large extent. The Chodhris were found chiefly in the talukas of Mandvi, Valod, Vyara and Mahuva. The Gamits were concentrated in Vyara and Songadh talukas and in west Khandesh. The Dhodiyas were to the south, in Mahuva, western Vansda, Chikhli, eastern Valsad, western Dharampur and Pardi. The Konkanis spread beyond the Ranimahals and into the Sahyadris, being found in

Vansda, Dharampur, the Dangs, Surgana and Nasik district. The Bhils, the largest of the western Indian tribes, were not found in Ranimahals to any large extent; their area started in Vajpur and Rajpipla state. An exception was in the Dangs where the ruling chiefs were Bhils, the mass of the peasants being Konkanis. The tribes of South Gujarat were culturally quite distinct from the Bhils; they were not a mere offshoot of this major tribe.

The adivasis of the Ranimahals were for the most part settled peasant farmers who lived in small hamlets (*faliyas*). Several faliyas normally made up one revenue village. The villages lacked any nucleus for they were without artisans and other specialist castes. In this the adivasi village provided a marked contrast to many of the so-called 'traditional' Indian villages with their hierarchies of Brahman priests, dominant castes, subordinate labouring castes, Baniya shopkeepers, artisan castes and untouchables. In most adivasi faliyas the members were exclusively of one tribe. They either owned or rented land and they normally possessed their own agricultural implements and draught bullocks.

As an example of an adivasi village we can take Sathvav in Mandvi taluka, which was surveyed in great detail in the early 1930s by the sociologist B.H. Mehta.[14] Sathvav had at that time a population of 588, divided into 114 families of which 106 were of the Chodhri tribe, 4 were Bhils, 2 Dhed untouchables and 2 Parsis. Mehta collected figures for the amount of land owned and/or rented by each family which enable us to compile the following table:

Land held	Families	
(acres)	No.	%
Nil	21	18
Under 5	21	18
5–10	14	12
10–20	34	30
20–30	12	11
30–40	5	4
40–50	3	3
Over 50	4	4
Total	*114*	*100*

The largest landholder was a Parsi who had 108 acres, while three Chodhris held 64, 60 and 52 acres respectively. According to Mehta at least twenty acres were required to provide an adequate livelihood for a family.[15] Eighty-eight (77 per cent) of the families were either landless or held farms below this acreage. It is likely therefore that the large majority of the adivasis of Sathvav were living in conditions of considerable poverty. We can conclude that not only were they poor, but also that by the 1930s there was a fair degree of differentiation in the villages. However the differentiation was a good deal less extreme than in the non-tribal villages of South Gujarat in which there were many bonded labourers working for high-caste landowners.

Despite these inequalities there was little exploitation of one adivasi by another. The worst exploitation was carried out by high-caste moneylenders and Parsi liquor dealers. The colonial bureaucracy also took its share of the fruits of the adivasi's labour, either through taxation or through forced labour and illegal levies. Policemen, revenue, excise and forest officers all took their cut. The moneylenders were mostly Baniyas, Parsis and Brahmans. Baniyas and Brahmans lived in the taluka headquarter towns. They lent their money either from their houses in the towns or from the weekly markets (*haats*) held at convenient centres throughout the adivasi tracts. Parsis, who tended to combine moneylending with liquor dealing, normally lived in the larger tribal villages. In these villages they had an exclusive right to sell liquor. We can get some idea about the numbers of the rural Parsis and their influence by noticing that there were 13 liquor shops in the 135 villages of Mandvi taluka, or an average of about one shop for ten villages. They quite commonly owned land in more than one village. By the early twentieth century some had accumulated huge estates and had retired to the towns, leaving their land to be managed by local agents. But many of the smaller Parsi landlords continued to live in the tribal villages. Their houses were double-storeyed and made of brick and tiles in contrast to the mud and thatch dwellings of the adivasis. They advanced liquor and toddy throughout the year, being repaid at greatly inflated rates in grain at harvest time. Landless adivasis paid back their debts by labouring in the fields of the Parsis.[16] There are numerous accounts of the heavy-handed methods used by the latter to control the adivasis.[17] Besides taking labour they took sexual advantage of adivasi women.[18] The tribal poor lived in constant fear. Any protest was met with a swift beating by the Parsi or his resident strongmen. Local officials and the police invariably took the side of the Parsis.

The position of the Parsis was strengthened considerably by the colonial liquor laws. Chief of these was the Bombay Abkari Act of 1878. Prior to this date the right to distil and sell liquor had been farmed out and the tax on liquor had been low. Liquor (known in Gujarat as *daru*) had been distilled in the villages, using as a base the sugary flower of the mahua tree. Toddy, which was fermented palm juice similar in strength to beer, was taxed through a small levy on toddy-bearing palm trees. The British disliked this system as it allowed considerable evasion of revenue on daru and toddy. The Act of 1878 banned all local manufacture of liquor, permitting only the operation of a central distillery at the headquarter town of a district. Central distilleries were run by district monopolists who had to pay a large annual sum to the government. This centrally taxed liquor was sold in the villages by men who paid an annual licence fee to the government. As it was felt that toddy might undercut the new more highly priced liquor, the tax on toddy trees was greatly enhanced and a more rigorous listing of the trees undertaken.[19]

Under this new system the excise revenue rose enormously, as the following table shows. The figures in the left-hand column are for percentages of the total revenue of Bombay Presidency and may be studied in comparison with the corresponding percentages in terms of the land revenue—the chief revenue earner—for the same years.[20]

Years	*Abkari* (*excise*)	Land revenue
1865–6	4.4	40.3
1875–6	4.2	38.8
1885–6	8.2	38.7
1895–6	7.7	34.7
1905–6	8.9	24.2
1915–16	13.7	31.4
1925–6	29.3	38.1

How the excise on country liquor and toddy rose over the years for one single district, namely Surat, can be seen from the amounts shown below in rupees.[21]

Revenue Years	Revenue (rupees)
1877–8	3,70,423
1885–6	7,94,221
1895–6	11,64,585
1905–6	11,67,718
1915–16	17,44,867
1925–6	34,36,291

The burden of this increase in Surat district fell on the lower castes and particularly on the adivasis. The liquor sellers did very well out of the new system. Although they had lost the right to distil liquor, they still had a monopoly of the sale of factory-made alcohol in extensive clusters of villages. Because they lived in the villages the liquor vendors were able to prevent most illicit distillation. Profits were made on the high-priced factory product by giving short measures, by watering it down, or by advancing amounts of it on credit against usurious rates of interest. While the shopkeepers lined their pockets thus by fraud and extortion, the excise officials could be bribed to look the other way.[22] According to Haribhai Desai of Surat, who testified before the Bombay Excise Committee in 1923, the excise officers always gave plenty of advance warning before visiting a liquor shop. Often the shopkeepers lent money to the officers and obliged them in other ways so as to keep them in their power. Desai continued:

> In fact, a liquor shopkeeper is, under the present system, a master in the village, whereas he was a pariah in the old regimes . . . To speak honestly and candidly, I have known the Abkari shopkeepers to be the only men of means in many of the villages. Their connection with the officials, coupled with this, makes them really dangerous as far as the internal affairs of a village are concerned. It is they who make and unmake quarrels, and under the warmth of official favour and countenance, they do not hesitate to ruin the reputation of many a respectable person. The less said about these shopkeepers the better.[23]

The profits made from moneylending and liquor selling were invested to a large extent in land. Before the land revenue settlements of the 1860s the adivasis had used land in the customary manner of shifting the area of cultivation from year to year. They did not think of themselves as owners of individual plots of land. During the 1860s however the tribal peasants of South Gujarat were given ownership rights on the land which they happened to be cultivating at the time, and for the first time land became a marketable commodity. Because they lacked political weight and were relatively docile (for they had never before been forced to defend their land), the adivasis were soon being deprived of their new proprietary rights by moneylenders and liquor dealers, and turned into tenants who, meek as they were, could be exploited with distressing ease.

This new system of exploitation rested therefore on the formation of property rights in land and on the liquor laws. Baroda and other adjoining princely states adopted similar measures in the late nineteenth century, so that the situation was much the same there. The colonial authorities soon noticed the dire effects their rule was having on the adivasis, but rather than question the system itself they laid the responsibility on the supposed moral depravity of the tribal peasants. In particular they blamed their 'addiction to drink'. In the words of a Deputy Collector of Surat district, writing about the Chodhris of Mandvi taluka in 1881:

> These Kaliparaj people are addicted to much drinking; in fact the whole Abkari revenue amounting to upwards of Rs 25,000 (for Mandvi taluka) is mostly derived from these people. If half the amount spent in drinking were used by them in improving their land and in supporting themselves with better means of cultivation, their condition will be gradually improved, whereas at present they give the superior produce of their fields such as rice, toovar etc. to their Sowcars towards the liquidation of their debt, reserving only kodra, naglee and other coarse grain for their subsistence.[24]

The answer it appeared was to educate the adivasis so that they would learn to appreciate the advantages of temperance and moderation. According to one Assistant Collector of Surat, 'Until they are sufficiently educated and are so much more advanced as to appreciate the rules of moderation, any attempt to emancipate them from their fancied thraldom must prove simply waste of labour.'[25] This sentiment was endorsed by another Assistant Collector writing seven years later:

> It is no exaggeration to say that the average Chodhra *cannot count above ten*, and he certainly abhors a school as a device of Brahmanism, but the inference that no perseverance would teach him anything is negatived by the example of Walod, which has been less neglected than Mandvi. That mahal boasts 2 or three purely Chodhra schools and actually two or three Chodhra schoolmasters, and I have observed that in those villages where there are schools—and in these only—there are Chodhras who live in brick houses, who feed on something better than *Kodra* and *Nagli*, who store up fodder against the hot weather, and who know that plough oxen cannot legally be carried off in payment of a debt.[26]

The colonial panacea for the pauperization of the adivasis was thus education.

Primary schools were opened in the adivasi villages. The experiment was not much of a success. High-caste teachers were unwilling to serve in remote tribal tracts and there were few adivasis either qualified to teach or indeed interested in promoting any education at all. Many believed that boys who went to school died young.[27] The schools were poorly attended and several had to be closed. The picture was not however entirely bleak, for Baroda state had had a small but important success in adivasi education. In 1885 after a tour of the Ranimahals Sayajirao Gaikwad ordered that a hostel for adivasi boys be opened at Songadh so that they could study full-time at the primary school in the town. Initially it proved hard to attract boarders. But the first superintendent, Fatehkhan Pathan, was determined to succeed and he went out to the villages to recruit pupils. The adivasis merely fled into the forest at his sight. The breakthrough came when he managed to persuade a prominent figure in the Gamit community to send two of his sons to the hostel. One of them, Amarsinh Gamit, was later to become a leading social reformer.[28] By 1900 the hostel was well attended and producing an annual quota of adivasis who had passed their seventh-standard Gujarati examination, which was the qualification required for a teacher. In 1904 the British decided to open a similar hostel of their own in Mandvi taluka. This institution—the Godsamba Boarding House—attracted boys from all over Surat district. Many of those who passed through the hostel were to become leading social reformers amongst the adivasis of the Ranimahals.

The most prominent of these social reformers was the ex-pupil of Songadh, Amarsinh Gamit (1873–1941). In 1905 he and Fatehkhan Pathan organized a conference for adivasis at his village in Vyara taluka. Resolutions were passed urging them to give up liquor, to acquire education, to abandon various superstitious practices and to free themselves from debts to moneylenders.[29] During the following years Amarsinh Gamit travelled from village to village encouraging the adivasis to reform their way of life. He tried to persuade them to take a daily bath, to keep their houses clean and to use modern medicine when they were ill rather than go to a shaman-healer.[30] He also campaigned against a big Parsi landlord, Ratanji Daboo, who was exploiting the tribals in a particularly blatant manner. The going was however hard and the success limited.

In the British areas, and in particular Mandvi taluka, young Chodhris educated at the Godsamba Boarding House began to form song-groups, known as *bhajan mandalis*, for the propagation of social reform ideas. A leading figure was Marvadi Master, a Chodhri who passed his Gujarati final examination from Godsamba in 1909. His father, who was from a village of Mandvi taluka, was a cultivator with about forty acres of land, so that Marvadi may be said to have come from a more prosperous Chodhri family. He became a school-master and taught in various villages of Mandvi taluka. He and some other ex-students of Godsamba organized a song-group to tour the villages on their days off, singing songs in praise of temperance, self-sufficiency and the need to stand up against alien moneylenders and Parsis. One such song went:

> Oh friends! Do not drink daru and toddy.
> Oh friends! If you drink the Parsi will plunder your property.
> If you go to the Parsi your wealth will be plundered.
> Oh friends! Do not drink daru.
> If you go to drink the Baniyas and Ghanchis will plunder your property.[31]

Once a crowd had been attracted by the singing the reformers gave lectures on these subjects in the Chodhri dialect.

Thus during the first two decades of the twentieth century young adivasis began to appear in the role of social reformers within their communities. Such men often came from the more prosperous adivasi families—the ones which could afford to release a son or two from fieldwork to attend school. From such families emerged a leadership capable of standing up against outside exploiters. Being educated these social reformers enjoyed considerable prestige among their people, and some of them initiated movements which anticipated the Devi movement. In 1905 for instance the Assistant Collector of Surat district reported:

> The last two months of the year were marked by a remarkable total abstinence movement among the Kaliparaj. The origin was in Baroda territory, where a schoolmaster said he had received from a god an authoritative prohibition of drinking any intoxicating liquor. The news went first to Bulsar, and prohibiting circulars were widely disseminated there. Some Anavla Patels energetically encouraged the movement. Mysterious letters from the god were alleged to be found in many villages. The Kaliparaj began to hold large meetings at which they decided after indulging in a big final debauch to abstain totally. Up to the present they have rigidly kept their pledge. . . . In adjoining native territory the abstainers have been severely threatened by the state, who feared the loss of Abkari revenue. But the people have replied that the god's command is greater than the state's and have continued to abstain. The movement is, I think, in no sense a strike against the high price of liquor, but is entirely a moral and religious one.[32]

In the following year the movement was reported to have died out. However a number of other movements of this type also occurred during this period, so that by 1922 they had become something of a tradition in the area.

III

The ground had thus been prepared for the coming of the Devi. This movement did not however start in the Ranimahals of South Gujarat, but in the coastal villages of Bassein, just to the north of Bombay city. The origins of the movement are undocumented and obscure, and my information comes entirely from interviews with old fishermen of the area.[33] It appears that early in the year 1922 the Mangela Koli fisherfolk were hit by an epidemic of smallpox. They believed this epidemic to have been caused by a goddess who had therefore to be propitiated. Ceremonies were held at which Mangela Koli women became possessed by the deity. Through these mediums she made it known to the community that she would be satisfied only if they gave up meat, fish, liquor and toddy for a limited period. The Mangela Kolis followed this advice. The women who were possessed were known as 'salahbai', meaning 'women (*bai*) who gave advice (*salah*)'. This propitiatory movement spread fast up the coast northwards to other fishing villages in Thana district, Daman and then Surat district. From the coastal villages of Daman, Pardi and Valsad talukas it spread to the Dhodiya adivasi villages of the interior. By this time the goddess herself had come to be known as 'Salahbai' and, as was the custom with adivasis, both men and women were becoming possessed. During this stage the cult spread comparatively slowly, as the ceremonies of possession took place in people's house and the attendance was small. As yet it had not come to the attention of the authorities. From Valsad and Pardi the movement spread east into Dharampur state where it took hold amongst the Konkani tribe. It then spread up the ghat into Surgana state and Nasik district and, at the same time, north-east into the Dangs. It reached this latter area around August 1922.[34]

In the Dangs the movement underwent an important change. Until then it had been conducted in a low key and there had been nothing in it which could be perceived as a challenge to the local status quo. In the Dangs groups of villages began to attend the meetings *en masse*, so that forest officials began to find it hard to obtain labour for the felling and transport of timber. The movement became better organized, with Dangi shamans, known as *gaulas*, carrying it from one group of villages to another. Many Dangi adivasis stopped drinking liquor so that the local Parsis were soon complaining to the authorities about a serious fall in sales and profits. From the Dangs the gaulas themselves carried the movement into Khandesh in the north-east and into Songadh taluka in the north-west. The first Devi meetings in these areas were organized by Dangi gaulas.[35] But after going a certain distance they turned back, leaving the movement to spread of its own accord. In Khandesh it did not go beyond the area covered by the gaulas, but in the Raṇimahals of South Gujarat it gathered momentum enough to spread westwards right up to the Arabian Sea.

In this area the movement was relayed from village to village either by those who had already been possessed by the Devi or by those who wanted to bring the Devi to their neighbourhoods. The local adivasis were already anticipating the coming of the goddess as a result of rumours which had been circulating for some time. When a meeting was convened—normally by the leading men of a village—large numbers would gather there from the surrounding hamlets. Once assembled, any man or woman could become possessed and speak the commands of the Devi. Many of those who were possessed were ordinary peasants with no personal history of possession and were never to be possessed in a similar manner again. The meetings usually continued for several days, with the participants either staying on at the meeting-ground or reassembling each morning. They freed or sold off their chickens and goats so as not to be tempted to eat them. They started to take daily baths. They were careful not to touch a drop of daru or toddy. Numerous cases were cited of unreformed individuals secretly persisting in 'impure' habits and then being detected miraculously by the Devi mediums and forced to make a public confession of their guilt. The meetings closed with a mass feast and a final ceremony of worship for the goddess.

This was a highly democratic movement in which any adivasi could, through possession, become for a time a respected leader with great authority. In its structure the Devi movement was not therefore what is known as 'messianic'.[36] Its central feature at this stage was that of possession by the deity. Throughout the world the poor and lowly have often chosen this method to voice their collective grievances and desires. I.M. Lewis has shown in his study of possession cults that tribes which have experienced the worst hardships over the past century have been particularly prone to outbursts of spirit possession.[37] Writing about India Richard Lannoy has argued that 'possession is not a mere chaotic hysteria but a structured, and in some cases a highly formalized phenomenon, which can be culture-creating and enrich the consciousness of the individual and the groups.'[38] The Salahbai phenomenon of 1922–3 needs to be understood in such terms. The wave of possession helped to articulate the deep-seated sense of wrong and the aspirations shared by the mass of the adivasis of South Gujarat.

IV

As could be expected in a movement in which authority was so dispersed, the commands of the Devi, as voiced by the spirit mediums, differed considerably from gathering to gathering. Some of these were clearly specific to local circumstances. For instance in Vyara taluka the Devi commanded the adivasis not to become Christians.[39] Vyara was a centre for missionary activities. However, in the midst of all the variety, it is possible to identify a core of commands and classify the material under the following heads:

1. Alcohol	(a)	Do not drink liquor or toddy.
	(b)	Do not serve in liquor or toddy shops.
	(c)	Do not tap toddy trees.
2. Meat and Fish	(a)	Do not eat meat or fish.
	(b)	Dispose of all live fowls, goats and sheep (kept for eating or sacrifice).
	(c)	Destroy all cooking vessels used for cooking meat.
	(d)	Remove and burn roofs of houses (normally of thatch in adivasi villages) as smoke from fires used to cook meat has passed through them.
3. Cleanliness	(a)	Take a bath daily (in some cases twice or thrice a day).
	(b)	Use water to clean up after defecation.
	(c)	Keep houses and compounds scrupulously clean.
4. Dominant classes	(a)	Boycott Parsis.
	(b)	Boycott Muslims.
	(c)	Do not work for anyone connected with the liquor trade.
	(d)	Demand higher wages.
	(e)	Take a bath when crossed by the shadow of a Parsi.

The commands demanded a profound change in the style of life of the adivasis. The drinking of daru and toddy was very much a part of their culture. Not only did these beverages provide a valuable food—important particularly during the hot season when foodstocks were low—but they were also used in religious and social functions, being consumed freely during many religious festivals and at marriages and funerals.[40] Likewise the sacrifice of live animals played an important part in adivasi rituals, the flesh of the animal being eaten afterwards. Daily bathing was not at that time a common practice for water supplies in the tribal villages were often very inadequate even for purposes of drinking. Not all the commands of the Devi were thus meant to make life easy for her followers and we need to examine more closely their underlying rationale.

Several observers at the time saw this as a movement for the 'purification' of the adivasis. The Gandhian leader Sumant Mehta, for instance, described it as *atmashuddhi*, or self-purification, by the adivasis.[41] This perception may be seen to underlie the concept of 'Sanskritization' put forward by M.N. Srinivas in the following manner:

> Sanskritization is the process by which a 'low' Hindu caste, or tribal or other group, changes its customs, ritual, ideology, and way of life in the direction of a high, and frequently, 'twice-born' caste. Generally such changes are followed by a claim to a higher position in the caste hierarchy than that traditionally conceded to the claimant caste by the local community. The claim is usually made over a period of time, in fact, a generation or two, before the 'arrival' is conceded.[42]

In terms of this concept Indian society is depicted as something like a very sluggish game of snakes and ladders. The game is entered in a state of impurity and a gradual advance is made over the generations towards the goal of Brahmanical purity. Many pitfalls lie along the way and most communities never make it to the top. There is no doubt however what the goal is: 'The Brahmanical, and on the whole, puritanical, model of Sanskritization has enjoyed an overall dominance, and even meat-eating and liquor-consuming Kshatriyas and other groups have implicitly conceded the superiority of this model to the others.'[43]

Srinivas continues: 'Sanskritization is not confined to Hindu castes but also occurs among tribal and semitribal groups such as the Bhils of Western India, the Gonds and Oraons of Central India, and the Pahadis of the Himalayas. This usually results in the tribe undergoing Sanskritization claiming to be a caste, and therefore, Hindu'.[44] In the case of the Devi movement it could be argued that in observing new rules of purity such as temperance, vegetarianism and cleanliness the adivasis of South Gujarat were advancing a claim to be accepted as clean castes within the Hindu hierarchy. It can therefore be seen as a dramatic example of the process of tribal Sanskritization.

There are however some difficulties in the use of this concept. In the statement quoted above Srinivas refers to the Oraons. A reading of S.C. Roy's classic work on reform movements among the Oraons reveals that Roy himself did not accept such an interpretation. He wrote that Hindu reformist groups, most notably the Arya Samaj, had attempted to win the Oraons to the Hindu fold by means of such things as *shuddhi* (purification) ceremonies, but had no success. For according to Roy, 'enlightened leaders among the Oraons naturally fight shy of such propagandists under the reasonable apprehension that orthodox official Hinduism with the religious and social exclusiveness of the twice-born castes, would relegate aboriginal converts to a very low, if not the lowest, stratum in the hierarchy of Hindu castes'.[45] Evidence from elsewhere also suggests that on the whole adivasis do not claim a rank in the caste hierarchy. It is true that in some cases they have demanded to be regarded as Kshatriyas.[46] This in itself is significant for Kshatriyas enjoy high status while continuing to practice 'impure' customs such as meat-eating and liquor-drinking. In other words adivasis who claim Kshatriya status are asking that they be accorded greater respect despite their 'impure' habits. But in modern times this has been the exception[47] and movements for purification such as that of the Devi clearly have adopted very different tactics. In such movements adivasis have adopted certain Hindu values without making an accompanying claim to caste status. There is no reason therefore why we should consider these as examples of acceptance of the caste system on the part of adivasis; we may just as well say that by adopting a way of life akin to that of a high caste the adivasis are claiming equality of status with high-caste Hindus.

A further drawback in the theory of Sanskritization is that it underestimates the amount of conflict involved in making good such claims and demands. Louis Dumont, in a discussion of Srinivas's theory, has pointed out that low castes or tribes which reform their way of life can hardly hope to enhance their status through such means alone. Higher castes have to be forced through political action to concede such a status. As a result there tends to be a correlation between the political power held by a community and its position in the caste hierarchy.[48] It would therefore be futile for adivasis to demand higher status or a position of equality without at the same time mounting a political challenge to the dominance of the higher communities. If we look at the commands of the Devi we find that this was indeed the case; the adivasi's programme combined adoption of certain high-caste values with a boycott of the dominant Parsi landlords and liquor dealers. The theory of Sanskritization in emphasizing only the aspect of 'purification' fails to take account of the sharp challenge to the existing social structure which forms a necessary part of such movements.

In addition the theory lacks any convincing historical dimension. Throughout time the goal towards which everyone is supposed to strive is that of Brahmanical purity. In Srinivas's words: '. . . the mobility associated with Sanskritization results only in *positional changes* in the system and does not lead to any *structural change.* That is, a caste moves up above its neighbours and another comes down, but all this takes place in an essentially stable hierarchical order. The system itself does not change.'[49] The theory thus represents a structural functionalist attempt to explain change in a society which it is believed does not itself change in its essentials.[50] To use our earlier analogy the game of snakes and ladders goes on but the board itself never alters. An alternative historical and dialectical approach would be to argue that any given social system is a synthesis arising out of pre-existing social systems. The interaction between tribal and Hindu society produces over the years a fresh synthesis which is neither purely tribal nor purely Brahmanical. Movements such as that of the Devi can thus be regarded as being specific to particular historical periods when the contradiction between tribal and non-tribal elements became particularly intense, leading to a strong thrust towards synthesis.

The evidence suggests that adivasi movements of this type started on a large scale in the late nineteenth century. They have continued to this day. In the past the adivasis had managed to isolate themselves to a large extent from the mainstream of Indian life; they were not expected to assimilate the values of the non-tribal élites and they did not feel compelled by their material circumstances to do so. Assimilation, where it did occur, was either extremely partial or affected only a small élite among the adivasis who then distanced themselves from their community by assuming prestigious designations, such as that of 'Rajput'. The change came with the conquest and subjugation of the tribal areas by the British, a process which had been largely completed by the middle of the nineteenth century. Rights in property were established, colonial laws were imposed and the tribal territories were opened up to economic exploitation. The historical context from which these movements issued was thus that of the process of the formation of the modern Indian state. Out of this emerged the adivasi reformers intent on forging that cultural synthesis which they believed would afford to their communities a respected position in the new society.

Another concept which has been used in connection with such movements is that of revitalization. This does not suffer from being undialectical. The idea, advanced originally by Anthony Wallace,[51] has been applied by Edward Jay to India in an article written originally in 1959.[52] Jay listed four main characteristics of the revitalization movement in the Indian context:

1. They are expressions of group solidarity and social cohesion and have acted as unifying forces for groups under conditions of social disorganization.
2. They represent attempts to establish a new moral order where the old one has been destroyed.
3. They have acted as mediators between the Great and Little Traditions of India, or, more broadly speaking, as catalysts of acculturation.
4. They have aided in the structuring of a new social system of which both Hindu and tribal societies are a part.[53]

Jay makes an important modification to Wallace's original statement. Wallace laid considerable stress on individual psychological disorientation leading to personal revitalization. Jay emphasizes the social disruptions which disorientate entire communities, leading to the revitalization of the group as a whole.[54] He does not find it fruitful to approach these movements in terms of the mental problems of individuals.

Although there is much that is good in Jay's approach, some reservations have to be made. Jay argues that there have been two basic types of revitalization in India, the resistive and the emulative. In the former the synthesis between the dominant and subordinate cultures is poorly worked out, there are serious barriers against integration, and the movements tend to develop into a state of violent resistance. In the latter the synthesis is better worked out, the barriers to integration are weak or non-existent, and the movements are peaceful.[55] On the surface this distinction may seem to explain the difference between violent movements such as that of Birsa Munda, and non-violent ones such as that of the Tana Bhagats or the Devi. In fact the distinction is of questionable value. All attempts at synthesis will encounter opposition from those who wish to maintain the status quo. Opposition will come from outsiders and from conservative members of the community itself. In this conflict there is always some potential for violence. Whether or not violence actually occurs depends on specific local conditions such as the relative strengths of the opposing groups, the political situation of the day, and community traditions of resistance to the upper classes (some tribes have a more militant tradition than others).[56]

A more serious drawback is that Jay fails to place the revitalization movement in a particular historical context. The examples which he cites all relate to the period 1850–1940. He does not however argue that the revitalization movement is specific to this period; the assumption is that such movements have been going on throughout Indian history. Jay's concept like that of Srinivas thus suffers from being ahistorical. The idea of a synthesis between the Great and Little Traditions is also problematic. Jay fails to spell out what is meant by the Great and Little Traditions in the Indian context, so that the statement remains vague. But even when set out more rigorously the idea does not take us very far, for although it explains how change occurs it fails to specify the direction of this change and why particular values are preferred to others.[57] In this respect Srinivas's concept of Sanskritization is more precise about preferred values. However the flaw in this approach lies in the assumption that there are values—such as those of Brahmanism—which do not change in their essentials over time, as in practice all value systems are in a constant state of flux and any attempt to define their essence invariably runs into difficulty. How do we overcome this problem?

The best approach appears to be to relate values to power. The values which the adivasis endorsed were those of the classes which possessed political power. In acting as they did the adivasis revealed their understanding of the relationship between values and power, for values possess that element of power which permits dominant classes to subjugate subordinate classes with a minimum use of physical force. To take an obvious example, the Brahmanical notion of 'purity' has provided a most potent means for the control of the supposedly 'impure' subordinate classes of India. By appropriating and thus democratizing such values the adivasis sought to deprive them of their power of domination.

We are not therefore dealing with value systems as such but with relationships of power. Once this central fact is grasped it becomes easier to understand the rationale underlying the various programmes adopted by adivasis in different areas. In many cases adivasis have adopted the values of the locally dominant classes among the indigenous population. In north-eastern Indian on the other hand adivasis converted to Christianity in large numbers because they associated the value system of the Christian missionaries with the power of the British. In South Gujarat they rejected the values of their direct exploiters, the Parsis, but endorsed the dominant regional culture of the Brahmans and Baniyas. The values which were appropriated could therefore be those of the colonial ruling class, or of a regionally dominant indigenous class, or of the actual local exploiters of the adivasis. The values endorsed differed profoundly. What they had in common was their association with the exercise of power.

One great strength of such programmes of assimilation of dominant values—as opposed to programmes of outright rejection of such values—was that they provided a meeting point between the adivasis and certain progressive members of the dominant classes. Amongst this latter group were the men of advanced liberal views: those who believed in national integration and the forging of a democratic Indian nation state. There were also the politicians who viewed the adivasis as a potential power base. Such men could play a vital role in convincing the colonial rulers and other members of their own class that the claims of the tribal peoples were reasonable and just. Adivasi movements of this type therefore took advantage of divisions amongst the élites.

Going back to the commands of the Devi therefore we can argue that they made up a mutually reinforcing package. On the one hand they sought to appropriate (and thus democratize and implicitly change) the values associated with the regionally dominant high-caste Hindus. In this respect it was significant that the commands never included any boycott of Baniya and Brahman merchants and usurers, even though they exploited the adivasis. The boycott was imposed only on Parsis and in a few cases Muslims. The logic of this was that the Baniyas and Brahmans lived the 'pure' way of life which the adivasis sought to assimilate whereas Parsis and Muslims were 'impure'. On the other hand the commands of the Devi represented an act of assertion against the most rapacious of the local exploiters, the Parsis. By refusing to drink liquor and by refusing to work for anyone connected with the liquor trade the adivasis were cutting the economic cords which bound them to the Parsis. Renouncing liquor was in this respect a far more effective act of assertion than resorting to subterfuge, such as illicit distillation, for the act of giving up had behind it a great moral force.

The commands of the Devi thus represented in this specific locality a powerful programme for adivasi assertion. The movement had unsettling implications for all those who wished to maintain the status quo in the Ranimahals, and in particular it sounded a challenge to the Parsi liquor dealers-cum-landlords. It is to the reaction of the non-adivasis to the movement that we shall now turn.

V

In the majority of cases possession cults do not pose any urgent threat to the status quo. I.M. Lewis has pointed out that they are often tolerated in an uneasy manner by the dominant classes. Possession is regarded as a safety valve through which the potentially subversive emotions of the lower classes can be worked off with least disruption to society.[58] The dividing line between purely ritual and more positive resistance can however be easily crossed. This is why the dominant classes keep a wary eye on such cults so that they can be quick to take action if things go 'too far'. In the case of the Devi movement the dominant groups sat up and took notice as soon as large groups of adivasis began to gather, for in such mass meetings lay the seeds of more active protest and subversion.

For the Parsis it soon became clear that the Devi movement was a disaster. Their trade in liquor dwindled to nothing, adivasis refused to tap their toddy trees, nobody would work in their fields or carry out domestic labour in their houses, and they were subjected to social boycott. To insult them even further adivasis who were crossed by the shadow of a Parsi took a bath to 'purify' themselves; some even told the Parsis that it would be better if they went back to Persia. The manner in which the latter reacted to the movement revealed how seriously they took the threat to their position. Their strongmen, assisted on occasions by excise officials, would seize an adivasi, hold him down and pour liquor down his throat, thus breaking his vow and making him ritually impure once again. Those who resisted were abused and beaten and even arrested on trumped-up charges.[59] In some cases Parsis poured toddy into village wells so that the tribals would be forced to take alcohol with their drinking water. So as to mock the 'purity' they urinated and defecated in the adivasis' shrines and holy places.[60]

The Devi movement was not popular with many local officials either. They had always regarded the adivasis as a debased and docile people whom they could exploit with little trouble and no qualms. Now with the new spirit of assertion they found that the supply of free goods, services and labour was not forthcoming as before. Their income from bribes dried up. They therefore did their best to undermine the movement, often aiding the Parsis in their efforts to break the spirit of the adivasis. In the British areas the local officials did not get any support from the higher authorities in this, whereas in the Baroda state areas they did. In the following pages we shall examine the differing reactions of the authorities to the movement in the Baroda state and British areas.

The first reaction by the Baroda officials of Vyara taluka was to instruct the police 'to bind down those people who come from the foreign limits and start this sort of gossip.'[61] Attempts were made to induce adivasis who had given up liquor to drink once more. When the Reverend Blunt of the Vyara Mission, a believer in temperance, heard about this he protested to C.N. Seddon, one of the leading ministers of the Gaikwad of Baroda. Seddon issued orders that officials were not to interfere with the Devi movement and that they were to allow it to spread from village to village.[62] In December 1922 a deputation of about twenty-five Parsis went to Navsari to request the district authorities to put a stop to the movement. Neither the police chief nor the Suba (equivalent of District Collector) were prepared to oblige.[63]

Soon after this the Dewan of Baroda, Sir Manubhai Mehta, came to a decision that the movement must be stopped. He later gave his reasons in a letter to the Gaikwad who was then on a tour of Europe.[64] He argued that political agitators and non-cooperators had taken advantage of the movement; Parsis were being intimidated and a racial feud had developed; the agitators were threatening to cut down a large number of toddy trees and this would damage the state excise revenue; many schoolmasters were supporting the campaign and were criticizing the excise police of the state in speeches at public meetings; the British authorities had started to take action against people involved in the movement; the operations of the forest department were being hampered; the adivasis were ruining themselves economically by not cultivating their land and by refusing to work for Parsis, thereby losing wages. Manubhai Mehta thus revealed a marked lack of sympathy for the aims of the movement. He showed a bureaucratic desire to maintain the excise revenue at any cost, a strong partiality towards the Parsi point of view (who was intimidating whom?), considerable ignorance of the movement (the adivasis never refused to work their own lands), and a fear that the nationalists of the state might use the movement to gain for themselves a firm base among the adivasis of Navsari district.

Orders were issued forbidding the holding of meetings in the Ranimahals. Government servants and schoolmasters were directed not to take part in Devi-linked activities. Cutting of toddy trees was forbidden throughout Navsari district.[65] Extra police were dispatched to Mahuva taluka, the area in which the conflict between Parsis and adivasis was most intense.[66]

The nationalists of Baroda state were not prepared to take this lying down. In Navsari town there had been strong support for the Gandhian movement for the past three years.[67] In early 1923 the leading nationalists of the town started a body called the Kaliparaj Sankat Nivaran Mandal (Kaliparaj Grievances Relief Association). The Baroda city leader Sumant Mehta agreed to be its president. Members of the committee began to go out to the villages in order to protect the adivasis from harassment by the authorities. In March 1923 Sumant Mehta came to Navsari to investigate for himself the repression being carried on by the state against the reformed adivasis. After his return to Baroda he saw the Dewan who was a relative and demanded that prohibition be brought into Navsari district. Manubhai Mehta rejected this plea on the grounds that prohibition had failed in the United States of America but he did agree to order the closure of a few liquor shops in the area in which the movement was strongest.[68]

In July 1923 the Baroda government prosecuted five of the leading members of the Kaliparaj Sankat Nivaran Mandal for holding meetings in the Ranimahals. The case was heard in early August, the leaders being defended by a prominent Vyara lawyer, Gopalji Desai. He managed to prove that the Navsari leaders had only had informal talks with some adivasis and had not held any meetings as such, and they were as a result acquitted.[69] Having failed to stop the urban leaders the Suba of Navsari then took out a case against some prominent adivasis. They were accused of forcibly preventing members of their community from working on the farms of Parsis and other non-adivasis. They were bound over to maintain the peace for varying periods.[70] Despite this repression the temperance movement and boycott of Parsis continued strongly in the Baroda Ranimahals, particularly Mahuva taluka.[71] If anything this demonstrated how marginal to the movement were the efforts of the outside nationalist leaders. Finally in frustration Manubhai Mehta issued an order on 1 November 1923 which continued the ban of meetings in the Ranimahals for a further six months and also prohibited all gatherings under the influence of Devis.[72] So finally the Baroda raj came to ban the Devi! Some of the sentiments expressed in Mehta's decree (issued under the name of the Suba of Navsari) throw an interesting light on the Baroda government's perception of the movement. There was an implication that the Devi had been manufactured by urban troublemakers:

> . . . certain intriguing people not knowing the true nature of the welfare of the ruler and the ruled, misrepresented matters to the Kaliparaj people, intimidated them and enticed them to hold large meetings. . . . these persons attempts to instigate the Kaliparaj against the officers of the state, thereby reducing the established authority of the Government, to undermine the faith of the Kaliparaj in the justice administered by the Government and to impress upon them that this Government is careless of the true welfare of their community.[73]

Rather inconsistently the decree also tried to make out that the Devi was an evil spirit misleading the people and that the 'wicked actions' of this goddess could not be tolerated. These statements were not only contradictory but revealed in a most transparent manner that this supposedly 'progressive' princely state had no time for movements of adivasi self-assertion. The state which had pioneered adivasi education in the late nineteenth century was not prepared to accept the consequences of this policy a generation later.

The Gaikwad himself proved to be rather more benevolent than his dewan. On 23 November 1923 he arrived back in India after a long sojourn in the health resorts of Europe. In December a deputation of over two hundred adivasis of Mahuva, Vyara and Songadh talukas came to Baroda to lay their grievances before the Maharaja.[74] Soon after this the suba of Navsari was relieved of his post and an order was issued permitting meetings in the Ranimahals for purposes of temperance and prohibition work. Local officials were ordered to cooperate with such activities.[75] In response to this new mood Sumant Mehta led a delegation on a tour of the Ranimahals in January 1924 during which he addressed large groups of adivasis. Conforming to the recent order these meetings were concerned purely with temperance. But this hardly mattered; what was important for the adivasis was that they were allowed to gather together once more to emphasize their solidarity in the struggle with the landlords and liquor sellers. Sumant Mehta found that the repression of the past year had failed to break the movement. The adivasis demonstrated to him an earnest desire for self-improvement and social reform. It was during this tour that Sumant Mehta became the first of the non-adivasis to question the use of the term 'Kaliparaj'. He remembered the bitter torment he had suffered in Britain when people had called him 'nigger' or 'blackie', and he decided to use henceforth the term 'Raniparaj' (people of the forest) to refer to the adivasis of the Ranimahals.[76] The term was soon accepted by nationalists throughout Gujarat. It provided a significant indicator of the increasing respect which the adivasis had earned, thanks to their self-assertion, from the more progressive members of the middle class of South Gujarat.

The British reaction to the Devi movement was of a different quality from that of Baroda state. In the past they had often adopted a tough policy towards popular anti-liquor movements. For instance when in 1886 large numbers of peasants of Thana and Kolaba districts resolved not to take liquor the local authorities promptly imprisoned the leaders of that campaign. The Abkari Commissioner for Bombay Presidency had justified this action in the following words:

> The question for decision is, shall we sit quiet and allow the movement to continue and to spread and thereby forfeit a large amount of revenue, or are measures to be adopted which will bring the people to their senses?[77]

By 1922–3 such a reaction was not to be expected. Under the Montagu–Chelmsford reforms excise had been made a transferred subject. The first popular minister was Sir Chunilal Mehta who had expressed his determination to 'combat the drink evil' at the very first meeting of the reformed council.[78] He had introduced a policy of gradual prohibition through increasingly rigorous rationing of supplies to liquor shops. He had also appointed a committee to consider the question of total prohibition in Bombay Presidency. The Collector of Surat, A.M. Macmillan, therefore had little choice but to show a benevolent attitude towards the temperance programme of the Devi.

Being foreigners the British were less concerned about the upset to the local hierarchy than with what looked like an emerging alliance between the adivasis and the Gandhian nationalists of Gujarat. Initially the movement was classified as 'religious' and not 'political', and therefore to be tolerated. But it was to be watched carefully lest it showed any tendency to 'drift into politics'.[79] Macmillan paid a visit to the Ranimahals as soon as he could to discover whether the nationalists of Bardoli had instigated the movement. He concluded after his tour that the movement was in fact 'spontaneous' and that it was 'doing the people no particular harm'.[80] However towards the end of December reports came that the Devi had started to advocate the burning of foreign cloth and boycott of government schools—both key features of the non-cooperation programme. So by January 1923 Macmillan began to have second thoughts on the subject:

> I am considering whether it is not time to get people of influence to put a brake on the Mata movement, as it is beginning to take objectionable forms, both through the interference of interested people and through the natural tendency of such a movement so long as it is entirely immune from the restraining influence of outside criticism and the exercise of ordinary common sense to assume crudely absurd exaggerated forms.[81]

In Jalalpor taluka a Devi medium was prosecuted for forcing a Parsi toddy-shop owner to pay a fine of Rs 120 to a local nationalist school.[82] He was judged guilty of extortion and sentenced to fifteen days' imprisonment and a fine of Rs 300.[83] In Jalalpor taluka the Devi movement was weak (it was not an adivasi area) and by early February 1923 the local police chief was able to report that the movement had died down as a result of the prosecution.[84]

In the Ranimahals the movement could not be crushed with such ease. Here Macmillan felt that it was best not to interfere. He felt rather that it was better to go along with the tribal people so that they would not be driven into the arms of the nationalists. In pursuit of this policy he persuaded the Excise Commissioner to allow sixteen liquor shops in the Ranimahals to be closed. Macmillan later argued in his annual report that his policy had been a success: 'Attempts were made by the local non-co-operation leaders to capture the movement for political purposes. Where it was superficial as in Jalalpor, they were fairly successful while it lasted but in Mandvi where it was deep and genuine, their efforts were more or less ignored.'[85] Can this verdict be accepted? Only partially, for the Gandhians linked up with the Devi movement with considerable skill. They did this by emphasizing those aspects of the programme which agreed with their own schemes and downgrading those which did not.

The Gandhians had been working among the adivasis of Bardoli taluka and Valod Mahal since late 1921. During that year Gandhi had insisted that before a campaign of civil disobedience be launched in these two sub-divisions, the adivasis must be brought into the nationalist movement. Until then the latter had shown no interest in the cause. As a result of a remarkable campaign in the tribal villages by the Congress leader Kunvarji Mehta, the adivasis not only became familiar with the name of Gandhi, but far more sympathetic to the movement.[86] It was not therefore surprising that in the following year the Devi mediums soon linked the name of Gandhi to that of the Devi. For many Gandhians the Devi movement appeared as an act of divine providence, for it seemed that at a stroke the adivasis had purified their way of life in accord with Gandhi's teachings. Soon after it began some of the Gandhian leaders of Bardoli taluka visited the adivasi areas and attended some Devi meetings. They suggested to some of the mediums that the usual list of the Devi's commands could be reinforced by such prescriptions as the need to wear khadi. Many of the mediums followed these suggestions.[87]

The Bardoli Congressmen decided to organize a Kaliparaj Conference at which Vallabhbhai Patel was to preside. They informed the adivasis that Gandhi himself was now in jail, but that his *gadi* (throne) was being occupied in his absence by Vallabhbhai Patel, and they invited them to come to the conference to hear Vallabhbhai and Gandhi's wife Kasturba. Large numbers promised to come. The First Kaliparaj Conference was thus held at Shekhpur in Mahuva taluka of Baroda state on 21 January 1923. About 20,000 adivasis attended—a large number if it is considered that their population was scattered and not very great (the total Chodhri population of Valod was for example only 8,000). The conference was very significantly divided into two separate sections. One of these was devoted to formal proceedings with speeches by Gandhian leaders addressed to a disciplined audience. The nationalists promised to give full support for a vigorous campaign to improve the condition of the adivasis and resolutions were passed advocating the cutting of toddy trees, the closure of liquor shops and propagation of khadi.[88] In the other section of the conference a large number of Devi mediums were brought together. They had been kept apart as it was feared that they might disturb the work of the formal conference. After the formal conference was over Vallabhbhai and Kasturba came to address the Devi mediums. As soon as they entered the mediums went into a state of mass possession, nodding their heads violently and waving red cloths in their hands. After ten minutes they quietened somewhat and Vallabhbhai began to speak, but as soon as they heard him they became once more possessed, shouting '*garam, garam, garam!*' (hot, hot, hot!). The meeting was considered a great success by all concerned.[89]

The First Kaliparaj Conference symbolized in a most striking manner the transition from the old style of politics to the new. Henceforth mass meetings of the adivasis of the Ranimahals were to become increasingly secular in tone. Less and less did authority flow from divine possession, more and more from resolutions put to a mass vote. In addition we see at this juncture the emergence of a new leadership among the adivasis. In the past bitter experience had made them wary of outside leadership. Too often they had been betrayed. From this time on however they began to place considerable trust in the Gandhian leaders and give them pride of place at their meetings.

Once accepted by the adivasis the Gandhians tried to modify the Devi movement still further. They believed that the chief value of the movement lay in the atmashuddhi, or self-purification, of the adivasis. By turning over a new leaf in this manner the adivasis would become worthy citizens of independent India. The Gandhians may be said to have anticipated the Sanskritization theorists in so far as they assumed that such purification would *in itself* bring about the uplift of the lower orders. They therefore poured cold water on that aspect of the movement which they felt not only to be less important but also socially divisive—and hence unhelpful for national integration—namely the adivasis' challenge to the dominance of the Parsis. When some Parsis came to complain about being boycotted the Gandhians responded by telling the adivasis that while they were right to refuse to carry out impure work for the Parsis, such as serving in liquor shops and tapping toddy trees, they were wrong to refuse to labour in their fields. When a second Kaliparaj Conference was held at Dosvada in Songadh taluka on 25 February 1923 Vallabhbhai Patel sent a message to be read out as follows:

> Everyone is surprised to see the awakening in your community. But you should be very careful. If you try to run too fast, you are likely to fall. Your decision not to work as labourers for Parsis and Muslims is very serious. Whatever steps you take should be well thought out.[90]

Kasturba Gandhi who was presiding over the conference was more blunt: she told the adivasis that they should go back to work for the Parsis.[91] The adivasis did not accept this advice. They argued in reply that the Parsis were extremely cunning and that they had been tricked many times in the past when they had tried to give up liquor. They feared that once they put themselves in the Parsis' power by labouring for them they would be forced to drink. The Parsis were prepared even to hand out free drinks so as to entice them. No longer were they prepared to be lenient to the Parsis. The complete boycott continued.[92]

It was perhaps this sort of disagreement between the Gandhians and the adivasis which Collector Macmillan had in mind when he reported that the adivasis had not accepted the leadership of the Gandhians. In other respects however a significant number of adivasis continued to show enthusiasm for the Gandhians and the Gandhian programme. They demonstrated most interest in khadi. Khadi production had not only economic attractions, but a somewhat magical significance for the adivasis. It may be remembered that when they had visions of Gandhi in the well he was seen spinning his charkha. It came to be believed by the adivasis that spinning of cotton on the wheel was a kind of ritual which would hasten both national independence and their own liberation.

Because of this interest in the charkha the adivasis asked for instructions to teach them how to spin and how to maintain the wheels. In 1924 a full-time khadi worker was sent to the Ranimahals. The man chosen was Chunilal Mehta, a Brahman from a village near Ahmedabad city. He went to live with an enthusiastic Chodhri social reformer of Vedchhi village in Valod taluka called Jivan Chodhri.[93] He started a training class in Vedchhi and toured the surrounding villages propagating khadi.[94] In January 1925 the Third Raniparaj Conference was held at Vedchhi (the Gandhians of the British areas had by now adopted Sumant Mehta's term for the adivasis). Gandhi, now out of jail, was president. He was particularly pleased to see large numbers of adivasis spinning khadi yarn.[95] Jivan Chodhri was chairman of the reception committee and in his speech he summed up what his community felt about Gandhi:

> We are satisfied and happy to have with us Jagatguru Bhagwan Mahatma Gandhi. We should worship the perfect god. From now on no other god can give us as much wisdom as this one can.[96]

Over the next two decades in 1928, 1930–1 and 1942 many Chodhris were to live up to this commitment by giving firm support to the Gandhian movement and the Indian national struggle against British rule. Macmillan was therefore wrong when he said that the adivasis had more or less ignored the Gandhians. The alliance between these two groups was fraught with difficulties but it was, still, a very real one.

VI

After a year many adivasis began to abandon their vows of temperance and vegetarianism. By mid-1924 Collector Macmillan was reporting an increase in the demand for liquor in the Ranimahals. He reopened four liquor shops in Mandvi taluka, one in Valod and one in Bardoli.[97] The temperance movement had been undermined not only by the Parsis and officials but also by people within the adivasi community. Opposition came from the many backsliders who failed to keep their vows and also from the adivasi shamans whose honoured position in the old society was threatened by the urge for reform. Many were still suspicious of placing their trust in non-tribal ways of life and leadership. Within a couple of years the conflict within the community had become acute. A divide emerged between the 'Varjelas' or those who followed the new way of life laid down by the Devi, and the 'Sarjelas' or those who had relapsed. The Varjelas tended to be firm supporters of the Gandhian Congress. In some cases they became an isolated minority shunned by other villagers, while in other cases, as in Vedchhi, they were in the majority. On the whole the Varjelas were in a minority. At times the conflict between the two groups became acute. In December 1929 for instance there was a pitched battle between Sarjelas and Varjelas at Pipalvada in Mandvi taluka when some Sarjela Chodhris tried to carry out an animal sacrifice to the Chodhri god Ahin.[98] Some of the commands of the Devi concerning purification continued to be held, however, by the mass of the adivasis. The habits of taking a daily bath, of using water to clean up after defecating and greater cleanliness in the home became general amongst adivasis of the area.

Although the movement for cultural reform thus had its limitations, as a movement for assertion against landlords, moneylenders and liquor dealers it can be judged to have had a considerable success. After the Devi things were never the same again for the Parsis, for just as the nationalist movement had undermined people's awe for the British so had the Devi undermined the adivasis' fear of the Parsi. The struggle was by no means over and during the following decades the Parsis attempted to make a comeback. But the nationalists proved good allies to the adivasis, and Indian independence brought land reforms which, in Gujarat, had greater force than in many other parts of India. For the most part the Parsis and high-caste Hindu landlords lost their estates to the tribal peasantry of the Ranimahals.[99] The misfortune of the Parsis was compounded by the imposition of prohibition in Bardoli and Valod talukas in 1938 and in the rest of South

Gujarat in 1950. This destroyed their liquor and toddy business. Since then the adivasis have enjoyed cheap daru distilled illicitly in their homes. However dubious this beverage may be, one thing is sure—liquor has ceased to be a major fulcrum of exploitation.

The Devi movement can thus be seen as a landmark in the struggle between the adivasis of South Gujarat and their exploiters. However, at the same time, it represented a stage in the growth of a class of richer peasants within the adivasi community. This process had already begun before the Devi movement but it was given a boost by the movement itself, for it helped the more substantial adivasis to achieve both economic independence and respectability within Gujarat society. Since then as the Parsis have declined, so have the richer adivasi peasants become one of the leading exploitative groups within the Ranimahals. There is no need therefore to romanticize this movement. One should rather recognize it for what it was—on the one hand a great liberation but on the other a movement which laid the foundations for new forms of exploitation.

Notes

1. To locate these sub-divisions, see the map provided with this essay.
2. B.P. Vaidya, *Rentima Vahan* (Ahmedabad, 1977), p. 177 Report by Collector of Surat, 14 December 1922, Maharashtra State Archives, Bombay (hereafter BA), Home Department (Special) (hereafter H.D. (Sp.)) 637 of 1922.
3. 'Kaliparaj'—meaning the 'black people'—was a derogatory term used to describe the adivasis of South Gujarat.
4. Report by Mamlatdar of Bardoli, 15 November 1922, BA, H.D. (Sp.) 637 of 1922.
5. *Land Revenue Administration Report of the Bombay Presidency, including Sind, for 1923–24* (Bombay, 1925), p. 39. A list for the year 1914 found in the record room of the Collector's office in Surat showed that there were 13 liquor shops in Mandvi and 8 in Valod, which suggests that all of the shops in Mandvi were closed.
6. Ibid., pp. 39–40.
7. The classic study of the Tana Bhagats is by S.C. Roy, *Oraon Religion and Customs* (1928; reprinted Calcutta, 1972), pp. 246–97.
8. Stephen Fuchs, *Rebellious Prophets* (Bombay, 1965), p. 240. T.B. Naik, *The Bhils* (Delhi, 1956), p. 324.
9. BA, H.D. (Sp.) 982 of 1938–42.

10. Fuchs, p. 79. L.K. Mahapatra and C. Tripathy, 'Raj Mohini Devi: A Social Reformer among Tribals of North Central India', *Vanyajati*, 4:4 (October 1956).
11. Fuchs, pp. 57 and 68; Surajit Sinha, 'Bhumij-Kshatriya Social Movement in South Manbhum', *Bulletin of the Department of Anthropology*, 8:2 (July 1959), pp. 16–19.
12. *Report of the Excise Committee Appointed by the Government of Bombay, 1922–23*, vol. I (Bombay, 1924), pp. 32–3.
13. Suresh Singh, *The Dust-Storm and the Hanging Mist: A Study of Birsa Munda and his Movement in Chhotanagpur (1874–1901)* (Calcutta, 1966).
14. B.H. Mehta, 'Social and Economic Conditions of the Chodhras, an Aboriginal Tribe of Gujarat', M.A. thesis, University of Bombay, 1933. The landholding figures have been compiled from the appendix volume of family schedules.
15. Ibid., p. 470. There were no irrigation facilities in Sathvav, so that the area needed for subsistence was greater than in many other regions.
16. *Gazetteer of the Bombay Presidency, Volume II, Surat and Broach* (Bombay, 1877), p. 190.
17. See, for instance, Sumant Mehta, *Samaj Darpan* (Ahmedabad, 1964), p. 340.
18. Dr U.L. Desai of Vyara to A.D.C. to Gaikwad of Baroda, 5 December 1923, Baroda Records Office (hereafter BRO), Confidential Dept., 301.
19. *Reports of the Excise Committee Appointed by the Government of Bombay, 1922–23*, vol. I, p. 43; vol. II, p. 301.
20. Figures from annual *Reports on the Administration of the Bombay Presidency.*
21. Figures from annual *Reports on the Administration of the Abkari Department in the Bombay Presidency, Sind, and Aden.*
22. *Report of the Excise Committee Appointed by the Government of Bombay, 1922–23*, vol. I, p. 49.
23. Ibid., vol. II, p. 526.
24. District Deputy Collector's report, 1880–1, BA, Revenue Department (hereafter R.D.) 1881, vol. 22, Comp. 1435.
25. Assistant Collector's report, 1893–4, BA, R.D. 1894, vol. 26, Com p. 1548.
26. Assistant Collector's report, 1893–4, BA, R.D. 1894, vol. 36, Com p. 1305.
27. I.I. Desai, *Raniparajma Jagrati* (Surat, 1971), p. 9.
28. Loc. cit.
29. Ibid., p. 10.
30. Ibid., p. 11.

31. The song was recited to me by a former member of Marvadi Master's song group, Dalubhai Chodhri of Salaiya (Mandvi taluka). The song, which I have translated from the Chodhri dialect with assistance from Professor I.P. Desai of Surat, uses the terms *Parha* for 'Parsis' and *Vange* for 'Baniyas'. Professor Desai says that these terms would have been regarded by Parsis and Baniyas as being highly insulting.
32. Assistant Collector's report, 1904–5, BA, R.D. 1906, vol. II, Comp. 511, pt. VI.
33. I am grateful for the help given me in this respect by Sudha Mokashi of the S.N.D.T. University, Bombay, who introduced me to the fishing villages of Bassein and Palghat talukas of Thana district.
34. Tracing the route of the movement proved to be a laborious—though fascinating—task, as the contemporary documents are very vague on the subject. It was necessary to start from Khandesh and work backwards village by village. Dates are difficult to establish by such a method, but according to the Collector of Surat at the time, the Devi was in the Dangs in August and September of 1922. *Land Revenue Administration Report of the Bombay Presidency for 1922–23*, p. 43.
35. For a description of such a meeting, see *Raniparajma Jagrati*, pp. 138–41.
36. Michael Adas has argued that the single most important feature of the messianic movement is the presence of a messianic or prophetic leader. See M. Adas, *Prophets of Rebellion: Millennarium Protest Movements against the European Colonial Order* (Chapel Hill, 1979), pp. 92–3 and 115. Adas relies here on an article by Normam Cohn, 'Medieval Millennarianism', in S.L. Thrupp (ed.), *Millennial Dreams in Action* (New York, 1970), pp. 32–43. Several tribal movements in India have had messianic-style leaders, most notably that of Birsa Munda. But the fact that many—such as the Devi—did not, suggests that we need to question this concept as an explanation for such movements. In this context, we may also take note of the writings of Stephen Fuchs. In *Rebellious Prophets* he describes several reformist movements amongst Indian tribals (though not the Devi) and labels them as 'messianic'. In his opening chapter he lists fourteen features of the 'messianic movement', which he says can be found either together or in part in such movements. The list is very comprehensive, and it is unlikely that all of these features would be found in one movement. Fuchs has not therefore provided us with a theory to explain such movements, for the essence of a theory is that the parts should fit together. The concept is thus a poor one which, beyond describing the nature of the leadership of certain tribal movements, does not advance our understanding very far.
37. The Shona of Zimbabwe provide an example: see I.M. Lewis, *Ecstatic Religion: An Anthropological Study of Spirit Possession and Shamanism* (Harmondsworth, 1978), pp. 141–3.

38. Richard Lannoy, *The Speaking Tree: A Study of Indian Culture and Society* (New York, 1975), pp. 198–9.
39. Police Report of 28 November 1922, BRO, Confidential Dept. 327.
40. *Papers Relating to the Revision Survey Settlement of the Mandvi Taluka of the Surat Collectorate. Selections from the Records of the Bombay Government*, no. CCCCXXVI—New Series (Bombay, 1904), p. 41. F.S.P. Lely to J.G. Moore, 22 May 1886, BA, R.D. 1887, vol. 7, Comp. 264. Assistant Collector's report, 1885–6, BA, R.D. 1886, vol. 32, Comp. 1548.
41. S. Mehta, 'Kaliparaj', *Yugdharma*, 2:3 (1923), p. 220.
42. M.N. Srinivas, *Social Change in Modern India* (Bombay, 1972), p. 6. This represents Srinivas's modified definition of Sanskritization which takes account of various criticisms made of his original statement in 'A Note on Sanskritization and Westernization', in *Caste in Modern India* (Bombay, 1962). For a critical discussion of Srinivas's theory and his changes in position, see Yogendra Singh, *Modernization of Indian Tradition: A Systematic Study of Social Change* (Delhi, 1973), pp. 7–12.
43. Srinivas, *Social Change*, p. 26.
44. Ibid., p. 7.
45. Roy, p. 293. Suresh Singh makes the same point for the Birsa Munda movement, pp. 198–9.
46. Fuchs gives brief histories of many adivasi movements in *Rebellious Prophets.* Only in two cases (cited on p. 67 and p. 69) did adivasis advance a claim to caste status, and in both it was for Kshatriya status.
47. During the medieval period there was probably a considerable amount of what Surajit Sinha calls 'Rajputization' of tribes—i.e. claims for Rajput or Kshatriya status ('Bhumij-Kshatriya Social Movement in South Manbhum'). With the failure of Rajput power over the centuries this model appears to have become increasingly less popular.
48. Louis Dumont, *Homo Hierarchicus* (London, 1972), pp. 244 and 283.
49. *Social Change*, p. 7.
50. Ramakrishna Mukherjee, *Sociology of Indian Sociology* (New Delhi, 1979), p. 51.
51. A. Wallace, 'Revitalization Movements', *American Anthropologist*, 58 (1956), pp. 264–81.
52. The version of the article referred to here is a revised and modified one of 1961. Edward Jay, 'Revitalization Movements in Tribal India', in L.P. Vidyarti (ed.), *Aspects of Religion in Indian Society* (Meerut, 1961), pp. 282–315.
53. Ibid., p. 282.
54. Ibid., p. 302.
55. Ibid., p. 304.

56. In this context it is interesting to note that in February 1898 Birsa Munda told his followers that they could adopt two tactics to fight for the Munda kingdom: either the 'religious' or the 'forcible' method. As there was a strong religious content to the 'forcible' method, what he meant was that they could choose to challenge the status quo either violently or non-violently. The violent method was chosen, leading to a disastrous defeat. After the outbreak was over the Mundas returned to non-violent methods. In the Munda movement we see a constant interchange, therefore, between violent and non-violent methods. Suresh Singh, pp. 82–3.
57. For a full discussion of this point, see Yogendra Singh, pp. 13–16.
58. I.M. Lewis, p. 128.
59. S. Mehta, *Samaj Darpan*, pp. 341–2.
60. S. Mehta, 'Kaliparaj', p. 222.
61. Report by Police Naib Suba, Navsari, 13 November 1922, BRO, Confidential Dept. 327.
62. Manubhai Mehta to Gaikwad, 7 June 1923, BRO, Confidential Dept. 273.
63. Report by Police Commissioner, Baroda, 16 December 1922, BRO, Confidential Dept. 327.
64. Manubhai Mehta to Gaikwad, 7 June 1923, BRO, Confidential Dept. 273.
65. Loc. cit.
66. S. Mehta, 'Kaliparaj ke Raniparaj', *Yugdharma*, 3 (1924), p. 444.
67. *Bombay Chronicle*, 27 April 1922.
68. Manubhai Mehta to Gaikwad, 7 June 1923, BRO, Confidential Dept. 273.
69. *Times of India*, 4 August 1923. *Servant of India*, 30 August 1923, p. 363.
70. *Times of India*, 18 September 1923.
71. Manubhai Mehta to Gaikwad, 5 October 1923, BRO, Confidential Dept. 273.
72. *Bombay Chronicle*, 30 November 1923.
73. Loc. cit.
74. *Bombay Chronicle*, 11 December 1923.
75. *Bombay Chronicle*, 28 January 1924.
76. S. Mehta, 'Kaliparaj ke Raniparaj', p. 446.
77. *Report of the Excise Committee Appointed by the Government of Bombay 1922–23*, vol. I, p. 45.
78. Ibid., p. 50.
79. M.S. Jayakar to Macmillan, 16 November 1922, BA, H.D. (Sp.) 637 of 1922.
80. Macmillan to Crerar, 1 December 1922, ibid.

81. Report by Macmillan, 19 January 1923, ibid.
82. Reports of 12 and 13 January 1923, ibid.
83. Report by Macmillan, 20 January 1923, ibid.
84. Report of 10 February 1923, ibid.
85. *Land Revenue Administration Report of the Bombay Presidency for 1922–23*, p. 43.
86. For details, see the biography of Kunvarji Mehta by B.P. Vaidya, *Rentima Vahan*, pp. 165–77.
87. Ibid., p. 170.
88. *Bombay Chronicle*, 7 February 1923. Report by Baroda Police Commissioner, 25 January 1923, BRO, Confidential Dept. 327.
89. *Rentima Vahan*, p. 171. *Raniparajma Jagrati*, pp. 25–6.
90. *Raniparajma Jagrati*, p. 20.
91. Loc. cit.
92. Ibid., p. 28.
93. Jugatram Dave, *Khadibhakta Chunibhai* (Ahmedabad, 1966), pp. 13–20.
94. *Raniparajma Jagrati*, pp. 52–3.
95. Ibid., pp. 53–4. By this time Chunilal Mehta had sold 520 charkhas to the adivasis of the area. Ibid., p. 72.
96. Ibid., p. 71.
97. *Land Revenue Administration Report of the Bombay Presidency for 1923–24*, pp. 39–40.
98. B.H. Mehta, 'Social and Economic Conditions of the Chodhris', p. 178. Divides such as these have often developed amongst adivasis as a result of reform movements. In some cases the reformed group has become a separate subcaste. For an example, see Roy, pp. 286–90.
99. The land was not necessarily distributed equitably; the bigger adivasi landowners benefited most, leading to a growing polarization between rich and poor adivasis in the years since independence. Ghanshyam Shah, 'Tribal Identity and Class Differentiations: A Case Study of the Chaudhri Tribe', *Economic and Political Weekly*, Annual Number, February 1979, pp. 459–64.

CHAPTER 3

Community, Patriarchy, Honour

Raghu Bhangare's Revolt

In 1872 a Marwari usurer called Hatichand Rupchand, who carried on his business from the village of Shervihire in the Sahyadri mountains of western Maharashtra, was visited by a group of Mahadev Kolis led by Honiya Kengle. The Kolis caught hold of Hatichand and three other Marwaris who were with him at the time and cut off their noses with their swords. The bandits burnt all of the account books and debt bonds which they could find, then set fire to the house and left the village with an estimated Rs 422 worth of the Baniyas' property.[1]

Two years on, despite all of the efforts of the police, Honiya Kengle and his gang were still at large, carrying out sporadic attacks on usurers. A British officer commented:

> Koli dacoity is, essentially, the rebellion of a race against our system of civil procedure; and Honya Naik is a national hero and a champion. The demands of dacoits and outlaws for provisions are readily complied with; and information to the authorities is either not given at all; or when the patels well know it is too late to be of any use.[2]

By the time Honiya was captured eventually in 1876, he had become a hero throughout the region. When he was tried in Pune, the jury returned a verdict of not guilty, despite the incriminating evidence against him. The British judge promptly ordered that Honiya be retried in Bombay city. The case was heard there two months later, and Honiya was transported for life.[3]

Honiya Kengle's life as an outlaw and his capture and trial are described in records kept in the Maharashtra State Archives in Bombay. There are many other records there about different Koli bandits who had taken similar punitive action against Marwari and Gujarati usurers in the second half of the nineteenth century. After reading through these records and some other sources I decided to visit the home region of the Mahadev Kolis, which stretches from the Bor Ghat (the pass through which the railway between Bombay and Pune runs) north to Nasik, to try to collect oral evidence about this tradition of banditry. There, I met up with some local social workers—Kusum Karnik, Anand Kapoor and Sadhana Dashishta—who agreed to introduce me to some of the Koli villagers. Together with two local Kolis, Jaibai Kengle and Dhadagu Langhi, we travelled up the mountain valleys. The Kolis whom we met could tell us plenty of stories about such people—whom they called *bandkaris*—who were active in the 1950s and 1960s. We drew a blank, however, over names from the nineteenth century which I had collected from various records. Except for one. When we mentioned the name Raghu Bhangare their eyes lit up. Yes, they knew about him. He was a Mahadev Koli from Akola taluka of Ahmadnagar district, to the north, but he had been active in Pune district as well. He was, we were told, so strong that he could defeat even ten to twelve people in hand-to-hand conflict.

In Jambhori village we were told a story about Raghu Bhangare. The police who were chasing him found out that he intended to worship at the Siddheshwar temple at Purshiroli in Junnar taluka at the time of Mahashivratri. They therefore kept a watch out for him. Raghu Bhangare came disguised in only a loin cloth and carrying a large and heavy copper pot with which he intended to bathe the Shiv linga at the temple. The police realized he must be there somewhere and tried to draw him out by abusing him, saying that although Raghu Bhangare was meant to be a devotee of Shiva he had failed to come. The tactic worked; Rahgu became angry and lashed out at them with his copper pot. The police were scattered and the people there helped him to escape.[4]

They told us also that there was a woman in Jambhori, Venubai Bhalchin, who knew a song about Raghu Bhangare. She was not around at the time, so some of us returned a few days later to meet her. She sang the song for us, which I recorded on tape:

Raghu plotted his revolt (*band*),
It was an awesome revolt,
He stormed the hill of Awu,

On top he raised his flag,
He took up the cause,
He struck hard,
At the gates of the fortress,
It was a spectacular revolt,
His mother, the brave Ramayi,
Concealed a knife in his *bhakri* (roti),
He was not deterred by sunlight,
Up to the crossroads of Bane,
Raghu has rid us of our afflictions,
Through dark and tortuous hill-passes,
From the treacherous slopes of Asud,
He reached the valley of Gugura,
Ramayibai proclaims,
My Raghu leads the revolt,
With ornaments of wild jasmine,
Chimayi tantalized the hero,
Raghu raised his revolt,
He stayed in the deep hollows of the Konkan,
Hid in the mango groves,
There was a big gun battle,
The rebels fought until they were victorious,
And the *gora's* (white man's) face was besmeared with blood.[5]

The song tells us that there was a great revolt in which Raghu, after raising his standard, went down from his mountain country into the Konkan and fought and defeated the British (*gora*). The song is suffused with a sense of pride and awe at Raghu's achievement. In places it is, however, so condensed that the meaning becomes obscure. Why did Raghu's mother Ramayi conceal a knife in his *bhakri*? Who was Chimayi, who tantalized the hero? What was 'the cause' for which Raghu fought? What were 'the afflictions' which Raghu rid the people of? Prior knowledge is assumed, and at the time, not having a proper understanding of the words of the song which I had recorded, I failed to probe the singer or her audience.

Raghu Bhangare was not one of the outlaws whose exploits had been described in the records of the Bombay archives. I had in fact obtained his name from the report on the Deccan riots of 1875, where he was described as a 'Bhil chief' who in 1845 had 'headed a large body of plundering Bhils, whose practice it was to cut off the ears and noses of Marwari sowkars wherever they could find them.'[6] G.S. Ghurye had mentioned Raghu Bhangare in his anthropological monograph on the Mahadev Kolis, written in the 1950s, but his information had come entirely from the nineteenth-century district gazetteers for Bombay Presidency.[7] Turning to this source, I found that the accounts in the gazetteers for Nasik and Ahmadnagar districts were virtually identical. They stated that the name of 'Raghoji Bhangria' was still fresh in the region:

> About the year 1845 Raghoji made a raid on some Marwari Vanis who applied to the police. During their investigation, the police asked Raghoji's mother where her son was hiding; and when she refused to tell she was put to torture. Enraged at this outrage, Raghoji gathered a band of Kolis, and wandering through the district cut off the nose of every Marwari he could lay hands on. Almost all village Marwaris fled in terror to the district towns, and the pursuit of the police was so hot that Raghoji had to break up his band and disappear. He escaped for some time, but was afterwards caught at Pandarpur, and, as some of his raids had been accompanied with murder, he was hanged.[8]

The Thane gazetteer gave a rather different account. The paragraph on 'Raghoji Bhangria 1844–8' started with a description of various crimes committed in 1843 and 1844, such as opium worth, in all, a lakh of rupees, stolen and carried down the ghats, the plunder of cloth-dealers and other merchants, the 'cutting-off' of officers' baggage and stopping of the post. The whole area, we learn, was 'infested by organised gangs of as many as two hundred robbers.' The terror was so great that the people of Bhiwandi town shut themselves in their houses. 'The leading spirit among the freebooters', we are told, was 'Raghoji Bhangria, the son of a robber chief who had once been an officer in the police.' In October 1843, this 'freebooter' descended from the Sahyadris with a large gang and committed several robberies. The hill police acted against him with great vigour, and although he escaped, many of his leading men were caught and the strength of his gang was much reduced. In 1845 he again appeared in Thana, burning villages and killing two village headmen who were known to have helped the police. A reward of Rs 4,000 was offered for his arrest, and a special party of police was established to track him down. By the end of 1845 four of his leading lieutenants had been captured. At the end of 1847, the police heard that he had left the hills and was heading for Pandarpur. They gave chase and captured him. He confessed, was tried for treason, and was sentenced to death in April 1848. The section in the gazetteer ended with a table which revealed that the total number of gang robberies in the district had fallen from 198 in 1844 to 45 in 1848, which, it was held, showed that the apprehension of the notorious outlaw had brought about a noteworthy decline in this form of criminal activity.[9]

According to the Nasik account, Raghu's career as an outlaw was a short one—only the year 1845 is mentioned. Although upset at the police torturing his mother, his only target of attack appears to have been the Marwaris. The Thane account, on the other hand, shows that he was active from 1843 to 1847 often escaping from the police—despite the supposed vigour of their operations. The attacks appear to have been directed against the state, for he burnt villages, killed village headmen, and was tried and eventually sentenced to death for 'treason'. At times the two accounts seem to be describing different outlaws.

For a time, I thought that I might have to be satisfied with these very fragmentary accounts of Raghu Bhangare. It was only subsequently, when I was looking through the Bombay Judicial Proceedings in the India Office Library in London, that I found an extensive body of material on the outlaw. Still later, I was told about an American doctoral thesis on social banditry in Maharashtra between 1818 and 1880 which had a lot of material on Raghu Bhangare.[10] Robinson, the author of this thesis, had consulted the records in the Bombay archives, the Peshwa Daftar in Pune, and the India Office Library, and although he had used all of these records to construct his narrative, his two chapters on Raghu Bhangare were based almost entirely on the India Office Library Proceedings. These records would appear, therefore, to be the most extensive relating to this outlaw.

Robinson's account of Raghu Bhangare fits into a narrative about the pacification of the region by the British which involved often tortuous dealings with local peasant leaders as well as frequent revolts. He shows in a very valuable manner how a tradition of revolt against the state gradually metamorphosed into a tradition of social banditry against usury. The account is however based entirely on the official records; Robinson made no attempt to tap any oral sources. In a later article—which was based on the thesis—he described Raghu Bhangare as 'a notorious band leader' who was 'briefly a hero to the people of the *mavals* [mountain valleys]'.[11] Briefly? Even a cursory acquaintance with the oral tradition of the Kolis would have caused him to avoid making such a statement. In the thesis itself Robinson dismisses the use of oral sources, stating that the written records 'are more valid than oral remembrances of events that occurred three, four, even five generations ago.'[12] In what sense 'valid'? The assumption is that written records which were created around the time of an event provide a more 'accurate' understanding of that event than memories which are passed from generation to generation by word of mouth. Such an argument fails to take into account that all sources, whether written or oral, are constructed by processing a mass of information for certain distinct ideological purposes. Colonial officials at each level of the hierarchy had their own particular agendas, and however rich their writings may have been as historical sources, most information was inevitably omitted so as to favour a particular reading of the event. Oral sources similarly provide an interpretation of an event. Both have to be used in an inevitably selective as well as critical manner by later historians in a way which reflects their own agendas.

The chief value of oral sources relating to events which occurred several generations back is not that they can ever provide an 'accurate' history—in a positivistic sense—but that they can open up to us alternative understandings which allow us to read the written sources in a different way. Oral sources are particularly valuable in the writing of subaltern history, for they allow the historian to engage with the subaltern classes' own understanding of their history. This understanding is inevitably coloured by the contemporary situation and struggles of each subaltern group, and by interacting with a particular group in this way, the historian can strive towards the writing of a more engaged history. The aim—we may say—is to establish a sympathetic rapport with the subaltern class in its life and struggles, both past and present.

At the same time, historians of the subaltern must be true to their profession, examining the available evidence from the past in a scrupulous and honest manner. From this dual exercise a history can be produced which brings out the complexities, contradictions, triumphs as well as tragedies of the past from a position which is both sympathetic and critical. As Eugene Genovese has stressed, the historian:

> must tell us, as best he [sic] can, how particular human beings solved and did not solve particular problems, adjusted and did not adjust to momentous changes, made and failed to make better lives for themselves and their children, honoured and dishonoured their God and their community. He must present some of the infinite grandeur of the human spirit—a grandeur no less for the inescapable frailty and evil that must forever go into the making of everything human.[13]

In this particular instance, my contact with the Mahadev Kolis helped me to understand that the legend of Raghu Bhangare played an important role in their construction of a sense of community. This was why I decided to seek out archival material on him, even though I had at the time much richer information on other Koli bandits, such as Honiya Kengle. This essay therefore concentrates on Raghu Bhangare and his revolt. I was aware, however, that although the oral tradition focused on the individual hero, it presented an expression of community identity. This related not only to the struggle of the community against outsiders—which gave expression to the Kolis' ideals of solidarity—but also to the construction of ideal relationships within the community, involving honourable behaviour, the role of the patriarch and the ideal mother–son relationship.

My aim therefore is to use the insights I gained from oral evidence to write a history of Raghu Bhangare's revolt using all the historical source materials available in a way that sheds light on evolving forms of community identity, politics and belief amongst the Mahadev Kolis. I shall examine the social base of Raghu's revolt, seeing how the solidarities which empowered the individual hero were forged; notions of honour, morality and patriarchy which informed the actions of Raghu and his supporters; also the limitations to solidarity which allowed the revolt eventually to be crushed. Finally, I shall try to explain why Raghu, rather than any other nineteenth-century outlaw, has survived in popular memory.

II

Venubai Bhalchin, in her song about Raghu, described his revolt as a 'band'. To begin, we need to say something about the concept of band. The word—spelt 'bund'—appears frequently in the documents in the India Office Library, as well as *bandwala* ('bundwallah') and *bandi* ('bundee'). In a petition to the government Raghu set out his terms for putting 'an end to the Bund'.[14] Here the term meant 'revolt'. In 1843 a Brahman is recorded as having exhorted the Kolis to make 'ghat bundee'—in other words to stage an uprising in the ghat region.[15] In 1844 a cowherd who was questioned by the British stated: 'When I was grazing my cows, the bundwallas came to me . . . and demanded milk . . . I gave them milk which they took to the bund—which were sitting on the hills . . .'[16] Here, the group of rebels is described as a band, and the members of it as bandwalas. The British themselves frequently talked about the 'bund' of Raghu Bhangare, meaning both 'revolt' and 'group of rebels'. Sometimes they used the English word 'rebels'. There was thus a consensus that this was a revolt.

According to a nineteenth-century Marathi-English dictionary, band meant either insurrection, sedition, or an insurgent, a rebel. A 'bandkhorvala' was a rebellious person.[17] Until the nineteenth century, the term appears to have been associated exclusively with revolts against the state or other ruling powers. Revolts by Brahmans, Marathas, Ramoshis, Mahadev Kolis and Bhils were all described as bands. Regions which were outside the control of the Maratha state were known as 'bandi mulk'. During the course of the nineteenth century the term evolved, being associated increasingly with the activities of peasants rebelling against social oppression. Today, the people of the mountain regions describe the Koli outlaws as bandkaris. This is not a word that appears in the nineteenth-century records. The term is applied now not so much to a rebel against the state, but to a person who has put himself outside the law to fight the social oppressors of his community. He thus enjoys the support of the community as a whole. In this, the bandkari is distinguished today from the daku, or dacoit, who is seen as being involved in illegal activities primarily for his own gain, and who does not enjoy popular support. In English, we may say that the contrast, as it now exists, is between the 'social bandit', as defined by Eric Hobsbawm, and the mere 'robber' or 'thief' who belongs to a professional underworld.[18] When outsiders wish to denigrate the heroes of the Kolis, they call them dakus.[19] In this section of the essay I shall examine the tradition of the band in the precolonial and early colonial periods, seeing how it had begun to change by 1830, and then go on in the following section to see how this tradition fed into the revolt of Raghu Bhangare.

The Mahadev Kolis are a sub-caste of the much wider Koli caste, which is found mainly in Gujarat and the Konkan. The region inhabited by this particular sub-caste stretches from Trimbak, near Nasik, in the north, to the mountains due west of Pune in the south, a distance as the crow flies of about 200 kilometres. In this area the Sahyadri mountains reach their greatest height. Some Mahadev Kolis live at the foot of the ghats in the coastal plains, but the majority are found on the eastern side of the scarp, where fast-flowing rivers run eastward down deep valleys towards the Deccan plateau. In the nineteenth century their villages could be reached for the most part only by footpaths.[20] In most of the above-ghat villages which they inhabited they made up the large majority of the population. The only other caste of any significance found in these villages was that of the Mahars, who carried out the most menial work, such as removing dead animals from the village. Mahadev Kolis did not take food or water from Mahars. As a rule there were only a few Mahar families in a Koli village. In the below-ghat villages in the Konkan, Mahadev Kolis often lived alongside Thakurs, but the two communities would inhabit separate hamlets.[21]

The Mahadev Kolis were in the past led by chiefs, known as nayaks. They existed, we know, as far back as the fourteenth century, for the state of Jawhar, below the mountains in the Konkan, was founded by a Koli nayak around 1300. When this region was under the nominal control of the kings of Ahmadnagar between 1490 and 1636, the Koli nayaks were left effectively independent. The Koli country was then known as the '*Bavan Mavals*', or '52 valleys'. Each valley was controlled by a Koli nayak. The *sirnayak*, or head chief, lived at Junnar, and presided over the *gotarni*, or caste council. The community was both cohesive and independent.[22] When the Mughals conquered the region in the 1630s they attempted to measure the land and fix a land tax. The Kolis rebelled in protest against this. When Shivaji began his revolt in the following decade, the Kolis were amongst the first to join him under the leadership of the sirnayak Khemi, and they played a leading role in helping Shivaji to consolidate his power. The Koli Tanaji Malsure is remembered in Maharashtra to this day for his courage in capturing the almost impregnable fort of Singhad for Shivaji.[23] In 1657 the Mughals sent an army which overpowered the Kolis. The prisoners were taken to Junnar and decapitated, their heads being piled in a pyramid. The whole of the sirnayak's lineage was thus destroyed. Subsequently the Mughals treated them with favour.[24]

In the eighteenth century, under the Peshwas, Kolis fought in the Maratha army, enjoying a high reputation as mountain warriors. They did not, however, become a cavalry force and thus did not participate in the cavalry-led expansion of Maratha power into other regions of India. The Kolis continued to fight from their home in the Sahyadri mountains. For example, in 1761 Gamaji Bhangare and Kheroji Pattikar led the storming party which took the hill fort of Trimbak from the Nizam of Hyderabad. At the same time, however, the Peshwas were trying to extend their control over the Koli region. In 1741–2 they grabbed the Koli hill fort of Kurag; in 1750–1 they annexed 14 Mahals with their hill forts which were controlled by Kolis in Surgana. These encroachments provoked a series of revolts.

The first, in 1769–70, was led by Javji Bamble, who was of an old nayak family. So as to restore order, the authorities agreed to grant Javji the right to police the area which later became Ambegaon taluka of Pune district. But the pressures continued, and in 1874 he went once more into revolt, joining up with Raganathrao, who was fighting to assert his claim to the Peshwaship. During this period Javji captured a number of hill forts. After Raganathrao's failure, he allied with the Maratha warlord, Tukaji Holkar. He handed over the forts which he had captured to Tukaji, and Tukaji then interceded with the Peshwa for his pardon. Javji and his leading colleagues, Khade, Bhangare and Pichad, were accepted back into the service of the Peshwa in 1776–7. Javji was granted responsibility for maintaining law and order in sixty villages around Rajur (Akola taluka). When the Koli brothers Kokata and Shilkunda rebelled soon after, Javji was instrumental in quelling their band.[25]

In 1798 Valoji Bhangare went into revolt, leading over a thousand men in raids on villages to the east and also below the ghat in the Konkan. He was captured eventually and executed by Hiraji Bamble, the son of Javji, who continued to support the Peshwa. The leadership of the band was then taken over by Valoji's nephew Rama Bhangare, patil of Devgaon village in Akola taluka and an able and daring commander, who proved more successful than his uncle. The Peshwas failed to suppress his rising, and eventually they offered him a pardon and an important police position. Rama was the father of Raghu Bhangare.[26]

Although the Kolis thus had a strong tradition of resistance, with each nayak family commanding the support of large numbers of subordinate Kolis, the nayaks themselves were often divided against each other. This was because their desire for independence was balanced against their need for recognition by the state. Their local authority was based not only on their position in Koli society, but also on the official posts they held from the Peshwas.[27] A revolt represented a fracture of a temporary nature, the aim being to exert sufficient pressure to force the state to settle for better terms. The state could counter this by offering perquisites to other nayaks on condition that they help suppress the revolt. A rebel could in turn counter this by allying with rival contenders for power at the centre, such as claimants for the Peshwaship or Maratha warlords like Holkar. Because the struggle could go several ways, and because disruption in any case served their interests, the nayaks who had not joined the revolt would often provide secret support to the rebels while at the same time protesting their loyalty to the state. Conflicts thus gave rise to a complex range of loyalties.

In 1817–18 the Kolis sided with the last Peshwa, Bajirao, against the British, helping him defend the mountain passes between Bombay and Pune.[28] After the Peshwa's final defeat and deposition in 1818, the British recognized the Koli nayaks as local police, holding them responsible for maintaining law and order in the hills. They were paid Rs 9 per month by the government. Other Kolis were employed as policemen under the command of the nayaks, being paid Rs 7 per month. The government provided these irregular forces, known as the *nayakwari* police, with a *karkun*, or clerk, who was invariably a Brahman. As the nayaks were illiterate, these Brahmans enjoyed considerable power.[29] The nayaks of the Ramoshis, who controlled the mountain regions to the south, were treated similarly. The British also established a small force of regular uniformed police ('red-coats'), who were recruited from all communities and who were based under their direct command in towns away from the hills. During the early years of British rule this force was far too small to exercise any significant control over the hills. In the 1840s, for instance, there were seventy-six such policemen responsible for the 347 mountain villages of Akola, Igatpuri, Nasik and Dindori talukas.[30]

Not all of the nayaks were thus employed by the British. Several of those who were not sought during the first decade of British rule to redress the situation through the tradition of the band, which in this case meant going into revolt and harassing the rulers into appointing them as police officers to buy them off. Initially, this tactic met with some success. The Ramoshi nayak Umiaji, who had been dispossessed by Bajirao Peshwa in 1803, and then ignored by the British, went into revolt in 1822. The British were unable to suppress his band, and eventually agreed in 1828 that if Umiaji would call off his revolt they would appoint him as head police officer of Purandhar and Bhimthadi talukas of Pune district on a salary of Rs 30 a month, as well as grant him 120 *bighas* of inam land. When the Mahadev Kolis to the north heard about Umiaji's success, a series of revolts were launched by disaffected nayaks with a similar motive.[31]

One of the principal figures in these revolts was Rama Bhangare. He had initially received an appointment under the British as an officer, a jamadar, in the nayakwari police, and had been considered initially to be a loyal and useful officer. However, the British took exception to his custom of demanding regular levies from the people of his charge. Rama claimed that he had been granted this right under the Peshwas, but he agreed to stop taking the levies if he was compensated with a rise in salary. This the British refused to give. He resigned in protest and in February 1829, encouraged by the success of Umiaji Nayak, went into revolt. He was joined by 500 to 600 dissidents, some of whom were Kolis who had either refused to serve under the British or who had been denied positions in the police. Arrows wrapped in bundles of dry grass were sent to villages, implying that they would be burnt down if they did not provide provisions and cash to the rebels. They carried out a series of attacks on Baniya usurers of the Akola region, destroying their account books and forcing them to reveal where their money was hidden. The British realized, rather late, that their treatment of Umiaji had sent out the wrong signals, and they decided to suppress Rama Bhangare's revolt in an uncompromising manner. Large numbers of troops were sent into the area, and Rama Bhangare was soon captured, tried for treason and transported for life. The revolt continued for some time under the leadership of Rama Kirve, who with some two hundred rebels raided villages in the south and in the Konkan. They even attacked and plundered the government treasury at Junnar. The rising ended after Rama Kirve was captured and executed in 1830.[32]

In this Koli revolt of 1829–30 we see the beginning of a shift to a new form of band. The revolt had been launched to gain titles, land and positions from the state, as had been the case with previous bands, but one of the targets of attack—the Baniya usurers, or *sahukars*—was a new one. Why the sahukars? To answer this question we need to look at the peasant economy of the Kolis at that time.

The mass of the Kolis were peasant farmers who lived by cultivating in the upper reaches of the valleys of the Sahyadris. They also kept cattle, which they grazed in the forests. They grew *nagli*, their chief subsistence crop, on the sides of the valleys, using shifting methods of cultivation. They constructed terraced fields on the floors of the valleys, irrigated by streams which ran off the mountains. In these fields they grew rice, most of which was sold. Their best rice enjoyed a high reputation amongst the élites of Pune and Ahmadnagar. In the eighteenth century, the Peshwas encouraged the extension of such agriculture through loans for the construction of new terraces and irrigation systems. The civil war in Maharashtra of the early nineteenth century led to a decline in demand for high quality rice and a drying up of assistance for such agriculture, and many of the terraces were washed away. The British, when they conquered the region in 1817, made no attempt to encourage or help the reconstruction of these field systems.[33]

During the early years of their rule in Maharashtra the British imposed large increases in land-tax. Hardly any money was set aside to fund agrarian improvements, which had been the practice of the Marathas in the eighteenth century. In 1821 agrarian prices collapsed, and continued depressed for the next three decades. The British refused to lower their land-tax demands, with the result that a lot of land went out of cultivation.[34]

The Koli peasants of the mountain regions mostly paid a plough tax, which varied according to the number of ploughs owned, the number of bullocks used to draw each plough (which could vary from two to eight bullocks), and the quality of the land which was ploughed. The amount of tax demanded changed from year to year, as a peasant bought or sold both ploughs and bullocks. The man responsible for making the assessment each year was the village accountant, or *kulkarni*, who was normally a Brahman who lived in a nearby town. Kulkarnis were given full discretion by the government to fix the assessments within the villages in their charge as they pleased. They were also allowed to collect money and grain from the peasants for their own pay. All that mattered, so far as the government was concerned, was that they paid the lump sum due from each village into the treasury in good time. This led to a situation in which the kulkarnis routinely abused their power so as to enrich themselves at the expense of the peasants.[35]

The class which benefited most of all at this time was that of the Baniya usurers. Traders-cum-moneylenders had for long been active in the region, buying fine rice and ghee from the Koli peasants, and providing credit in return. Under colonial rule the Koli peasants became increasingly dependent on the usurers for the cash needed to pay the high rates of land tax which were being demanded by the British. In return, the sahukars appropriated more and more of the Kolis' produce. The high profits so earned encouraged many Marwari and Gujarati Baniyas to set up shop in the towns and villages of the region. In Rajur, for instance, there were by the 1830s four households of Gujarati Baniyas who were lending money in thirty-six surrounding villages. They provided loans on favourable terms to the Koli nayaks, and in return enjoyed the protection of the nayakwari police. The sahukars also enjoyed the support of the colonial civil courts, which could order the confiscation and sale of the property of any peasant who failed to repay a loan promptly. The Baniyas used the courts to harass the peasants, threatening to take out a case if they did not hand over the large bulk of their produce at each harvest. Within little more than a decade of the establishment of British rule, the majority of Koli peasants had been pauperized by the usurers.[36]

Many Kolis who joined the band of 1828–30, which was led initially by Rama Bhangare, did so not because they wanted posts in the police or other perquisites, but because they saw this as the only way in which they could obtain money to pay off their debts to the Baniyas.

Their chief aim was therefore to appropriate cash and valuables from moneyed people of any class. When they had the chance, they also attacked the Baniyas directly, destroying their account books and any other papers they could lay their hands on. This was a new feature of the Koli band. After that, the Baniyas of the region got into the habit of keeping duplicate sets of accounts with partners elsewhere.[37]

III

Raghu Bhangare's revolt, which began a decade later, had elements of both the old and the new forms of band. Raghu Bhangare was born around 1820,[38] and must have therefore been around ten years old when his father, Rama Bhangare, rebelled against the British and was as a result transported for life. Raghu was allowed to succeed to the patilship of Devgaon, but he was not granted his father's old post of jamadar of police. The post was given instead to a Brahman called Amritrao Bhatt. Raghu's family appears to have had to live modestly at that time, surviving mainly through cultivation. In the early 1840s Raghu shared a small house in Devgaon with his mother, wife and brother.

In October 1843 Amritrao Bhatt came with a party of police to this house, caught Raghu and others in his family, and tortured them. According to a statement made later by Raghu, they 'applied cupping horns to the breasts of women and the testicles of men'.[39] The reason for this action was that Amritrao suspected Raghu of being involved in a raid on a village in the Konkan. Amritrao was accompanied by Abaji Bamble, a Koli nayak. Raghu later described both Abaji and Amritrao as 'my enemies'—suggesting that the enmity was long-standing.[40] Raghu was arrested, taken to Rajur, and locked up there. That night his mother brought him a bowl of food, in which a knife appears to have been concealed.[41] Raghu cut the leather cords binding him and escaped. The chief nayak, Javji Bamble—a cousin of Raghu—was in overall command of the guard, and appears to have connived in his escape.[42]

During the next two months, Raghu visited villages around Rajur, recruiting men to take part in a rising. Some of his chief lieutenants, such as Devji Mahar of Devgaon, Bhau Dungar of Chinchavane and

Khundu Sable of Parosi (all villages of Akola taluka), joined him at this time. The recruits were mostly Kolis, though Devji was a Mahar, and another called Gangaji was a Thakur. In common with Raghu, most appear to have been in their twenties and married, with families.[43] They were thus rooted within their communities.[44] They were armed with swords, iron-tipped staves, bows and arrows, and a few muskets.

Raghu's chief aims at the start were to avenge himself on Abaji and Amritrao, and to regain the position of jamadar for his family.[45] Raghu appears to have calculated that the latter ambition could be achieved in one of two ways: either he could make himself so troublesome to the British that they would be forced to concede his demand, or his revolt would feed into a wider uprising against the British in which he would be rewarded by the successful rebels with extensive perquisites. In trying thus to have things both ways, he was acting like many a Koli rebel before him. The first sort of demand was seen in a petition which he sent to the government in early 1845:

> I Ragoojee Naik Bangra beg to present my most respectful compliments and represent that formerly we were employed as Sirdars in the service of the 22 sirdars who resided in the Mawul Country depending on the protection of the Rajah Sahoo Chutruputtee[46] and enjoyed certain villages in Surunjamee Inam. In the same manner let us now be entrusted with the police duties of the North Conkan, the 14 Mahals in Jooneir, and the districts in Nassick and be allowed 45 villages in Inam as heretofore, that is 20 villages in the Conkan, 10 in the 14 Mahals, and 15 in the Nassick districts. This should be done without any delay and then we will put an end to the Bund, so as to restore peace.[47]

This aspiration reflected what had been a common practice under Maratha rule and, indeed, early British rule.[48]

The other possibility was for a general revolt which he could take advantage of. There were at the time many rumours about a forthcoming general uprising to restore the raja of Satara, Chhatrapati Pratapsinh, the heir of Shivaji, who had been deposed by the British in 1839. These rumours led to a series of minor revolts in the region during the early 1840s, most notable of which was the one led by Narsappa Dattatraya Petkar of Satara district, who raised a band in

1841 on what he claimed were the orders of the deposed raja, then exiled in Banaras. There were other revolts which continued in the mountains of Satara district up until 1844.[49] In 1843 a former confidante of the deposed raja, called Atma Baniya, circulated a document which prophesied the foundation of a Maratha government which would drive the British from India. In September 1843 a Maharashtrian Brahman called Antoba Lotekar brought a *sanad* in the name of the Maratha ruler of Gwalior state, Sinde, which enjoined the nobility, Marathas, Koli nayaks, Bhils and Ramoshis to rebel against the British. The sanad claimed that the Hindu religion was failing because under foreign rule Brahmans, temples and charities were no longer being patronized. Those who rebelled would receive generous rewards once Maratha rule was re-established. Atma Baniya and Antoba Lotekar visited Akola takuka together and encouraged the Kolis to 'make ghat bundee'—in other words stage an uprising in the ghat region.

On 29 January 1844, after Raghu had recruited his band from villages of Akola taluka, he and his followers met Antoba Lotekar in the forest near Padoshi. The Brahman showed the gang the sanads which he claimed were from Sinde, the ruler of Gwalior. They had on them impressive black seals, as large as limes. He read out the message, in which the Kolis were enjoined to join in Sinde's service, close the ghats, raise bands, plunder the country, and stop the English from passing from the Deccan to the Konkan, seizing them if they tried. They decided to begin their rebellion in the time-honoured manner—by looting a moneyed man so as to provide the funds to finance their campaign.[50] They accordingly went that night to Sonamba village, where they caught hold of a rich Marwari, beat him up, robbed him of his property and set his house on fire.[51]

In February, Raghu and about thirty followers descended the ghat to the Konkan, attacking and looting moneylenders and village Patils (headmen). They returned to the above-ghat region at the end of April, and in May attacked and robbed villages in Akola, Igatpuri and Khed talukas. In the meantime, Raghu's cousin, Bapu Bhangare (of Satewadi village of Akola), led his own gang on a series of raids on villages in the Konkan. He based his gang in the petty state of Jawhar, in the Konkan, where he stayed with his brother, Ramji, who was married to the sister of the raja of the state. It is probable that Bapu and his gang were shielded by this Koli raja.

In July 1844, Raghu and his band captured three policemen at Chichondi village of Akola taluka, took them into the forest and killed them in cold blood. In September they ambushed a party of eleven policemen near Bhimashankar, which was at the top of the ghat in Ambegaon taluka. Because of the heavy monsoon rain, the police were unable to fire their matchlocks, and eight were killed and three captured. Raghu released them, saying: 'Go and ask the Saheb why he sends black people after me, let him send white people, when I will kill them and hang their caps on the trees of the Ran Mulla Jungle.'[52]

Raghu also told the three policemen that he was a *sardar* (army commander) of Sinde.[53] He therefore continued to project himself as an ally of the ruler of Gwalior state. In October 1844 it was reported that Raghu was telling people that an army from Gwalior was about to arrive in the Deccan to link up with him. Few appear to have doubted that this was the case.[54] Others were inspired by this belief to form their own bands to take advantage of the anticipated change of power. In 1844–5 the sheer number of bands which were active throughout the region reinforced the belief in an imminent general insurrection.

The revolt was at its height during the period between November 1844 and March 1845. In November, Raghu took his own gang back into the Konkan, and over the next few months travelled around the villages levying tribute. When pressed by the police, he ascended the ghat, and did the same there. Many of the new bands pretended to be led by Raghu when they raided villages, knowing that the villagers would be terrified into complying with their demands. For a time it thus appeared that Raghu was everywhere, both in the Konkan and above the ghats. Bapu Bhangare, for his part, linked up with a Koli from the Konkan called Bhau Kengle and levied tribute in that area. In January they went so far as to attack the police station at Vada, but were driven off with gunfire, two of the attackers being killed.

Raghu levied tribute both to sustain his revolt and to impress his authority on the people. In late 1844 he put out a proclamation announcing his intention:

> An order to all persons entrusted with any power or authority in the state to the ryuts and to the 18 sects forming the community of the zillah of Ahmednuggar.
>
> You are not to pay the revenue for the present year to the English Government under penalty of having your noses and ears cut off. You are therefore enjoined to transmit the revenue due on the black soil to Ragojee Naique Bangria Sirdar. Be careful of this, and do not be afraid that you will be exposed to hardships from the English but be assured that the English shall not be allowed to exercise their rule. Take a copy of this and forward it from village to village in order to proclaim it to all.[55]

When he was finally captured, Raghu admitted that he had gone from village to village, taking provisions and sums of money from the Patils and villagers—varying from Rs 20 to Rs 25—according to what they could afford, and ordering the Patils not to pay their land tax to the government. He described this activity as 'levying khund'.[56]

Khand meant literally a division or share of the produce, and, by extension, tribute due to a ruler. By paying such tribute to a person, peasants were considered to be recognizing his authority. It was normal for such a demand to be backed by the threat of force. This did not in any way invalidate the claim: what mattered was whether the threat could be made good. In 1844–5 Raghu had this power, and thus a recognized claim to the khand of the peasants.

Raghu went about his task in a systematic way. He would first send an arrow and a cake of cowdung to a village, demanding that money be ready when called for. The arrow and cowdung intimated death and fire in the event of refusal.[57] He and his band would then come to the village and have the Patil brought before them. The frightened officer was questioned as to the amount of land tax paid by the village, and asked whether or not any instalments had already been paid. If paid, he was ordered to hand it over; if not, he was ordered to collect it forthwith. He and his menials, accompanied by a few members of the band, would then go from house to house collecting the tax, and hand it over to Raghu. When the services of a captured scribe were available, a receipt would be written out and handed over.[58] If the Patil prevaricated or showed any reluctance, he was likely to be beaten up. This does not, however, appear to have happened often.

In certain respects Raghu Bhangare's revolt was typical of those of the pre-colonial period. It had grown out of his alliances and rivalries with other Kolis of leading families. He hoped that it would form a part of a wider revolt against the state in which he would be able to manoeuvre to his own advantage. He travelled around expropriating tribute like a feudal lord. However, in launching his band at the time he did, he became—perhaps unintentionally—the leader of a much wider insurrection of the ghat peasantry as a whole against the British and their local representatives and allies, in particular the Baniya usurers, local officials and the regular police. It is to this popular dimension of the revolt that we shall now turn.

IV

Initially the Marwari and Baniya sahukars formed the chief target of attack for Raghu and his band. To begin with the attacks were almost certainly carried out for loot to finance the revolt rather than because Raghu himself had any particular enmity against the usurers as a class. It was clear however that such attacks were very popular amongst the mass of peasants who were suffering from the exploitation of these usurers. For example, when Raghu and his band raided Saralambe village of Shahpur taluka in the Konkan in March 1844, they were welcomed into the village by the watchman and headman, and given food. Raghu took pains to explain that he and his men had come only to rob the usurers and burn their books, not to cause any trouble to the peasants. Both the watchman and the headman were in debt to the two Baniyas and were in sympathy with him in this. They then led Raghu and his followers to the houses of the two Baniyas. They beat up the Baniyas, cut off their noses and burnt their account books and houses.[59] In another case, a Baniya managed to flee before Raghu and his band reached a village, but the headman himself led the outlaws to the place where the Baniya was hiding.[60]

There is evidence from later bands to show how the rebel leaders had sometimes to be reminded by villagers to take particular types of punitive action against sahukars. In 1879, some Ramoshis led by the rebel Vasudev Phadke carried out a raid on a village of Purandhar taluka of Pune district. They went to the house of a Baniya to loot him, as they needed money to carry on the revolt. They found two Baniyas asleep there. Phadke wrote in his diary:

> They were arrested and told to give up what they had, which they refused. We commenced beating them, and Pandoo Ramoshi cut the ear of one Bania, and the Nama Bania was also wounded . . . Every one in the village was much dissatisfied with Nama who was making a great zoolum on them. They therefore said 'If you will take revenge we will be very grateful to you'. We punished him well; and when the people reminded us, we burnt all his papers, books etc.[61]

This evidence shows that rebel leaders whose agendas were often somewhat different to those of the mass of the peasants would agree to act as the latter demanded so as to maintain the support base which was crucial if they were to sustain their revolt.

By late 1844 Raghu had taken it upon himself to act as a spokesman for the peasants against the usurers. In a letter to the Collector of Ahmadnagar of late 1844 he gave voice to the prevailing feelings about the Baniyas and their tool, the civil courts: 'The Ryots are greatly distressed by the court and harassed by the Wanees and as I have dealt with them, therefore so I will deal with you . . .'[62] Raghu was also reported to have once issued a threat to the British that as the Baniyas took too much interest on their loans, 'if the Sahib did not make some arrangement in the matter, he would cut off the Banian's noses'.[63]

The mode of attack which proved so popular with the peasants was to humiliate the usurers in public, by giving them a thrashing or by cutting off the tips of their noses. The latter was a common form of punishment in Maharashtrian society. According to Mountstuart Elphinstone, writing about the government of the Peshwas: 'Mutilation was very common, and the person who had his hand, foot, ears or nose cut off, was turned loose as soon as the sentence was executed and left to his fate.'[64] In colonial times, it was a form of punishment used in Jawhar state, which was ruled by a Mahadev Koli chief.[65]

In feudal-patriarchal society honouring and dishonouring was associated with actions applied to the body. Honour was given by conferring items of dress, such as a shawl or turban. Dishonour was conferred through bodily humiliation, such as enforced grovelling, thrashing, perhaps with a shoe, or, as a more permanent sign of shame, through mutilation. The nose, in particular, was seen as a seat of a person's honour, one term for dishonouring a person being 'to cut their nose'. A woman who committed a supposed sexual transgression often had her nose cut in this way. A British judge who tried some members of the band in 1845 commented on this practice in a manner which revealed his own feudal-patriarchal sentiments in the matter:

> Mutilation by cutting off the lower part of the nose has certainly been a characteristic of the dealings of the bunds which have lately harassed this part of the country; but this particular kind of mutilation is common, and is the usual mode of revenge of an injured husband upon an unfaithful wife and judging from the healthy appearance of all the mutilated persons who have lately come before this court, as well as of the wives who have from time to time testified against their husbands, it is intended to cause mental rather than bodily pain; and in the case of erring wives to destroy the temptation to seducers.[66]

By so directing his attack on the body of the Baniyas, cutting off the tips of their noses and in some cases ears as well, Raghu won widespread support for his band from large numbers of peasants who derived great satisfaction from seeing the hated usurers thus shamed. Raghu quickly became the terror of the Marwari and Gujarati usurers. This he achieved with what appears to have been a relatively sparing use of such violence.

Raghu started his revolt in January 1844 by attacking a Marwari, at Sonamba in Akola, beating the usurer and burning his house. He then went into the Konkan, where in the course of the next four months he is recorded as having looted the houses of five Baniyas, two of whom had their noses and ears cut off and one of whom was killed. In the latter case there was a rivalry between the Baniya, a Marwari, and a local Koli who had joined up with Raghu temporarily. This man had encouraged Raghu to attack the village, and he and not Raghu put the Marwari to death.[67] In May 1844 Raghu seized four Baniyas of Ghurad in Khed taluka of Pune district, later releasing them—no doubt after they had paid ransoms. In early 1845 he cut off the noses of five Baniyas of Savargaon and the nose and ear of a Baniya of Mutkhal, both of Akola taluka. In the latter case, the villagers had given information to the British about Raghu's movements, and the attack was in revenge. No other attacks on Baniyas which were specifically by Raghu and his band are mentioned in the records. This may have been due to some under-reporting. It seems however that after the first attacks, the Baniyas fled from the villages and small towns, taking refuge in the larger towns of the region for the duration of the revolt. As a result, there were few left to loot, beat up or mutilate.

Raghu was also popular amongst the people for his attack on the official representatives of the government at the local level, the local tax collectors and the regular police. Any kulkarni or other subordinate tax official who was caught by Raghu was likely to be beaten severely and even to lose his nose.[68] Thus, in December 1844 a kulkarni and a Patil's clerk who were on their way to a village in the Konkan to inspect the crops to fix the tax assessment were met by Raghu and his band. Raghu asked them why they were carrying out such duties after he had ordered officials not to do so. He had their noses cut off, after which they were allowed to go. The band then went to the village, seized the kulkarni's papers and burnt them.[69] As a result of such attacks, the subordinate tax officials tended to keep away from the villages while the revolt continued.

Although the regular police were few in numbers, they also were extremely unpopular. Raghu's own torture by the police jamadar Amritrao in October 1843 must have been an experience not uncommon at the time. The British, in their operations against the bands, freely admitted the use of 'some little coercion' to obtain information from captured Koli outlaws.[70] The police raided and plundered their houses, beat them up and abused them sexually. They also arrested and detained the wives, mothers and sisters of known outlaws or people from whom they wanted information. Once in their power these women were an easy prey to sexual harassment and attack.

Raghu felt a particular sense of outrage against the police for the way in which they tortured his mother and other women of his family in October 1843. In the following year the police arrested his mother, wife and sister-in-law and confiscated all of their property. Raghu felt keenly his failure to protect them. In his petition to the Governor of Bombay of December 1844, he complained bitterly of their detention, as well as that of the families of other leading members of his band, such as Devji Mahar, Bhau Dungar and Rama and Dharmia Mundia: 'It will be well if their families are released and the attachment [of their property] removed, otherwise as above written I will not fail to lay waste the country, because according to the Sirkar's custom only he who has committed crimes should be punished. His family have no connection with it.'[71] Khundu Sable was another member of the band who suffered in this way. At his trial in September 1846 he told the court: 'that he has already been punished, as after he joined the bund his wife was apprehended by the Sirkar and has since died in their custody'.[72]

Kolis who were not themselves outlaws also suffered in this manner. The police detained many Koli women, in an attempt to force their husbands to reveal the hiding places of the outlaws.[73] Arbitrary detention such as this had no sanction in the law of Bombay Presidency,[74] and it caused extreme distress. The peasants, bitter at their treatment, gave even greater support to the band in consequence.

This accounted for the high and escalating level of violence against the police during the revolt. From mid-1844 onwards, Raghu and members of his band tended to kill policemen when they could, rather than beat and mutilate, as was their normal practice with usurers and local officials. In all, Raghu was personally involved in the killing of twelve policemen. In January 1845 a member of Raghu's band called Padaji Nirmal led an attack on a party of police led by Amritrao Bhatt, the jamadar who had arrested and tortured Raghu and his family in October 1843. Padaji appears to have taken on this responsibility because of a personal insult he had received from the jamadar, who during a quarrel had knocked his turban off his head. Amritrao was put to death and other policemen in the party maimed.[75] By taking revenge in such a spectacular fashion, the rebels sought to avenge not only their own honour, but the honour of their mothers, wives and other female relatives, and—by extension—Koli women in general.

Raghu received support, shelter and sustenance from the mass of the peasants throughout his revolt. Stores of grain were left by villagers in the forest for the use of the gang. Whenever they were in need, Raghu had only to send a couple of members of his gang into a village, meet the Patil, after which food would be collected from house to house and carried by the villagers to the gang's hiding place nearby. In one case reported by the British, some peasants provided daily supplies to the gang in this manner, while a party of police searching for Raghu were stationed in the next village, entirely ignorant of what was happening.[76] In another case, a Patil of a village in the Konkan welcomed the outlaws to his village, 'not only feasting them but actually furnishing them with warlike weapons'.[77] Villagers used to help the rebels also by helping them carry their equipment from village to village while in their area.[78] They also passed on information about police movements so as to allow them to escape.

It was reported in May 1844 that in nearly all cases of robbery of usurers or village officials there was collusion between the residents of the village and the outlaws.[79] When the houses of usurers were about to be set alight, the outlaws would go around the village telling the people to watch their own houses to prevent them from catching fire.[80] Often, the peasants actively encouraged the bands to carry out such attacks. For example, in April 1844 a Koli of the Konkan persuaded Raghu to come with his band to raid a village near to his. He wanted to avenge himself on a local usurer who had bought up the liquor rights for the area and refused to allow any Kolis to run liquor shops.[81]

The peasants did not support Raghu and the other bands lightly. They fed them from their often meagre stocks of grain and, in addition, handed over to them considerable sums of money in khand. They also opened themselves to possible retribution by the British, for in providing food and shelter for the rebels they were considered to be 'aiding treason and rebellion'. Many villagers were convicted on this charge during the course of the revolt and sent to gaol.

The support for Raghu came not only from his own caste of Mahadev Kolis, but from a major caste of the region below the ghats, the Thakurs. This community took a collective oath never to give any information about Raghu to the authorities, or to give him up.[82] In the words of Morris, Commander of the Khandesh Bhil Corps: '. . . I can safely state that on no similar duty have I met so confirmed a combination against our endeavours as exists in both the Cooly and Takoor population.'[83] Solidarity in the revolt stretched, therefore, beyond ties of caste alone.

The strength of this solidarity explains another feature of the revolt, which was the high degree of support which it received from the Koli nayaks. In the past, the state had been able to undermine bands by dividing the nayaks against each other by either threatening them with loss of perquisites or by promising rewards. In late 1844 the

British tried to intimidate them by arresting and jailing the chief nayak Javji Bamble. This had no effect, the nayaks remained solidly behind Raghu. Even his rival, Abaji Bamble, gave him full support.[84] This was not because they had any particular regard for Raghu as a person. One nayak, Syaji Bamble, even went so far as to describe Raghu in contemptuous terms as 'his sheep' whom he allowed to stay in 'his jungle'.[85] It was, rather, because the nayak's own authority was under threat from the developments associated with colonial rule.

The nayaks resented the growing power of the regular police, subordinate officials and Baniya usurers. As the power of these groups increased, their own declined. Despite this, ordinary Koli peasants who were being exploited by local tax officials and pauperized by the usurers were looking to them for help, and the authority of the nayaks over this class depended on their being able to provide some remedy. After Raghu's escape from custody in October 1843, Javji and other nayaks appear to have advised him to form a band and attack the usurers.[86] The sheer popularity of the resulting revolt amongst the mass of the ghat peasants meant that the nayaks had to continue in their backing for it if they were to maintain their authority over the peasants.

Thereafter, the nayaks went out of their way to help Raghu. They advised him on the targets for his raids.[87] One nayak is recorded as having accompanied Raghu on a raid in which a village was burnt. In the words of some local people, he went to see 'the tamasha'.[88] The nayaks also helped Raghu to avoid the police. They either prevented messages about Raghu's whereabouts from reaching the authorities or delayed them, giving Raghu time to escape.[89] In one case, when a village headman told two nayaks where Raghu was hiding they retorted: 'Why do you give such correct information, why not let him alone.' When the Patil told them some eight or ten days later that Raghu was still hiding in the same place one of them said: 'What are you afraid of, what have you to lose. If the bund are in your jungle let them be in it. If Government wish they may be seized.' After this the headman held his tongue, fearing that if he told the government, the nayaks would injure him.[90] If ordered by the British or the regular police to pursue Raghu, they would deliberately do so slowly, allowing him to get away. Sometimes, as soon as such an order was received, they made themselves scarce. Morris of the Khandesh Bhil Corps complained in August 1845 that although many outlaws had been captured or killed that year, not one had been put out of action by the Koli police.[91] Raghu was as a result able to shelter for months in the area under the jurisdiction of the nayaks without being captured.

V

In both the colonial and people's narratives of the revolt, Raghu's mother Ramayi played a crucial role. In the colonial account, Raghu's hatred of the police was seen to have stemmed above all from the way they had treated Ramayi. They had tortured her when he was first captured, then had imprisoned her. Later, when he was on the run, she had sent money to those who were sheltering and feeding him.[92] In turn, Raghu sent his followers to kill the policeman who had tortured her, thus redeeming her and the honour of the family. In the people's account, as seen in Venubai Balchin's song, Ramayi was depicted as being entirely supportive to her son throughout, helping him to escape from the police by concealing a knife in his bowl of food, and later celebrating his deeds with maternal pride. The strength of this bond between mother and son in a time of hardship and suffering comes through the stories of the revolt in a powerful manner.

The feelings of the peasants were engaged and moved in this respect by sentiments which were rooted firmly in feudal-patriarchal notions of honourable behaviour. The actions of Ramayi and Raghu were seen to conform to and, in the process, reinforce this cultural construct. This, in turn, fed into notions of community identity. As Elizabeth Fox-Genovese has stated:

> Gender relations constitute the foundations of any society and lie at the core of any individual's sense of self, for gender relations map the most fundamental relations between any individual and the other members of society. We do not experience our gender in the abstract, but in relation to others: to be a woman is to be a woman in relation to men. Just as societies have characteristic social relations, so they have characteristic gender relations. Societies have also tended to promote distinct roles for women and men. Those gender roles constitute the activities through which women and men are encouraged to contribute to the collectivity and in which they are encouraged to find their identities—their deepest sense of who they are.[93]

To understand the power of such sentiments in Koli society we need to examine notions of gender and family honour in the peasant communities of western Maharashtra.

The central unit in this society was the family, which can be defined as a joint household in which members of a lineage and women who had married into that lineage subsisted from a common pool of resources and income. Each peasant community represented a moral space in which values were shared and in which families struggled continually to enhance their relative standing within the group. As David Pocock has argued, *jatis* did not as a rule have any particular overall organizational unity or common body of custom. Although there was a general feeling of loyalty to the jati which emphasized the value of solidarity against outsiders, within the group there was a continual competition amongst families to appear better and more 'honourable' than others. There were no fixed defining features to indicate the correct form of 'honourable' behaviour, for the rules were flexible and were applied differentially to different members of the caste. A person from a highly respectable family would commonly have been able to get away with behaviour which would not have been tolerated from a member of a family of low standing within the group.[94]

Within a peasant community there was accordingly a hierarchy of honour. Positions in this hierarchy were never secure, they had constantly to be asserted and vindicated in a public way. A reputation took a long time to build and consolidate, but it could be destroyed in a moment. The more vulnerable a family was within the group, the more it needed to protect its reputation and honour with great zeal. Well-respected families did not have to defend their honour at every turn, whereas those of questionable status had to be very sensitive to a wide range of points of honour. 'Thus,' says Pierre Bourdieu, 'poverty, far from contradicting or prohibiting respectability, makes doubly meritorious the man [sic] who, though particularly exposed to outrage, nonetheless manages to win respect.'[95]

In each community there was continuous rivalry between families, each of which sought to enhance its honour at the expense of others. This rivalry was often vicious and full of bitterness, breeding that climate of petty gossip and innuendo which was one of the features of village life. Peasants sought constantly to undermine the worth of their neighbours. Fear of being thus gossiped about ensured that people generally conformed to the broad code of 'honourable' behaviour. Gossip was however a weapon which had to be used with caution, for it was considered disreputable to have a reputation for constant malevolent gossip-mongering.[96]

So long as slander remained at the level of gossip, there was little that a person could do directly to rebut the slur. If, however, an insult—whether verbal or physical—was offered to a person's face in public by a member of the same community, honour could be saved only through aggressive action by one or more males of the family. It was considered that only members of a family 'without shame' (*besharam*) would not retaliate when thus provoked.[97] Arson and cattle poisoning were popular forms of retaliation in nineteenth-century Maharashtra. Very commonly, the retaliation was directed by males against women of the rival family. It was reported from Satara district that 'a man thinks nothing of burning the house and wife and children of a man with whom he has had some trifling difference a few days before.'[98] Confrontations and attacks such as these—in which women 'of' the perceived rival were the most notable target—led often to long running family feuds and vendettas.

Family honour was seen to be located in the blood, being an inheritable quality transmitted from ancestors through the legitimate union of males of the family with females of another family of honourable status. It was therefore crucial to try to maintain or strengthen the blood of the family by marrying into families of high reputation. In this way—so it was believed—future generations would be mothered by women of quality and virtue. If a mother was rumoured to have lost her virginity before marriage or afterwards to have been guilty of adultery, or even flirting outside the family, her children were considered to be tainted with dishonour and the reputation of the family was sullied, whatever its wealth.

A mother who bore sons and remained pure in her life could in time achieve a place of honour within the family. As the sons married and brought in their own wives to live under the common roof, she might become a leading power within the household, symbolizing the physical and moral centre of the peasant household. A man of honour was expected to revere his mother and to follow her advice. It was considered particularly humiliating for a man to have the honour of his mother questioned or insulted in public.

Any attack on a woman of a family, whether verbal or physical, was seen as an attack on the honour of the family as a whole. It called into question the honour, and thus manliness, of the males of the family. It was believed that only men deficient in this quality would allow such insults or attacks to go unpunished and unrevenged. Vengeance had to be taken on the perpetrator of the act, again leading to violence and possible death. But worse than this, it was often suspected that a woman of the family thus accused or violated had somehow brought the shame upon herself, and she herself would then be punished by members of her own family. In cases of rape or adultery, a woman might even be turned out of the house, or put to death. Murders of this particularly gruesome sort were common in the early twentieth century.[99]

The honour of a man and a woman was thus judged by very different standards. Males were expected to maintain the honour of their family in an assertive, fearless and 'masculine' manner, which often involved physical violence. A man's decisiveness and courage in this respect was seen to reflect on his sexual potency. Men who acted promiscuously might be admired for their virility rather than denigrated. Women on the other hand were expected to maintain family honour in a passive way, by conserving their purity through the strict avoidance of any potentially shaming situations.

Raghu Bhangare clearly believed that he was from a family of superior blood and honour, and it is likely that many of the Kolis accepted this self-evaluation, though it appears that some of the superior nayaks did not. He sought through his revolt to restore the official position which he believed was his family's due. Also, as a man of honour, he saw it as his patriarchal duty to avenge the insult to his mother by having the person who had assaulted her put to death.

Raghu was a very 'masculine' hero, renowned in popular legend for his huge strength. He was, according to the story I was told in

Jhambori, so strong that he could defeat ten to twelve people in hand-to-hand combat. Even his victims respected him for his 'honourable' male bearing. A Baniya who was attacked by the band in April 1844 described Raghu as a man of fine and superior presence. During the raid he was ordering his followers to: 'seize, strike, wound'.[100] Others mentioned his stout bearing, his air of authority, his intimidating manner, his fierce temper. When angered on one occasion by a question from a member of his band, he turned in a rage and slashed him on the thigh with his sword.[101] On another occasion, when Raghu suspected a band member of treachery, he himself killed the man by cutting off his head with his sword.[102] To be fierce and quick tempered were qualities commonly associated with men of honour. Although his dress, in common with other members of his band, does not appear to have been particularly striking, consisting of a drab dark red shirt and turban and a white dhoti, he carried accoutrements which made him stand out as a leader, such as a striking handkerchief—which was described by some as 'English', others as 'Karnatak'—and a sword with a silver-plated handle. Appearance is to a large extent a construct in the mind of the beholder. The British—who sought to deny Raghu the status he claimed—described him at the time of his capture as merely 'a small slight man'.[103]

Women, by contrast, were expected to behave as good mothers and wives, nurturers of the masculine heroes. Ramayi Bhangare, above all, was celebrated for this quality. Koli women were expected to shelter the outlaws and ensure that stores of food were available for their use.[104] They were expected also to encourage their husbands or sons to join the rebels if they were in a position to do so. There is at least one case recorded in which a Koli was given a sword by his mother and told to join Bapu Bhangare's band. He obeyed her command.[105]

The position of Koli women both during the revolt and afterwards was a particularly vulnerable one. During the revolt their houses were raided and plundered by the police, often leaving them destitute. They were abused by the police sexually and they were likely to be dragged off by them to detention centres in the towns, where many died of cholera. In August 1845, some Koli women who had been thus detained complained to the Collector of Ahmadnagar:

> For the last six or eight weeks we have been brought to Kusba Rajoor and put into confinement. Our husbands have been despatched by Government to seize the rebels. There is no one at our houses to bring us food our cattle wander in the jungles and several of them have died. There is no one to take care of them. Our fields are lying uncultivated. We have nothing to eat here. We have no grain at our houses. We are obliged to remain without food some times for a day and some times for two days. We get no Batha [*bhatta*, or rations] from Government. Several of us died of the cholera which lately broke out here. Although Government cares for the protection of its ryuts, we have been greatly oppressed. We do not think that our imprisonment will lead to the apprehension of the rebels. If Government is aware of an instance in which rebels have been seized through the medium of women, we beg that we may be imprisoned in Ahmednuggar and be allowed Batha. If Government is tired of us women and children, we beg that we may all be removed to Ahmednuggar and be hanged there. But we do not wish to be kept here. We are poor women and we pray your Honor in Council to have compassion upon us and to issue such orders as may be deemed proper.[106]

After the revolt was over, the property of many of the outlaws who were caught and jailed was ordered to be confiscated by the courts. Although by law a portion of this property was meant to be set aside for the maintenance of the family of the convict, in practice the police often took everything. For example, in June 1846 the police came to confiscate the property of Kima Gauli, a convicted Koli outlaw of Ambedara village of Ambegaon taluka. They made a careful inventory of the meagre belongings of his family, consisting of three cows, one bed cover, one women's dress, one copper pot, one iron pan, one koita (machete), two implements for cutting grass, one and three-quarter maunds of nagli and half a maund of rice. They took all of this away and sold it, realizing a total of Rs 14.8.7, from which they deducted Rs 0.2.6 for their expenses.[107] The families of captured outlaws were thus stripped not only of their means of livelihood and subsistence, but even their bedding and clothes. If they owned land, that also was likely to be taken. The misery caused to these families could not have been greater.

Koli women thus suffered much, and they, unlike the men, did not have recourse to becoming outlaws themselves. The records do not mention any women as being active members of the bands. Such a life was not generally considered suitable for women of honour. It was only when the male rebels went to ground and were in hiding that their wives or lovers sometimes went to be with them.[108] In situations of danger, however, the men would often flee, allowing the women to be captured. Thus, an outlaw who was sheltering with his two wives deep in the forest in May 1845, ran off as soon as he heard a dog bark, taking his gun, but leaving his wives to be taken by the police.[109] It was considered the duty of an honourable woman to accept such misfortune for the good of the cause.

Just as the patriarch and man of honour sought to defend the women of 'his' family from the assaults of rivals, so it was common for rivals to seek to shame a family by raping, torturing or killing women members. In March 1845, for example, one of the Koli bands murdered a man in the Konkan and cut off the noses of his wife and brother.[110] In May 1844 Bapu's band 'committed violence on the women' of three villages in the Konkan.[111] A Koli band whose leader was unknown is recorded as having 'much annoyed the women' of a Patil's family in the Konkan in December 1844.[112] This probably involved sexual abuse, if not rape. In February 1845 another unnamed band was feasted by a Patil of a village in the Konkan and allowed by him to take away the wives of two Kolis who were serving in the much-hated regular police. They took them into the forest, where they were kept all night and 'grossly ill used' and 'outraged'—which must have meant raped.[113]

There is no evidence, however, that Raghu Bhangare himself was ever involved in such a rape. Even when he had Baniya or other women in his power when he was raiding a village, he hardly ever laid a finger on their bodies. The only exception which appears in the records was when he seized the two wives of a village Patil of the Konkan, and tortured them by setting fire to their hair, so as to force them to reveal where the family wealth was hidden. They were not raped.[114] It is possible that Raghu followed standards of behaviour which set him apart from other outlaws in this respect. Venubai Bhalchin's song told of how Raghu was tantalized by Chimayi with garlands of wild jasmine. Chimayi, whose name does not appear in any of the records, was depicted as a seductress-figure of a sort commonly found in popular legends tempting a male hero. The assumption in the song is that

Raghu resisted such temptation. What was believed to have been his sexual restraint in all of these respects must certainly have enhanced his reputation amongst the people.

As defenders of family and community honour, the leaders of bands were expected, however, to punish sexual transgression from within the family or community.[115] Thus, in March 1845 a Koli whose wife had fallen in love with another man asked his brother, a member of one of the bands, to take suitable action. He caught the two lovers and cut off their noses.[116] Around the same time, Raghu had a member of his own band put to death along with a woman who was with him. The reason was not stated, but a violation of the code of community honour seems to have been the likely cause.[117] Raghu's patriarchal defence of the honour of the women of his community thus gave rise, conversely, to a ruthless punishment of women who were seen to be bringing what he and other Kolis considered to be 'shame' to the community.

Ramayi and Raghu Bhangare were thus seen as exemplifying in their lives certain standards of 'honourable' behaviour which provided a model for other Koli women and men. They were celebrated not only for their defence of the community against outsiders but also for their assertion of a particular code of patriarchal values within.

Over and above this, there was a further popular validation of Raghu—as a great devotee of God. In the story which I was told about him in Jambhori, he was described as being prepared even to risk capture by the police to worship Shiva at Purshiroli at an auspicious time. The records bear these sentiments out. During his career as an outlaw Raghu is recorded as having worshipped at Bhimashankar, Vrajeshvari, Trimbak, Nasik and Ujjain. In late April 1845 he made a special journey into the Konkan to worship a local goddess to whom he had long promised to make an offering.[118] He was captured while fulfilling his desire to make an offering to Vitthal of Pandarpur on the *ekadashi* which fell at the start of 1848. Although his worship was thus eclectic, incorporating Shiva, Krishna (in the form of Vitthal) and mother goddesses, he had a reputation for a particular devotion to Shiva. In common with many followers of this god, he often took *bhang* and smoked *ganja*.[119]

As a devotee, Raghu was popularly believed to enjoy divine protection. He always carried two silver charms in a tiger skin bag slung over his shoulder. These, his long hair and sword were believed to give him the power to escape from his enemies, however tight the situation. It was believed that if these were taken from him he would lose his power. Raghu was said to be strongly under the influence of Devji Mahar, his chief lieutenant, who was said to have the facility of second sight. Raghu paid careful attention to whatever Devji advised him.[120] It is likely that his band carried small *murtis* of a variety of divinities, who were believed to provide protection.[121]

In the eyes of the people, Raghu's revolt appeared to enjoy divine blessing and protection, and his life was viewed as one of morality. His devotion was seen to sustain him and give him confidence and courage in situations of great danger and difficulty. The death of Devji Mahar in an encounter in May 1845 appeared to have robbed him of his chief adviser and spiritual mentor. The revolt promptly collapsed, and people must have drawn a connection between the two events. This belief explains, perhaps, Raghu's subsequent wanderings to many places of pilgrimage in the guise of a Shaivite *gosai*; he was attempting to regain supernatural powers which appeared to have failed. He was not successful in his mission. A peasant who met Raghu in late 1847 gives the impression that Raghu lacked the aura which had previously so impressed his followers and admirers.[122] He was captured eventually by the British because, it was said, he was persuaded to abandon his charms and allow his hair and beard to be shaved so that he could travel in disguise to Pandarpur. The fierce-looking ganja-smoking Shaivite, with long unkempt hair and beard, was replaced by the meek smooth-shaven Vaishnavite bhakta. In the words of one peasant: 'I had understood from common report that if Raghoo Bangria's hair, his sword, and silver boxes containing certain plants, by means of which he could escape from among 25 men, were taken away from him he would have no more power.'[123] When apprehended by the police at Pandarpur early in the morning of the ekadashi, Raghu made no attempt to escape, but surrendered quietly. He had not yet had the chance to worship Vitthal, and was seen to be at that moment particularly exposed, unprotected and powerless.[124]

VI

The British knew that Raghu's revolt could be broken only if the people could be induced to inform them about the movements and hiding places of the outlaws.[125] The regular police were certainly not up to the task of suppressing the revolt. They were few in numbers, often incompetent, and hampered by the disinformation they were fed constantly by the Koli nayaks as well as peasants. The rebels on the other hand were always kept informed by the people about police movements, so that they could avoid them with ease. Only if in very superior numbers would the rebels attack a party of police. The British set about trying to break the solidarity of the people in a number of ways. They offered large rewards for the capture of the leading rebels. Raghu had Rs 4,000 on his head, others lower amounts. They also tried to frighten the people by arresting those suspected of helping the rebels, by detaining their families and, in the case of Patils and nayaks, by dismissing them from office.

These tactics had some success, for there were always those who for one reason or another were prepared to act as informers. Some hoped for reward. Others had personal grudges to pay off. There were those, such as the village Patils, who feared loss of office if they failed to cooperate with the government. In 1844 it was reported that about fifty Kolis of twenty-three villages of Akola taluka were passing on information about the bands. By August 1844 twenty-eight members of Bapu Bhangare's band and sixty-five other outlaws had been captured with their help.

Raghu himself appears to have been very aware that his greatest danger lay in such treachery from members of his own community.[126] In mid-1844 it was reported that he had become cautious about accepting new members into his band for fear of possible betrayal.[127] Around this time he was told that a member of his band was plotting to kill him. He seized the man and found that his gun was loaded ready to be fired. This seemed to confirm the suspicion, and he immediately cut off the man's head with a sword.[128] He also set about silencing informers by attacking some of the more notorious ones.

On 9 October 1844 Raghu raided Titavi village in Akola taluka with the aim of killing a Patil who had been helping the police. The informer managed to escape, but his family were beaten up and his house looted. News of the attack frightened informers throughout the region; many thereafter made a habit of taking their families out of their villages each night to sleep in hiding places in the forest.[129] Others who had earned rewards for helping in the capture of outlaws, refused to accept any money for fear of thereby exciting the hostility of the bands. In many cases, parties of police had to be stationed where informers lived to protect them.[130] With the informers thus isolated, there was a drying up of information during the winter of 1844–5, when Raghu was raiding the Konkan.

Raghu kept up his campaign of terror against informers throughout this period. On 24 February 1845 he and eleven followers went to Mutkhel, a village in Akola taluka where the people had refused to provide food for the band and, still worse, had on more than one occasion told the police about their movements. After cutting off the nose and ear of the Baniya, the outlaws went round the village setting houses on fire. In all, about two-thirds of the houses were destroyed and several animals burnt to death.[131] A month later, word came to Raghu that Padaji Patil of Kumbhefal, near Akola, was relatively unprotected. The British considered Padaji their most valuable informer in the region; no less than 117 people had been arrested with his help. Because the outlaws knew of his activities, the British had posted a party of police in the village to protect him. In March 1845 the people of Kumbhefal, whose sympathies lay with the bands rather than with Padaji, sent word to Raghu that all except one of the police party had left the village for a few days to celebrate Holi. Raghu, with thirty of his followers, went immediately to the village and killed the informer.[132]

A few days later there was an even more terrifying attack on an informer, this time not by Raghu but another band. The outlaws surrounded the village of Vachape in Ambegaon taluka and searched every house until they found the Patil, an informer. They dragged him to the shrine of Vitthal and sacrificed him there. They went on to attack Ambegaon, where they burnt the government kacheri.[133]

It was at this juncture, when the morale of the local police and informers was particularly low, that the government mounted a far more determined operation against the bands. The police were reinforced with troops of the regular army and a contingent of the Khandesh Bhil Corps. The latter were known as experienced mountain troops, a foe far more formidable to the rebels than the demoralized and corrupt regular police. Their commander, W.J. Morris, met the mamlatdars—the officials in charge of the talukas—who complained that the people had lost all confidence in the power of the police and were obliged to side with the rebels.[134] Morris was determined to win over sufficient informers—whether by punitive action, threats or bribes—to break the solidarity of the ghat peasantry and restore the power of the government.

Large numbers of Kolis of the above-ghat villages who were suspected of helping the bands were called into Rajur and ordered to give active help to the authorities, while their families were detained as so-called 'security' to ensure that they carried out this task. These Koli peasants were forced to abandon their villages at the time when they should have been busy preparing their fields for the first rains. The conditions in the detention centres were moreover notoriously bad: the prisoners suffered from malnourishment and there were deaths from cholera. Put into this intolerable situation, many gave information about the hiding places of the rebels.[135] By 21 June 1845 around 150 outlaws had been either captured or killed. Most prominent amongst them was Devji Mahar, Raghu's closest comrade and confidante, who, after a tip-off, was surrounded while asleep and shot dead where he lay.[136] Bhau Kengle was also captured at that time. Raghu fled with a few of his closest colleagues to Nasik, and then to the north. In August Bapu Bhangare was double-crossed by a member of his gang, and after being severely wounded, surrendered to the police.[137]

Although this brought an effective end to Raghu's revolt, he himself continued to be sheltered by his supporters. A Koli Patil of his own village of Devgaon let him, Bhau Dungar and Khundu Sable hide out in a cattle shed which he kept in the mountains of Baglan, on the border with Khandesh. In September, after the monsoon was over, Raghu returned to Akola, where he remained in hiding. He was still protected by the Koli nayaks—a Patil who told them where Raghu was hiding was ordered by them to remain silent.[138] In December W.J. Morris tried to force a Koli of Akola taluka who he knew was sheltering Raghu to lead him to the hiding place. The Koli took Morris's party up a precipitous mountain, and at the top flung himself over a cliff, preferring death to an act of betrayal which would have brought a lasting stigma for him and his entire family.[139]

In February 1846 Raghu had another narrow escape, but lost his remaining comrades, Bhau Dungar and Khundu Sable. He had returned to Baglan to hide out with them again in a cattle shed. While there, Bhau Dungar was recognized by a Patil from Akola taluka, who used to graze his cattle in the area. He went to the place with another Patil and a policeman They found Bhau and Khundu asleep in the shed. The policeman later claimed that the two tried to resist and he had to cut them down with his sword. They were taken to Nasik, where Bhau soon died of his wounds. Neither said anything about Raghu, and the authorities did not at the time know how close they had come to capturing him.[140]

Raghu fled north to Malwa, in Central India, and wandered from place to place as far as Bhopal. He disguised himself as a gosai, or holy man, with long unkempt hair and beard, and lived in a temple for three months. He then returned, travelling to Surat, then back into the Konkan by June 1847. He hid out in the forest in Mokhada taluka during the monsoon. In September 1847 Raghu decided to return to his village to see his mother, wife and other relatives. He reached within about five kilometres of Devgaon, but hearing that the place was under surveillance, he went back to the Konkan without seeing them. In October and November he travelled around villages near the foot of the ghat, meeting up with old gang members and other Kolis who could form the nucleus of a new gang. On 24 November he was almost caught near Devgaon by Lieutenant Gell of the Ghat Light Infantry. Other members of the new gang were arrested immediately afterwards.

Having failed in this endeavour, Raghu decided to go on pilgrimage to Pandarpur. He persuaded a Koli Patil of Ambivali, in the Konkan, to organize a party of pilgrims in which he could travel in disguise. Gell was tipped off about this, and after a forced march to Pandarpur, captured Raghu on 2 January 1848, just as he was entering the town.[141] The records do not tell us who Raghu's betrayer was.

After his capture, Raghu was taken in chains to Thana, where he was jailed. In April 1848 he was tried on a charge of treason. He tried to persuade a local lawyer, a Parsi, to defend him. The Parsi refused, and as a result he had no legal representation. In the brief, one-sided trial, Raghu admitted to levying khand in the Konkan, but denied that he had used violence or had killed anyone. He said that the worst depredations had been committed by others using his name. He was convicted largely on the evidence of the three policemen whose lives he had spared near Bhimashankar in September 1844. The judge sentenced him to death. Next day he petitioned the Governor of Bombay that his case had not been heard properly, and that he had been convicted on the evidence of his adversaries. The petition was rejected, and he was hanged.

VII

Raghu was dead, but the revolt against usury continued. I have already mentioned the revolt of Honya Kengle between 1872 and 1876. Although sometimes described in the records as 'Honya Naik', Honya Kengle was not a member of a family of Koli nayaks, but an ordinary cultivating Koli. His revolt was not—as with Raghu's—driven by any desire for élite position. He cut off the noses of at least six Marwaris and for a time drove the moneylenders from the region.[142]

There were further revolts against usurers between 1892 and 1902. One of the Koli rebels was called Dagadu Deshmukh. Like Raghu, he became an outlaw as a result of an insult to his family honour. 'It is said that he was infuriated by his *savkar* saying in the market place that he (the *savkar*) would strip off Dagadu's wife's *choli* [bodice, thus exposing her breasts] if his debt was not paid. . . . Dagadu's primary object was revenge'.[143] Another was Chimanya Bhavani, a Koli of Kochargaon (Dindori taluka). He was originally persuaded to attack the usurers by a Patil of Peint taluka who told him: 'I will give you food, but you must cut the noses of the Wanis who have oppressed us poor fellows and burn their documents'. Chimanya agreed to do this, and the Patil arranged for him and his band to be supplied with arms.[144] That year—1898—various Koli bands attacked forty-five moneylenders in Nasik, Ahmadnagar and Thana districts, cutting off the noses of seventeen. One, a Gujarati Baniya, was killed.[145]

Because of these attacks, moves were made in the early years of the twentieth century to classify the Mahadev Kolis as a 'criminal tribe'. When the Inspector-General of Police for Bombay Presidency,

M. Kennedy, produced his *Notes on Criminal Classes in the Bombay Presidency* in 1908, he described them as a group with so-called 'criminal propensities'. He stated:

> The Koli is not a burglar or thief in the ordinary sense. Though given to petty thieving, he is a source of trouble and anxiety only when he takes to outlawry, and then he commits dacoity robbery, grievous hurt and sometimes murder.
>
> In the matter of criminal tendencies, Kolis bear a strong resemblance to Bhils. The predatory instinct and love of adventure is still strong in them. A season of scarcity, the grasping avariciousness and exacting demands of moneylenders, or some domestic grievance drives individuals into outlawry and once an outlaw has established a reputation as a successful freebooter he soon attracts others, with or without some grievance fancied or real, to his standard. Unless speedily dispersed, captured or disposed of, the gang thus formed increases and multiplies and soon creates a reign of terror. They raid villages and extort black-mail, known as khand, in the shape of food, gunpowder or money; loot Marwaris, and burn their accounts; cut off noses and slit ears; hold up solitary policemen and forest peons, whom they beat, tie to trees and rob, and generally harry and terrorize the countryside by crimes of violence.
>
> Such crimes are difficult to deal with by reason of the fact that the outlaw gangs are sheltered, through sympathy or fear, and assisted by their caste fellows, while the Kolis' intimate knowledge of every jungle path and hiding place, and their hardiness and activity, enable them to successfully evade pursuit and capture by the police.[146]

According to Kennedy the 'only effective way to deal with outbreaks in the ghats' was to hunt down criminal Kolis swiftly before they could gain a significant following. He made no attempt to address the social causes of their discontent, such as 'the grasping avariciousness and exacting demands of moneylenders'.[147] The Government of Bombay accepted this line of thought, for in 1914 the Mahadev Kolis were notified as a 'criminal tribe' under the Bombay Criminal Tribes Act of 1911.[148] Around 700 'notorious' Kolis were required to attend a roll-call each day which was designed to stop them from travelling away from their villages to commit crimes. Although not many were directly affected, the classification stigmatized the community as a whole. Shivaji's proud mountain warriors were now classed by the colonial state as a despised 'criminal tribe'.

The application of the Act to the community failed to bring any halt to Koli revolts. In 1920–1, for example, a Koli band which was about twenty-strong carried out nearly fifty attacks on sahukars and other moneyed people in the mountain villages of Nasik district and the adjoining parts of the Konkan below the ghats. They achieved fame as the 'Devali band' on account of the silver images of gods that some of the members wore around their necks.[149] In 1939–40 a band was formed in Junnar taluka of about forty Kolis led by a Maratha called Kondiya Navle, with the avowed aim of looting all the Gujarati sahukars of the region, who were charging exorbitant rates of interest. They carried out thirteen raids on sahukars in Pune, Ahmadnagar, Thana and Kolaba districts in the first half of 1940. The police caught up with the band in July 1940, Kondya Navle being killed in the ensuing encounter, and several of his followers being captured.[150]

One of the most celebrated of the band leaders of the 1950s was Satu Marade of Khed taluka, who led an attack on a notorious sahukar, in this case a Muslim called Amin Sheth. This usurer was notorious for lending money for marriage celebrations on condition that the bride spent her first night with him. The rebels tortured him by twisting his testicles before they beat him to death.[151] It seems that he was particularly hated, and was as a result treated far more viciously than the Marwaris and Gujaratis normally were.

Satu Marade, like Raghu Bhangare, is remembered as a great devotee. According to the oral tradition, it was while he was travelling around his area performing *kirtans* to Vitthal of Pandarpur that he was told of Amin Sheth's goings on. He took a vow in the name of Dnyaneshwar—the thirteenth-century devotee of Vitthal—to kill the usurer. He thus became what was by now known as a bandkari out of a sense of moral duty. The people's narrative tells of how his brother's wife eloped with a Katkari from the Konkan. Katkaris were considered by the Mahadev Kolis to be of inferior caste. Satu Marade lured the lovers back and killed them. When charged with the crime he is reputed to have said: 'I did it for my honour. I am a bandkari and I could not tolerate my own sister-in-law being taken away by a Katkari'. It was said that as he was being led away by the police he recited a sloka: 'Whatever I did was with good intention, but in the process I might have hurt some people, so please forgive me.' He wept, and the whole village wept with him. At the trial, it was said, Satu asked the judge whether he would be angry with him if he put a question. The judge told him to do so. He asked: 'Imagine that tonight you have to send your wife to me.' The judge realized that Satu was in the right and set him free. He returned to his village, where he lived a life of religious devotion until his death.[152]

Although this story is far-fetched, it shows that in popular consciousness the bandkari continued to be viewed not only as a defender of the community from outsiders, but also as a defender of the patriarchal honour of the community from within. He was seen to undertake this task out of a sense of moral duty and at considerable cost to his own happiness in life. There was in this a sense of proud dignity which, quite clearly, struck a chord deep in popular imagination. The dignity was that of the patriarch who is forced to be cruel for a supposed good.

Since the 1960s there have been no further bands. A combination of Koli self-assertion and anti-usurer legislation has helped to curb the worst excesses of the sahukars. Today the threats to the Kolis—who are now classed as an exploited and impoverished 'scheduled tribe'—come from other directions: from Maratha Kunbi peasants who are buying up their lands, from large dam projects which are submerging their best fields in the valleys, even from tourist development schemes which seek to replace their villages with wildlife sanctuaries.

VIII

We may end by asking why only Raghu and no other nineteenth-century Koli rebel continues to live in popular memory. To some extent it must be because Raghu's band was the greatest of the Koli revolts of the colonial period. The degree to which he drove the sahukars and kulkarnis to ground and the losses which he inflicted on the hated police were never matched by later Koli rebels. He, more than anyone, put the godas and their local collaborators to shame.

As important as this, perhaps, was the fact that Raghu's revolt marked a transition. In the pre-colonial period the band had represented an assertion of power by a particular family of nayaks and their followers. There were powerful solidarities within the revolt, but the Koli community as a whole tended to be divided. Raghu's revolt grew in part from such politics; his chief personal ambition was to avenge himself on his enemies, one of whom was a Koli, and to regain his families' lost jamadarship. There were however new forces coming to the fore. Under the British, the mass of the peasants had been pauperized by a combination of high taxes, a slump in agrarian prices and unprecedented state support for usurers. When Raghu attacked the usurers and local tax collectors, he struck a chord which resounded amongst the people. A new solidarity was born which cut across old divisions. Raghu's revolt thus inaugurated a new form of subaltern political organization and action. By celebrating Raghu in story and song, later Kolis paid tribute to this fact.

Raghu, in addition, was seen as a defender of family honour, the dutiful son of a devoted mother, and the righter of sexual transgressions from both within and without the community. He appears to have conformed to a code of moral behaviour which set him above the other rebels of his time. He was seen as being deeply religious, protected by god in his adventures until the final, last betrayal.

In all these respects, Raghu's name served as a signifier. The invocation of his name by later generations represented a statement and celebration of the qualities of, amongst other things, assertive power and courage, community solidarity, patriarchal honour, the bond between mother and son, devotion to god. The assumption, for storyteller, singer and audience, was that it was in the continuing interest of the community to maintain, assert and strengthen these qualities in the present day.

NOTES

Abbreviations used in footnotes: BJP—Bombay Judicial Proceedings; BA—Bombay Archives (Maharashtra State Archives, Bombay); IOL—India Office Library, London; J.D.—Judicial Department; R.D.—Revenue Department. When referring to talukas I use the present-day names and boundaries, so that places can be located on modern maps.

1. A.B. Portman, District Superintendent of Police, Pune District, 3 March 1872, BA, J.D. 1876, 50/1876.
2. W.F. Sinclair, 4 April 1874, BA, J.D. 1874, 52/353.
3. Case against Honiya Kengle, October 1876, BA, J.D. 1876, 50/1876.
4. Interview with Javji Soma Kengle, Chandav Krishna Pardhi, Govind

Maruti Sable at Machchiwadi hamlet of Jambhori (Ambegaon taluka, Pune District), September 1991.

5. I am very grateful to Indra Munshi Saldhana for a rough initial translation, and to Padma Anagol for this full translation made later in London from the tape recording.
6. *Report of the Committee on the Riots in Poona and Ahmadnagar 1875* (Bombay, 1876), p. 7.
7. G.S. Ghurye, *The Mahadev Kolis* (Bombay, 1963), p. 13.
8. *Gazetteer of the Bombay Presidency*, vol. XVI, *Nasik* (Bombay, 1883), pp. 314–15; *Gazetteer of the Bombay Presidency*, vol. XVII, *Ahmadnagar* (Bombay, 1884), pp. 417–18. The quotation is from the Nasik Gazetteer; the wording in the Ahmadnagar Gazetteer differs slightly.
9. *Gazetteer of the Bombay Presidency*, vol. XIII, *Thana* (Bombay, 1882), pp. 636–7.
10. I am grateful to Sumit Guha for drawing my attention to this thesis. Frederick Bruce Robinson, 'Adaptation to Colonial Rule by the "Wild Tribes" of the Bombay Deccan, 1818–80: From Political Competition to Social Banditry', unpublished Ph.D. thesis, University of Minnesota, 1978 (hereafter 'Robinson thesis').
11. F. Bruce Robinson, 'Bandits and Rebellion in Nineteenth century Western India', in Anand Yang (ed.), *Crime and Criminality in British India* (Tucson, AZ, 1985), p. 60.
12. Robinson, 'Bandits and Rebellion', p. 41. Later, on p. 68, he accepts that there must have been 'ballads and songs' about some of the bandits, but states rather patronizingly that: 'To endeavour to collect remnants of such popular lore remains a worthy but extraordinarily time-consuming task.' As archival research is also very time-consuming it is clear where his priorities lay.
13. Eugene Genovese, 'On being a Socialist and a Historian', in E. Genovese, *In Red and Black: Marxian Explorations in Southern and Afro-American History* (Knoxville, TN, 1984), p. 12.
14. Petition by Raghu Bhangare, January 1845, IOL, BJP 1845 P/403/40, no. 2270.
15. Sanad of 3 September 1843, IOL, BJP 1845 P/403/38, no. 35.
16. Statement by Vithuji Kanavkar, no date, IOL, BJP 1844 P/403/34, no. 5584
17. Baba Padamji, *A Compendium of Molesworth's Marathi and English Dictionary* (Bombay, 1875), p. 380.
18. E.J. Hobsbawm, *Bandits* (Penguin, 1972), pp.17–18.
19. I noticed this in an exchange in 1991 in a Mahadev Koli village between

some Kolis and a bus driver who was a Maratha from outside the area. The former talked about the bandkaris, the latter about dakus.

20. H.F. Silcock, 11 May 1888, BA, R.D. 1888, 345/1813.
21. In Akola, which was Raghu Bhangare's home taluka, the Mahadev Kolis were the single largest caste. According to the 1881 census, there were 22,110 Kolis, making up 36.4% of the population. There were 5,385 Mahars, making up 8.8% of the population. There were however 21,821 Kunbis (35.9% of the population), living chiefly in the eastern part of the taluka in the lower reaches of the valleys. So even in their heartland, Kolis hardly outnumbered Kunbis. In Ahmadnagar district as a whole, Kunbis made up 40.5 % of the population, while Kolis, who were confined almost entirely to the one taluka of Akola, made up only 3.6 % of the population. *Gazetteer of the Bombay Presidency*, vol. XVI, *Ahmadnagar* (Bombay, 1884), pp. 46, 86, 193, 589–90.
22. *Gazetteer of the Bombay Presidency*, vol. XVII, *Ahmadnagar* (Bombay, 1884), pp.195 and 208.
23. Robinson, 'Bandits and Rebellion', p. 50.
24. Ibid., pp.195–6. Ghurye, *The Mahadev Kolis*, p. 11.
25. *Gazetteer of the Bombay Presidency*, vol. XVII, *Ahmadnagar*, pp. 404–6; Ghurye, *The Mahadev Kolis*, pp. 11–12; Robinson thesis, pp. 229–33.
26. A. Mackintosh, 'An Account of the Tribe of Mhadeo Kolis', *Transactions of the Bombay Geographical Society*, vol. 1, 1836–8, pp. 245–58.
27. Ajay Skaria has noted a similar state of affairs among the Bhil chiefs of the Dangs. 'A Forest Polity in Western India: The Dangs 1800s–1920s', unpublished Ph.D. thesis, University of Cambridge 1992, p. 116.
28. Robinson, 'Bandits and Rebellion', pp. 4 and 9.
29. J.D. Inverarity, 5 November 1844, IOL, BJP 1844 P/403/36, no. 6593; W.J. Morris, 14 August 1845, IOL, BJP 1845 P/403/50, no. 8098; W.J. Morris, 19 January 1846, IOL, BJP 1846 P/403/57, no. 2241.
30. C.E.F. Tytler to H.P. Malet, 10 January 1845, IOL, BJP 1845 P/403/38, no. 540.
31. Robinson, 'Bandits and Rebellion', pp.188–216.
32. *Gazetteer of the Bombay Presidency*, vol. XVII, *Ahmadnagar*, p. 416; Mackintosh, 'Account of the Mhadeo Kolis', pp. 234–5; Robinson, 'Bandits and Rebellion', pp. 236–46.
33. Mackintosh, 'Account of the Mhadeo Kolis', pp. 211–12. Robinson argues in his thesis on pp. 15–16 that the agriculture of the Kolis was always very 'primitive' with yields so low that they had to become warriors and looters so as to 'supplement the meagre fruits of their agricultural endeavours'. This appears to be based on observations of the economic

state of the Kolis during the colonial period; the evidence from Mackintosh suggests that the condition of their agriculture was by no means so bad in the pre-colonial period.

34. For details, see Sumit Guha, *The Agrarian Economy of the Bombay Deccan 1818–1941* (New Delhi, 1985), pp. 17–26.
35. *Gazetteer of the Bombay Presidency*, vol. XVII, *Ahmadnagar*, pp. 483–6.
36. Mackintosh, 'Account of the Mhadeo Kolis', pp. 232–5.
37. Ibid., pp. 234–5.
38. The judicial records of 1848 describe him, variously, as aged 26, 27 and 31. This puts his date of birth as between 1817 and 1822. Proceedings before I.S. Gell, 11 January 1848, IOL, BJP 1848 P/404/29, no. 1567; Statement of Raghu Bhangare, 7 February 1848, IOL, BJP 1848 P/404/30, no. 2012 C; Trial of Raghu Bhangare, April 1848, IOL, BJP 1848 P/404/32, no. 3129.
39. Loc. cit.
40. Petition by Raghu Bhangare to Governor of Bombay, December 1844, IOL, BJP 1845 P/403/38, no. 79.
41. Testimony of Vithu Patel of Devgaon (Akola), no date, but probably 1844, IOL, BJP 1846 P/403/57, no. 2244.
42. J.S. Law, 11 March 1844, IOL, BJP 1844 P/403/29, no. 1963. Javji Bamble was the son of Tuljabai, the sister of Raghu's father Rama Bhangare. Robinson, 'Bandits and Rebellion', p. 283.
43. For instance, the average age of some members of the allied band led by Bapu Bhangare who were captured in 1844 was nearly 26. The youngest was 20, the eldest 40. Proceedings against 22 Koli prisoners, no date, but around June 1844, IOL, BJP 1844 P/403/34, no. 5584.
44. This contradicts Hobsbawn's argument that social bandits tend to be young unmarried men who are not yet tied down with family responsibilities. *Bandits*, p. 30.
45. So he said in a petition to the Governor of Bombay of December 1844, in which he asked for the jamadarship to be given to his brother Ravji. IOL, BJP, 1845 P/403/38, no. 79.
46. Shahu II, Raja of Satara 1777–1810, and heir of Shivaji.
47. Translation of petition from Raghu Bhangare to the British Government, received in February 1845, but written most probably in mid-January 1845, IOL, BJP 1845 P/403/40, no. 2270.
48. It was reported in 1845 that many Kolis had joined the insurrection 'the ultimate object being permanent Government employment, which has been granted on similar occasions, and under similar circumstances'. J. Liddell to J.D. Inverarity, 4 April 1845, IOL, BJP 1845 P/403/41, no. 2859 B.

49. See *Source Material for a History of the Freedom Movement in India (Collected from Bombay Government Records)*, vol. I, *1818–1885* (Bombay, 1957), pp. 55–9.
50. Deposition of Dhundi Sable, 14 November 1844, IOL, BJP 1844 P/403/36, no. 7167; Deposition of Kavaji Bhangare, February 1848, IOL, BJP 1848 P/403/30, no. 2012 B.
51. Deposition of Gyaniram Marwari, February 1848, ibid.
52. Testimony of Nana Sawant, one of the policemen who was released by Raghu, in proceedings against Raghu Bhangare, February 1848, IOL, BJP 1848 P/404/30, no. 2009.
53. J. Liddell to J.D. Inverarity, 20 September 1844, IOL, BJP 1844 P/403/34, no. 5250.
54. C. Giberne to H.A. Harrison, 5 October 1844, IOL, BJP 1844 P/403/35, no. 6062.
55. Proclamation by Raghu Bhangare, received by the British in November 1844, IOL, BJP 1845 P/403/38, no. 47.
56. Statement by Raghu Bhangare, 7 February 1848, IOL, BJP 1848 P/404/30, no. 2012 C.
57. H.P. Malet to W.H. Harrison, 15 December 1844, IOL, BJP 1845 P/403/38, no. 345.
58. H.P. Malet to W.H. Harrison, 7 January 1845, IOL, BJP 1845 P/403/38, no. 518; Evidence of Vasudev Dattar, November 1845, IOL, BJP 1845 P/403/52, no. 9014; Evidence of Sukh Patil, 7 February 1848, IOL, BJP 1848 P/404/30, no. 2092.
59. Lieutenant Mellersh, 25 April 1844, IOL, BJP 1844 P/403/30, no. 2612.
60. John Liddell, 1 February 1845, IOL, BJP 1845 P/403/39, no. 1427.
61. Diary of Vasudev Padke, entry for 29 March 1879, *Source Material for a History of the Freedom Movement in India (Collected from Bombay Government Records)*, vol. I, *1818–1885*, p. 121.
62. Raghu Bhangare to H.A. Harrison, no date, but received 23 November 1844, IOL, BJP 1844 P/403/36, no. 6951.
63. Raghu told a soldier whom he met by chance to convey this threat to his superiors. Robinson, 'Bandits and Rebellion', p. 321.
64. M. Elphinstone, 'Report on the Territories Conquered from the Peshwa', in G.W. Forest (ed), *Selections from the Minutes and Other Official Writings of the Honourable Mountstuart Elphinstone* (London, 1884), p. 311.
65. *Gazetteer of the Bombay Presidency*, vol. XIII, *Thana*, p. 707.
66. Proceedings before John Warden, Sessions Judge, Pune, 9 September 1845, IOL, BJP P/403/51, no. 8581.
67. Proceeding before I.S. Law, 2 and 3 February 1848, IOL, BJP 1848 P/404/29.

68. C.E.F. Tytler to H.P. Malet, 24 December 1844, IOL, BJP 1845 P/403/38, no. 271
69. I.S. Law, 24 December 1844, IOL, BJP 1845 P/403/38, no. 117.
70. F.G. Fraser, 28 May 1844, IOL, BJP 1844 P/403/32, no. 3954.
71. Petition by Raghu Bhangare to Governor of Bombay, December 1844, IOL, BJP 1845 P/403/38, no. 79.
72. Trial of Khundu Sable, 2 September 1846, IOL, BJP 1846 P/404/8, no. 8397.
73. W.R. Simpson to J.W. Langford, 24 September 1845, IOL, BJP 1845 P/403/49, no. 7759.
74. When the Governor of Bombay had these detentions brought to his notice in November 1845 he condemned them strongly, and ordered all the women and children to be released forthwith. Minute by the Governor, 14 November 1845, IOL, BJP 1845 P/403/51, no. 8582.
75. W.F. Curtis, 4 January 1845, and C.E.F. Tytler, 10 January 1845, IOL, BJP 1845 P/403/38, nos. 63 and 540.
76. C. Giberne to H.A. Harrison, 19 August 1844, IOL, BJP 1844 P/403/34, no. 5129; W.R. Simpson to G.I. Blane, 6 April 1845, IOL, BJP 1845 P/403/46, no. 5291.
77. F. Gordon to R. Travers, 24 February 1845, IOL, BJP 1845 P/403/40, no. 1840.
78. D. Costello, 18 March 1845, IOL, BJP 1845 P/403/40, no. 2226.
79. F.G. Fraser to I. Holland, 28 May 1844, IOL, BJP 1844 P/403/32, no. 3954.
80. J.S. Law, 11 March 1844, IOL, BJP 1844 P/403/29, no. 1963.
81. Deposition of Bhagwan Bhangsali, 2 February 1848, IOL, BJP 1848 P/404/29.
82. W.R. Simpson to G.I. Blane, 6 April 1845, IOL, BJP 1845 P/403/46, no. 5291; W.J. Morris, 4 June 1845, IOL, BJP 1845 P/403/44, no. 4548.
83. W.J. Morris to the Collector of Thana, 21 June 1845, IOL, BJP 1845 P/403/47, no. 5566.
84. Deposition of Gangaji Patil, no date, IOL, BJP 1846 P/403/57, no. 2249.
85. Deposition of Birji Patil, no date, IOL, BJP 1846 P/403/57, no. 2248.
86. According to Vithu Patil of Devgaon (Raghu's village), the Koli nayaks of Rajur were informed that Raghu was engaged in this activity in November and December 1843, but they did nothing to stop him. Deposition of Vithu Patil, no date, but probably 1844, IOL, BJP 1846 P/403/35, no. 6062.
87. For instance, Raghu was told by them in March 1844 that Rs 14,000 was lying in the treasury at Akola, and he was encouraged to plunder it. He did not on this occasion take the advice. Ravji Bhangare (brother of

Raghu), quoted in C. Giberne to H.A. Harrison, 5 October 1844, IOL, BJP 1844 P/403/35, no. 6062.

88. *Tamasha* was a form of popular drama, but the term also means a show, sport or fun. J.D. Inverarity, 5 November 1844, IOL, BJP 1844 P/403/36, no. 6593.
89. For an example, see F.G. Fraser, 11 May 1844, IOL, BJP 1844 P/403/32, no. 3954.
90. Deposition of Gangaji Patil, no date, IOL, BJP 1846 P/403/57, no. 2249. See also deposition of Vithu Patil, IOL, BJP 1846 P/403/57, no. 2244.
91. W.J. Morris, 14 August 1845, IOL, BJP 1845 P/403/50, no. 8098.
92. Statement of Mahadev Patil of Tale, June 1844, IOL, BJP 1844 P/403/34, no. 5584.
93. Elizabeth Fox-Genovese, *Within the Plantation Household: Black and White Women of the Old South* (Chapel Hill, 1988), p. 29.
94. D. Pocock, *Kanbi and Patidar: A Study of the Patidar Community of Gujarat* (Oxford, 1972), pp. 66–9.
95. Pierre Bourdieu, *Outline of a Theory of Practice* (Cambridge, 1977), p. 61.
96. M.N. Srinivas, *The Remembered Village* (Berkeley, 1976), p. 279.
97. Insults by powerful superiors not of the community, such as officials, policemen, landlords or usurers, were suffered in silence. Only the most reckless peasant dared retaliate against such superiors; though such revolts—on the rare occasion when they did occur—were the stuff of peasant legend.
98. A. Shewan, Assistant Collector, annual report 1874–5, BA, R.D. 1875–6, 8/608. What seemed 'trifling' to the official was clearly a matter of considerable concern to the arsonist. As Helen Lynd has remarked in *On Shame and the Search for Identity*: 'It is peculiarly characteristic of these situations . . . that they are often occasioned by what seems a "ridiculously" slight incident. An ostensibly trivial incident has precipitated intense emotion. . . . It is the very triviality of the cause—an awkward gesture, . . . an untimely joke . . . a mispronounced word, ignorance of some important detail that everyone else surprisingly knows—that helps to give shame its unbearable character.' Quoted in Eugene Genovese, *Roll, Jordon, Roll: The World the Slaves Made* (New York, 1972), pp. 330–1.
99. For examples from Gujarat and Karnataka, see D. Pocock, *Kanbi and Patidar* (Oxford, 1972), p. 75 and M.N. Srinivas, *The Remembered Village*, pp. 156 and 159.
100. Deposition of Bhagwan Bhangsali, 2 February 1848, IOL, BJP 1848 P/404/29.
101. The man had asked him where he had been hiding while on the run in

1846 and 1847. I.S. Gell to C.D. Mylne, 27 November 1847, IOL, BJP 1848 P/404/27, no. 288.

102. Deposition of Bhavanji Ranaji, no date, but probably early 1848, IOL, BJP 1848 P/404/30, no. 2012.
103. I.S. Gell to C.D. Mylne, 10 January 1848, IOL, BJP 1848 P/404/28, no. 928.
104. F.G. Fraser to I. Holland, 28 May 1844, IOL, BJP 1844 P/403/32, no. 3954.
105. Statement of Mahadev Patil of Tale, June 1844, IOL, BJP 1844 P/403/34, no. 5584.
106. Full text (in translation) of petition by the wives of certain Kolis suspected of assisting Raghu Bhangare's gang, no date, received 9 August 1845, IOL, BJP 1845 P/403/49, no. 7757.
107. Yad from Police Amildar of Khed Pargana, 5 June 1846, IOL, BJP 1846 P/404/10, no. 463.
108. I.S. Gell to C.D. Mylne, 27 November 1847, IOL, BJP 1848 P/404/27, no. 288.
109. R. Travers to Scott, 17 May 1845, IOL, BJP 1845 P/403/43, no. 4136.
110. I.S. Law to W.H. Harrison, 25 April 1845, IOL, BJP 1845 P/403/43, no. 4066.
111. Proceedings against Bapu Bhangare and others, no date, but 1844, IOL, BJP 1844 P/403/34, no. 5584.
112. Petition by Vakils of Murbad, 6 December 1844, IOL, BJP 1856 P/403/38, no. 113.
113. F. Gordon to R. Travers, 24 February 1845, IOL, BJP 1845 P/403/40, no. 1840.
114. J.S. Law, 11 March 1844, IOL, BJP 1844 P/403/29, no. 1963.
115. This came out clearly in interviews which I conducted in the region in September 1991.
116. J. Liddell to J.D. Inverarity, 4 April 1845, IOL, BJP 1845 P/403/41, no. 2859 B.
117. W.R. Simpson to G.I. Blane, 6 April 1845, IOL, BJP 1845 P/403/46, no. 5291.
118. Evidence of Sukh Patil, 1848, IOL, BJP 1848 P/404/30, no. 2092.
119. J.D. Inverarity, 21 September 1844, IOL, BJP 1844 P/403/34, no. 5249.
120. Ibid.
121. A group rounded up by the police in May 1845 was identified as a band because they had with them a small tin box containing images of their gods. Ordinary peasants, it was said, never went about with such a box—only a band did. A.J. Etheridge to Morris, 17 May 1845, IOL, BJP 1845 P/403/43, no. 4158.

122. Raghu told the Patil that he wanted to approach a British saheb so that he could put his case, but that he lacked the confidence to do so. Evidence of Sukh Patil, 1848, IOL, BJP 1848 P/404/30, no. 2092.
123. Ibid.
124. I.S. Gell, 10 January 1848, IOL, BJP 1848, P/404/28, no. 928. In respect of Raghu's supposed loss of power along with his hair and beard, there are interesting parallels with the brilliant short story by Saadat Hasan Manto about a don of the Bombay underworld who was seen to have lost his charismatic power after his huge and imposing moustache was shaved. Saadat Hasan Manto, 'A Question of Honour', in *Kingdom's End and Other Stories* (New Delhi, 1989).
125. C. Giberne to H.A. Harrison, 19 August 1844, IOL, BJP 1844 P/403/34, no. 5129.
126. Hobsbawm has argued that the careers of social bandits have most commonly been brought to an end through betrayal by colleagues or members of their community, rather than by the police. *Primitive Rebels* (Manchester, 1974), p. 14.
127. C. Giberne to H.A. Harrison, 19 August 1844, IOL, BJP 1844 P/403/34, no. 5129; C. Giberne to H.A. Harrison, 5 October 1844, IOL, BJP 1844 P/403/35, no. 6062.
128. Deposition of Bhavanji Ranoji, March 1848, IOL, BJP 1848 P/404/30, no. 2012.
129. C. Giberne to H.A. Harrison, 14 October 1844, IOL, BJP 1844 P/403/35, no. 6070.
130. C.E.F. Tytler to H.P. Malet, 10 January 1845, IOL, BJP 1845 P/403/38, no. 540.
131. C. Giberne to G.I. Blane, 25 February 1845, IOL, BJP 1845 P/403/40, no. 2168.
132. W.S. Simpson, 24 March 1845, IOL, BJP 1845 P/403/41, no 2608; C. Giberne to G.I. Blane, 25 March 1845, IOL, BJP 1845 P/403/42, no. 3072.
133. J.D. Inverarity, 1 April 1845, IOL, BJP 1845 P/403/41, no. 2758
134. W.J. Morris, 19 January 1846, IOL, BJP 1846 P/403/57, no. 2241.
135. W.R. Simpson to J.W. Langford, 24 September 1845, IOL, BJP 1845 P/403/49, no. 7759.
136. This was the version given by a woman companion of Devji, who was sleeping with him at the time. The police denied the charge, claiming that Devji charged at them waving his sword, whereupon he was shot dead. J.W. Simpson to G.I. Blane, 11 May 1845, IOL, BJP 1845 P/403/43, no. 3737; Rupsingh Havildar to Captain Liddell, 20 May 1845, IOL, BJP 1845 P/403/47, no. 5936.

137. Havildar Rupsingh to Captain Liddell, no date, but probably August 1845, IOL, BJP 1845 P/403/48, no. 6580; W.F. Curtis to I.J. Law, 29 September 1845, IOL, BJP 1845 P/403/50, no. 8252. In November 1845 Bapu Bhangare, Bhau Kengle and two others were tried for treason and Bapu and Bhau were sentenced to death. Court proceedings, 26 November 1845, IOL, BJP 1845 P/403/52, nos. 9009, 9014, 9016, 9017, 9019 and 9022.
138. Deposition of Gangaji Patil, no date, but probably late 1845, IOL, BJP 1846 P/403/57, no. 2249.
139. W.J. Morris to J.W. Langford, 13 December 1845, IOL, BJP 1846 P/403/54.
140. C.E.F. Tytler to H.P. Malet, 19 February 1846 and H.P. Malet to W.H. Harrison, 23 February 1846, IOL, BJP 1846 P/403/56, no. 1782; Statement of Raghu Bhangare, 7 February 1848, IOL, BJP 1848 P/404/30, no. 2012 C.
141. A description of the chase is given in I.S. Gell to C.D. Mylne, 10 January 1848, IOL, BJP 1848 P/404/28, no. 928.
142. See BA, J.D. 1874, 52/353 and 1876, 50/1876.
143. Collector of Ahmadnagar, 14 February 1899, BA, J.D. 1900, 139/508.
144. Deposition of Chimanya Bhavani, 25 October 1898, BA, J.D. 1899, 88/630.
145. The figures are from January to the end of October 1898 for Nasik and Thana districts, and from the end of May to 22 October 1898 for Ahmadnagar district. BA, J.D. 1900, 139/508.
146. M. Kennedy, *Notes on Criminal Classes in the Bombay Presidency* (Bombay, 1908), pp. 90–4.
147. Ibid., pp. 95–6.
148. Notification of villages coming under Criminal Tribes Act, 1911, Bombay, 27 March 1914, IOL, BJP 1914, no. 9605.
149. *Police Report of the Bombay Presidency including Sind for the Year 1921* (Bombay, 1922), p. 23.
150. *Police Report of the Bombay Presidency including Sind for the Year 1940* (Bombay, 1941), p. 22. Kondiya Navle was still remembered by the people of Ambegaon taluka when I travelled in the area in 1991.
151. Interview with Ganpat Lohokare, Bhimashankar (Ambegaon taluka), 9 September 1991.
152. Interviews with Ganpat Lohokare, Bhimashankar (Ambegaon taluka), 9 September 1991 and Madanlal Prabhakar, Vada (Khed taluka), 11 September 1991.

CHAPTER 4

The Quit India Movement in Gujarat

In Western India, the Quit India Movement was less dramatic than in Bihar or the United Provinces, but it lasted far longer. In the rural areas there was in August 1942 no mass insurrection. The agitation gained momentum slowly, but once under way it continued strongly into 1943, and in some cases even longer. In districts such as East Khandesh, Satara, Broach and Surat large numbers of peasants took part in guerilla-style attacks on government property, lines of communication, and people known to be sympathetic to British rule. Because it had mass support, the movement in such areas proved hard to suppress. The agitation was remarkable also for the strength and duration of protest in towns such as Pune, Ahmadnagar and Ahmedabad.[1] One commentator even went so far as to label Ahmedabad in 1942 as 'the Stalingrad of India'.[2] Western India took the lead, furthermore, in bomb and sabotage activities. Of the 664 bomb explosions recorded in India from August 1942 to January 1944, 447—or 76 per cent—occurred in Bombay Presidency.[3]

The pattern suggests that the movement in this part of India was, on the whole, better organized than elsewhere. In this essay we shall concentrate on Gujarat which was perhaps the best-organised province. At that time, Gujarat was divided into a large number of different territories. There were five districts under the Government of Bombay (Ahmedabad, Broach, Kheda, Panchmahals and Surat), four districts under Baroda state (Amreli, Baroda. Mehsana and Narsari), some large princely states such as Bhavnagar, Jamnagar, Junagadh and Kutch, and a mass of small princely states, some of which covered little more than a few villages. The Quit India Movement did not affect the whole of this region. It was strong only in the districts under British

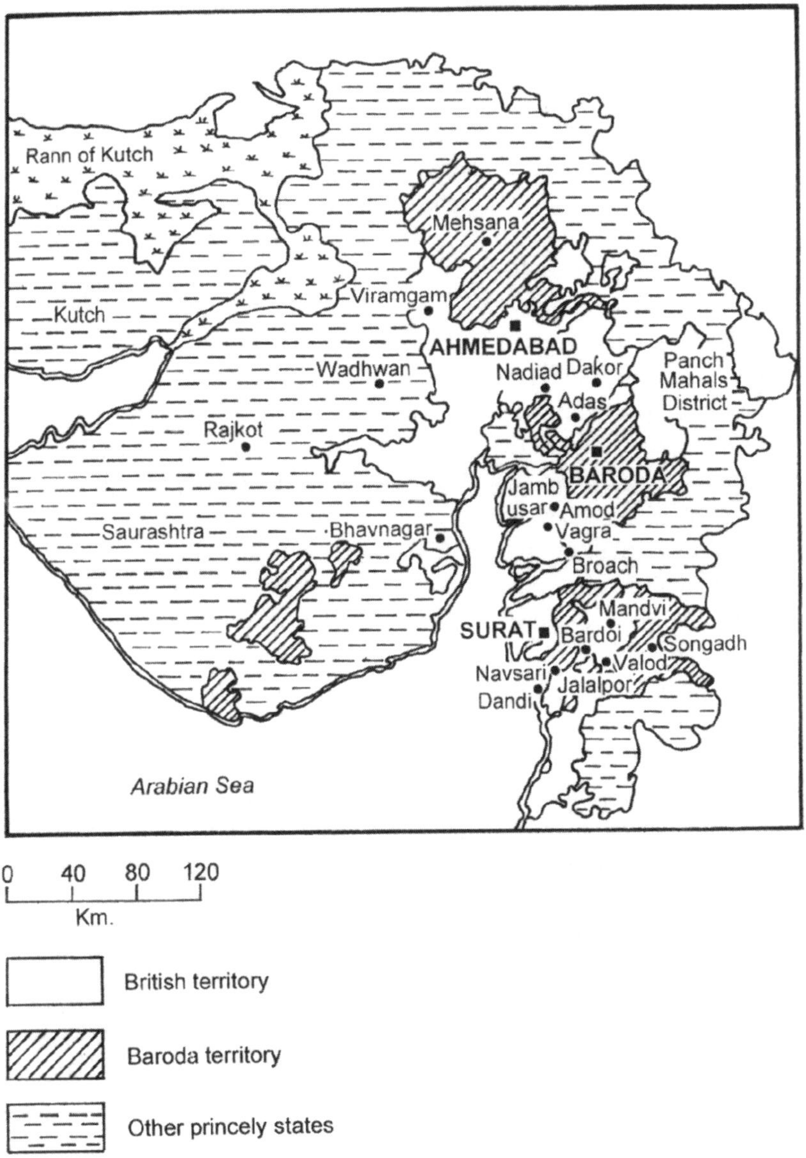

Map 2: Gujarat in 1942

and Baroda rule, and it is on these areas that we shall focus our attention.

II

The Gujarat Provincial Congress Committee (GPCC) was renowned for its organization. It had been responsible for some of the more notable Congress successes during the 1920s and 1930s, such as the Bardoli Satyagraha of 1928, and the salt march to Dandi and the Dharasana salt raids of 1930. The GPCC revolved around Vallabhbhai Patel, its president from 1921 to 1946.[4] Patel kept in direct touch with town, taluka and village level leaders who had, during the course of the movement, proved themselves to be able local political organizers. In the towns, these tended to be the leaders of the local petty bourgeoisie, and in the rural areas they were often leaders of particular peasant castes. By giving these men a relatively free hand at the local level, Vallabhbhai Patel was able to maintain an organization which continued to operate in a dynamic manner even after he had been arrested during campaigns of civil disobedience. The areas of the Congress's greatest strength were Ahmedabad, Baroda[5] and Surat cities, the districts of Kheda and Surat, and the Jambusar taluka of Broach district.

Although Vallabhbhai Patel became increasingly involved in all-India politics during the 1930s, he did not relinquish his hold over the Gujarat Congress. One rather hesitant attempt was made by Morarji Desai, the rising star of Gujarat politics, to elect an alternative president in 1934, but he made a quick retreat when it became clear that Patel opposed the move.[6] Patel's hold was strengthened further by the sweeping success of the Congress in Gujarat in the elections of 1937.[7] Another, rather different, challenge came from the socialist group in the Congress. The leaders were for the most part youths who had taken part in the Civil Disobedience Movement of 1930–4, and who had become disillusioned with the reformist tactics of the right wing of the Congress during the closing stages of this struggle. Many became socialists while serving jail sentences. In July 1934, they founded the Gujarat Congress Socialist Party. The members of the socialist group were mostly young men from a high-caste background, and they tended to be urban based, being strongest in Ahmedabad and Baroda cities. Their crusade against Gandhian ideals earned them the severe disapproval of Vallabhbhai Patel, and as a result they had no say over the running of the GPCC. It was generally believed that the socialist group in Gujarat had very little support. From 1937 they ran, however, a large number of study classes, and there was considerable sympathy for their ideas amongst some of the more able of the younger nationalists of Gujarat.

The Morarji Desai and socialist groups represented, at best, potential bases which could become important once Patel was removed from the scene through arrest. Even then, the majority of nationalists of Gujarat were firmly loyal to Patel. This was particularly true for the Patidar-based rural organizations, and also for the strong Congress youth organizations of the cities.

One group somewhat apart from this, but important for the events of 1942, was the Gujarat Vyayam Pracharak Mandal (Gujarat Society for the Propagation of Physical Training). This organization had strong nationalist leanings. Its leader, Chhotubhai Purani of Broach (1885–1950), had been associated with nationalist terrorist organizations in the early twentieth century, and although he had later become an active member of the Gandhian Congress, he never accepted the principle of non-violence. He founded a network of gymnasiums throughout Gujarat in which boys and young men were taught that they should train both their bodies and minds to fight the British. Besides being taught scouting, cross-country hiking and long-distance running, they were encouraged to perform manual labour and community service. There were frequent debates at the gymnasiums on current affairs and other political and social topics.[8] The boys were mostly Brahmans, Baniyas, Patidars and Anavil Brahmans from urban middle-class and prosperous rural families. Gandhi approved of these activities in part because Purani refused to allow right-wing Hindu and anti-Muslim sentiments to be voiced in his gymnasiums.[9] The heyday of this movement was in the 1930s, and by 1942 there were as a result a large number of young men in Gujarat who were mentally and physically prepared to support a violent struggle against the British.

III

Sir Roger Lumley, who was Governor of Bombay from 1937 to 1943, had since his arrival in India considered Gujarat to be '. . . the spiritual home of the Congress'.[10] He acknowledged that it was the Congress rather than the British which enjoyed mass support in this region of Bombay Presidency.[11] That there was deep distrust among Gujaratis as regards the motives and intentions of the British Government was revealed very clearly after the outbreak of war in 1939. British information about the war was ignored in favour of Hindi broadcasts from Germany and Japan and various, in Lumley's words, 'fantastic rumours'[12] which related to British disasters and impending attacks on India. In July 1940, Lumley reported:

> Amongst the Gujarati bania element . . . there is much disloyalty—in fact, some of those loyal Indians with whom I have contacts are not a little disturbed at the sentiments which they hear frequently expressed in Gujarati bania circles. There is much gloating over German successes and our reverses, and a good deal of talk to the effect that they would be no worse off under Hitler and that they see no reason why India should be apprehensive of a German victory.[13]

In May and June 1940, at the time when the Germans were winning sweeping victories in Europe, there was a run on banks and much hoarding of gold and silver in Gujarat.[14] After the German advance was halted the excitement subsided. There was then a lull in alarmist rumours until late 1941, when once more the war situation became critical. The entry of Japan into the war brought '. . . a fresh wave of pessimism and defeatism'.[15] The scare-mongering increased as victory after victory mounted up for the Japanese. In December 1941 there was a rush on banks, renewed hoarding of precious metals and a spate of rumours. In early 1942 many Gujarati families of Bombay, fearing bombing and subsequent chaos, left the city for their ancestral homes in Gujarat.[16] The evacuees brought with them the stories and rumours current in Bombay. In March the first air raid practice in Ahmedabad was followed by an exodus from the city. 'Extreme nervousness' was reported amongst those who remained. In Surat city many merchants buried their valuables or hid them in wells.[17]

The merchants and businessmen of Gujarat were terrified that if the Japanese advanced into India the British would carry out a scorched earth policy to prevent the Japanese gaining control of factories and resources which would be of value to them in their war effort. Their fears were reinforced by reports of what had happened to Gujarati businessmen in Rangoon when the city was evacuated.[18] They had heard from Gujaratis who had fled from Singapore how the British had, during the evacuation, favoured whites over coloureds, and they were warned not to depend on the British in such times of crisis.[19] By May it was feared that the Japanese fleet would attack the west coast of India at any moment, and there was in consequence widespread hoarding of food throughout Gujarat and Saurashtra.[20] The hoarding, coupled with the severe shortage of transport available for foodstuffs, produced a rapid rise in food prices in June and July 1942, which added to the feeling of impending catastrophe. News of the fall of Tobruk in June made it seem that India was vulnerable now from both the west and the east, and it was widely believed that the British collapse was imminent. In July the authorities in Gujarat reported a feeling of great insecurity in the villages and a big demand for weapons for self-protection.[21] It was in this explosive atmosphere that the Congress leaders launched the Quit India Movement. In acting as they did, they proved to be very much in tune with the mood of the people of Gujarat.

The initial preparation for the struggle in Gujarat was carried out by Vallabhbhai Patel during the second half of July 1942. Of all the leading Congressmen of the province, Patel was most enthusiastic for the coming confrontation with the British.[22] He believed that the time was ripe for a massive revolt which would force the British to hand over power to Indians, after which the latter could organize popular resistance to the Japanese. As he said at the time: 'This will not be a long struggle. It must produce quick results. We must get independence before the Japanese come here,'[23] He believed that there had to be mass civil disobedience with maximum disruption of all government, and strikes in which industry and communications would be paralysed. In his words: '. . . if there is your wholehearted support, the struggle will be over and won in a matter of days'.[24] 'When the leaders are gone to jail, the entire field will be open to you. Remaining within non-violence, break down all government authority'. '. . . do not wait for any programme. Invent your own.'[25]

Many Congress leaders both in Gujarat and other parts of India feared such an opening of the floodgates. Morarji Desai, for instance, believed that all of Gandhi's work for non-violence would be undone and that Vallabhbhai, in advising his followers as he did, was tacitly allowing the socialist element within the Congress to indulge in violence. Kanaiyalal Desai, president of the Surat District Congress Committee, agreed with Morarji in this.[26] Reading between the lines, we can see Morarji Desai's fear that such a movement would greatly strengthen the socialist element in Congress.

Arguments such as Morarji's were rejected at the Congress Working Committee meeting at Wardha on 14 July 1942, and the decision was taken to launch civil disobedience. After the meeting was over, Patel returned to Gujarat, where he delivered a series of fighting speeches in Ahmedabad, Kheda district and Surat district. He held discussions with Congress workers from all parts of Gujarat and Saurashtra, and met the nationalist leaders of Baroda state and pressed them to join the agitation.[27] According to Sir Roger Lumley: 'It was common talk, both in Ahmedabad and Bombay, amongst Congressmen, that Patel, in these private meetings, told them that on this occasion they would go all out, and were not to be too squeamish about non-violence.'[28] This is borne out by a report of a Congress meeting in Ahmedabad on 25 July, when Patel said of the forthcoming struggle:

> It would not stop even if there was civil war or anarchy in the country and that it would shake the whole world. It would be carried on by the masses even if all the leaders were arrested by the Government. . . . The Congress would not interfere if some people lost their temper and took dangerous and drastic steps against the Government during this struggle, nor would Gandhi show his disapproval in that connection.[29]

On 27 July he told another meeting in Ahmedabad:

> If all the leaders are arrested tomorrow and there is no time to meet you again, you should carry on the programme set forth before you by Gandhi from 1919 to 1942. Die but do not fall back. In this struggle, if instances like Viramgam occur or the railway line is removed or an Englishman is murdered,[30] the struggle will not be stopped. If the scorched earth policy is sought to be pursued here, as in other countries, do not allow it to be carried out. Face it boldly, even at the cost of violence. Carry this message to every nook and corner of Gujarat. You should put aside the constructive programme now and be ready to carry out Gandhi's *farmans*. Acts of violence even of the type of Chauri Chaura will not stop the movement.[31]

On 1 August, Vallabhbhai Patel travelled on to Bombay to prepare for the All India Congress Committee (AICC) meetings of 7 and 8 August, at which the 'Quit India' resolution was passed. In Bombay he formulated plans for a campaign of sabotage, and in the early hours of 9 August, just before he was arrested, it appears probable that he passed on these plans to a Congressman from Gujarat who left immediately for Gujarat and escaped arrest. T. Wickenden, in his official report on the agitation, later wrote about Patel: 'It is likely that he had a more personal part in the actual issue of instructions of sabotage than any of the other leaders.'[32] During the next few days these sabotage plans appeared in underground Congress bulletins issued from both Bombay and Ahmedabad.[33] The outburst of violent protest in Gujarat thus occurred with the full support and according to the well-publicized plans of the president of the GPCC, Vallabhbhai Patel.

IV

As soon as the news of the arrest of Gandhi broke, Vallabhbhai Patel and the other Congress leaders reached Ahmedabad city on the morning of 9 August, the millworkers downed their tools, the merchants closed their shops, students left their schools and colleges, and large crowds flocked into the streets. They began to molest policemen and anyone wearing that symbol of colonial culture, the solar topi. A police station was attacked and set on fire. In the ensuing battle between the police and people, one demonstrator was shot dead. The crowd was eventually dispersed with tear-gas, and troops were posted to prevent further violence.[34] On the following day about 2,000 students took out a procession. When the police tried to break it up with lathi charges, the students counter-attacked, throwing bricks. One student was killed and many others injured before they were dispersed.[35] Demonstrations and clashes with the police continued at a high pitch for another two weeks. The mills and shops remained closed and the students stayed away from their schools and colleges.

In Kheda district there were demonstrations and *hartals* from 9 August onwards in most of the towns and Patidar villages which had a history of support for the Congress. Many of the demonstrations took a violent turn when the police tried to break them up with lathi charges. The crowds fought back in actions that often led to police firings. The first such incident was on 11 August, one person being killed when the police opened fire. On 13 August, a more serious incident occurred in the noted Congress centre of Dakor, where a crowd of 2,000 counter-attacked, killing two policemen and injuring two others. In the resulting firings, two demonstrators were killed and many others injured. One of the dead was the Secretary of the local taluka Congress Committee.[36] There were further clashes over the next four days, during which two more agitators died at the hands of the police. The next serious incident occurred at Adas railway station, where a party of students who had come from Baroda to distribute Congress propaganda were shot at by the police on 18 August. Four students were killed and five seriously injured.[37] In all, a total of ten agitators were killed by the police in Kheda between 11 and 19 August. These were the highest recorded casualties for all of Gujarat during that period. In addition to the open clashes, there was widespread cutting of telegraph wires and other minor acts of sabotage on public property. According to Sir Roger Lumley, Kheda was the most disturbed district in Bombay Presidency during August. He dispatched two companies of British troops with orders to march through the district as a warning to the agitators.[38]

In contrast to Kheda, Surat district—that other great centre for rural nationalism during the 1920s and 1930s—was subdued during the first weeks. Surat city was peaceful on 9 August. On 10 and 11 August, boys from the schools and colleges took out processions and there was a partial hartal. The processions were dispersed by the police. On 12 August, most of the shops reopened and only rather feeble attempts were made to hold meetings. By 14 August, the students were returning to their schools and colleges.[39] On 23 August the Collector of Surat commented that Surat city had been remarkably quiet.[40] The rural areas were more militant, particularly Jalalpor taluka and, to a lesser extent, Bardoli and Valod talukas. There were demonstrations and acts of railway sabotage. For instance, on 17 August two hundred peasants from four Patidar villages converged on the railway station at Timbarva in Bardoli taluka, burnt the records, smashed up the equipment and removed several railway lines.[41] Two days before this, a large crowd attacked a party of policemen at Amalsad, an Anavil

Brahman village of Jalalpor taluka. After the police took shelter at the railway station, the crowd, by now 3,000-strong, smashed up the station, removed some rails and sacked the post office.[42] On 21 August there was a clash between villagers and police at Matvad, a coastal village of Jalalpor taluka inhabited by Koli peasants. Two villagers and one policeman were killed and four other policemen seriously injured. Elsewhere in Surat district there were no serious disturbances during the first two weeks.

In Broach district there were processions and demonstrations in the towns, and in the Patidar village of Sarbhan (Amod taluka) a police party which tried to break up a procession was beaten up by a large crowd on 13 August.[43] In the Panchmahals district there were demonstrations in the towns but little disturbance in the rural areas.[44] The same was true for the small towns and villages of Ahmedabad district.

In Baroda state, the agitation was most intense in Baroda city, Baroda district, Mehsana district and in Navsari town (which adjoined Jalalpor taluka of Surat district). The nationalist party of Baroda city, the Praja Mandal, was not banned immediately by the state authorities and processions were permitted until 18 August. There was one clash on 9 August, when demonstrators attempted to march on the British Residency, which was in an enclave of British territory.[45] During the following days there were frequent processions, and officials and topi-wearers were harassed. The millworkers went on strike, there was a partial hartal, and the students stayed away from their schools and colleges. By 17 August, the moderate Praja Mandal leaders were forced by popular pressure to declare their open support for the Quit India Movement, and on 18 August the body was banned and the leaders arrested. In the turbulent demonstrations which followed, two were killed and many others injured in police firings.[46] Police and troops then moved in force into the Raopura area—the storm centre of the agitation in the city—and carried out house-to-house searches.[47] As a result of the strong bandobast crowds were unable to gather, and by 24 August an uneasy calm had descended on the city. The strike by students and millworkers continued.[48]

In Baroda district there were hartals, school strikes and processions in small towns and in many Patidar villages. These continued at a high pitch until the end of August. Conditions were similar in Mehsana district, which also had a strong Patidar element in the rural population. In several cases, large numbers of Patidar peasants flocked into the nearest towns to take part in demonstrations. There were also many cases of railway sabotage.[49]

In the other princely states of Gujarat there were few disturbances. On the whole, protest was confined to demonstrations in towns by the urban middle classes. Only in Bhavnagar, Rajkot and Wadhwan states was there sustained agitation.[50] The people of Bhavnagar were most militant, and attempts were made there to hinder the war effort. On 15 September a demonstrator was killed in a lathi charge after a crowd tried to prevent the loading of a steamer with goods destined for the war. This was the only death caused by police action throughout the whole of Saurashtra during the Quit India Movement. Rajkot was the headquarters of the British Resident for the states of western India, and protests there were chiefly staged outside his office. There, and in Wadhwan, demonstrations were largely peaceful. The middle-class nationalists of Saurashtra failed to win support from the peasantry. In fact, the one demonstration of any significance in Porbander was suppressed by the police with the help of peasants brought into the town in buses by the Maharaja. Generally, people in the rural areas of Saurashtra knew little about the nationalist movement.[51] This obviously served to greatly weaken the protest there.

In all, during the first two weeks of the agitation in Gujarat, three policemen and sixteen demonstrators were killed. Of the latter, ten were killed in Kheda district, and two each in Ahmedabad city, Baroda city and Surat district. During this initial phase the violence was less than in Bombay city (where 33 people were killed in firings in the first four days) and northern and eastern India. By the standards of previous movements in Gujarat since 1920, the casualties were however very high, and the psychological impact on the agitators was profound.

By now new leaders were emerging to replace those in jail. The two most important among them were B.K. Mazmudar and Chhotubhai Purani. Mazmudar (1902–81) was a Kayastha of south Gujarat who had studied at the Banaras Hindu University and London School of Economics. He settled in Ahmedabad in 1930 to work as secretary to the prominent millowner, Kasturbhai Lalbhai. Mazmudar was a leading figure in socialist intellectual circles in the city during the 1930s.

He was thus in close touch with both the socialists and capitalists of Ahmedabad. He was a good friend of Achyut Patwardhan for the two had studied together at Banaras. During the movement he maintained firm links with Patwardhan and other leaders of the All India Secret Committee, such as Jayaprakash Narayan and Ram Manohar Lohia. During the course of the struggle he travelled secretly to Bombay and Pune to meet these leaders and to formulate strategy.[52] Chhotubhai Purani, the leader of the Gujarat Vyayam Pracharak Mandal, went into hiding in the villages of northern Broach district. Like Mazmudar, he was in contact with the All India Secret Committee. But as he was a well-known public figure, he was unable to travel as freely as Mazmudar. In addition to organizing a powerful underground movement in the villages in which he was staying, Purani called on his followers throughout Gujarat to take an active part in sabotage activities. The response to this call was very positive. Under these all-Gujarat figures there were the local leaders, such as Jayenti Thakor in Ahmedabad—a Congress socialist—and Thakorbhai Desai in Surat district—a member of Morarji Desai's group. They combined a programme of open mass demonstrations with secret sabotage work. The strength of these men stemmed from their position as leaders within existing Gujarat organizations which functioned within the broad ambit of the Congress Party. They were able to use these existing networks, drawing on the loyalties which had been built up within them, to carry on the movement in a highly effective manner.

Their activities were financed in part by voluntary donations, in part by exactions. In some cases the nationalists resorted to outright robbery and looting, in others they put intense moral pressure on people to donate money. Much of the money was given willingly. In Ahmedabad, Jayenti Thakor issued a directive from his so-called 'Azad Government' that all houseowners should contribute to nationalist funds at a rate of one anna for each fifty rupees earned. By early November this 'tax' had brought in Rs 7,000.[53] Amongst other things, the money was used for collecting arms and making bombs and other sabotage weapons, and also for financing the extensive publicity that was required during the agitation.

The chief organ of publicity was the patrika (bulletin). Patrikas were printed and cyclostyled on a large scale and distributed by hand throughout Gujarat by Congress workers. The main centre for patrika production was Ahmedabad city, where an underground Congress publicity organization ran four cyclostyling machines, kept in different places to avoid detection.[54] Other towns throughout British Gujarat and Baroda state also had secret presses and cyclostyling machines.[55] In the patrikas the people were told what they should do to support the movement, and news was published about the struggle in Gujarat and other parts of India. Some of the patrikas followed the orthodox Gandhian line of non-violence, others endorsed sabotage, terrorism and violence. This did not represent any divide in the movement in Gujarat, for the two types of patrika were put out by the same organizations. Rather, it reflected the desire of the underground leaders to win support from all shades of nationalist opinion.[56]

In the patrikas, factual news and rumours were often jumbled together. Rumours played an important role in the struggle, for they helped to rouse emotions and often gave an impression that the movement was on the verge of success. Some rumours found chalked up on a notice board in Baroda city during the first week of the agitation give a good impression of the exaggerated stories which circulated in Gujarat at this time. It was said that soldiers had been raping and shooting women and murdering children; that American soldiers had laid down their weapons and were refusing to fight unarmed Indians; that the British were in such a perilous state that the Viceroy was preparing to leave for England.[57] It was also widely rumoured that Mahadev Desai, who died suddenly on 15 August, had been tortured to death in jail by the British in an attempt to make him divulge information about secret negotiations between the Congress and the Japanese.[58]

British officials were much impressed by the thoroughness and depth of the organization of the agitation in Gujarat.[59] It was this which in a large measure gave such prolonged power to the movement there. In the next two sections we shall examine how the agitation continued in the months after August 1942, looking first at the cities of Ahmedabad and Baroda, and secondly at the rural areas.

V

In Ahmedabad city leadership of the movement was taken up by a young Congress socialist called Jayenti Thakor (b. 1913). He became known as the *Shahersuba*, or 'head of the city'. Under him were nineteen *ward nayaks* (ward leaders) in charge of the fourteen municipal wards of the city.[60] Under them were *pol nayaks*, who were leaders of the enclosed caste-based enclaves known as pols which honeycombed the old part of the city. The pol provided one of the basic units of solidarity within the city. Through this chain of command, Jayenti Thakor could pass orders to activists throughout the city within hours. Thakor was also in close contact with leaders of other groups within the city, such as the heads of the student group, the women's group sabotage groups and the children's group (Vanar Sena), and they also followed his directives.

The core of the support for the movement in both Ahmedabad and Baroda cities came from middle-class people of higher castes. Their localities provided the centres for the agitation. In Ahmedabad, business came to a virtual halt as a result of the closures of the retail, wholesale and share markets in protest at the government repression. These closures were enforced by the Mahajans, or unions, of traders for each locality of the city. The Mahajans were dominated by Baniyas, but membership cut across caste lines. In a few cases, caste councils also demanded that their members support the agitation; but this was not a very important means of enforcing solidarity.

The chief unit of solidarity was, rather, the pol. As people living in a pol tended to be largely of one caste, this represented a form of caste solidarity. Underground workers were able to hide in the pols with little fear of capture, for no body of policemen could enter a pol without alarms being raised. Fugitives could thus flee from back entrances or over the rooftops long before the police reached their hiding places. In some cases the police were actively prevented from entering pols.[61] In Ahmedabad the authorities tried to counter pol solidarity by removing the huge wooden gates from the entrances to sixteen of the most troublesome pols. But this had little effect.

The pols which gave most trouble to the authorities were situated in Khadia and neighbouring areas of Ahmedabad and in the Raopura area of Baroda. Khadia was considered a centre of intellectual life in Ahmedabad. The people of the locality had a reputation for their independence of mind and their suspicion of authority. The chief castes of Khadia were the Nagars and the Brahmo-Kshatriyas, two of the best educated communities of Gujarat. Members of these two castes often served in government administration. The top leaders of Ahmedabad in 1942 were all from Khadia. Jayenti Thakor was a Brahmo-Kshatriya of the locality. In Baroda the Panch Pols (five pols) of Raopura were considered by the state authorities to provide much of the power behind the agitation in the city. The Panch Pols were inhabited largely by Patidars who had migrated to Baroda from Kheda district during the late nineteenth and early twentieth centuries. In common with the Patidars of Kheda, they had a strong commitment to the nationalist cause, and they gave firm support to the Quit India Movement. Most of the big processions in Baroda originated from these Panch Pols.

The pols provided an ideal hiding place for underground saboteurs in the two cities. In Ahmedabad, the chief sabotage group was formed by thirty young men of Khadia on 13 August, under the leadership of K.G. Prabhu. They resolved to cut telegraph lines and damage railways and other government property. They signed an oath of secrecy using their own blood as ink. Others joined soon after, bringing the total strength to about 150. They travelled to the princely states of Saurashtra to purchase revolvers, bullets and explosives, and to Bombay to buy chemicals for bombs. Besides equipping themselves, they passed on weapons and explosives to other sabotage groups in Gujarat. They hid their equipment in private houses, mostly in Khadia.[62] Bombs were made in the house of a perfumer and hair-oil manufacturer called H.K. Dyer. The first bomb was thrown in Ahmedabad on 17 September. There were nine more cases during that month.[63] But the bombers suffered more than the bombed. Between 25 and 30 September, four saboteurs were blown up by their own bombs in the city.[64] Besides, the bombs tended not to be very effective as they were mostly made of gunpowder, a low explosive which made a lot of noise but did minimal damage to masonry. As a result, the authorities did not feel greatly threatened by their activities. In the words of Sir Roger Lumley: '. . . I cannot help being impressed by the feebleness of the attempts at sabotage with which we have had to cope.'[65]

More effective were the big mass protests. In the cities, the chief forms of such protest were processions, the holding of special days of protest and the continual harassment of the authorities, often by many acts of coordinated petty sabotage. The processions were often very rowdy affairs, with the police attacking with lathis and the demonstrators fighting back with stones and brickbats. On the whole, the police refrained from using firearms against the crowds, and when they did fire it was done to frighten rather than inflict casualties. As a result, the numbers killed and wounded in such clashes were very slight by most twentieth-century Indian standards. No policemen were killed, and in all only five demonstrators died (four in Ahmedabad and one in Baroda). Officials of the Bombay Home Department felt that the Ahmedabad police were being too gentle with the demonstrators, and that this was the reason for the continuing militancy of the people of the city. The Ahmedabad police chief replied that the demonstrators were suffering considerable punishment in lathi charges, and this was an adequate deterrent.[66]

Notably absent from these demonstrations were the Muslims, who made up twenty per cent of the population of Ahmedabad and fifteen per cent of the population of Baroda. Ever since the breakdown of the Congress–Khilafat alliance of 1920–2, the Muslims of Gujarat had played little part in the nationalist movement. Before the late 1930s they had not, however, adopted a position of outright hostility to the Congress. In the 1937 Legislative Assembly elections, the Muslim League had managed to win only four of the eight seats in Gujarat reserved for Muslims. All this changed over the next few years. As a counter to the Congress mass contacts movement in Bombay Presidency, Jinnah launched his own Muslim League mass contacts movement in mid-1937. Branches of the Muslim League were established all over Gujarat and an intense campaign of propaganda was launched. Soon, the Muslims of Gujarat were regarding the Congress ministry in Bombay and Congress-controlled local authorities with profound suspicion. In February 1938 the Bombay Presidency Muslim Association met in Ahmedabad and passed resolutions which expressed complete lack of faith in the Congress ministry.[67] The Muslims became extremely aggressive. In March 1938 there were riots during Muharram in two places in Kheda district, and over the next two years there were further disturbances in Kheda, Ahmedabad and the Panchmahals districts. In 1938 the Congress-controlled Ahmedabad municipality caused a storm in the city when it tried to close down a Muslim graveyard.[68] A Congress inspector who visited Ahmedabad in July 1940 reported back to the AICC: '. . . the influence of the Moslem League among the Moslem masses is so great that they will not listen to you if you are a Congressman.'[69] In January 1941, Lumley reported to Linlithgow: 'In Ahmedabad, the Muslim League has improved its position and can now be said to have nearly all Muslims in the City within its fold. In the recent Municipal elections, all the Muslim seats were secured by Muslim Leaguers . . .'[70]

In April 1941, the Muslims of Ahmedabad launched a massive attack on the Hindu localities of the city. After four days of furious rioting, 76 lay dead and over 300 more were injured.[71] Most of the casualties were Hindus.[72] There was a particularly fierce battle in Khadia, in which the Hindus counter-attacked with considerable ferocity. After that, few Muslims dared enter the area. Lumley commented on the riots: '. . . I do not think that there can be any doubt that the basic origin of these riots is political and is due to the preaching of Pakistan and the counter-preaching of the Hindu Maha Sabha and to some extent to the civil disobedience movement, which the Muslims regard as an attempt to coerce us into granting a Hindu Raj.'[73] Afterwards, the Muslim League paid the fines of convicted Muslim rioters and the Congress paid the fines of convicted Hindu rioters.[74]

It was hardly to be expected, therefore, that the Muslims of Gujarat would show any sympathy for the Quit India Movement. This was particularly so in Ahmedabad, where it was the Hindus of Khadia who supported the agitation most strongly. In mid-August 1942, the twelve Muslim members of the municipality were the only ones who refused to support a motion condemming the arrest of the Congress leaders.[75] In October 1942, when some stones thrown by Congress supporters at the police happened to fall into a Muslim area, the Muslims retaliated by looting a Hindu-owned shop and robbing a passing Hindu woman. A major riot was prevented by prompt action by police and troops.[76] In February 1943 there was a more serious clash after some Congress nationalists attacked a Muslim policeman.[77] In Baroda city, the Muslims met at the Jama Masjid on 26 August 1942 and resolved not to take part in the Quit India Movement.[78] They believed that the

Baroda Praja Mandal was a communal organization representing only Hindus.[79]

The relationship between the working classes of Ahmedabad and Baroda and the middle class nationalists was, on the whole, a happier one. In 1942 there were in Ahmedabad 75 textile mills with about 116,000 workers; in Baroda 5 mills with about 12,000 workers. In Ahmedabad, work within the mills was divided on communal lines. The majority of the spinners were Harijans, originally from villages in north Gujarat. The weavers, on the other hand, were for the most part Patidar immigrants from north Gujarat and Muslims whose ancestral home was the city.[80] The most powerful of the labour unions in both cities with the Majur Mahajan, which had been closely connected with the Gandhian Congress for over two decades. In Ahmedabad, this union had a membership of around 50,000 in 1942.[81]

During the war Majur Mahajan had managed to negotiate a series of favourable wage rises for the textile workers and, as a result, in Lumley's words: 'Their hold over labour in Ahmedabad is impressive.'[82] On 9 August 1942 the textile workers struck work in protest at the arrest of the Congress leaders. In Baroda city, the strike began on 13 August. There were, in addition, strikes in mills in the smaller towns of Nadiad, Petlad, Viramgam, Kalol, Kadi and Broach. The strike was purely political, not being connected with any demand for higher wages. The workers intended to remain out only for a short period. It was a time of shortages and soaring prices, and they could not hope to survive long without wages. The Gandhian leaders of the Majur Mahajan had other ideas, however. A strong campaign was mounted to persuade the workers whose ancestral homes were outside the city to return to their villages, where they could be fed by their families. As a result, about two-thirds of the millworkers left the city. The large majority of those who remained were Muslim weavers.[83]

Although the millowners were losing considerable profits from the closure of the mills during the boom period of the war, they made no effort to persuade the workers to return to work. Many of them had nationalist sympathies. Vallabhbhai Patel, who had considerable influence over them, had in July 1942 encouraged them to take the lead in paralysing the textile industry.[84] During the first week of August 1942, the Ahmedabad Millowners Association donated huge sums of money to the Congress in response to an appeal by Vallabhbhai Patel.[85] The influential millowner Kasturbhai Lalbhai, who was in close contact with the underground leader B.K. Mazmudar, took the lead in persuading his fellow millowners to agree to a long-term closure.[86]

The millowners were frightened that if the Japanese advanced into India, the British might destroy their textile mills as they retreated. They therefore had little to gain, so it seemed, from all-out cooperation with the British war effort, and they had considerable sympathy for the Congress suggestion that the Indian people should negotiate a separate peace with Japan. Even if the British were victorious, the millowners saw little to be gained from supporting them to the hilt, for they realized that the Congress would most probably form a government in India after the war, and that it was in their long-term interests not to alienate that party at this critical juncture.[87] Besides fearing damage to their factories and plants through war action, the millowners were in addition frightened that if they did not keep their mills closed nationalist saboteurs might bomb or burn them down.

Although the millowners thus supported the Quit India Movement to the extent of keeping their factories shut, they never came out in favour of it openly. In talks with the British between August and November they always held that the workers were responsible for the closures as they refused to return to work. Even Kasturbhai Lalbhai took this line in public.[88] To a large extent, therefore, the millowners were sitting on the fence, waiting to see how the conflict would shape before making a definite move one way or the other.

Within days of the closure, the millworkers who had remained in Ahmedabad began to demand that the factories reopen. Being Muslims for the most part, they had no sympathy for the agitation.[89] The communist union of the city, which already had a sizeable following,[90] put out an appeal for the workers to demonstrate at the mill gates with the cry 'Give us Work or Bread!'[91] During September there were a series of such demonstrations. Communist workers toured the villages of north Gujarat to persuade the spinners to return to the cities. The Majur Mahajan countered by sending its own representatives to tell the workers that the mills were not about to open, so that it would be futile to return. The millowners and merchants of the cities tried to pacify the workers by opening half-price grain shops and by giving loans which were to be repaid after the mills reopened. Large numbers of workers took advantage of these arrangements.[92]

During October the millowners' resolve to keep their factories closed began to weaken, for huge profits were being lost. Cloth prices were rising rapidly at this time, in part as a result of the continual closure of the Ahmedabad mills. Between August and December prices rose threefold.[93] In addition, the British were threatening to punish them for keeping their mills idle. The collector of Ahmedabad said that he would cut off their supplies of coal and Lumley hinted that he might cancel their government contracts and demand compensation for orders which had not been fulfilled.[94] By early November, it was also becoming clear that the war was turning in Britain's favour and that the time for sitting on the fence was over.[95]

On 13 November, the Majur Mahajan leaders suddenly came round to the demand for reopening. On 11 and 12 November there had been demonstrations outside the Majur Mahajan offices by spinners demanding an end to the lockout. The spinners had shouted anti-Congress slogans. The Majur Mahajan leaders, fearing that they were rapidly losing their hold, agreed to return to work from 23 November.[96] The middle-class nationalists of the city were bitterly upset by this capitulation. Over five hundred young volunteers were dispatched to the villages of north Gujarat to tell the workers not to return to work. Their message combined an appeal to patriotism with warnings that those who went back would suffer severely. The workers were told that the factories might be blown up by nationalist saboteurs while they were in them.[97] But by now the workers were desperate for work, and by 18 November large numbers were returning to the city.

The authorities were concerned lest there be clashes on the one hand between the workers and middle-class nationalists, and on the other hand between Hindu and Muslim workers. Troops were therefore kept at the ready and a cordon was thrown around the old city to prevent middle-class nationalists from reaching the mill areas. As it was, bombs were exploded by underground activists in five electrical substations which served the mills on 22 November, in an attempt to sabotage the return to work on the 23rd. The damage was however slight, and did not stop the mill sirens from sounding again next morning after a silence of three and a half months. Within days the mills were functioning at full strength. This dealt a serious blow to the movement in

Ahmedabad. Soon after, many markets and shops which had been shut since 9 August reopened, and by early December the economic life of the city was returning to normal.[98]

The middle-class nationalists had not yet lost heart. Unruly demonstrations and clashes with the police continued. On 10 December large crowds attacked the police in several areas of the city. In the resulting firing one man was killed and three injured. There was similar violence on 9 January 1943, when the police killed one and injured four, and on 10 March 1943, when one was killed and one injured. These were the last casualties: thereafter the demonstrations became less intense and less frequent. It was, however, only after August 1943 that the agitation died away completely in Ahmedabad city.

VI

In August the protest in rural areas was strongest in Kheda district. Surat district was initially less militant. From September this changed, with the agitation in Kheda becoming increasingly muted while the agitation in south Gujarat became more and more powerful. This turnabout was heralded with an event which caught the imagination of nationalists throughout Gujarat—the raid on the Vedach police station in Jambusar taluka on 22 September.

The Congress leader Chhotubhai Purani had gone into hiding in the villages of this area. With him was another leading Congressman of Broach called Chandrashankar Bhatt and a Rajput called Meghji, a dacoit who during the 1930s had become a Congressman. On 22 September Meghji and Bhatt captured the Vedach police station in a surprise attack, and appropriated all of the muskets kept there. This action signalled the beginning of a campaign of rural terror directed against officials, policemen and local supporters of British rule in Broach district, Surat district and the Baroda district of Navsari. In Broach district this campaign was at its height from late September to late December 1942. The places chiefly affected were the northern talukas of Jambusar, Amod and Vagra. Villages were attacked and the village records and record offices were burnt. There were a large number of robberies and dacoities directed against anti-nationalist elements. In many villages of Jambusar taluka the underground Congress workers rather than the British were in effective control, and cases were reported of Congress flag-hoisting ceremonies which the authorities were powerless to prevent.[99] Even though the British dispatched armed police and troops to the area in late September, they were unable to restore order, for the villagers refused to provide any information on the whereabouts of the underground Congress workers. On 4 December they managed to kill two members of Meghji's group in a gun battle.[100] But this had little effect on the nationalists, for on 15 December they carried out another daring raid on a police station, this time at Sarbhan, a Patidar village of Amod taluka. Meghji, Purani and Bhatt led this raid in which the police sentry was shot dead and all the policemen inside were captured and stripped of their uniforms. The station was vandalized and all the guns and ammunition were taken. As a direct result of this, all the minor police stations of Broach district were closed down, as they were considered too vulnerable.[101] On 18 December a company of troops arrived in the district and carried out demonstration marches in the three northerly talukas. The dacoity died down abruptly thereafter. In January and February 1943 some of the dacoits were arrested, though the three leaders escaped. Purani and Bhatt left Gujarat to carry on underground work in Bombay city and, later, in eastern India.

In Surat district, strong pressures were brought to bear on village headmen (*patels*) who refused to resign. Initially, many resigned voluntarily, particularly in Bardoli taluka. Many more refused to resign, and from early October onwards direct action began to be taken against them. Attacks were mostly directed against their property. Ripening crops were destroyed and mango trees were cut down. Mango was an important cash crop in the area. In several cases the houses of patels were set on fire. In only one case was the attack physical: a patel who had been a particularly notorious opponent of Congress for many years was—along with his wife—severely injured in a bomb blast in his house in a village of Bardoli taluka.[102]

In Jalapor taluka of Surat district, Thakorbhai Desai and Lalbhai Nayak, who were Anavil Brahmans of Morarji Desai's group, organized a series of raids on village *chavdis* (government record offices), post offices and other offices and other government properties. They broke in and burnt records and furniture. In several cases they set the chavdi on fire. Except for lathis, they carried no arms and they were careful not to injure anyone physically.[103] The members of the gang were local Anavil Brahman and Koli peasants who carried on their normal work during the day, and participated in raids at night. They began their attacks in November: from 4 to 12 November they raided 27 different villages. A company of troops was rushed from Bombay to patrol the area.[104] This had little effect, for the troops patrolled only the roads, whereas the saboteurs moved on country tracks, avoiding the motor-roads. During November, December and January this and some other allied groups carried out a total of 76 raids on 60 different villages. In early January, sixteen leading members of the gang were captured in Baroda territory.[105] Thereafter there were fewer raids: nine in February, four in March and one in April. Thakorbhai Desai was captured eventually in May 1943 and Lalbhai Nayak surrendered in October 1943.

In South Gujarat the local adivasis also took part in the movement. In the predominantly adivasi talukas of Mahuva, Valod, Vyara, Songadh and Mandvi, some adivasis who had been organized by Congress nationalists and also, in some cases, by Kisan Sabha workers during the 1930s carried out a series of attacks on loyalist patels, Baniya moneylenders and Parsi liquor and toddy shopkeepers. The Parsis were ruthless exploiters of the adivasis and, over the years, many had become big landlords by expropriating adivasi land. They were known to be strong supporters of British rule. In 1942 the adivasis raided the villages in which there were loyalist patels and Parsis. They burnt their haystacks, cut down their toddy trees, smashed their toddy pots and set alight their liquor and toddy shops. They broke into and looted their houses and set them on fire. In addition, they raided the houses of Baniya moneylenders and destroyed their account books, hoping thereby to wipe out their debts. As a result many patels resigned and many Parsis closed down their liquor and toddy business during the period of the attacks. These raids came to an end on 8 February 1943, when the Navsari district police captured about 200 of the adivasi dacoits and in the process recovered substantial amounts of loot.[106]

The only other area of Gujarat in which there was any degree of continuing rural violence was the Panchmahals district. In February and March 1943 there were four dacoities by a gang led by an underground worker called Bhimsinh Parmar, who had linked up with a local dacoit. Parmar had informed the local adivasis that British power was on the wane and that the time had come to strike against the local usurers. The adivasis rose up and looted the houses of the moneylenders, taking cash and clothes and, in all cases, burning the account books. No physical harm was done to the moneylenders. In late March the police broke up the gang and arrested many of its members.[107] The only other major incident in the Panchmahals was a raid on a police outpost by a gang led by an underground Congress worker in May 1943. Two police muskets were captured.[108]

In Kheda district the movement died down considerably after the first one and a half months. There were few demonstrations, and loyalist patels, government officials and liquor dealers were not attacked. Protest was confined largely to acts of petty sabotage by groups of high-caste youths, many of whom were associated with Purani's gymnasiums. Telegraph wires were cut, schools were vandalized, post boxes were destroyed, postmen were ambushed and, in a few cases, village record offices, post offices, and other government offices were damaged.[109] In February 1942 the police chief for Gujarat, J.W. Rowlands, commented: 'Kaira might have been one of the worst districts in the Province. In the event it has turned out to be one of the least troublesome . . .'[110]

One of the most noticeable differences between the rural agitation in 1942 and earlier Congress agitations in Gujarat was that in 1942 the peasants did not refuse to pay their land revenue and other taxes. Revenue refusal was on the nationalist agenda in 1942, and the British anticipated such a campaign in Gujarat, and we therefore need to ask why this form of protest never occurred. An important reason was that land revenue collections started only in December and January, so that the movement had begun to flag before the land revenue became due. However, a considerable number of collective fines were levied on villages which had given violent support to the struggle but in only five out of fifty cases was any attempt made to refuse to pay this fine, even though in most cases it was demanded soon after the start of the movement. The evidence suggests that even if the movement had continued strongly into 1943, there would not have been a no-revenue campaign.

The single most important reason for this was that the last such campaign, in 1932–4, had ended in failure. Considerable amounts of land had been confiscated from peasant activists of Kheda, Surat and

Broach districts. Although this land had been returned by an Act of 1938 passed by the Congress ministry in Bombay, the peasants who had lost land had suffered severe hardships during the preceding six years, and they had no desire to repeat an ordeal still fresh in their memories. The 'no-revenue' campaign was no longer considered to be such a potent weapon as it had been in the heady days after the Bardoli Satyagraha of 1928. This was somewhat ironic, for in fact the British were not prepared to confiscate land in 1942, as they knew that it would be returned by law as soon as the Congress returned to power.[111] Draconian measures were however planned for the supression of any no-revenue movement, and in both Kheda and Surat districts British troops were ordered to march through previously troublesome villages at the time the land revenue became due. This show of strength ensured that the revenue was paid up promptly.[112]

A further reason was that the richer peasants of Gujarat were making big profits from the high wartime prices. Prices were rising rapidly in late 1942, coinciding with a bumper harvest for the year. At the end of August 1942, the Collector of Kheda predicted:

> So far as I can gather there will be no movement for non-payment of Land Revenue when it falls due after three months. The crops are excellent and so are prices. The cultivator is expecting to realise for his crops almost double of what he got last year, and is in no mood to cooperate in a non-tax campaign.[113]

Although the no-revenue campaign never got off the ground, there was, as we have seen, considerable rural protest in Gujarat. The class support for this protest differed from area to area. In Kheda and Mehsana districts the protest was confined almost entirely to the Patidar peasantry, whereas in Broach, Surat and Navsari districts the more substantial Patidar and Anavil Brahman peasants were united with the poorer Koli and adivasi peasants in their opposition to British rule. To understand these regional variations we need to review briefly the history of these areas.

In Kheda and Mehsana districts, rural wealth was concentrated in the hands of the Patidar peasantry. The poorer peasants were to a large extent of lower castes who considered themselves to have been dispossessed by the Patidars over the centuries. These lower castes were often in conflict with the Patidars. The chief of these lower castes were the

Baraiyas, Patanvadiyas and Thakardas (the last found mostly in Mehsana district). During the period 1923–30, the Baraiyas and Patanvadiyas of Kheda had been sympathetic to the Gandhian movement.[114] This sympathy was put under great strain during the Civil Disobedience Movement of 1930–1, and over the next decade relations between the Patidar and Baraiyas and Patanvadiyas deteriorated. The two low castes were angered in particular by the Act passed by the Congress ministry in Bombay in 1938 returning lands confiscated for revenue refusal during civil disobedience. Those who had lost land were for the most part Patidars, and in many cases poor Baraiyas and Patanvadiyas had acquired the land at throwaway prices. Afterwards, they refused to part with the land voluntarily, and had to be forced to give it up by legislation.[115] This convinced them that the Congress was essentially a Patidar party.

The Baraiyas and Patanvadiyas claimed Kshatriya status and in 1937 they had formed a Kshatriya Association as a rival to the Patidar-dominated Kheda District Congress Committee.[116] This proceeded to link up with the Gujarat branch of the Kisan Sabha, which had been started in the same year. The Kisan Sabha was fighting for land to the tiller, lower rents, lower revenue and a moratorium on debts. All of these demands held great appeal for the Baraiyas and Patanvadiyas. In 1940 there were peasant marches and a no-rent campaign in a petty state within Kheda district in which the majority of the peasants were of these two castes.

The hostility between the Patidar-dominated Congress and the low caste movement was revealed very sharply in August 1942, when a meeting of Baraiyas and Patanvadiyas was called to protest against the killing of two police constables by Congress activists. The two policemen happened to be Baraiya by caste. The 10,000-strong crowd who attended this meeting resolved that they would give no support to the Quit India Movement. A pro-nationalist Baraiya held a counter-meeting, but few turned up.[117] Attempts made by Patidars to persuade the Baraiyas and Patanvadiyas to support the agitation largely failed.[118] The widespread opposition by the Baraiyas and Patanvadiyas of Kheda undoubtedly helped to dampen the rural protest in this district in 1942, for it was too risky for the Patidars to launch a widespread campaign of sabotage when a large proportion of the peasantry would almost certainly have been prepared to inform on them.

A similar pattern was observed in Mehsana district of Baroda state, where the Patidar peasantry were firm supporters of the Baroda state Praja Mandal. In August 1942 they came out in processions and demonstrations, causing considerable trouble to the Baroda authorities. The lower castes of the district took a directly opposite line. In September 1942 there were meetings by Thakardas and Rabaris in different parts of the district in which the Praja Mandal and Quit India Movement were condemned, and resolutions of loyalty to the Gaikwad of Baroda were passed.[119]

The situation turned out very differently in the northern part of Broach district, even though the social composition of this area was similar to that of Kheda, with a richer Patidar peasantry and poorer Baraiya and Patanvadiya peasantry. The Patidars had given firm support to the Congress for the past two decades, and in 1942 they came out strongly in favour of the agitation. The Baraiyas and Patanvadiyas of this area had not come under the influence of the Kshatriya or Kisan Sabha movements during the 1930s, and in 1942 they also supported the struggle. Here, therefore, there was rural unity and, as we have seen, the British virtually lost control of this area in late 1942.

In Surat and Navsari districts the agitation enjoyed strong support from all classes of peasants. The Anavil Brahman and rich Patidar peasants had been strongly pro-Congress since the end of the First World War. The somewhat poorer Koli peasants of the coastal areas had given firm support to the nationalist movement since 1929. Dandi, the scene of the famous salt satyagraha of 1930, was a Koli village in this area. The adivasis of the eastern tracts had been won over to the Congress cause in the early 1920s,[120] and they had given support to the Bardoli Satyagraha and Civil Disobedience Movement of 1930–1. During the 1930s the Kisan Sabha had made inroads amongst the adivasis by championing their demands for lower rents and land to the tillers. The Kisan Sabha leaders taught them that violence against their exploiters was justified. In this area the chief exploiters were Parsi liquor dealers-cum-landlords, who were pro-British, rather than high-caste nationalistic peasants, so that in this area there was no contradiction between the demands of the poor peasantry and the nationalist movement. As a result, in 1942, local activists, including Kisan Sabha workers, took the lead in encouraging nationalist dacoities by the adivasis against the Parsis and other exploiters. In 1942, there was thus a considerable degree of peasant unity in South Gujarat in the struggle against British rule.

VII

In Gujarat, the Quit India Movement came as a culmination of intense nationalist activity over a period of nearly twenty-five years. It was above all a political protest against continuing British rule in India, launched at a moment when it was felt that the edifice of the Raj was about to crumble, and it demonstrated the continuing strength of the Indian National Congress in the political life of Gujarat. The Congress Party depended for its strength on its ability to mean many things to many people, championing as it did the demands of the urban middle classes, prosperous dominant peasants, struggling subordinate peasants, Harijans and adivasis. In 1942 members of all of these classes supported the struggle in considerable numbers in different parts of Gujarat. In cases in which there was no immediate clash between the class interests of these disparate groups, the national front forged during the 1920s and 1930s stood firm during the period.

It did not, however, stand firm everywhere. Whereas in the past the subordinate peasantry of central and northern Gujarat had been mildly sympathetic towards the Congress, in 1942 they were extremely hostile. The same was true for the Muslims. In both cases there had been a noticeable change in consciousness, with a conviction growing amongst them during the 1930s that the Congress Party was working against their interests. In this respect, there was less unity in the nationalist movement in Gujarat in 1942 than there had been in 1920–2 and 1930–1.

Also, despite all the rhetoric, the movement in Gujarat was not socially very radical. The first patrika of August 1942 told the people to 'create a revolution'.[121] The words 'revolution' (*inkilab*) and 'freedom' (*azadi*) were however used almost interchangeably. 'Revolution', in other words, meant no more than the removal of British rule. Although the means by which this was to be done were spelt out in great detail in the patrikas of this period, little was said about what was to be done once this freedom was gained. One patrika said that 'the people's administration will be formulated parallel to Government administration'.[122] But no guidelines were laid down as to the form which this alternative administration should take.

Even then, a very successful parallel government was established in Ahmedabad. To some extent this body duplicated the existing administrative structure, with underground leaders in charge of each municipal ward, but it was also more comprehensive, stretching as it did to the level of the pol, and taking within its fold organizations such as the women's group, the Vanar Sena, the student organization, and the groups of saboteurs. This 'Azad Government' not only organized frequent demonstrations, but also took more positive administrative initiatives, such as levying taxes, issuing information in patrikas, collecting intelligence through a network of spies, and punishing certain notorious policemen.[123] Although the leadership was in the hands of young Congress socialists, this body drew its legitimacy from the broad mass of the Hindu middle classes of the city. The working classes were less under its sway, as was revealed in November 1942 when they returned to the mills in defiance of its orders. This was the only parallel administration established in Gujarat in 1942. No attempts were made to set up such bodies in the rural areas, as happened in Satara district of Maharashtra or Medinipur district of Bengal. The reason for this was that the movement in rural Gujarat was for the most part controlled by members of dominant castes, such as the Patidars and Anavil Brahmans, who had an aversion to the concept of 'parallel government'. For such people it was an idea loaded with radical implications, and they had no desire to upset the rural status quo. Azadi for them meant a transfer of power, and they confined their activities in 1942 to sabotage and punishment of people loyal to the British. As a result, when the rural underground activists were hounded down by the police in early 1943, the peasantry had no alternative programme to turn to.[124] Thereafter the movement in the countryside soon petered out. Only in the adivasi areas of south Gujarat were there indications of a more radical movement, for there the struggle was directed chiefly against Baniya moneylenders and Parsi landlords-cum-liquor dealers. Local high-caste Gandhian leaders proved very sensitive to the implications of such activities, and did their best to discourage them.[125] Yet even though the Baniyas and Parsis had fled away in terror to the towns by early 1943, no attempt was made to establish an alternative administration. The organization in the area proved too disjointed for any such move.

We cannot therefore describe the movement in Gujarat as being 'revolutionary' in a socialist sense. Morarji Desai's fear that it would strengthen the Left in Gujarat was not borne out in practice. In this, Vallabhbhai Patel proved the shrewder judge of his fellow-Gujaratis. He knew their capacity for forceful protest, and he knew also that they were unlikely to turn *en masse* to more radical programmes and doctrines in the course of such a movement.

As it was, the Quit India Movement strengthened the hold of the Gandhian Congress over Gujarat. Although the agitation began to wane by early 1943 and was dead by the middle of that year, this failure did not bring in its wake a decline in Congress popularity, as had happened in 1922 and 1931. In these years Gandhi had called an abrupt halt to movements which were in full spate, thus generating a sense of betrayal among the people. In 1942–3 the movement was crushed in a very uncompromising manner by the British, and the popularity of the Congress was enhanced. The people felt bound together with their jailed leaders in a continuing struggle against British rule. This was revealed in 1944, when the Congress swept the polls in the Gujarat local elections of that year with huge majorities and then refused to operate the councils which they now controlled. Law and order may have been restored, but British prestige very clearly had not; the majority of Gujaratis still had full faith in the party of Gandhi and Vallabhbhai Patel.

Notes

1. Sumit Sarkar, *Modern India 1885–1947* (New Delhi, 1938), p. 397. The movement started very strongly in Bombay city, but faded rapidly.
2. Govind Sahai, *'42 Rebellion* (Delhi, 1947), p. 124. A Government of India report of 5 September 1942 singled out the closure of the Ahmedabad mills as being the only element of the movement in Bombay Presidency which was causing an important interruption to the British war effort. N. Mansergh (ed.), *The Transfer of Power 1942–47*, vol. II (London, 1971), p. 905.
3. Francis Hutchins, *Spontaneous Revolution: The Quit India Movement* (New Delhi, 1971), p. 338.
4. See my book *Peasant Nationalists of Gujarat: Kheda District 1917–1934* (New Delhi, 1981), pp. 115–17.

5. For a history of the nationalist movement in Baroda state, see pp. 123–31 of my essay 'Baroda: The Structure of a "Progressive" State', in Robin Jeffrey (ed.), *People, Princes and Paramount Power* (New Delhi, 1978).
6. Kalyanji Mehta to Vallabhbhai Patel, 27 August 1934, Private papers of Kunvarji Mehta.
7. Congress won all of the 19 general seats and 3 out of 5 of the special seats in Gujarat in 1937. It failed to win any Muslim seats; *Return Showing the Results of the Elections in India, 1937. Great Britain, Parliamentary Papers 1937–38, Vol. XXI* (London, 1937), pp. 29–38.
8. Interviews with Chinubhai Shah (Secretary of Gujarat Vyayam Pracharak Mandal) in Rajpipla, Nirubhai Desai in Ahmedabad, Chandrashankar Bhatt in Broach.
9. In this, there was a marked contrast with the gymnasiums of Maharashtra. For Gandhi's opinion about Purani's gymnasiums, see *Navajivan*, 15 June 1924.
10. Lumley to Linlithgow, 18 December 1937, India Office Library (hereafter IOL), L/P & J/5/155.
11. Lumley to Linlithgow, 1 January 1940, IOL, L/P & J/5/160.
12. Lumley to Linlithgow, 9 July 1940, ibid.
13. Lumley to Linlithgow, 19 July 1940, IOL, L/P & J/5/161.
14. Fortnightly report from the Government of Bombay to the Government of India for the first half of the month (hereafter FR1) June 1940; Fortnightly report from the Government of Bombay to the Government of India for the second half of the month (hereafter FR2) May 1940, IOL, L/P & J/5/160.
15. Lumley to Linlithgow, 3 October 1941, IOL, L/P & J/5/162.
16. Tokyo Radio was announcing forthcoming bombings of Bombay in its Hindi broadcasts, and British air raid precautions added to the apprehension; Lumley to Linlithgow, 5 March 1942, IOL, L/P & J/5/163.
17. FR1, March 1942, ibid.
18. FR2, March 1942, ibid.
19. Rajabali Jumabhai, President of the Indian Merchants Chamber in Singapore, gave speeches to this effect in Ahmedabad in mid-April; FR2, April 1942, ibid.
20. FR1, May 1942, ibid.
21. FR1, July 1942, ibid.
22. Patel was probably the most enthusiastic of all of the top Congress leaders in 1942. He threatened to resign from the Congress Working Committee in June 1942 if a decision was not taken in favour of civil disobedience; P.N. Chopra, *Quit India Movement: British Secret Report* (New Delhi, 1976), pp. 197 and 233.

23. Narhari Parikh, *Sardar Vallabhbhai Patel*, vol. II (Ahmedabad, 1956), p. 474.
24. Ibid., p. 475.
25. *Conscience*, Ahmedabad, 7 August 1942, in National Archives of India, Home Political Department (hereafter NAI, H-Pol), 49/9/43.
26. Morarji Desai, *The Story of My Life*, vol. I (Madras, 1974), pp. 177–80; B.G. Kunte (ed.), *Congress Activities 1942–46 (Collected from the Maharashtra State Records)* (Bombay, 1977), p. 40.
27. P.N. Chopra, *Quit India Movement*, p. 245; Dewan of Baroda to British Resident, 3 June 1943, quoted in ibid., pp. 290–1.
28. Lumley to Linlithgow, 27 August 1942, IOL, L/P & J/5/163.
29. P.N. Chopra, *Quit India Movement*, p. 56.
30. Patel is referring here to three instances of violence which occurred during the Rowlatt Satyagraha of 1919. In Viramgam, in the words K.L. Gillion, '. . . a crowd of over a thousand people attacked the railway station and other government buildings. Six rioters were shot dead by the police, and an Indian official who was believed to have ordered this firing was caught by the mob, had kerosene poured over him and was burnt to death.' At Nadiad, in Kheda district, a train carrying troops was derailed after nationalists sabotaged the tracks, and in Ahmedabad a European police sergeant was murdered; K.L. Gillion, 'Gujarat in 1919', in Ravinder Kumar (ed.), *Essays on Gandhian Politics: The Rowlatt Satyagraha of 1919* (Oxford, 1971), pp. 137 and 142.
31. P.N. Chopra, *Quit India Movement*, pp. 197–8.
32. Ibid., pp. 199–200 and 292.
33. Examples of these bulletins (patrikas) were given in the appendix to this essay in its original form, but are omitted here. See D. Hardiman, 'The Quit Indian Movement in Gujarat', in Gyanendra Pandey, *The Indian Nation in 1942* (K.P. Bagchi, Calcutta 1988), pp. 109–21.
34. Maharashtra State Archives, Bombay, Home Department (Special) (hereafter BA, H.D. (Sp.), 1110(6)—A(3) of 1942.
35. J.R. Shukla, 'Ek hazar nav so betalisni Hind chhodoni ladatma Ahmadavadnu paradhan' (Ph.D. thesis Gujarat University, 1975), pp. 79–84.
36. *Conscience*, Ahmedabad, 7 August 1942, in NAI, H. Pol, 49/9/43; NAI, H-Pol, KW V to File 3/15/43, p. 16; Interviews in Dakor.
37. NAI, H. Pol, KW V to File 3/15/43, p. 35.
38. Lumley to Linlithgow, 27 August 1942, IOL, L/P & J/5/163.
39. Reports by Collector of Surat, 9-14 August 1942, BA, H.D. (Sp.), 1110(6)—A(7) of 1942.
40. BA, H.D. (Sp.), 1110(109)—G of 1942–3.

41. Report by Collector of Surat, 24 August 1942, BA, H.D. (Sp.), 1110(8) B(3) of 1942.
42. Loc. cit.
43. Report by Collector of Broach and Panchmahals, 14 August 1942, BA, H.D. (Sp.), 1110(6) A(5) of 1942.
44. Report by Collector of Broach and Panchmahals, August 1942, BA, H.D. (Sp.), 1110(6) A(6) of 1942.
45. Baroda Records Office (hereafter BRO), Huzur Political Office (hereafter H.P.O.) Pol. Dept. 38:97.
46. Baroda Press Note, 21 August 1942, ibid.
47. *Praja Mandal Pegam No. 3*, 21 August 1942, ibid.
48. Police Report, 24 August 1942, ibid.
49. BRO, H.P.O., Pol. Dept. 38:100.
50. Following information on the states of Saurashtra is from the weekly reports by the Resident for the States of Western India, IOL, C.R.R. R/1/1/3804.
51. This ignorance was remarked on by Gital Steed, who carried out research in a village of Saurashtra in 1949–50; 'Notes on an approach to a study of Personality Formation in a Hindu village in Gujarat', in McKim Marriott (ed.), *Village India* (Chicago, 1955), p. 114.
52. *Shri B.K. Mazmudar Sahebna Samman Prasange Abhivancana* (Atul, 1974).
53. Report by C.I.O. Bombay, 3 November 1942, NAI, H-Pol, 3/6/42. When Linlithgow heard about this, he refused to believe that there could be such a tax, for the collectors would be arrested. The Bombay Government had to inform him that the collectors enjoyed popular support and that the report was, regrettably, true. Linlithgow to Lumley, 10 November 1972 and comment by Bombay Government, 24 November 1942, ibid.
54. Interview with Jayenti Thakor.
55. J.R. Shukla mentions Baroda, Navsari, Mehsana, Attarsumba, Dabhoi, Varnama, Itola and Sinor, among other places, J.R. Shukla, 'Quit India Movement in the Vadodara State', paper presented to the Gujarat Itihas Parishad, 1976, pp. 2–3.
56. Interview with Jayenti Thakor. See also: Report by Baroda Resident, 17 August 1942, in which the British Resident noticed that there were two types of patrika circulating in Baroda city, one advocating sabotage and violence, the other tax refusal and non-violence. IOL, C.R.R.R/1/29/2431.
57. Note on Praja Mandal Agitation in Baroda State by C.K. Daly (Resident), 17 August 1942, ibid.

58. Report by Collector of Broach and Panchmahals, 26 September 1942, BA, H.D. (Sp.), 1110(6)—A(5) of 1942; Note by British censor, 28 November 1942, IOL, C.R.R.R/1/13804.
59. For instance, see comments by Collector of Ahmedabad, quoted by Lumley to Linlithgow, 24 September 1942, IOL, L/P & J/5/163.
60. A list of the ward nayaks reveals that 5 were Brahmans, 5 were Baniyas, 5 were Patidars, 1 was a Brahmo-Kshatriya, 1 was a Harijan, and 2 were of unknown caste; Shukla, 'Ek hazar nav so betalisni', p. 68.
61. For an example from Baroda, see Police Report, 1 October 1942, BRO, H.P.O. Pol. Dept. 38:97.
62. Shukla, 'Ek hazar nav so betalisni', pp. 286–9.
63. Ibid., p. 292.
64. Ibid., pp. 294–7.
65. Lumley to Linlithgow, 24 September 1942, IOL, L/P & J/5/163.
66. Note by Add. Sec. H.D. (Sp.) 14 November 1942 and note by Police 1110(109)—D of 1942–3. By mid-November, 34 demonstrators had been killed in Bombay City, 10 in Kheda district, 9 in Thana district, but only 2 in Ahmedabad city.
67. FR2, February 1938, IOL, L/P & J/5/156.
68. Collector of Ahmedabad to Commissioner, Northern Division, 5 May 1941, BA, H.D. (Sp.) 844 H VII of 1941.
69. AICC Inspection Report by R.K.L. Nandkeolyer, 29 August 1940, Nehru Memorial Library, AICC File 14 of 1939.
70. Lumley to Linlithgow, 3 January 1941, IOL, L/P & J/5/162.
71. *Times of India*, 19, 23 and 25 April 1941.
72. FR2, April 1941, IOL, L/P & J/5/162.
73. Lumley to Linlithgow, 1 May 1941, ibid.
74. FR2, May 1941, ibid.
75. Shukla 'Ek hazar nav so betalisni', p. 170.
76. FR1, October 1942, IOL, L/P & J/5/163.
77. Report by DSP Ahmedabad, 4 February 1943, BA, H.D. (Sp.) 1110(6)—A(3) III of 1942.
78. Police Report, 27 August 1942, BRO, H.P.O. Pol. Dept. 38:97.
79. Baroda FR1, June 1940.
80. In 1930 it was estimated that only 20 per cent of the millworkers of Ahmedabad were born in the city. Sixty per cent came from other parts of Gujarat; Sujata Patel, 'The Capitalist Class and Labour Politics: A Case Study of the Ahmedabad Millowners Association', unpublished Ph.D. thesis, Jawaharlal Nehru University, Delhi, 1984, p. 50a.
81. Figures in *Times of India*, 20 November 1942. For a history of this union, see Sujata Patel, 'The Capitalist Class and Labour Politics'.

82. Lumley to Linlithgow, 5 March 1940, IOL, L/P & J/5/160.
83. Shukla, 'Ek hazar nav so betalisni', p. 132.
84. FR2, July 1942, IOL, L/P & J/5/163.
85. FR1, August 1942, ibid.; Kunte, *Congress Activities in 1942–46*, p. 51.
86. Dwijendra Tripathi, *The Dynamics of a Tradition; Kasturbhai Lalbhai and His Entrepreneurship* (New Delhi, 1981), p. 181; Howard Spodek, 'On the Origins of Gandhi's Political Methodology: The Heritage of Kathiawad and Gujarat', *Journal of Asian Studies*, 30:2, February 1971, p. 366.
87. This appreciation of the millowner's point of view is based on a report by the British police officer, Roderick Parkes; R. Parkes to E.C. Gibson, 18 August 1942, IOL, C.R.R.R/1/1/3804. Linlithgow gave similar reasons for the millowner's attitude in a letter to provincial Governors of 2 November 1942. Mansergh, *The Transfer of Power*, vol. III (London, 1971), p. 190.
88. Lumley to Linlithgow, 24 September 1942, IOL, L/P & J/5/163.
89. Report by DSP Ahmedabad, 27 August 1942, BA, H.D. (Sp.) 1110(6) A(3) of 1942.
90. After the ban on communist organization was lifted by the Congress ministry in 1937, the communist millworkers' union in Ahmedabad managed to build a solid position for itself. Its most notable success was a strike it initiated in November 1937; FR1, October 1937, FR2 November 1937, Lumley to Linlithgow, 18 December 1937, IOL, L/P & J/5/155.
91. Shukla, 'Ek hazar nav so betalisni', pp. 134–5.
92. Ibid., pp. 136–40; *Ahmedabad Millowners Association General Body Minutes* 1942, Reports of 15 September 1942 and 26 December 1942. I am grateful to Sujata Patel for this reference.
93. Shukla, 'Ek hazar nav so betalisni', pp. 144–5 and 162.
94. Lumley to Linlithgow, 24 September 1942, IOL, L/P & J/5/163.
95. The victory at E1 Alamein came at the end of October 1942, and in the east the impetus of the Japanese advance had clearly been halted by the arrival of large Allied reinforcements in India.
96. Shukla, 'Ek hazar nav so betalisni', p. 142; Police Commissioner, Bombay Presidency, 19 November 1942, BA, H.D. (Sp.) 1110(109) D of 1942–3; Lumley to Linlithgow, 18 November 1942, IOL, L/P & J/5/163; DSP Ahmedabad, 14 November 1942, BA, H.D. (Sp.) 1110(6) A(3) (II) of 1942.
97. BRO, H.P.O. Pol. Dept. 38:98; Shukla, 'Ek hazar nav so betalisni', p. 146.
98. Four of the five mills in Baroda city had already opened by the end of October. The fifth reopened on 9 December. The mills at Nadiad, Petlad

and Viramgam reopened on 23 November. The mills at Broach, Kalol and Kadi were by then already functioning.

99. Reports by Collector of Broach and Panchmahals, November and December 1942, BA, H.D. (Sp.) 1110(6) A(5) of 1942.
100. Loc. cit.
101. Report by DSP Broach and Panchmahals, 16 December 1942, ibid.
102. Report by Collector of Surat, 7 October 1942, BA, H.D. (Sp.) 1110(6) A(7) of 1942.
103. According to Lalbhai Nayak, during August 1942 he and Thakorbhai Desai tried to prevent the movement in their area from becoming violent, but when they realized that the people were thirsting for violent action against the British, they decided to channel these energies into a programme of comparatively mild acts of sabotage of government property in which nobody got hurt. Interview with Lalbhai Nayak in Navsari.
104. H.V.R. Iengar to Collector of Surat, 10 November 1942; BA, H.D. (Sp.) 1110(109) G of 1942–3.
105. Police Report, 8 January 1943, BRO, H.P.O. Pol. Dept. 38:101.
106. BRO, H.P.O. Pol. Dept. 38:99 and 38:101.
107. Report by Collector of Broach and Panchmahals, 6 and 22 March 1943; Addl. Sup. Police. Broach and Panchmahals, 22 March 1943, BA, H.D. (Sp.) 1110(6) A(6) I of 1942; J.R. Shukla, 'Hind Chhodo Ladatna Panchmahal Jilla', *Pathik*, June 1976.
108. BRO, Confidential Section, Daftar 7, File 158.
109. NAI, H-Pol, 3/15/43.
110. Rowlands to Inspector General, Poona, 19 February 1943, BA, H.D. (Sp.) 1110(109) E of 1942–3.
111. Lumley to Linlithgow, 15 October 1942, IOL, L/P & J/5/163. For details about the return of confiscated lands in 1938–9, see BA, Revenue Department 7159/33-I.
112. Lumley to Linlithgow, 18 November 1942. FR1, November 1942, IOL, L/P & J/5/163; Lumley to Linlithgow, 8 February 1943, IOL, L/P & J/5/164.
113. Collector of Kheda, 30 August 1942, BA, H.D. (Sp.) 1110(8) B (1).
114. See my *Peasant Nationalists of Gujarat*, pp. 45–50, 173–8, 198–200 and 206–7.
115. Lumley to Linlithgow, 15 November 1937 and 18 December 1937, IOL, L/P & J/5/155.
116. John Wood, 'The Political Integration of British and Princely Gujarat: The Historical-Political Dimension of Indian State Politics', Ph.D. thesis, Columbia University, 1972, p. 324.

117. Ghanshyam Shah, *Caste Association and Political Process in Gujarat: A Study of the Gujarat Kshatriya Sabha* (Bombay, 1975), p. 39.
118. The Patidars of the prestigious Patidar village of Dharmaj offered to dine together with the Baraiyas if they agreed to support the movement. The offer was rejected. Collector of Kheda. 7 October 1942, BA, H.D. (Sp.) 1110(109) E of 1942–3.
119. Report of 22 and 23 September 1942, BRO, H.P.O. Pol. Dept. 38:100.
120. For details, see my paper, 'Adivasi Assertion in South Gujarat: The Devi Movement of 1922–3', in this volume.
121. *Azad patrika* no. I, reproduced in Report by Collector of Broach and Panchmahals, 13 August 1942. BA, H.D. (Sp.) 1110 (6)–A(5) of 1942.
122. 'Programme given to the Provincial Committees and Public from the All India Congress Committee, published by the Gujarat Provincial Committee', in E.C. Gibson to Political Department, Delhi, 1 September 1982. IOC C.R.R. /1/1/3804.
123. Interview with Jayenti Thakor. Thakor said that they only harassed and threatened such policemen. They refrained from killing them—which they could easily have done—as this would have invited military rule, as happened in 1919.
124. The peasant movement in Satara district suffered similar reverses in early 1943, but the local activists turned this defeat to advantage by changing tactics and establishing parallel governments. See Gail Omvedt, 'The Satara Prati Sarkar', in G. Pandey, *The Indian Nation in 1942*, pp. 223–61.
125. An important underground leader of this area, Lalbhai Nayak (an Anavil Brahman), told me in an interview that the adivasis were wrong to attack landlords and moneylenders, who were fellow-Indians. The movement was meant to be against the British only. He felt that such actions would alienate—in his words—'the public', and he did his best to stop the adivasi movement.

CHAPTER 5

From Custom to Crime

The Politics of Drinking in Colonial South Gujarat

I

The history of drink and drinking during the colonial period in India has been a subject of almost complete neglect. This may seem surprising, seeing that during the later years of British rule the revenue from country drink was second in importance only to the land revenue.[1] Two reasons can be suggested for this lacuna. On the one hand the brunt of the taxation on drink was borne by the lower classes, and few historians have felt moved to examine their plight. On the other hand drinking has been in the eyes of orthodox Hindus, Muslims and Jains a disreputable and degrading habit. Whereas high levels of land revenue were seen as crippling the 'honest agriculturists' on whom the wealth of India depended, high taxes on drink have been commended as helping to check a supposedly pernicious habit. Together, these considerations have ensured that while colonial policy towards land has been a respectable subject of enquiry, the history of drink has been considered taboo.

For anyone with an interest in the history of the subaltern classes, such a state of affairs can only be deplored. Even if our desire is merely to obtain a balanced view of the impact of colonial taxation on the people of India, we need to place far greater emphasis on this history. But there is of course more to drinking than taxation alone. All the evidence suggests that drink has occupied and continues to occupy a central position in the life of large numbers of Indian peasants. Over the past century peasant drinkers have demonstrated a remarkable ability to resist moves made by colonial officials and their Indian heirs to restrict the consumption of village-manufactured alcoholic drinks. This fact in itself is worthy of study. How have the subaltern classes proved so tenacious in their rejection of both state initiatives and élite values? To answer this question we have to relate the drinking habits of the peasantry to their conditions of life. In doing this we must avoid the trap of trying to understand peasant drinking culture in terms of our own form of rationality (which has in many cases a highly economistic content). The culture of the lower classes has possessed, according to Hans Medik, '. . . that sensuous physical character . . . [which] distinguishes itself from the "public realm of reason" of the educated bourgeoisie and from the seigneurial, ceremonial self-display of the aristocracy . . .'[2] Drinking has thus to be regarded as a customary action which related to existing forms of perception, social rules and morals, and also to the material conditions of life.

While carrying out such a study, we need to take into account changes in drinking habits. We find for instance that the types of drink consumed in India have, over the past century, changed considerably. Also, in most regions peasant manufacture of country drinks has become a furtive occupation, banned by law. In looking at such developments we are, like it or not, brought face to face with the fact that in the capitalist era drinking cannot be studied as some quaint form of 'social history'. The matter has become suffused with politics. This is because drink, which previously was to a large extent obtained freely by custom, has in the bourgeois epoch become a most important commodity. As such it provides a profitable item of manufacture for capitalists and a lucrative source of taxation for governments. This development could be brought about only by political means, that is by the formulation of liquor controls by modern states and the enforcement of these controls by the police. Through their experience of this process, peasants have been made to feel the power of both the capitalist classes and the state in a most direct and striking manner. For them it has been a political education. In this respect a history of drink provides a means towards a better understanding of the relationship between peasants and the dominant classes in colonial and postcolonial India.

There is a further dimension to the problem. The bourgeoisie have always had an ambiguous attitude towards drink. As a marketable commodity drink could yield huge profits; but drink was also 'the root of all evil'. A lower class given to drinking could hardly—in such a view—become a disciplined and industrious workforce. In Britain this consideration weighed heavy with many capitalists during the period of the industrial revolution and, after the reforms of 1832 brought greater parliamentary representation for this class, there was for nearly a century after this a powerful temperance lobby in the House of Commons.[3] In India temperance was advocated strongly from the mid-nineteenth century onwards by middle-class social reformers. Although they took their cue from the British champions of temperance, they adapted the movement to India by arguing that drink was alien to Indian culture. In this they confused their own élite values with Indian culture as a whole. Be that as it may, this middle-class propaganda had its effects on certain elements among the subaltern classes. From the late nineteenth century onwards there was a growing number of popular social reform movements in which one of the key items in the programme was to give up drink. By studying these movements we can observe the extent to which élite values were assimilated, the form in which assimilation occurred, and, just as important, the extent to which such values were rejected by the subaltern classes.

In this essay I shall try to throw some light on these problems through an examination of drink and drinking in one region, that of South Gujarat. For the purposes of this essay 'South Gujarat' can be taken to be the area covered during the colonial period by the British district of Surat, the Baroda state district of Navsari, and the petty princely states of the Dangs, Dharampur, Sachin and Vansda (spelt 'Bansda' in colonial records), all of which can be found on the accompanying map.

II

For centuries the people of South Gujarat have been known for their love of toddy and country liquor (*daru*).[4] William Finch, who stayed in Surat from 1608 to 1610, described this as 'a goodly countrey and fertile, full of villages, abounding with wild date trees, which generally are plentifull by the sea-side in most places; whence they draw a liquor called tarrie . . .'[5] In the hilly region to the east of Surat city he found that 'heere is made much wine of a sweete fruit called mewa . . .'[6] This clearly refers to daru made from the *mahua* (or in Gujarati *mahuda*) flower. Peter Mundy, who was in Surat from 1628 to 1630, wrote of the local toddy: 'The best sort thereof may be compaired to new white wyne, both in colour and taste, pleasant and wholseome'.[7] His enthusiasm was shared by Jean de Thevenot, who visited South Gujarat in 1666: 'The best *tary*... is of an acide sweetness, which leaves in the mouth the flavour of a chesnut, which is very agreable.'[8] The toddy was both cheap and intoxicating. In the words of John Ovington, who was in Surat in 1669: 'A quart of it may be got for a pice or two, and is so strong that it turns the brain as soon as *English* beer...'[9]

The partiality of the people of South Gujarat for their drink continued into the colonial period. During that time South Gujarat had the highest rates for per capita consumption of alcohol in the whole of Bombay Presidency. Although in terms of population Surat was a rather small district (ranking sixteenth out of the twenty-one districts of the Presidency), more toddy was consumed there each year than in any other district. In 1919–20 the consumption was 3,872,214 gallons of toddy. The average consumption per district for that year was a mere 713,150 gallons. The only district to rival Surat was Thana, where 2,189,067 gallons were consumed. In the same year the average per capita consumption of country liquor in Surat district was 0.46 gallons. In Bombay Presidency, only Bombay city had a higher consumption rate (0.70 gallons per head), and the average consumption was only 0.16 gallons per head.[10] Within Surat district, per capita consumption was highest in the predominantly tribal talukas of Chikhli, Mandvi, Pardi, Valod and Valsad, and in Surat city. It was lowest in the talukas of Chorasi, Jalalpor and Olpad, in which there were many high-caste cultivators.

A survey of eight villages of South Gujarat carried out by a team of sociologists from Bombay University in 1951 found that 72 per cent of all families had one or more members who drank. However, whereas 80 per cent of the families of tribals, untouchables and other low-caste people contained one or more drinkers, only 7.5 per cent of high-caste families did so.[11] The general pattern was that Brahmans, Baniyas (Jain and Hindu) and 'respectable' peasant castes such as the Patidars and Anavil Brahmans did not consume liquor or toddy. The local Muslims, who might have been expected from their religion to have abstained from drink, were found by the survey team to have drinkers in 59 per cent of their families.[12] That this was no new phenomenon is revealed by the account of John Ovington, who visited Surat in 1669 and reported that the local Muslims consumed large amounts of toddy.[13]

The castes which generally abstained from drink made up about 20 per cent of the population of the region. Population figures by caste for Surat district for 1872 were as follows:[14]

	Population	%		Population	%
Adivasis	180,107	29.67	Other Brahmans	23,838	3.93
Kolis	78,651	12.95	Fishing castes	20,749	3.42
Muslims	52,157	8.59	Parsis	12,841	2.11
Patidars	47,157	7.77	Rajputs	8,439	1.39
Untouchables	31,001	5.11	Herdsmen and shepherds	7,639	1.26
Artisan castes	30,565	5.03	Others	59,332	9.77
Baniyas	28,458	4.69			
Anavil Brahmans	26,153	4.31	Total	607,087	100.00

The Parsis of South Gujarat were well known for their love of toddy and country liquor. Peter Mundy, in his account, mentioned only one occupation of the Parsis of the region: that of the cultivation of toddy trees.[15] At that time a large area of countryside around Surat was cultivated in this manner by Parsis on a commercial basis.[16] They were connoisseurs of fine country liquors, preferring old spirits to those freshly made. They often laid down stocks of high quality daru to mature in their own houses.[17] Parsi distillers of Surat manufactured fine mahua-based liquors which were flavoured with such delicacies as Mozambique lemons, pineapples, mangoes, falsa fruits, roses, jasmine, mogra flowers, cardamoms, currants and aniseed. In some cases they allowed these drinks to mature for over forty years before consumption.[18]

Such drinks were however drunk only by a minority. The large majority of the people of South Gujarat preferred to drink toddy if it was available, and home-made mahua liquor when it was not. On the whole they drank in moderation. In the words of a collector of Surat district, W.T. Morison: 'It is common to find the low caste people on holidays and ceremonial occasions making themselves "cheerful", seldom drunk, with liquor.'[19] Another collector, A.S.A. Westroppe, reported similarly: 'drinking to intoxication is a matter of great rarity in the district'.[20] A.N. Solanki, who lived for many years in a Dhodiya village of Chikhli taluka, reported:

> Dhodias did drink a lot of toddy and some got properly tipsy during festivals and weddings but only a very few of them were real addicts. In fact the Dhodias themselves criticized and looked down on and called the addicts '*Pidhel*'. Such persons had little credit amongst the common people and they were made the laughing stock at assemblies.[21]

These impressions are borne out statistically by the Bombay University survey of 1951, which found that 75 per cent of those who drank indulged themselves less than ten times a month.[22] By most non-Indian standards, the poorer peasants of South Gujarat were not therefore very heavy drinkers.[23] In the words of W.C. Shepherd, and *Abkari* commissioner for Bombay Presidency:

> Even the Bhils whose fondness for liquor is notorious, often go for two or three months without touching it. Generally speaking it may be said that liquor is only drunk on festival occasions, or in certain areas at certain seasons of the year. At some festivals, notably at the Holi there is excessive drinking, but many persons who drink even to excess on such occasions do not touch liquor at any other time except at a marriage or other private ceremony. The total amount consumed per head is so small that it is obvious that it can rarely be used to an excessive extent by more than a comparatively small number of persons.[24]

It was noticeable that the high rates of consumption of alcohol in South Gujarat did not lead to crime and acts of violence. The crime rates in Surat district were amongst the lowest in Bombay Presidency, and the peasantry were renowned for their peaceful and law-abiding ways.[25]

The Bombay University survey of 1951 allows us to get some idea about drinking patterns within the family. In the families in which drinking went on it was found that in all cases the male head of the family was a drinker; 54.9 per cent of the wives drank, 44.3 per cent of sons, 32.9 per cent of daughters, 85.4 per cent of other males and 84.7 per cent of other females. The percentages of children drinking in such families were, by age: 0–5 years, 22 per cent; 6–10 years, 23 per cent; 11–15 years, 29 per cent; 16–20 years, 43 per cent.[26] That child drinking was no new phenomenon is shown by a petition from some toddy sellers of Surat city to the governor of Bombay in 1885:

> The labouring classes . . . look upon toddy as an element of life and their infants, nay sucklings, are nurtured on toddy, so that by the time they have attained their understanding they are capable of consuming several drachms of it at a time without the least sign of intoxication.[27]

Although they did not necessarily drink every day, most poor and landless peasants of South Gujarat would have felt deprived without a fairly regular supply of country liquor or toddy. Such drinks occupied a central place in their culture. In marked contrast to the Brahmanical, Jain and Islamic faiths, tribal religion accorded great honour to spirituous drinks. The adivasis believed that their deities were extremely fond of daru and toddy and that they could be appeased by such offerings.[28] It was common to pour a libation before starting to drink. Alcohol was considered a 'food of the gods' and drunkenness incurred during the act of worship a sacred condition.[29] In local legend, liquor was believed to have been given originally to the people by the gods.[30] In the words of one local proverb: 'God gave the Brahman ghi and the Bhil liquor.'[31] A British report of 1872 describes how the local Chodhri adivasis celebrated their annual memorial service to the dead by sacrificing goats, sheep and chickens and drinking to excess:

> . . . and then men and women joining promiscuously in a wild fantastic dance, [go] in circles round the deities. These orgies of theirs are so timed that they fall in the toddy-drawing season, so that there may be an 'ad libitum' supply of spirits to fortify and sustain their religious enthusiasm.[32]

Likewise, the tribal spirit-mediums, who divined the causes of diseases and other misfortunes while in a state of trance, often enhanced their state of possession with the help of alcohol.[33] It was normal, also, to pay these mediums for their services with chickens, goats and liquor, which they then consumed. The sanction provided by religion made drinking respectable in tribal and low-caste culture, and daru and toddy were accordingly consumed without any feeling of guilt.

Religious drinking was however the exception rather than the rule, being confined to certain periodic festivals and celebrations. In the words of Donald Horton:

> With occasional exceptions, and despite the fact that the drinking of libations, ritual offerings to the gods, and other religious rites are often a part of the drinking pattern (usually only at the beginning of the 'drinkfest', when people are still sober enough to make their bow to tradition), drinking is predominantly a social and secular activity with essentially social motives.[34]

Drinking provided an important means by which the peasants expressed their mutual solidarity. To drink together was considered a mark of friendship, and it was considered impolite not to offer drink to a guest. Drinks were served at meetings of village or tribal panchayats to put a seal on the discussion.[35] A group about to carry out a daring exploit would boost its morale and stress its solidarity with a ceremonial drink.[36] Drinks were served to celebrate the birth of a baby and to mark the successful conclusion to marriage negotiations.[37] A free flow of drink was considered a necessity at any major celebration, such as weddings and dances, and was also required during funerals. On the evening before a wedding it was the custom for men and women to drink together and dance the night away with free and often promiscuous abandon. At Holi the peasants merged their individuality into a joyful and light-hearted communal celebration. There was night-long drinking and dancing around the Holi fire, followed by festivities lasting up to a week. Young men toured the surrounding villages dressed in gay costumes, performing dances in return for donations, which were spent on drinking bouts in the evening. Huge quantities of daru and toddy were consumed during this celebration. In 1886 it was reported that sales from a liquor shop in a tribal village of Pardi taluka rose from a normal average of four gallons a day to 121 gallons a day during the Holi festival.[38]

Drinking was considered a necessity in other ways also. It provided a welcome relief to the poor and landless after a hard day's work in the fields. According to a liquor contractor called A.M. Dalal:

> What wine is to a Frenchman and the other wine-drinking people of the West, and beer to the German or an Englishman, toddy is to a poor husbandman, a Bhil, a seafaring Kharwa, a Koli and a hardworking labourer. Under toddy booths and shades of trees situated in the open field, pure unadulterated, undiluted and undoctored toddy, with the simple and homely

and nourishing food, is an ideal meal and drink of the poor making him and his family contented and happy.[39]

Not only did it allow them to relax, it also helped them to revive their strength, for toddy in particular had important nutritional values. It was full of calories and also contained many vitamins important for good health.[40] F.S.P. Lely, then an assistant collector in Surat district, reported in 1884 that toddy was an important element in the diet of the poor and landless of South Gujarat. It provided both a substitute for more solid foods and acted also as an aid to the digestion of the coarse and heavy unleavened breads which these classes ate. Lely reported a universal belief among them that toddy was beneficial to their health. It was taken as a medicine during illness.[41] Daru was also considered beneficial, providing, it was believed, protection against malaria, cholera and plague.[42] The adivasis of Mandvi taluka maintained that without daru they could not digest their coarse foods.[43]

Toddy was particularly important during the hot season. At this time food was at best in short supply, and often hardly available at all. For several months the poor of South Gujarat virtually lived on toddy.[44] In some cases it provided a substitute for both food and water. In 1872 it was reported that in Mandvi taluka there were hardly any wells and tanks and that most villages suffered from an annual water famine. What little water there was was so bad that the local adivasis were reluctant to drink it. Instead, they drank toddy. According to a British official: 'It seems to me, however much we may rail at the immorality of drunkenness amongst these poor people, that the stimulant is absolutely necessary for the preservation of life during a good half of the year.'[45] High-caste officials serving in this area who refused to drink toddy often went down with fever at this time of year, and it was believed—whether rightly or not—that this was because of their abstinence from toddy. Likewise during years of famine toddy was often an important saver of lives.[46]

Daru and toddy thus occupied a central place in the lives of the peasants of South Gujarat. They were acculturated into drinking at an early age, and knew how to take their drink—with moderation on the whole, but with gusto when the occasion demanded it. In all spheres of their life, drink had positive associations. It was a food of the gods which possessed an element of divine power; it set a seal on negotiations and legitimized family ceremonies; it enhanced the pleasures of social gatherings and public festivities; it provided succour during times of scarcity. Drink, we may say, lubricated the whole cycle of life of the peasants.

Before the colonial period, most of this country drink was produced in a customary manner. Most, but not all—for Gujarat had achieved a considerable degree of commercialization long before the establishment of British rule,[47] and drink had not escaped the attention of merchant capital entirely. In the next section we shall examine how daru and toddy were made and, in certain cases, sold, in the period before strict controls over these processes were imposed by the colonial authorities.

III

Toddy is the fermented juice of any kind of palm tree, such as coconut, brab, palmyra or date-palm. In South Gujarat the date-palm (*Phoenix sylvestries*), known locally as *khajuri*, was the tree used chiefly for toddy production. This tree grew freely throughout the district. In 1867–8 it was recorded that there were 195,901 date-palm trees in Surat district which were fit to be tapped, compared to 47,810 brab-palm trees. Of these trees, 489,395 date-palm and 16,739 brab-palm trees were recorded as having been tapped for toddy during that year.[48] The sap of the palm was collected in earthen pots. When collected in cleaned and lime-washed pots, there was no immediate fermentation and a non-alcoholic drink called *nira* was the result. The poor and landless peasants of South Gujarat did not, however, relish nira. They preferred, rather, to draw the palm-sap in old pots in which was left a little old toddy. This caused the sap to ferment in a matter of hours. After about four hours sweet toddy (*mithi tadi*) was produced, with a content of under five per cent alcohol. After twenty-four hours a much stronger sour toddy (*khati tadi*) was produced, with an alcohol content nearer eight per cent. Further fermentation did not make the drink any stronger, but this by now very sour liquid could be heated and spiced to make bitter toddy (*kadvi tadi*), which was much appreciated by heavy drinkers.[49]

In South Gujarat most of the tapping of the palm-trees was carried out by the peasants who tilled the land on which the trees grew. The tapper and his family drank most of the toddy themselves and sold any surplus. Little skill was required to climb and tap the date-palm, for the trunk of this variety of tree was seldom more than twelve to twenty feet high. Brab and palmyra palms, the chief toddy-producing trees of the Konkan and South India, were far taller trees which required greater skill to climb and tap. This, most probably, explains why specialist toddy-drawing castes were found in the Konkan and South India, but not in South Gujarat.[50]

A date-palm began to yield juice when it was about eight years old, and it could be productive for about twenty years or more. The juice could only be taken for a limited period each year, a total of about three months being the maximum duration which a single tree could bear. Within this period the tree had, in addition, to be given regular rests from tapping.[51] It was also considered advisable to allow a tree to remain fallow every second year.[52] The most productive period for a tree was between November and March each year, but a lot of toddy was tapped from April to June when the need for toddy as a food substitute was greatest. The toddy tapping season can thus be said to have continued from about November to June each year. Yields differed considerably according to the quality of the tree. In the toddy plantations around Surat city, which were managed by Parsi businessmen, trees could in 1884 be made to yield 90 to 100 gallons of toddy a year. However, the large majority of trees grew in a semi-wild state on land belonging to peasant agriculturists. Such trees yielded at most 30 gallons, more commonly only about 15 gallons a year. Most of the trees came into the latter category.[53] In 1940–1 the average yield for toddy trees throughout Surat district was calculated at 24 gallons per year.[54]

As a rule, toddy trees were considered to be the property of the man on whose land the trees grew. Before the liquor laws of the late nineteenth century, peasants did not require a license to draw and consume toddy. If they sold any surplus, they were meant by law to sell it to a licensed toddy dealer, who was usually a Parsi. In the period between 1830 and 1867 the number of licensed toddy shops in Surat district fluctuated between 124 and 183. As well over half of these shops were located in Surat city and adjoining villages, and as there were over 850 villages in the district, only about one-tenth of the villages could have had an authorized shop. Because toddy was a highly perishable commodity which could not be transported far in those days of poor communications, there was in practice widespread bartering between peasants.[55] Although this was technically illegal, the authorities made little attempt to prevent such infringement of the law. On the whole, therefore, the landowning peasants obtained their toddy free from tax (except in some cases, where a light annual tree tax had to be paid, as will be described in the next section). The Halis, or bonded labourers of rich high-caste peasants,[56] were generally allowed to draw toddy freely from the trees on their master's land.[57] The urban poor had on the whole to buy toddy from licensed shops. In Surat city the Parsi-owned toddy shops of the Jhanpa bazaar were famous. Because of this demand from the city, commercial cultivation of toddy trees was a major business in the countryside surrounding the city, and large profits were made.[58] The toddy sold in these shops was not, however, expensive. The normal practice was for a customer to be allowed to drink as much toddy as he wanted for two to four pies.[59]

Being an easily obtained natural product, toddy was the most popular drink in South Gujarat. In the five years 1885–6 to 1889–90, the volume of toddy consumed in Surat district per head of population was twelve times that of daru.[60] Toddy was of course a weaker drink, containing about one-seventh the alcohol found in a similar volume of the type of daru which formed the basis for this calculation.[61] Even taking this into account, the ratio still favoured toddy. A rough estimate such as this cannot be made for the period before 1880 as no statistics are available, but it is almost certain that toddy would have been favoured even more, for, as will be explained in the next section, the liquor law of 1878 had already by 1885 caused a noticeable decline in toddy drinking in the area.

Daru was made chiefly from the flowers of the mahua tree. This process was, in India, one of great antiquity. Mahua liquor is mentioned in the *Vishnudharma Sutra* (c. AD 100–300),[62] and, at a more local level, in medieval times it appears to have been an important product of the kingdom of Baglan, which lay in the hills due east of Surat.[63] The mahua tree flowered in the March–April period, and the sweet, sugary flowers were collected and stored until required. In the words of Ruskin Bond:

> The *mahua* tree bursts into full bloom at the very beginning of the hot weather, when the fortunes of the tribal people are usually rather low. As it is the slack season among cultivators, the gathering of the *mahua* is a welcome task, the whole village often turning out to bring in the crop. Sometimes the grass under the *mahua* tree is burnt away so that the blossoms may be gathered more easily. The women equip themselves with baskets, piling them one on top of the other on their heads, and the children carry brooms so that after all the blossoms have been gathered the ground can be cleared in readiness for the next fall.
>
> During the short period—only about fifteen days—that the *mahua* falls, the villagers practically live in the jungle, the men carrying away the crop as fast as the women and children can collect it.
>
> Laid out to dry on a smooth bare patch of ground that has been especially cleared and prepared, the blossoms become quite dry and shrink of half their normal size, changing from white to brown.[64]

In years of scarcity mahua was a valuable food for both the peasants and their cattle. The surplus was either made into liquor or sold. Liquor was made by first soaking the flowers in a big earthen pot for a week or more. Fermentation occurred, and a mash was produced. This was then boiled in an earthen pot, the neck of which was joined to a tube of bamboo with a seal of earth. The vapour from the boiling mash passed through this tube into another pot, which was immersed in water so as to cool and thus liquify the vapour, which became liquor. Country liquor of this sort was a fairly mild spirit, containing about 15 per cent to 30 per cent alcohol.[65] As the equipment for this process was extremely simple and cheap, country liquor could be made by any peasant with ease. In South Gujarat mahua trees grew on a large scale only in the hilly eastern regions, inhabited largely by adivasis, and it was only in this area that daru rivalled toddy as a popular drink. Most of the daru made by professional liquor manufacturers (who were mostly Parsis) was made from mahua imported into the area from North Gujarat, Khandesh, the Central Provinces and the Konkan.[66]

Manufacture and sale of liquor was, by law, permitted only to those who had been given permission by a government liquor farmer. This system, which will be described in the next section, had been continued from the preceding Maratha period. In 1830–1 there were 282 liquor distilleries and 285 liquor shops operating under this system in Surat district. In almost all cases the distillery and shop were together under the same manager. There was therefore a ratio of about one shop-cum-distillery for every three villages.[67] The village dealers were normally Parsis.[68] It is likely that Parsis were operating in villages throughout South Gujarat long before the advent of British rule. The Parsis of South Gujarat were originally peasant cultivators, and during the fifteenth and sixteenth centuries many had fled into the tribal interior to escape persecution at the hands of the sultans of Gujarat.[69] It is probable that a number stayed on and combined agriculture with the manufacture and sale of liquor. The *Surat District Gazetteer* of 1877 noted that some Parsi families had retained the liquor farms of the same villages for several generations.[70] A report from Rajpipla state mentioned that Parsis were running stills and liquor shops in some tribal villages of that region during the eighteenth century.[71] Thus, even before the colonial period, daru was to some extent a marketed commodity.

In the mid-nineteenth century British officials found Parsis established throughout the tribal tracts. A report of 1854 by M.S. Mansfield, the collector of Khandesh and political agent for the Dangs, mentioned that there were many Parsi distilleries operating on the western frontiers of the Dangs. The Parsis came into the Dangs each year to purchase the mahua flowers which grew there in abundance.[72] A forest officer who toured the Dangs in 1856 came across a Parsi who had paid a local tribal chief for the right to sell liquor in the area.[73] As the Dangs were the most remote tract of South Gujarat, it is fair to assume that Parsis were found in even greater numbers in the villages nearer the coast. C.J. Prescott, writing in 1865, reported that there were a good number of Parsi liquor dealers in the forests of Chikhli taluka.[74] As yet the Parsis do not appear to have been particularly rapacious exploiters of the adivasis. W.B. Mulock, who served as an assistant collector in Surat district from 1864 to 1869, reported of his experiences at that time:

> The sale of mowra liquor in a certain village or group of three or four villages is sold to a Parsee who has all Abkari rights therein. He sells at the proof and price and with the measures that he deems best. . . . He is obliged to sell generously at low prices with large measures and of good proof. The Parsee liquor farmer however of the village in which I camped did not even trouble himself to distil liquor or to open a shop. He allowed the Bheels

> themselves to distil and he levied twelve annas on every maund of mowra flower as it stood soaked previous to distillation.
>
> From a maund of mowra flowers a maund (four gallons or twenty-four bottles) of fairly strong liquor can be distilled so the price per bottle to the Bheels who themselves collected the mowra flowers in the jungle was ° anna or six pies per bottle.[75]

Although the liquor was very cheap, the adivasis tended to be in debt to the Parsis. In Mulock's words: 'The land of the village was mortgaged or even sold to the liquor vendor. He took in exchange for his liquor jewellery, clothes and grain, and almost every soul in the village was in debt to him for a liquor bill.'[76] Whether or not this was the case before the mid-nineteenth century is hard to discover, but it would seem likely that as long as there were Parsi liquor dealers operating in villages there were villagers in debt to them. However, there appear to have been some popular checks against excessive profiteering. An example of this occurred in 1876–7, when a Parsi liquor seller of Rajpipla state raised the price of liquor in his shops from eight to nine pies a bottle. According to the report:

> Immediately the Bhil panch assembled and decided that no one was to drink liquor till it was sold at its usual price and whoever drinks it will be excommunicated. They succeeded in their resolve. The shops remained closed for 3 months and the shopkeeper suffered a loss of thousands. On constant entreaties the panch reassembled, who were appeased by a present of a herd of sheep and pots of liquor and the selling price was again lowered to 8 pies and then only they commenced drinking, and the shop began working.[77]

Rajpipla was, however, a remote region. In most of British South Gujarat the balance had already by that time swung against the adivasis.

Before the 1860s the Parsis were unable to turn the indebtedness of their adivasi clients greatly to their advantage. Land in adivasi villages was then plentiful and the peasants had shifted their area of cultivation from year to year. Adivasis did not therefore own distinct plots of land. During the 1860s the British mapped out the land and gave ownership rights for the fields which a peasant happened to be cultivating in that particular year. Land became a marketable commodity. The adivasis were soon being deprived of their new title deeds by the Parsis in settlement of their drinking debts. By the 1870s the situation had become such as to encourage a fresh influx of Parsis into the tribal villages of the region. The *Surat District Gazetteer* of 1877 reported:

> Leaving his family in some town in Surat or Baroda territory, the Parsi liquor-contractor chooses some good spot in one of the larger aboriginal villages. Here he builds a large brick house, two stories high, apart from the village and surrounded by an enclosure of from two to three acres in extend. Inside of the enclosure are out-houses and stables for cattle, of which the liquor seller has almost always a good supply. Investing their savings in land, these Parsis have in several cases acquired considerable estates. Their profits are almost entirely derived from dealings with men of the dark races, or *kaliparaj*. Catering to their passion for strong drink, the Parsi advances them liquor, to be repaid, if the customer is a cultivator, in grain at the time of harvest; if he is a labourer, making him clear off his debts by working in the liquor-seller's fields. In this way it is that the Parsi's lands are tilled, for neither he nor his family personally take any part in the actual work of cultivation. So great authority does he gain, that the Parsi moneylender is commonly called the master, or *seth*, of the village. His people obey his orders in preference to the summons of the headman of the village or of an officer of government. Of the liquor-seller's dependents some are bound to work for a time to clear off a particular debt, and others have permanently sunk into the position of servants. While they are working off their debt, men of the first class generally receive each day a few pounds of grain. The latter class of labourers are said to be entirely in their master's hands, and being kindly treated, seldom, if ever, leave his service.[78]

While reading the extract above it should be borne in mind that as yet the adivasi did not have to buy his drink from the Parsi. Toddy continued to be available free of charge for most peasants, and many adivasis had as a result not yet fallen into the clutches of Parsi liquor dealers. This situation was to change radically with the implementation of the Bombay Abkari Act of 1878.

IV

Prior to British rule the Marathas had farmed out the right to distil and sell spirits in certain of their Gujarat territories. Toddy was taxed in some areas by a levy on toddy trees. The great majority of trees escaped taxation. The revenue from liquor and toddy was not large, although it did increase during the eighteenth century.[79] The British took over and continued this system in its essentials until the last quarter of the nineteenth century. The same was true in the Baroda and other adjoining princely ruled parts of South Gujarat. Under this system the liquor rights for each area were sold by auction for a period of one year. The successful bidder—invariably a Parsi—was responsible for selecting village-level liquor dealers who distilled and sold country liquor and collected and sold toddy. From them he collected the duty which they were required to pay on any liquor which they made. In practice the liquor farmer took a lump sum from the local dealer which bore little relation to the actual quantity of liquor manufactured and sold. Little control was exercised over the local distilleries, and much of the duty was evaded.[80] In 1830–1 the excise revenue for Surat district was Rs 148,220. Of this, Rs 63,144 was collected from Surat city alone; the revenue from the rural areas being only Rs 85,076. Land revenue collections during that year were Rs 1,418,972, so that rural Abkari brought in a sum equivalent to only six per cent of the land revenue.[81] Toddy trees were taxed as a part of the land revenue in certain areas. There was no tax in the talukas of Chikhli, Bardoli, Valod, Chorasi and Jalalpor. In Olpad and Valsad trees were taxed in a few selected villages. The tax rarely exceeded a rate of one anna per tree. In Mandvi taluka a tax of from Rs 5-0-0 to Rs 6-4-0 per 100 trees was levied, and in Pardi taluka a tax of Rs 10 per 100 trees.[82]

The British disliked this system as it provided an opportunity for widespread evasion of revenue. The obvious remedy was to ban village-based manufacture. Such a measure had already been carried out in another colonial territory of theirs, Ireland. During the eighteenth century there had been a mass of petty distilleries in Ireland manufacturing whiskey, and evasion of duty had been rampant. In 1779 small-scale distilleries had been banned by law so as 'to draw the trade as in England into the hands of persons of respectability and capital'.[83] Such a policy could not be carried out in India initially, for the British lacked effective control at the local level. In many parts of the Bombay Presidency even the land revenue was collected through intermediaries until the 1860s. Only after the suppression of the revolt of 1857–8 did the Government of India feel that the time was ripe for the initiation of a policy of centralization. In 1859 a circular was sent to the provincial governments suggesting that central distilleries should be established in all populous regions.[84] In this way drink could become a standardized commodity, paying regular rates of excise.

In addition to this pecuniary concern, there was a further objection to the liquor-farming system, which was moralistic. Here the evangelical voice of the British Raj was heard at its most strident. This particular objection to drink had its roots in the English experience. According to Sydney and Beatrice Webb:

> This movement came . . . from several distinct but converging currents of public opinion—the new-found Evangelical zeal of saving men's souls, the growing dislike of the propertied class of the insecurity of life and property, the alarm both of the financier and the ratepayer at the increasing burden of the poor rate, and last but not, we think, least, the half-conscious desire of the rising class of industrial capitalists to drive the manual workers out of the ale-house and gin-shop into the factory and workshop.[85]

During the course of the nineteenth century this local ideological requirement of the British bourgeoisie became translated into an absolute moral value to be imposed on all subjects of the British empire. It was not a value which had much to do with rural India, but this consideration did not prevent temperance reformers from trying to apply their dogmas to the Indian peasantry. Their views found an early voice in a directive sent out by the Bombay government to its districts in 1838:

> It cannot be too strongly urged on the Collectors that the object which Government has in views is to restrain and, if possible, to correct and diminish the total actual consumption of spirituous liquors, being fully persuaded that any amount of revenue that may be lost by the efficiency of the system for this will be repaid a hundredfold in the preservation and advancement of moral feeling and industrious habits among the people.[86]

Under the liquor-farming system it was not possible to regulate the manufacture and consumption of alcoholic drinks in an effective manner. Proper control could be exercised only if liquor was made in a limited number of factories under the close supervision of excise officers. In this wish for central distilleries, the moral ideals of the colonial administrators turned out, in best Victorian fashion, to be in complete accord with their financial needs.

In 1864, in response to the Government of India circular, the Government of Bombay appointed a commission to examine the Abkari laws and make recommendations for future policies. After various setbacks the report was completed eventually in 1869 by C.W. Bell. He recommended that central distilleries similar to the one already operating in Surat city should be established to manufacture and supply spirits for liquor shops throughout each district. He believed that such distilleries would produce more wholesome spirits at less cost than the village distilleries, and that the excise rates could as a result be raised.[87] It proved very difficult however for the government to devise ways in which the system could be thus standardized, as existing practices varied so much from area to area. Also, there was considerable opposition to the proposal from the liquor farmers of the Konkan, who were in many cases big landlords. As a result no immediate action was taken on Bell's recommendations. It was left to Charles Pritchard to put forward the scheme which eventually found favour with the government.

Pritchard was serving in 1875 as Collector of Salt Revenue and supervisor of the distilleries at Uran in Thana district, near Bombay. Thana district and the Konkan provided particular problems for the implementation of a central distillery system, for there most of the liquor consumed was cheap *arak* (distilled toddy). As toddy had to be processed into arak within twelve hours of tapping, distilleries had of necessity to be localized.[88] Pritchard's plan was gradually to replace arak with mahua daru, which could be made in central distilleries with no difficulty. In this manner the price of liquor and government revenue could both be greatly enhanced.[89] To do this he intended to raise the tax on toddy trees to such an extent that arak would not be able to compete with the daru produced in the central distilleries. The measure was to be phased over a number of years, with the tree tax being raised annually, while village distilleries were closed down area by area to be replaced by central distilleries. Through such means customary drinks such as toddy and locally-made arak were to be replaced by a mass-produced commodity. Pritchard's proposals found favour with the Government of Bombay, and they formed the basis for Act V of 1878. This Act laid down that liquor manufacture was to be confined to central distilleries, that excise duty was to be levied on this liquor before it left the distillery, that no toddy was to be drawn from trees except by permission of the collector and under licence, that each toddy tree that was tapped was to pay tax under licence, that each toddy tree that was tapped was to pay tax under excise (rather than land revenue, as had been the case before), and that liquor and toddy were to be sold in licensed shops, with licences to be auctioned as before. These measures were to be brought in gradually over a number of years.[90] Pritchard himself was appointed in 1878 as the first Abkari Commissioner for Bombay Presidency so that he could personally supervise the implementation of the Act.

In Surat district the central distillery system came into effect in the talukas of Chorasi, Olpad, Valsad and Pardi in 1879. Liquor was supplied to Chorasi and Olpad talukas from the Surat city distillery, and to Valsad and Pardi talukas from a distillery in Valsad town which had been established in 1873–4. The system was extended to Bardoli, Jalalpor and Chikhli talukas in 1880, and to Mandvi taluka in 1883. Strong pressure was brought to bear on the adjoining princely states to implement a similar policy in their areas. By 1888 the Baroda district of Navsari and the states of Sachin, Vansda, Dharampur, Surgana and Rajpipla were all covered by central distilleries. The Baroda distilleries were at Navsari and Kathor (both opened in 1881).[91] Sachin took its liquor from Surat city from 1879, and the other states all had distilleries in their capital towns. In 1888 a central distillery was opened at Ahwa to cover the Dangs.[92] Thus by 1888 the whole of South Gujarat was covered by the new system.

Initially the central distillery in Surat city continued to operate under the rules which had existed since its foundation in 1816. Eight Parsi distillers were permitted to operate their stills in a factory which was managed by the government. They made both the renowned *Surti masala daru* as well as cheap unspiced daru for mass consumption. With the extension of the market for their product after 1878, the government felt justified in demanding from them higher rates for the privilege of operating stills in the central distillery. However, through private negotiations and bargains with other Parsi distillers in both the British and princely areas of South Gujarat, the Surat distillers managed to restrict the bidding at the annual auctions held by the government for still rights, and they thus managed to hold down the rates.

Even worse, so far as the government was concerned, was the fact that they managed to evade considerable amounts of duty on the liquor which they made, either by smuggling it out of the factory with the connivance of the guards, or by declaring low alcohol content for their strongest liquors (duty was paid according to alcohol content). These irregularities were discovered in 1883, after Pritchard sent a special investigator to Surat to make enquiries. Prosecutions were launched, and as a result two distillery officials and three Parsi distillers were convicted and jailed.[93]

Pritchard decided that the moment had now come to establish a district monopoly for the manufacture of liquor in Surat district. He therefore sent for a Parsi of Bombay called Dadabhai Dubash. Dubash already held the liquor monopoly for Poona district, and he was in addition a big coal merchant and dockyard contractor of Bombay who had nearly 10,000 men in his employment in the city.[94] He had in 1876 given valuable help to Pritchard when the latter was trying to persuade the Uran distillers who supplied Bombay city to accept an increase in duty rates on their liquor; their opposition had been broken after Dubash dispatched large quantities of liquor from his Poona distillery to Bombay to be sold at the new, higher, prices.[95] Pritchard told Dubash that he was prepared to give him a complete monopoly for the manufacture and sale of country liquor in Surat district for three years in return for an annual payment of Rs 475,000. In addition to this, duty would have to be paid on the liquor. Dubash expressed some reluctance about accepting this offer, for the existing liquor farmers of Surat district had paid between them only a total of Rs 346,044 in the preceding year.[96] Dubash also realized that he would incur the wrath of the Parsi liquor farmers and distillers of South Gujarat if he took the monopoly. Pritchard argued that once the new system began to operate smoothly, and the adjoining princely states had all been brought into line, large profits would be made.[97] Dubash accepted the offer after a day's consideration.

Dubash did not himself run the central distillery in Surat. He sent an agent, Manekji Framji Lakdawala, to carry on the day-to-day management of the Surat monopoly. Lakdawala was an experienced liquor farm manager who had been operating previously in Sholapur.[98] He promptly standardized liquor manufacture at Surat and Valsad and established his own private force to detect and prevent illicit distillation.

On the whole he allowed the existing Parsi shopkeepers to continue to sell liquor under licence, so that he managed to keep on good terms with this influential class. However, the destruction of the spiced liquor industry created a furore amongst Parsi connoisseurs of South Gujarat and Bombay city, who found the taste of ordinary mahua daru 'positively disgusting'.[99] Even more serious opposition came from the deposed liquor farmers, who formed a company and bought up all of the liquor farms of the Navsari district of Baroda state. They proceeded to sell cheap liquor at shops along the border with British Surat district, thus destroying the trade of the Surat monopolist. As the two areas were much intermingled, this strategy proved extremely effective. Dubash and Co. had to lower their own prices to compete and ended up by selling much of their liquor at a loss. Protests by the British government to the Baroda authorities were to little avail.[100] Between October 1884 and July 1885 Dubash and Co. incurred losses of Rs 126,584. Dubash claimed compensation from both the British and Baroda governments, but in the end was mollified with an extension of the Surat monopoly for a further three years at the same rates.[101] As by 1886 his company was beginning to make a profit in Surat, this proved to be a good bargain. By then Lakdawala had discovered various ways in which he could make money on the side for the company, such as by taking illegal payments from shopkeepers for the goodwill of their liquor shops and by bribing petty excise officials to look the other way when liquor on which no duty had been paid was being smuggled out of the distillery.[102]

Dubash and Co. continued to hold the monopoly for Surat district until 1915.[103] In addition to Surat the company held the monopoly for the districts of Poona, Ahmadnagar, Khandesh (including the Dangs) and for Cambay state. In 1896–7 the company paid Rs 1,726,566 to the British government for all of these district monopolies.[104] The liquor produced by Dubash and Co. was notoriously bad, being the subject of frequent complaints from consumers of all classes.[105] Although attempts were made to manufacture spiced liquor, the end product turned out to be sugary and weak and was not approved of by sophisticated Parsis, who turned increasingly to the consumption of foreign-made liquors.[106] Thus disappeared a once-famous product of Surat.

Daru was still not, however, the most important drink in South Gujarat, and it was the devastating effect of the new law on toddy which was of far greater consequence for the majority of the people of the area. The British had been trying to discourage toddy drinking since the 1860s, as it was believed that excessive consumption was retarding the development of the district.[107] As a result a large number of trees on government land were cut down in 1865–6.[108] The effects of this were however minor compared to the results of the imposition of the new tree-tax rates under the Abkari Act of 1878, which were introduced on 1 August 1879. Rates were graded according to the proximity of an area to Bombay or Surat. Pritchard had introduced punitively heavy tree-tax rates in Thana district (so as to destroy the arak business), which ranged from Rs 5 per tree in the vicinity of Bombay to Re 1 per tree in the area bordering South Gujarat.[109] In order to prevent toddy from the southern taluka of Pardi from flooding the market in Thana district, Pritchard tried to enforce a rate of Re 1 per tree in this taluka also, but after protests by a former collector of Surat district he agreed to a rate of twelve annas per tree.[110] The rate for Surat city and the adjoining villages in which there were commercial toddy plantations was fixed at Rs 1-8-0 per tree. Rates for the district as a whole were as follows:[111]

Area	Pre-1879 rate (paid as land revenue) (rupees per tree)	1879 rates (paid as excise) (rupees per tree)
Surat city and adjoining area	No tax	1-8-0
Pardi taluka	0-1-7	0-12-0
Olpad taluka	0-2-0*	0-8-0
Chorasi, Chikhli, Jalalpor, Valsad talukas	No tax	0-8-0
Bardoli and Valod talukas	No tax	0-4-0

*Only a few villages in Olpad paid this tax; the majority paid no tax.

Under the new law, toddy tapping could be carried out only by those who had a licence from the government. Licences were given to those who undertook in advance to tap the largest number of trees in an area, thereby paying the highest amount of tax. Once the licence had been granted, the licensee had to specify the trees which he intended to tap that year, and the village *talati* (government accountant) would then paint numbers on these trees. Only these numbered trees could then be tapped that year. The tapping was carried out by local peasants hired by the licensee for the season. The licensee also had a monopoly for the sale of the toddy in his area, and he was allowed to sell it at any price he pleased. Toddy shops and liquor shops were henceforth to be separated.[112]

Frederick Lely, an assistant collector of Surat district, wrote about the effects of this new policy in 1886:

> . . . the change of 1879 was a small social revolution, in that it drove the people out of the fields to the shop. Previously, every man who had trees in his fields, tapped them and gave thereof to his acquaintances with little fear of the farmer who asked no questions. No doubt they often drank more than was good for them, but at any rate it was sound juice taken straight from the tree and only half fermented. The customers at the shops were, as a rule, strangers and travellers only. Upon such a state of things fell the order that no toddy was to be got except at a licensed place, and not even there without payment of cash. To a people whose wages were one anna per day paid in kind, this was really a prohibition, except on very rare occasions. It made no practical difference to them whether the price was two pice per pint or twenty. Both rates were hopelessly beyond their reach.[113]

V

The new toddy regulations and tree-tax rates brought immediate protests from toddy merchants, tree-owners and toddy consumers alike. In the months after August 1879, many tree-owners made their displeasure felt by refusing to allow their trees to be tapped. Some of the strength of feeling of the peasants at this time can be appreciated from a petition to the Government of Bombay by the Kolis, Bharvads (shepherd caste), Dublas, Machhis (fishermen) and Dheds (untouchables) of six villages of coastal Olpad taluka. By occupation they were poor peasants, landless labourers and fishermen.

> Toddy is our food, giving us relief when tired, our chief supporter, and the principal thing at the time of marriage and death ceremonies. By imposing heavy tax on toddy it has become exceedingly dear and we thereby suffer greatly. Without toddy we labour half starved, have no other means to give us relief when tired, our constitution is much weakened. Our marriage

> festivities are now without any pleasure. At the time of death toddy was chiefly taken to give consolation. That practice is now ceased. In short, we have lost our chief happiness and it will be very difficult to pass our half remaining life without toddy.[114]

Not all of the petitions reached Bombay as this one did. In Pardi taluka some leading peasants petitioned the collector and assistant collector, but the petitions were returned with an endorsement that the tax of twelve annas a tree must be paid. They were then told, in the words of Frederick Lely,

> that the district officers had no longer any influence and that the only means of getting at the ear of Government was to fee a barrister (pronounced 'banlister'). A large number of villages combined to raise a fund. I have the original subscription list and the accounts now before me. The total amount collected seems to have been Rs 222-14-0. Charged with this money 17 or 18 of these simple people left their villages and took the rail to Bombay. They were headed by the Koli Patel of Motivada, a man of some means and intelligence, who was understood among them to know the world. They went to an office where they sat on the ground floor while two of their number went upstairs and interviewed 'a gora barrister'. The whole body then returned home and it would appear that a petition was drawn up if not presented, as in the accounts there is an item of Rs 2-10-0 for pay of a man who took it round the villages for signature. It is said that no answer has ever been received. The net result of this attempt to reach Government by the modern channel was that they spent their Rs 222, and got a receipt (now in my possession) signed by a firm of Bombay attorneys for Rs 100 'as a first advance'. They have not tried again.[115]

Despite the barrage of complaints from South Gujarat—which included protests from local British officials—Pritchard refused to be shaken in his determination to price toddy out of the market. In 1881 he doubled the tree-tax in all talukas of Surat district (with the exception of Surat city and its vicinity where the tax was raised from Rs 1-8-0 to Rs 2-0-0).[116] In the following year the assistant collector reported after a tour of the rural areas of the district that toddy was hard to obtain, and that the people were in a state of distress. The collector raised the matter with Pritchard. Pritchard merely censured both officers severely, and continued with his plan to impose another new tax, namely a toddy shop licence fee of Rs 10 per 25 trees in Pardi taluka and Rs 20 per 25 trees elsewhere in Surat district. The measure was implemented in 1883.[117] In July of that year the same assistant collector reported that a significant number of tribal peasants were relinquishing their land in Surat district and migrating to Baroda areas, one of the reasons being their annoyance with the new toddy regulations.[118] Although the Baroda government had, under British pressure,[119] started to charge a tree-tax in 1881, rates were lower than in the British areas and tree-owners were permitted to sell their toddy in their fields.[120] When the commissioner for the northern division of Bombay Presidency toured the tribal areas of Surat district in the same year, complaints about government Abkari policy came thick and fast. Although he reported the matter to Pritchard, the Abkari commissioner failed to offer any satisfactory reply.[121]

In his annual report for 1882–3 Pritchard had to admit that the tax on toddy trees had proved a controversial issue, as many people, including government officials, considered that toddy was a harmless and nutritious beverage. He acknowledged the fact that he had received protests from many experienced officers. He also admitted that there had been continuing opposition by the people to the tree tax. As a concession he permitted owners of toddy trees in Pardi, Valsad, Chikhli, Bardoli and Valod talukas to tap up to ten of their own trees on payment of the full tree-tax rates. They were permitted to sell any surplus toddy at the foot of the tree.[122] In 1884 the concession was extended to Jalalpor and Chorasi talukas. In the same year, however, Pritchard raised the tree-tax in Valsad taluka from Re 1 to Rs 1-8-0, in Chorasi, Chikhli and Jalalpor talukas from Re 1 to Rs 2, and in Pardi taluka from Rs 1-8-0 to Rs 2.[123]

In Jalalpor taluka this fresh increase proved to be the last straw. Many trees in this taluka were owned by Parsis and Anavil Brahmans who had in the past made good money by exporting toddy to the adjoining Baroda district headquarter town of Navsari. There was a big market for toddy in the town. After the imposition of the tree-tax they found that their toddy could no longer be sold at competitive prices in Baroda territory, where the tree-tax rates were less. The toddy trees of Jalalpor taluka were on the whole of a poor quality, and did not yield sufficient toddy to justify the ever-increasing rates of tax. In addition,

Anavil Brahmans who had in the past allowed their Halis to tap any trees on their lands freely were not now prepared to pay so dearly to continue this custom. The bonded labourers were the chief sufferers—no longer did they receive free toddy—but their paternalistic masters were not happy at having to cut off a benefit which had helped so much to reconcile the Hali to his menial position in life. A concerted campaign was therefore launched by the toddy dealers and tree-owners of the taluka to refuse to pay the tree-tax. The agitation had a strong impact: in 1883–4 the old tax of Re 1 per tree brought in Rs 55,525, in 1884–5 the new tax of Rs 2 brought in a mere Rs 10,603.[124]

This agitation, and the general strength of feeling against the toddy regulations in Surat district, made a deep impression on a new assistant collector of the district, Frederick Lely. Lely represented a very different school of colonial thought to that of Pritchard. The latter was very much the man of 'progress' who wanted to transform relations of production in India in the English image with utmost speed, and who felt it a positive good if 'inefficient' peasants were driven from the land or converted into the paid labourers of more 'efficient' cultivators as a result of the implementation of British policy.[125] Lely was of a more sensitive school which believed that each society evolved in its own unique way. Rules and regulations which were enlightened and progressive in one region might not prove so in another. Thus, utilitarian principles which were suited to England had had an often disastrous effect when applied to India in a rigid manner. Progress could be achieved best through policies which took account of the values and institutions of the particular society.[126] Lely believed that in the India of his day there was '. . . absolutely no organic union between Government and its subjects.'[127] Brash and unsympathetic interference with many time-hallowed customs was causing grave unrest in India, producing a ferment which might in the end lead to rebellion. Being sympathetic to the needs of the people, men of this school had their ears to the ground. They were prepared to heed what they considered the legitimate grievances of the people and to act as their champion in official debates.

Lely mounted his defence of popular drinking customs by writing in September 1884 to Pritchard that the tribal peasantry and Hali labourers of Surat district had been very hard-hit by the new regulations, as they were quite unable to afford to pay the tree-tax. Their trees were usually of an extremely low quality; most adivasis would be lucky to obtain fifty gallons of toddy in a year from half a dozen of their trees. Village moneylenders and employers of Hali labour were not prepared to pay the tree-tax for the poor and landless. As a result they were having to spend most of the little money which they could scrape together on toddy. In the past they would have spent this money on food, clothes, salt and other necessities. Since the tree-tax was introduced there had not been, most fortunately, a year of scarcity. But when such a year came—as it must in time—the lack of toddy would have extremely serious consequences. Lely had received several petitions against the regulations, and 'innumerable verbal complaints', for this was the only way in which the majority of the tribal peasants knew how to go about complaining. Lely proposed that the adivasis and Halis should be allowed to tap up to ten trees per family on payment of a charge of two annas per tree.[128]

Pritchard replied immediately in an irate manner, denying that the toddy regulations were at all oppressive. He demanded proof from Lely and also evidence to back up his assertion that toddy was used as a food by the poor.[129] Lely wrote out a detailed reply which showed how the tribal peasantry and Halis were suffering severe deprivation from the lack of cheap toddy. He produced evidence that they had tried to complain, but to little avail due to their lack of good contacts and experience in petitioning.[130] Although Pritchard tried to fob off Lely's reply, the matter was brought to the notice of the Governor of Bombay, Sir James Fergusson, who was much impressed by the strength of Lely's case. Fergusson commented: 'I must say that I have no sympathy with those who philosophise about drink not being necessary to the poor man when they probably have got to regard it as so for themselves.'[131] He felt that the poor and landless peasants of Surat district were suffering real hardships and that Lely's proposal should be accepted. On 15 December 1884 the Government of Bombay ruled that the Kaliparaj people of Surat district should be allowed to tap one tree per two adult family members, up to a maximum of ten trees, on payment of two annas for each tree tapped.[132] This so-called 'Kaliparaj concession' applied only to the talukas of Pardi, Valsad and Chikhli, where the hardship was believed to be greatest. It was estimated that about fifty thousand people would be affected. Lely was not altogether happy with this; he felt that Halis should be allowed to tap trees on their master's lands at the same concessionary rate.[133]

In February 1886 Lely was directed by the Bombay government to carry out further investigations on the effects of the toddy regulations on the people of Surat district.[134] Lely discovered that toddy was increasingly being replaced by daru as a popular drink. The high tree-tax rates were causing toddy shopkeepers to make a loss, and many toddy shops had been closed down in consequence. As a result people were often unable to buy toddy even when they could afford it. The toddy which was on sale was often old, sour and vile-smelling, as it had to be carried to the few isolated shops from a long distance. People were therefore either going to toddy shops in adjoining princely states or turning to country liquor. Figures drawn up by Lely which compared the number of toddy trees tapped with the quantity of country liquor sold in the three talukas of Pardi, Valsad and Chikhli during the period of the operation of the Abkari Act proved—in Lely's opinion—extremely revealing:[135]

	Pardi Taluka		Valsad Taluka		Chikhli Taluka	
Year	Toddy trees tapped	Daru sold (gallons)	Toddy trees tapped	Daru sold (gallons)	Toddy trees tapped	Daru sold (gallons)
1879–80	10,565	13,732	40,772	61,629	12,603	–
1880–1	30,597	29,936	57,851	56,752	18,031	–
1881–2	16,032	37,537	49,000	32,074	12,690	6,780
1882–3	18,739	33,966	32,933	69,416	12,100	15,225
1883–4	13,030	31,563	34,596	67,131	11,501	17,448
1884–5	4,793	46,645	17,108	103,404	9,743	35,968

Lely reported that the people to whom he had spoken had told him that they did not like the factory-made liquor which they now had to drink. They felt that it was bad for the health, in contrast to toddy which was wholesome and nourishing. Toddy, in their words, 'fills our bellies and liquor does not'.[136]

The Collector of Surat at this time was, however, W.B. Mulock, a supporter of Pritchard's policy. He provided his own evidence to refute

Lely from a hunting expedition in Mandvi taluka (the only taluka in which the toddy regulations had not yet come into effect).

> While shooting in Mandvi in the hot weather I was a large employer of the labour of these castes [the tribal people] for driving the jungles. Sometimes two or three hundred of these people were collected at my camp, and I supplied them with grain and money as wages. It was almost impossible to persuade them to remain in camp. Morning and evening they ran home to their villages for their toddy and after their drink they were most of them useless for any exertion on the hill-side and many of them were drunk . . . To my mind it incontestably showed that where the [abkari] act was not in force intemperance was largely promoted.[137]

Mulock took no account of the fact that this was the hot season, when toddy often served as a major item in the diet of the tribal peasants. He also had no right to expect them to show great eagerness to beat the forest for tigers, leopards and wild boars, a frightening and dangerous task which few men would enjoy. Yet it was on the basis of this kind of 'evidence' for the 'demoralizing' effects of toddy that Mulock felt justified in trying to water down the concessions which had been granted to the people of the South Gujarat area over the past seven years. He was extremely niggardly in issuing licences for the sale of small amounts of toddy at the foot of the trees—the concession granted by Pritchard in 1883.[138] Petitions by the adivasis of Bardoli and Valod talukas that the two-anna concession be extended to them were ignored.[139] Lely had by this time been transferred hundreds of miles away to serve as administrator of Porbandar state, where the local maharaja had been causing trouble to the British. He was not, therefore, in a position to champion the cause of the poor peasants of Surat district at that juncture.

In 1889 Pritchard launched a fresh attack on the toddy concessions in Surat district. He demanded that the tree-tax be raised and that the two-anna concession be abolished so as 'to check the excessive consumption that now prevails and the drunkenness and demoralization occasioned by that excessive consumption . . .'[140] In response the Government of Bombay resolved in the following year that the distinction between adivasi and other toddy-tree owners should be gradually phased out. To start with, the concessionary rate was raised from two to four annas per tree. Ordinary rates of tree-tax were also raised.[141] The adivasi rates were doubled yet again in 1892, and raised to ten annas in 1893–4. They remained at this level for the next decade as a result of a prolonged period of successive bad harvests and famine. In 1907 the authorities returned once more to the attack. Even though there had been an agrarian crisis during the previous decade in which thousands of adivasis had died of starvation and during which huge tracts of adivasi land had passed into the hands of moneylenders and liquor dealers, the collector, A.S.A. Westropp, justified this move by arguing most perversely that there had been 'a considerable increase of material prosperity among the Kaliparaj during the last 20 years'.[142] The concessionary rates were accordingly raised to Re 1 per tree in Chikhli taluka, Rs 1-4-0 in Pardi and eastern Valsad talukas, and Rs 1-8-0 in western Valsad taluka. These rates continued till 1924, when the Kaliparaj concession was abolished. Henceforth the adivasis of these talukas had to pay the same rates of tree-tax as everyone else.[143]

In the end, therefore, the protests of the peasants brought no lasting changes in the system laid down by Pritchard. Why were their protests so ineffective? To a large extent the reason would appear to be that the poor peasants of South Gujarat were unaccustomed to fighting for their rights in an aggressive manner. They had no tradition of rebellion, as did the Bhil and Koli peasants to the north. In the past this population had been relatively scattered, and it had been possible to make an adequate living from cultivating the land—which was quite fertile—in a customary manner. The peasants had not needed to rob to supplement the fruits of their agriculture; nor had they needed to fight to control their territory. Thus in the 1880s, when their plight moved them to protest, they chose methods which came naturally to them, such as voting with their feet by migrating to adjoining princely areas, or by going in groups to complain to any sahib who happened to be touring their area. A few rather more sophisticated peasants attempted to petition the government, but this proved a heartbreaking process. The British authorities, who in those years of interlude between the crushing of the revolt of 1857 and the emergence of popular nationalism were at their most confident and arrogant, paid little heed to these protests. The few concessions which were granted were gained largely through the crusade of one sympathetic officer, F.S.P. Lely, and they were soon reversed after he had quit the scene.

VI

Over the next decades the tax on drink increased in South Gujarat by leaps and bounds as the excise on country liquor, the charge for the district monopolies and the toddy-tree rates ever rose. The following figures are for Surat district, Navsari district of Baroda state, and the petty state of Vansda (lying entirely in adivasi territory). Land revenue figures are provided also to show how Abkari came gradually to equal land revenue as the most important tax in the region.[144]

	Surat District		Navsari District		Vansda State	
Year	Abkari revenue Rs	Land revenue Rs	Abkari revenue Rs	Land revenue Rs	Abkari revenue Rs	Land revenue Rs
1877–8	3,72,874	23,20,049	99,277	17,41,248	6,348	89,663
1887–8	8,43,994	23,52,724	4,39,411	18,82,095	58,745	1,01,505
1897–8	11,70,352	23,98,876	6,04,953	17,29,113	1,58,364	1,29,732
1907–8	14,60,434	25,62,358	6,43,432	17,22,173	2,21,308	1,12,530
1917–18	22,34,180	26,41,342	15,78,325	18,79,685	3,39,407	1,28,713
1927–8	29,30,025	28,67,623	16,03,432	19,73,579	4,07,217	1,96,795
1937–8	23,57,423	24,83,209	12,83,500	19,46,000	2,85,396*	2,22,227*

* Figures are for 1935–6 as 1937–8 figures are not available.

As a result of the ever-increasing tax the price of daru soared over the years.[145] Before the 1878 Act a quart bottle of mahua daru cost from five to six annas. Afterwards it cost seven to eight annas.[146] By 1928 a quart bottle cost Rs 2-8-0, which represented a fivefold increase in price.[147] In the words of Frederick Lely: '. . . throughout a great part of the Bombay Presidency the native of India now pays as much, relatively, for common country liquor as the Englishman does for champagne.'[148] What was worse, the product itself was continually deteriorating in quality. Village-distilled daru had been drunk at the strength at which it came out of the still. Factory-made liquor was distilled at a high strength and then sent by rail and road to bonded warehouses in different parts of each district, where it was diluted with water to conform to the liquor strengths laid down by government regulation. This was a very unpopular practice. According to the *Bombay Excise Commission Report* of 1922–3:

> There is a strong popular belief among all classes of country liquor drinkers that the liquor should be distilled weak and not reduced by the addition of water. They consider that liquor distilled weak is healthier and lasts longer, than liquor diluted after distillation. The latter soon becomes unwholesome, turns sour, and affects the liver and digestion. The reduction of liquor by the addition of water is regarded as very harmful.[149]

In addition, the water used to dilute the liquor was often not very pure. The adivasis of South Gujarat also had certain religious objections to the diluted liquor.[150] No doubt they believed that their gods were not satisfied with the offering of this inferior product. The liquor made by Dubash and Co. proved, however, to be better than that produced by the successors as district monopolists in 1915, Carew and Co. of Calcutta. According to a mamlatdar who had served in Surat district, '. . . the supply of liquor by Messrs. Carew and Co. . . raised a great hue and cry among the liquor consumers about the badness of the stuff'.[151] Many peasants stopped buying liquor for some months in protest.[152]

In 1922 the Surat distillery was closed as no private contractor could be found who was either willing or had sufficient resources to carry on such large-scale manufacture of liquor. Thereafter country liquor was supplied to Surat from government-operated distilleries outside the district. From 1922 to 1926 the liquor came from the government distillery in Godhra, in the Panchmahals district of Gujarat, and after that from the government distillery in Nasik in Maharashtra. The Nasik liquor was no more popular than the old Dubash and Carew spirits. By 1931 the Abkari commissioner, J.P. Brander, had to report that the liquor distilled in the modern stills at Nasik had such a bad taste that people were increasingly turning to better-tasting illicit daru. Attempts were therefore being made to improve the flavour by mixing some of the mass-produced spirit with a little daru made in the old manner using an earthenware still. This, Brander believed, would restore the authentic mahua daru flavour to the liquor.[153] But, judging by the ever-falling sales of licit daru over the decades, it does not appear that this tactic had much success. The average annual sales of centrally distilled liquor in Surat district by decades were as follows:[154]

	Gallons of liquor sold (proof strength)
1890–1 to 1899–1900	315,026
1900–1 to 1909–10	294,545
1910–11 to 1919–20	272,810
1920–21 to 1929–30	160,341
1930–31 to 1939–40	90,480

The reasons for this remarkable decline will be discussed in more detail below.

Toddy fared little better than daru. Because the tree-tax was so high, it proved uneconomical for most dealers to provide pure toddy for their customers. Watering of toddy by shopkeepers became the general practice. Government rules laid down that all toddy sold had to be less than a day old. Rather than throw out their stocks of old, sour toddy, the dealers often added sugar to make it sweet once more.[155] The resulting mixture was low in alcoholic content and it lacked the characteristic thickness and froth of pure, fresh toddy. To overcome this problem, dealers added small quantities of chloral hydrate or opium to induce a feeling of intoxication, and soap to make the toddy appear frothy. Although drinkers often vomited after imbibing such concoctions, this in itself was often taken as a sign that the toddy was of correct strength.[156] In this manner many were to forget the taste of true toddy.

It had been anticipated by those who framed the Abkari Act of 1878 that the central distillery system and rigid new controls would undermine the local powers of the Parsi distillers-cum-dealers. In fact this class not only adapted to the new regulations with ease but even turned them to its advantage. As each shopkeeper continued to enjoy exclusive rights for the sale of liquor or toddy in a cluster of villages, the peasants had little recourse against them when they diluted and adulterated the drink and gave short measures. This was done quite easily, as daru and toddy were normally stored in earthen pots in the shop, being poured into the customer's drinking-pot or glass from a gourd ladle.[157] As the peasants were often deep in debt to the Parsi, they hardly dared complain. The Abkari inspectors and police were often in league with the shopkeepers in any case, being bribed to turn a blind eye to malpractices. In the words of a mamlatdar who had served in Surat district: 'The Abkari officers request them [the shopkeepers] to send their carriages when they want to visit their shops. They even go to the length of borrowing money from them and coming under their obligation in hundreds of ways.'[158] Thus, far from feeling any pinch, the Parsi liquor dealers went from strength to strength under the new regulations, and grabbed more and more land from the peasants in debt to them. By the early years of the twentieth century many had acquired large landed estates. A report on Mahuva taluka of 1913 revealed that the 281 Parsi landowners of the division owned 10,721 acres of land, which represented an average Parsi holding of 38 acres. The average holding of the adivasi and Koli peasants was by contrast a mere 3.75 acres. Amongst the Parsis, the largest landowner was the liquor dealer, Ratanji Faramji Daboo, who owned two entire villages and 1,344 acres of land scattered around seven other tribal villages.[159]

As their estates became larger, the Parsis became more rapacious. They maintained their own strongmen to coerce the poor and landless into labouring in their fields for nominal payment.[160] Peasant girls were forced to work in their houses and gratify their sexual demands.[161] Any protest by the peasants was suppressed with the help of the local police. For instance, when in 1920 some poor adivasis of a village in Vyara taluka refused to labour for the local Parsi for only an anna a day in wages (the going rate elsewhere being about ten annas a day), they were hauled before the taluka court by the police and prosecuted for sedition. The case dragged on for three years, causing the adivasis extreme inconvenience and anxiety.[162]

In desperation, peasants throughout South Gujarat increasingly sought to obtain their drink illicitly. In effect this meant either resorting to illicit distillation or buying cheap liquor in princely states or Portuguese territory and smuggling it over the border. Illicit tapping of toddy trees was not very practical, for a tree had to be tapped for at least two months at a stretch, and with a pot hanging high up on the trunk for all to see it was the easiest possible crime to detect.[163] A few ingenious people may have strapped a long bamboo tube to the tree, down which the sap could run into a pot buried under the ground at the base of the tree. Such tubes were not easily noticed.[164] But this does not seem to have been a popular practice for it was much easier to make illicit drink by distilling daru. Even here there were problems, for it was hard to manufacture liquor in complete secrecy. Mahua flowers and a good supply of firewood had to be procured, and the smoke from the fire was very visible. The smell of the liquor also carried far. On the whole, therefore, liquor could only be made either in villages in which there were no Parsis or high-caste peasants who would report the matter, or with the connivance of the local authorities. Parsis in particular had a vested interest in preventing illicit distillation as it affected the sales of their own government liquor. They were very sensitive as to whether or not illicit distillation was going on in their area, and if they did have any suspicions they were able to call on either the police or the private detective force of Dubash and Co. This latter company put considerable effort into stopping illicit distillation in the district.[165]

Despite this a considerable amount of illicit distillation was carried on in South Gujarat. Amongst the poor and landless no stigma was attached to breaking the law in this manner; rather, it was considered admirable to thus outwit the Parsi and the police. In villages in which there were no Parsis, high-caste peasants or other outsiders, it was possible for a peasant to make daru in his own house.[166] In addition, a large amount of daru was made by peasant distillers just inside the borders of Dharampur state and the Portuguese territory of Daman, where security was lax. Liquor from these stills supplied the southern part of the region.[167] Elsewhere, peasants found it safest to make daru in gullies along the river banks or in the forest. If the police came they could easily run away, abandoning their cheap equipment. It was hard for the police to track down the culprits, especially as local villagers normally refused to give any information.[168] In 1902–3, for instance, the Abkari police and detectives of Dubash and Co. discovered 134 abandoned stills in Surat district, but in not a single case could prosecutions be made.[169] Even when guilt was proved, prison sentences rarely exceeded three months.

As the price of country liquor went up over the years and as the quality of the licit liquor continually deteriorated, illicit distillation became increasingly popular. The Bombay government tried to reverse this trend by imposing strict controls on the supply of the chief raw material—mahua flowers. The idea of mahua control was first proposed by Charles Pritchard, who was disturbed by the huge amount of illicit distillation going on in Thana district, using as a base mahua flowers imported from elsewhere (mahua did not grow there).[170] Pritchard proposed that collection and sale of mahua flowers should be banned. This caused an outcry from officials throughout Bombay Presidency, who argued that mahua flowers were eaten by poor peasants and their livestock during the summer months of scarcity, and that a ban would cause intense suffering and even loss of life. As a result, the Government of India under Lord Ripon vetoed Pritchard's proposed legislation in 1882.[171] The Abkari commissioner was not, however, prepared to give up his plans. In 1892 Pritchard, by now Sir Charles and a member of the Viceroy's Council, took up the matter once again. He put forward new proposals in which a vacation was to be granted from the mahua controls during the period 15 February to 15 April each year, so that the peasants would be able to consume fresh mahua. At all other times the storing and selling of mahua was to be banned. The Mahua Act was passed in December 1892 and was applied initially only to the Thana and Kolaba districts.[172] By 1900 the Abkari department was demanding an extension of the Act to Surat district, due to the rapid increase there of cases of illicit distillation. Frederick Lely, by then a member of the Bombay Governor's Council, fought this proposal on the grounds that it would lead to increased harassment of the common people.[173] This was particularly true for the eastern areas of South Gujarat, where there were numerous mahua trees and where many adivasis made ends meet during the hot season by picking and selling to merchants the mahua which they did not consume. Lely made, however, an exception in the case of the three southern talukas of Pardi, Valsad and Chikhli. There, mahua trees did not grow to any great extent, and the people did not use the product as a natural resource. Most of the cases of illicit distillation were in any case in these three talukas.[174] As a result in 1906 the Mahua Act was extended to these three talukas.[175]

Mahua control stopped the supply of mahua to the southern part of Surat district, and it brought about a dramatic decrease in cases of illicit distillation. Whereas the average number of such cases had been 223 per year during the five years 1900–1 to 1904–5, during the following five years the annual average fell to 25.[176] The low figures continued until the 1920s, when the Bombay government began to ration supplies of liquor with a view to bringing in eventual prohibition.[177] By the end of that decade the number of cases of illicit distillation were back to the pre-1906 rates.[178] In 1927 it was reported that the distillers were becoming more crafty: '. . . a large number of scouts are thrown out to watch the movements of the excise officers with the result that it is getting very difficult to catch distillers red handed'.[179]

In 1930 the Mahua Act was extended to the remaining talukas of Surat district in the hope that this would check the growing incidence of such 'crime'. Although the statistics suggest that this policy had considerable success,[180] the likelihood is that after a temporary check illicit distillation became more and more common during the 1930s. The chief reason for this was that licit liquor was becoming harder to obtain from licensed liquor shops, as shops were being closed down as a part of the government prohibition policies. Whereas in 1880–1 there had been 274 liquor shops in Surat district (representing on average one shop to 2.8 villages), by 1940–1 there were only 103 shops (representing on average one shop to 7.5 villages). Not only was it therefore becoming much harder to obtain licit liquor, but it was also less likely that illicit distillers would be reported by Parsi shopkeepers, who by 1940 were becoming few and far between.[181]

The other major way in which the liquor laws could be circumvented was by smuggling liquor and toddy from foreign territory into Surat district. As a rule, prices in the princely states and in the Portuguese territory of Daman were lower than in British India. The liquor was also stronger and of better quality. Poor peasants were prepared to walk miles to obtain cheap liquor in this manner, and as the borders of the different territories were much intermingled it was impossible to prevent such smuggling. The implementation of the Mahua Act in the southern talukas in 1906 saw a marked rise in smuggling from Portuguese territory. Large amounts of cheap daru were manufactured in Daman from mahua and sugar and sold by Parsis at shops along the border with Pardi taluka.[182] In addition, a good deal of liquor was taken by fishing boats from Daman to the coastal villages of Surat district. The liquor was carried in barrels tied to the undersides of the boats.

Another radically different solution to the problems brought about by British Abkari policies was to give up drink altogether. In Brahmanic Hindu culture abstention from spirituous drinks was considered a great virtue, and it is probable that even before the colonial era there were certain tribal and low-caste peasants who refused to drink in the belief that this would raise their status in the wider society. In 1893 Frederick Lely reported that he had heard of adivasi families 'in which teetotalism had long been an inherited custom'.[183] These families tended, however, to be the more prosperous ones which were trying to distance themselves from other members of their community, for refusal to drink together in a community in which such drinking represented a symbol of mutual solidarity could be considered a gesture of renunciation of membership of the community. The difference between this isolated type of renunciation and the popular temperance movements which started in the late nineteenth century was that in the latter case entire communities which were undergoing a process of pauperization attempted to give up liquor and toddy. Through such radical cultural reform they hoped to save themselves from further impoverishment and also to enhance the status of their community in the region as a whole. Although this hope was not altogether realistic, the strategy had some real strengths. Faith in the old culture had been undermined and it was felt that a fresh start was required. Refusal to drink represented both a moral stand and a new symbol of commitment to the cause of communal advance. It provided a badge of solidarity in the peasant's struggle against the Parsi and, in addition, it cut the economic cord which bound the peasant to the liquor dealer.[184]

In the decade following the implementation of the Abkari Act of 1878, cases began to be reported from Surat district of low-caste people getting together and taking vows to give up liquor and toddy. Only rarely did such efforts survive beyond the first marriage or feast day.[185] The first movement of this sort to affect the whole of South Gujarat occurred in 1895, when Lely was collector of Surat district. In his annual report he commented:

> The only other special Abkari feature of the year was the formation of total abstinence leagues almost throughout the District. The movement began in Surat and Nowsari and spread to the outlying villages. It was most vigorous in Surat where an organised crusade against drink was carried on for

> a while by means of public meetings and caste-pressure. Some of the promoters acted with the childish purpose of embarrassing Government. The great mass of those who joined did so under the persuasion that they would thereby force down the prices of liquor and toddy while a few were roused by a sincere desire to diminish drunkenness.[186]

The movement was, however, short-lived, collapsing rapidly after several influential caste leaders were found to be drinking secretly.

The next major temperance movement occurred in 1905, and this time it originated in the tribal territory of Vyara. It was started by an educated adivasi called Amarsinh Gamit. Mass meetings of the adivasis were held and vows were taken to abstain from daru and toddy. The movement spread throughout Navsari and Surat districts, causing a sudden slump in sales of liquor and toddy and a remarkable decrease in the number of cases of illicit distillation. In Surat district twenty liquor shops had to be closed for lack of custom, and sales of toddy fell by 114,712 gallons during the year.[187] Although longer lasting than any previous movement, it suffered a severe setback after the harvest failure of 1905, which forced many peasants to turn to toddy for subsistence during the following months. By the end of March 1906 consumption of daru and toddy was back to normal in the region.[188] Over the next few years spasmodic attempts were made to revive the movement. The results were on the whole poor. It was only after a further decade and a half that such a movement again affected the whole region, and this was the greatest anti-liquor movement known in the history of South Gujarat—the Devi movement of 1922–3.

This movement has already formed the subject of a recent essay and I do not intend to describe it again here.[189] It is sufficient to say that it represented a major attack on the Abkari system throughout South Gujarat, as well as on the Parsi liquor and toddy dealers. Parsis were subjected to a rigorous social boycott which destroyed their prestige in the region. Even though the majority of the peasants began to drink again in the late 1920s, the Parsis never recovered from this blow. Through the Devi movement the adivasis of South Gujarat found their political voice; never again were they to form the passive object of colonial policy. During the course of the movement an influential element among them forged an alliance with the middle-class Gandhian nationalists of Gujarat, thereby gaining on their side a group of most vocal champions. The common platform was that of abstention from daru and toddy, and it is therefore to the Indian nationalist policy towards drink which I shall now turn.

VII

The Indian National Congress had from its earliest years put forward the view that the chief concern of the British in their excise policy was to raise as much revenue as possible in a manner which went against the best interests of the people.[190] It was argued that although officials claimed that high prices discouraged drinking, in practice the local revenue officers did their utmost to stimulate the consumption of liquor. This appeared to be borne out by the history of an anti-liquor movement in Kolaba and Thana districts in 1886. Eight of the leaders of this peasant movement were arrested by the authorities, and the movement was crushed. The Abkari commissioner, J.G. Moore, had justified this action in the following terms: 'The question for decision is, shall we sit quiet and allow the movement to continue and spread and thereby forfeit a large amount of revenue, or are measures to be adopted which will bring the people to their senses?'[191] The nationalists also argued that the government had allowed many liquor shops to be opened in places in which they had never existed before, often in defiance of local opinion.[192]

There were broadly two schools of thought on the subject. One school—represented chiefly by Parsi nationalists of Bombay—believed that colonial policy was distorting the existing healthy drinking culture of the people, in particular causing the mild and harmless drink of toddy to be replaced by hard spirits. Dinshaw Wacha (Congress President in 1901) and P.B. Dantra were the leading lights of this school, and they took much inspiration from the activities and writings of Frederick Lely.[193] They were supported and financed in this work by rich Parsis, and the government tended to write them off accordingly as mere spokesmen for Parsi liquor and toddy interests. There was no doubt, however, that they were voicing a popular grievance, as was recognized by the British Liberal MP, W.S. Caine, who said about the excise on toddy in a speech in the House of Commons: 'This tax is undoubtedly one of the most unpopular that was ever levied upon a poverty-stricken people, and has led to endless dissatisfaction and even rioting.'[194]

The other school of nationalist thought, and the predominant one, demanded complete prohibition in India. In the words of David Mandelbaum:

> Many of the political leaders held the belief that an independent India had to be a pure India, and one way to advance national purity was by legal prohibition. This seemed to be quite in the sacred tradition, but in fact it was in one respect a radical departure from it. The Sanskritic tradition did not rule out alcohol for all in society but only for the most spiritually elevated.[195]

G.K. Gokhale was one of the leading spokesmen for this school during the early nationalist phase. He favoured prohibition because liquor drinking was 'contrary to the sentiment of the great majority of the people of India'.[196] He argued that the British were stimulating the liquor trade, and that liquor consumption was increasing rapidly. Demands for complete prohibition became more vociferous after the highly successful First All-India Temperance Conference held in Bombay in 1904. This brought together 301 temperance associations which already existed scattered over India.[197] These associations were, however, largely urban based, with predominantly high-caste members. They showed little interest in the popular temperance movements which were becoming increasingly important; instead they preferred to lobby the government for a change in policy.[198] It was only with the emergence of Gandhi within the Congress after 1918 that positive attempts were made to link the temperance activities of the middle classes with the anti-liquor movements of the masses. In 1921 Gandhi gave his blessings to a campaign to picket liquor and toddy shops. As a result sales of drink decreased significantly in many areas.[199]

While the Gandhian nationalists were carrying on their agitation at the shop-doors, the old-school Congressmen who had no taste for such assertive forms of protest were at last getting a chance to put their programmes into practice through the powers established under the Montagu–Chelmsford reforms of 1919. Under these reforms provincial Abkari came under the control of an elected minister. The first of such ministers in Bombay was Sir Chunilal Mehta. At the very first meeting of the reformed Bombay Legislative Council he expressed his determination to 'combat the drink evil'.[200] He inaugurated a policy of rationing of supplies to liquor shops. Supplies were reduced initially by five per cent and further reductions were proposed year by year. He also appointed a committee to examine the operation of the liquor laws in the Presidency, which was instructed to report on the feasibility of implementing complete prohibition. The committee started work in January 1922 and reported in November 1923. During this period the members travelled all over the Presidency and examined a large number of witnesses. Opinions were divided between on the one hand government officials and liquor contractors who favoured the existing policy, and on the other non-officials who favoured either greater restriction on liquor production and sale or, in many cases, complete prohibition.

British officials who testified before the committee maintained that the liquor laws had achieved their stated aim, which was to increase revenue while at the same time bringing down consumption. The Abkari commissioner of the day, W.C. Shepherd argued that consumption of liquor had fallen since 1878. He produced figures for country liquor consumed in Bombay Presidency, exclusive of Bombay city:[201]

Year	Gallons of country liquor consumed	Drams consumed per head of population
1867–8	2,884,442	14.0
1907–8	2,704,354	8.9
1920–1	2,371,488	7.6

Consumption per head had thus, Shepherd argued, halved during this period. He roundly condemned any suggestion of prohibition. Such a policy would lead to a mushroom growth of illicit distilleries. 'At present illicit distillation is carried on entirely by ignorant members of the lower classes, using small stills, and supplying a limited clientele.'[202] Such illegal practices were not, he argued, a great problem to the authorities. Prohibition on the other hand would see the emergence of big-time bootleggers making illicit hooch on a large scale. Enforcement of prohibition would become increasingly expensive and hazardous. Shepherd believed that the existing policy was effective both in raising revenue and in checking excessive consumption. He therefore felt that there should be no substantial change in the liquor policy.

The non-officials who testified before the committee were overwhelmingly in favour of greater restrictions on the consumption of liquor. Many favoured complete prohibition. In the report the committee summarized their arguments in the following terms. Drinking was a vice and the government had no right to derive revenue from it (one-third of the revenue of Bombay Presidency came from excise). The majority of Indians did not drink. The traditions, customs, sentiments and religions of India were opposed to it. Drinking was an exotic habit—not indigenous. Only the lowest members of Indian society used to drink before the British came. Liquor shops provided a temptation for all: 'The masses being illiterate cannot withstand the temptation.' The implementation of greater restrictions or, ideally, prohibition would be in the best interests of the 'drinking classes', who were mostly poor people who were being ruined by their craving for liquor. Gradual imposition of prohibition would be unlikely to cause mass discontent. Illicit distillation could be stopped if there was a will to do so.[203]

The 'Indian' case for prohibition was put in a particularly explicit form by Mavji Govindji Sheth, a businessman, theosophist and nationalist of Bombay city. His statement to the committee revealed a characteristic high-caste contempt for all those who drank, coupled with an equally characteristic ignorance of the facts of Indian history.

> At no period of Indian history—Vedic, Buddhistic, Rajput, Mahomedan or Moghul—had the masses of the country the temptation of drinking liquor flung so violently and so assiduously in their faces, as in the British period. Whereas in former days wine was to be found at the table of some stray renegade aristocrat, or occasionally in the haunts of the lowest and vilest outcastes, to-day we find a net-work of liquor shops spread over the whole length and breadth of the land, taking it, as it were, to the very doors not only of the village people but even to the hill tribes. A village may be without a school or a temple, a sarai or a masjid, but there is scarcely a cluster of villages today in India where there is no grog shop.
>
> Whereas India, this sacred land of ours, should have set an example to the rest of the world in complete eradication of the drink-evil, the United

States carried the palm and, in unequivocally declaring for prohibition, have amended their constitution (requiring three-fourths majority of all the States) and have steadily gone on suppressing it.

That the evil is a potent factor in promoting crime, in ruining happy homes, in causing perpetual indebtedness and consequent bondage and physical condition of the nation, is now universally accepted.

The Government policy as laid down on paper sounds altruistic enough but its carrying out has evidently been in the opposite direction.[204]

In this exchange both British officials and Indian nationalists claimed to have the interests of the masses at heart. The masses themselves were not, however, a party to the debate. The committee even had to admit somewhat sheepishly that only two 'poor people' had testified before it, and they were industrial workers who believed in prohibition. Attempts to get millworkers who drank to appear had failed as, it was argued, they were ashamed to admit their degrading habit in public. More probably they were frightened of being cross-questioned by a committee of sahibs. In any case no attempt appears to have been made to gather evidence from agrarian drinkers, such as the rural poor of South Gujarat. They had to be spoken *for* by European officials and high-caste social workers. Despite this grave lacuna in the evidence submitted to the committee, it came to the conclusion in its final report that the Indian people *as a whole* wanted prohibition. It therefore recommended the implementation of a policy of prohibition in Bombay Presidency.[205]

The chief problem appeared to be that of finance. The Bombay government could hardly give up one-third of its income there and then. Another committee therefore had to be appointed in 1926 to seek alternative sources of revenue. This committee, which reported in 1927, recommended a long-term plan for gradual tax substitution, to be spread out over a period of at least twenty years.[206] The Bombay revenue department objected to this on the grounds that the education and development projects of the government would all be sacrificed for the cause of prohibition. As yet, Indian ministers did not control the Bombay government as a whole, only certain departments, and they could not therefore prevent the government from declaring in 1928 that it did not intend to change the existing Abkari policy.[207] Following this the rationing policy was relaxed.

The ball was therefore back in the nationalists' court. During these years the Gandhian Congress had been working hard to demonstrate that there was a mass demand for prohibition. They had been particularly successful in South Gujarat, linking up first with the adivasi abstainers during the Devi Movement of 1922–3 and then leading a powerful anti-drink movement amongst the Koli peasants of the coastal region. As a result of a strong agitation in 1929, the excise revenue of Surat district fell by Rs 350,000. In Jalalpor taluka large numbers of Koli peasants chopped down their toddy trees, and there was intense picketing of liquor and toddy shops.[208] Those who continued to drink suffered severe social boycott.[209] The agitation was carried on in Navsari district by the Baroda State Praja Mandal, under the direct guidance of Vallabhbhai Patel.[210] The campaign continued during the Civil Disobedience Movement of 1930–1, becoming if anything stronger. To all appearances it seemed by the 1930s that the demand for prohibition was in South Gujarat a genuinely popular one. In fact there were already signs of a reaction against the reformers, as we shall see below.

In the late 1930s it at last became possible for the nationalists to bring in prohibition, after autonomy was granted at the provincial level under the Government of India Act of 1935. The first elections were held in 1937 and a Congress ministry came to power. It was decided to implement prohibition in stages over a period of three years. Ahmedabad city and certain rural areas were declared dry in 1938. In Surat district prohibition came into effect in Bardoli taluka in 1938 and in Valod taluka in 1939. The move was financed through an urban property tax and various other levies. Bombay city was declared dry in 1939—bringing a storm of protest from Parsis. Parsi liquor contractors took the matter to court and various aspects of prohibition were ruled *ultra vires*. But even before these judgements were made, the Congress ministry had resigned in protest at India's involuntary involvements in the Second World War, and the governor of Bombay, Sir Roger Lumley, took the opportunity to abandon some of the more controversial aspects of the policy. As a result, until the Congress returned to power in Bombay after the war in 1946, prohibition was not pursued with much energy in the Presidency.[211] In 1946 a programme was launched for total prohibition in four years. This culminated in the Bombay Prohibition Act of 1949. Complete prohibition was introduced in Surat district on 1 April 1950.[212] Prohibition has remained in force in the region to this day.

Contrary to the expectations of the Congressmen and other high-caste nationalists prohibition did not in South Gujarat bring about a significant decline in the consumption of spirituous drinks. The survey conducted by the University of Bombay in the year after the introduction of prohibition in Surat district found that 72 per cent of the population continued to drink.[213] The Tek Chand report on the working of prohibition in India (1964) found widespread consumption of liquor in South Gujarat and made the remark that 'Gujarat's biggest problem district is Surat'.[214] Clearly, the nationalists and prohibitionists had made miscalculations about the tenacity of the anti-drink movements of the preceding decades. In fact from about 1925 onwards a reaction had begun to set in against such cultural reforms. This counter movement occurred in a particularly demonstrable form in the years after the Devi Movement of 1922–3.

Even during the Devi Movement there were many peasants who did not accept the need to change their habits. As soon as they were able, they began to drink once more. During the movement they had been told that they would incur divine displeasure and suffer great misfortune if they acted in such a manner. But when it was seen that they were living quite happily, others began to follow their example.[215] In many areas almost the entire population was drinking again within a year. However, in the areas inhabited by Chodhri and Dhodiya adivasis, such as Mahuva, Mandvi and Valod talukas, the movement had a more lasting impact. This because there was there an influential class of upwardly mobile adivasis which was determined to sustain the challenge to the Parsi landlords-cum-liquor dealers. As these men were often leading figures in their villages, they were able to prevent the movement from flagging for a number of years. Groups of them used to tour the villages, holding meetings and singing reformist *bhajans*. They sought and obtained help from the Gandhian nationalists, which took their movement onto a new level.

Gradually, however, opposition began to build up against the reformers from adivasis who felt that drinking was a part of their culture, a custom hallowed by tradition, something indeed which was a part of their very identity. What had been good for their fathers, they felt, was good for them. These sentiments received encouragement from several quarters. The Parsis were eager to see an end to the social reform movement and were active in persuading adivasis to renounce their vows. In many cases they gave away free daru and toddy, a temptation which few could resist. Some Parsis argued that the Devi was a false goddess whose demands were unreasonable. Likewise, adivasis who depended on the patronage of Parsis, such as assistants in drink-shops and toddy-tappers, did their best to persuade their neighbours to drink once more.[216] The spirit-mediums, whose position as mediators between the adivasis and their gods was threatened by the movement for religious reform, used their considerable influence to persuade the adivasis to return to their old habits. In a few cases meetings were organized at which adivasis became possessed by the Devi; the command this time being that they could once more eat meat and fish and drink daru and toddy.[217] A name—Sarjela—was coined for those who wanted to return to the old ways of life. This word stemmed from *sarjan*, meaning 'primordial creation'; the argument being that Sarjelas took whatever had been created by the gods—which included chicken, goat, fish, daru and toddy. The reformers were labelled as Varjelas, stemming from the word *varjan*, meaning 'giving up'. The Sarjelas began to boycott the Varjelas. They refused to marry into Varjela families or attend their funerals.[218]

In time the rivalry between the two groups became quite fierce, in some cases even leading to violence. One such clash occurred in December 1929, when a group of three hundred Sarjelas decided to carry out their customary annual sacrifice of goats and chickens to the adivasi god Ahin, who was located on a hilltop near Pipalvada village in Mandvi taluka. A local group of militant Varjelas surrounded the place of sacrifice and prevented the Sarjelas from reaching the sacred place. They had to return without making the sacrifice. A few days later the Varjelas announced that they would hold a meeting at Sarkui village of Mandvi taluka to preach temperance and the abandonment of blood sacrifices. The Sarjelas decided to take their revenge. Before setting out for Sarkui they took a feast of chicken and toddy, which emphasized both their solidarity and their belief in the old customs. They then went to Sarkui and laid an ambush for the reformers. As soon as the Varjelas appeared they set upon them, beating them with lathis and, more symbolically, with the possession-sticks decorated with rings which were used by the spirit-mediums. In some cases they rubbed the Varjelas with meat or poured daru and toddy over them. The Varjelas, being in a minority, had no choice but to flee.[219] After this they were very much on the defensive in the area.

A similar though generally less dramatic reassertion of older values has occurred throughout South Gujarat over the past fifty years. This fact was brought out quite clearly in an investigation of eight villages of the region carried out in 1975 by Harish Doshi and Vidyut Joshi.[220] The aim of this study was to show 'the benefits of prohibition', but when they tried to find 250 non-drinking families in these eight villages so that they could document the supposed benefits, their best efforts were unable to uncover more than 213 such families. Families of drinkers were found in abundance! Doshi and Joshi reported that '. . . most of the drinkers strongly believe that there is nothing wrong in drinking'.[221] Many said that they drank out of customary habit and that they felt obliged to offer drinks to other members of their community as a form of hospitality. People who tried to give up drinking were teased as *bhagats* (meaning, in this context, that they were being excessively zealous), or as still being under the effects of the Devi (*Devi-no va*) long after the Devi had gone.[222] Some forms of customary drinking were found to have declined. For instance it had become almost unknown for drink to be served at meetings of caste or tribal councils. In many cases tea had replaced drink at betrothal ceremonies, death ceremonies and other such public gatherings. However, three-quarters of the Dhodiya adivasis who were questioned said that they felt obliged by custom to serve drink when a child was born in their family. About half of the Machhis said that it was necessary to serve drink at births, betrothal ceremonies and marriages. It was also found that large amounts of daru were consumed during major festivals such as Holi, Dashera and Diwali. Very few people were found to drink excessively. Most drank only during their leisure time—normally in the evening before going to bed.[223]

The study went on to show that in the adivasi villages people largely distilled their own daru. Often this was done on a reciprocal basis, with families taking it in turn to distil some daru, which was then supplied to everyone who was a party to the arrangement. Such daru was not made for sale. In coastal villages on the other hand it was found that drink was being distilled by organized gangs who sold the product both in the villages and nearby towns.[224] That this is still the practice I myself discovered in 1983 on a visit to a fishing village on the coast near Surat city, where I saw large numbers of stills being worked in the open, outside the doors of the people's cottages, in a most brazen manner. As a result daru is obtained with no difficulty at very cheap rates throughout South Gujarat. The police turn a blind eye to much of this manufacture and sale in return for regular considerations.

This illicit liquor is not for the most part particularly tasty or wholesome. It has to be made in haste and various harmful ingredients are commonly added to the wash to speed the process of fermentation. The basic ingredient used is no longer mahua, but country sugar (*gur*). As a result the characteristic mellow taste and flavour of the traditional mahua daru is lost. Thus, although the poor peasantry and working classes no longer have to pay the exorbitant prices which prevailed under British rule and no longer fall into the clutches of Parsi liquor and toddy dealers, they have to drink an extremely inferior liquor and they are, moreover, liable to police harassment at any time. Today, little toddy is drunk in South Gujarat. Toddy trees have died and have not been replaced. Pritchard's policy of replacing toddy with daru has thus met with success in the region, though not in a way which he would have appreciated.

A large majority of the population of South Gujarat thus breaks the law on a regular basis. Although prosecutions are few in relation to the total amount of such lawbreaking, the figures are still striking when compared with similar figures for the first decade of the twentieth century. In 1980 there were 26,366 prosecutions for violation of prohibition in Surat district, and 10,846 more in Valsad district and the Dangs. Between them these three districts accounted for 37 per cent of such prosecutions in the nineteen districts of Gujarat.[225] By contrast, between 1900–1, and 1909–10, the annual average number of offences against the liquor laws in Surat district (such as illicit distillation, smuggling, illicit tree-tapping and so on) was a mere 235.[226] Prohibition has thus been a major catalyst of what is now classified as 'crime' in this region.[227] Nowadays it is in fact 'crime' which has become the custom. In all, therefore, the policy of the ruling Congress towards drink has proved hardly more satisfactory than that pursued by their British predecessors.

VIII

In this history there have been two distinct elements to the 'drink question'. On the one hand there was the impact of colonial policies on a society which had until then a remarkably balanced attitude towards spirituous drinks. As a result of the changes wrought by colonial policy the traditional drinks of mild toddy and cottage-made daru were replaced with sour and adulterated toddy and expensive mass-produced hooch. There was widespread protest which won some short-lived relaxations of the liquor laws, but the general tendency was towards evasion of these laws and a growth in the 'crimes' of illicit distillation and smuggling. Over the years the peasantry increasingly gave up toddy in favour of daru. This process was brought to its unhappy conclusion with the advent of prohibition, which made illicit gur-based daru the chief drink consumed in South Gujarat.

In this manner a popular and nourishing natural product, obtained at almost no cost to the poor, has been replaced by a dubious and unhealthy spirit. The mass of the people of South Gujarat break the prohibition laws on a regular basis, being turned thus into so-called 'habitual criminals'. This has occurred in a region which during the nineteenth century was renowned for its remarkably low rate of crime. The most equitable solution would appear to be to attempt to reverse the whole process by allowing the peasants once more to tap their own trees for toddy and make daru to the old standards in cottage distilleries.[228] But although prohibition is likely to be lifted in Gujarat sooner or later, it is unlikely that there will be a return to such a satisfactory system. The state will want its excise and the capitalists will want a captive market for their hooch. The system imposed in 1878 will almost certainly continue, therefore, to provide the basis for government policy towards drink. In such a circumstance 'crime' connected with drink is likely to continue on a large scale.

The other distinct element to this history concerns changing attitudes towards drink over the past century. On the one hand the nationalist leaders of India evolved a demand for total prohibition, fired by a belief that the Indian nation should be ritually pure. This ambitious desire to build a nation of the orthodox became linked during the Gandhian era with popular temperance movements. These movements were fuelled in part by resentment against the colonial Abkari laws, but were also a part of a widespread movement throughout India in which low-status communities began to demand to be considered equal to those of higher social status. Despite its many successes in a number of fields, this movement has failed to promote temperance of a lasting nature amongst the mass of the poor of India.

These two aspects to the history of drink in South Gujarat were to some extent interrelated, though rather less so than many of the more vocal observers believed. Thus, the colonial officials argued that the Abkari laws had caused a reduction in the amount of drink consumed, whereas the nationalists argued that the laws had in fact promoted mass consumption of drink. In fact this legislation probably had little long-term effect on the general amount of drink consumed; its impact was rather on the type of drink consumed. In themselves the laws did not promote either temperance or so called 'drunkenness'. The popular movements for temperance were based on rather different considerations, which related to the general pauperization of peasants and workers under colonial rule and the impact of middle-class reform movements on the consciousness of the leaders of low-status communities.

On the whole the drinking customs of the peasants of South Gujarat have proved remarkably resilient under attack. There is little reason to believe that the traditional moderation and congenial attitude of the people of the region towards their drink has as yet been destroyed. In fact, with the loss of momentum of the social reform movements of the colonial period and with the increasing tendency amongst the middle classes of the region to take Indian-made 'foreign-style' liquor, it is becoming generally more respectable to drink. Out of this as yet slight convergence between élite and subaltern values a more equitable solution to the 'drink problem' in Gujarat may perhaps eventually emerge.

NOTES

1. In 1930–1 the proportion of total revenue made up by land revenue and excise (most of which was derived from country drink) was, by leading provinces:

	Land revenue (%)	Excise (%)
Bombay	43	33
Madras	41	31
Bengal	24	17
UP	65	12

2. Hans Medik, 'Plebian Culture in the Transition to Capitalism', in Raphael Samuel and Gareth Stedman Jones (eds), *Culture, Ideology and Politics* (London, 1983), p. 86.
3. Sidney and Beatrice Webb, *The History of Liquor Licensing in England Principally from 1700 to 1830* (London, 1903), pp. 50–2 and 128–36.
4. The terms 'country liquor' and 'daru' will be used interchangeably throughout this essay. Together, country liquor and toddy (in Gujarati: *daru-tadi*) will be referred to as 'country drink'.
5. William Foster (ed.), *Early Travels in India 1583–1619* (London, 1921), p. 175.
6. Ibid., p. 136.
7. Peter Mundy, *The Travels of Peter Mundy in Europe and Asia 1608–1667, Vol. II. Travels in Asia 1628–1634* (London, 1914), p. 32.
8. S. Sen (ed.), *Indian Travels of Thevenot and Careri* (New Delhi, 1949), p. 24.
9. J. Ovington, *A Voyage to Suratt in the Year 1669* (London, 1696), p. 238.
10. *Reports on the Administration of the Excise Department in the Bombay Presidency, Sind and Aden, 1919–20* (Bombay, 1921), (hereafter *Excise Admin. Report, Bombay*).
11. *Report of the Study on the Socio-Economic Effects of Prohibition* (*Rural*) (Bombay, 1953), pp. 6 and 16.
12, Ibid., p. 16.
13. Ovington, *A Voyage to Suratt*, p. 238.
14. *Gazetteer of the Bombay Presidency, Vol. II. Surat and Broach* (Bombay, 1877), pp. 47–55. (Hereafter *Surat District Gazetteer*). The chief tribes amongst the adivasis of South Gujarat were the Chodhris, Dhodiyas, Gamits, Dublas, Konkanis, Naikas and Bhils. It should be noted that although they made up less than a third of the population, adivasis were

found chiefly in the more sparsely populated eastern regions, and in large areas of South Gujarat they made up the vast bulk of the population.

15. Mundy, *Travels*, vol. II, p. 306.
16. The large toddy orchards around Surat were noticed by both Mundy (ibid., p. 32) and William Finch, who stayed in Surat between 1608 and 1610; Foster, *Early Travels in India*, p. 175.
17. *Excise Admin. Report, Bombay*, 1883–4, p. 22.
18. Byramji Jijibhai and others to Sec. to Govt. of Bombay, 28 October 1886, Maharashtra State Archives, Bombay (hereafter BA), Revenue Department (hereafter R.D.) 1887, vol. 7, Comp. 810.
19. Collector's Report, Surat district, 1903–4, BA, R.D. 1905, vol. 23, Comp. 177.
20. Collector's Report, Surat district, 1904–5, BA, R.D. 1906, vol. 11, Comp. 511.
21. A.N. Solanki, *The Dhodias: A Tribe of South Gujarat Area* (Vienna, 1976), p. 259.
22. *Report of the Study on the Socio-Economic Effects of Prohibition*, p. 19.
23. For a comparison with another peasant society, we may note E. Le Roy Ladurie's calculation that in sixteenth-century Languedoc farm workers consumed on average about two litres of wine a day. In Surat district the average per capita consumption of toddy in the period 1885–6 to 1889–90 was 5.65 gallons per year. If we assume that only about half the population drank toddy regularly, this represented 11.3 gallons (51.57 litres) per drinker per year, or 0.14 litres per head per day. Toddy is less alcoholic than wine (about 6 per cent alcoholic content, compared to the 8 per cent of wine), so that comparative consumption in South Gujarat was far less than in sixteenth-century Languedoc; see E. Le Roy Ladurie, *The Peasants of Languedoc* (Urbana, 1976), p. 63; *Excise Admin. Reports, Bombay*, 1885–6 to 1889–90. For a comparison with an industrialized society we may note that in Britain in 1897 the average annual consumption of alcoholic drinks per head of the population was 1.03 gallons of spirits, 0.40 gallons of wine and 31.4 gallons of beer. Again, consumption was far higher than in South Gujarat; Sydney and Beatrice Webb, *The History of Liquor Licensing in England*, p. 134.
24. *Report of the Excise Committee appointed by the Government of Bombay 1922–23, Vol. I* (Bombay, 1924), p. 165 (hereafter *Bombay Excise Committee Report*).
25. *Surat District Gazetteer*, p. 235; *Police Reports of the Bombay Presidency including Sind for the year 1875* (Bombay, 1876).
26. *Report of the Study on the Socio-Economic Effects of Prohibition*, pp. 12–14.
27. BA, R.D. 1886, vol. 9, Comp. 842.

28. Testimony of Reverend Enok Hedberg, April 1923, *Bombay Excise Committee Report*, vol. II, p. 256; S.L. Doshi, *Bhils: Between Societal Self-Awareness and Cultural Synthesis* (New Delhi, 1971), p. 106; Solanki, *The Dhodias*, p. 259.
29. Such beliefs are found in many tribal cultures; see Donald Horton, 'The Functions of Alcohol in Primitive Societies: A Cross-Cultural Study', *Quarterly Journal of Studies on Alcohol* 4:2 (September 1943), p. 246. James Campbell, the editor of the Gazetteers of Bombay Presidency, believed that inebriation was seen by primitive people as a form of possession by divine power; James Campbell, *Notes on the Spirit Basis of Belief and Custom* (Bombay, 1885), p. 128.
30. For such a legend, see T.B. Naik, *The Bhils: A Study* (Delhi, 1956), pp. 219–20.
31. Quoted in *Excise Admin. Report, Bombay*, 1924–5, p. 18.
32. *Mandvi Taluka Settlement Report, 1872* (Bombay, 1904), p. 41.
33. B.H. Mehta, 'Social and Economic Conditions of the Chodhras, an Aboriginal Tribe of Gujarat', unpublished M.A. thesis, University of Bombay, 1933, p. 214.
34. Horton, 'Functions of Alcohol in Primitive Societies', p. 247.
35. This is reminiscent of the ancient Teutonic custom of drinking over an agreement as a mark of reconciliation and friendship; Edward Baird, 'The Alcohol Problem and the Law, I. The Ancient Laws and Customs', *Quarterly Journal of Studies on Alcohol* 4:4 (March 1944), p. 550.
36. B.H. Mehta reported that in 1929 a group of Chodhris of Mandvi taluka took a feast of toddy and chicken before carrying out a violent attack on a rival group; Mehta, 'Social and Economic Conditions of the Chodhras', p. 178.
37. T.B. Naik, *The Bhils*, pp. 220–1; Solanki, *The Dhodias*, p. 259.
38. F.S.P. Lely to J.G. Moore, 22 May 1886, BA, R.D. 1887, vol. 7, Comp. 264. Partha Chatterjee has noted how drinking bouts in medieval Europe could help to reinforce communal solidarity. European peasants indulged in periodic joyful destructions of wealth in the midst of privation, in a manner which rekindled the sense of brotherhood and group cohesion; P. Chatterjee, 'More on Modes of Power and the Peasantry', in R. Guha (ed.), *Subaltern Studies II* (New Delhi, 1983), pp. 336–7. Horton, in his study of drink in tribal societies, mentions the frequently found custom of communal labour being carried out with a free supply of drink. Such labour has both a practical and festive content, and it promotes group solidarity; 'Functions of Alcohol in Primitive Societies', p. 248. In South Gujarat adivasis often carried out communal labour without payment (see Mehta, 'Social and Economic Conditions

of the Chodhras', p. 490), but I have no evidence regarding whether or not this was accompanied by drinking. It may well have been.

39. Testimony of A.M. Dalal, April, *Bombay Excise Committee Report*, vol. II, p. 303.
40. For a report on the food value of toddy by a nutritionist see: Tek Chand, *Report of the Study Team on Prohibition*, vol. I (New Delhi, 1964), pp. 182–3.
41. F.S.P. Lely, 13 October 1884, BA, R.D. 1884, vol. 9, Comp. 1735.
42. *Bombay Excise Committee Report*, vol. I, p. 29. This belief is not of course accepted in western medical theory.
43. Assistant Collector's Report, Surat district, 28 July 1884, BA, R.D. 1884, vol. 32, Comp. 1548. In nutritional terms distilled liquor provides calories, but it lacks vitamins, minerals and proteins as these are destroyed in the process of distillation. It is not therefore such a valuable food as toddy; Horton, 'Functions of Alcohol in Primitive Societies', pp. 208–9.
44. That it is possible for a community to survive almost completely on palm-juice products is shown by James Fox's study of the Indonesian islands of Roti and Savu; *Harvests of the Palm* (Cambridge, Massachusetts 1977), pp. 24–7.
45. *Mandvi Taluka Settlement Report, 1872*, p. 57.
46. Letter by P.B. Dantra to *Indian Spectator*, 24 July 1887, in BA, R.D. 1890, vol. 262, Comp. 179.
47. Frank Perlin, 'Proto-Industrialization and Pre-Colonial South Asia', *Past and Present* 98 (February 1983), p. 70.
48. *Surat District Gazetteer*, p. 39. In the mid-nineteenth century there were probably even more date-palm trees in Surat district, for a large number of trees growing on government land were destroyed in 1865–6 as part of a campaign to reduce toddy consumption. See *Jalalpor Taluka Settlement Report, 1868* (Bombay, 1900), p. 27.
49. *Bombay Excise Committee Report*, vol. I, pp. 120–1. Solanki, *The Dhodias* p. 259.
50. W.R. Pratt to R.D. Bombay, 26 June 1879, BA, R.D. 1879, vol. 6, Comp. 249.
51. *Surat District Gazetteer*, p. 40.
52. C.W. Bell, *Report on the Abkaree System in Force in the Presidency of Bombay* (Bombay, 1869), p. 55. (Hereafter Bell, *Abkaree Report*).
53. F.S.P. Lely to C.B. Pritchard, 22 September 1884, BA, R.D. 1884, vol. 9, Comp. 1735.
54. Excise Superintendent, Surat, 1 June 1942, Surat Collector's Office Records, Daftar MAG/ADM, A class.

55. Bell, *Abkaree Report*, pp. 55 and 120–3.
56. For a description of the Hali system, see Jan Breman, *Patronage and Exploitation: Changing Agrarian Relations in South Gujarat, India* (California, 1974).
57. *Surat District Gazetteer*, p. 199.
58. *Chorasi Taluka Settlement Report, 1866* (Bombay, 1897), p. 39.
59. F.S.P. Lely, 15 December 1885, BA, R.D. 1886, vol. 9, Comp. 842. There were 12 pies to one anna, and 192 pies to one rupee.
60. In these five years the average per capita consumption of toddy in Surat district was 5.65 gallons per year. I have calculated this figure by taking the average number of trees tapped each year and multiplying it by the average yield per tree in the district (24 gallons per year) and dividing the total by the population in 1891. The average per capita consumption of daru containing 43 per cent alcohol by volume was, during the same five years, 0.47 gallons per year. Figures for toddy trees tapped and daru con-sumed from *Excise Admin. Reports, Bombay*, 1885–6 to 1889–90.
61. Country liquor was sold in Surat district in two strengths: 25 per cent under proof and 60 per cent under proof, which contained respectively 43 per cent and 23 per cent alcohol by volume. For comparative pur-poses, consumption figures in the *Excise Admin. Reports, Bombay* were expressed in terms of the amount of liquor which would have been con-sumed if it had all been sold at a strength of 25 per cent under proof (43 per cent of alcohol by volume).
62. Om Prakash, *Food and Drink in Ancient India (From Earliest Times to c. 1200 A.D.)* (Delhi, 1961), p. 152.
63. Foster, *Early Travels in India*, p. 136.
64. Ruskin Bond, *The World of Trees* (New Delhi, 1975), pp. 31–2.
65. That the people of South Gujarat preferred weaker spirit is shown by the figures for the sale of government liquor in 1924–5. 78 per cent of all country liquor sold in Surat district was 60 per cent under proof, which contained 23 per cent of alcohol by volume; *Excise Admin. Report, Bom-bay*, 1924–5, p. 67.
66. *Excise Admin. Report, Bombay*, 1879–80, p. 34.
67. Bell, *Abkaree Report*, p. 120. In addition there were sixty-four liquor shops in Surat city in 1830–1, served by one central distillery.
68. The Parsis occupied a position in South Gujarat similar to the Jews of Tsarist Russia. Tavern-keepers in Russia were often Jews who had the local population in their debt. Charles van Onselen writes: '. . . many Ukrainian folk songs of the time bemoaned the peasant's indebtedness to the local Jew'. This fed popular anti-Semitism in Russia at that time. The parallels with the Parsis of South Gujarat are striking; C. van Onselen, 'Landlords and Rotgut', *History Workshop* 2 (Autumn 1976), p. 35.
69. *Gazetteer of the Baroda State*, vol. II (Bombay, 1923), p. 698. Manek

Pithawalla, 'The Gujarat Region and the Parsees: A Historico-Geographical Survey', *Journal of the Gujarat Research Society* 8:2 and 3 (April and July 1945).

70. *Surat District Gazetteer*, p. 189.
71. Limji Jamsetji to E.V. Stace, 31 March 1886, BA, R.D. 1886, vol. 1, Comp. 139.
72. Report by M.S. Mansfield, June 1854, in *Selection from the Records of the Bombay Government No. XXVI—New Series* (Bombay, 1856), p. 165.
73. Report on tour of the Dangs by J. Davidson, 5 June 1856, *Forest Reports of the Bombay Presidency of the Years 1849–50 to 1855–56* (Bombay, 1857), p. 98.
74. *Chikhli Taluka Settlement Report, 1865* (Bombay, 1899), p. 51.
75. Collector's Report, Surat district 1886–7, BA, R.D. 1887, vol. 26, Comp. 1548.
76. Collector's Report, Surat district 1885–6, BA, R.D. 1886, vol. 32, Comp. 1548.
77. Limji Jamsetji to E.V. Stace, 31 March 1886, BA, R.D. 1886, vol. 1, Comp. 139.
78. *Surat District Gazetteer*, pp. 189–90.
79. Bell, *Abkaree Report*, p. 3. With the emergence of more centralized polities in Europe and western Asia in the late medieval period, more positive attempts were made by rulers to control and tax drink. But in practice their control was limited as drink could be manufactured easily in every village, and as a result revenues tended to be small; see Edward Baird, 'The Alcohol Problem and the Law', pp. 545–4 and R.E.F. Smith, 'Drink in Old Russia', in E.J. Hobsbawm and others (eds), *Peasants in History: Essays in Honour of Daniel Thorner* (New Delhi, 1980), pp. 45–52. The Maratha state of the eighteenth century appears to have followed in this late medieval tradition.
80. *Bombay Excise Committee Report*, vol. II, p. 301.
81. Bell, *Abkaree Report*, p. 120. The collections from Surat city were high because it was the only place in the district in which the central distillery system operated. A central distillery had been established by the British in 1816, duty being levied before the liquor was allowed to be sent out to the city shops.
82. W.B. Mulock, to R.D., 30 October 1886, BA, R.D. 1887, vol. 7, Com p. 264; *Pardi Taluka Settlement Report, 1871* (Bombay, 1904), p. 47.
83. K.H. Connell, 'Illicit Distillation', in K.H. Connell (ed.), *Irish Peasant Society: Four Historical Essays* (Oxford, 1968), pp. 36–7.
84. Tek Chand, *Report of the Study Team on Prohibition*, vol. II (New Delhi, 1964), p. 393.

85. Sidney and Beatrice Webb, *The History of Liquor Licensing in England*, pp. 50–1.
86. *Bombay Excise Committee Report*, vol. I, p. 40.
87. Bell, *Abkaree Report*, pp. 18–21.
88. *Excise Admin. Report, Bombay*, 1882–3, pp. 4–5. Hardly any arak was consumed in South Gujarat.
89. Pritchard argued that there was 'unfair competition between toddy and mhowra spirit', because toddy spirit could be distilled easily and cheaply in villages; ibid., p. 9.
90. *Acts Passed by the Governor of Bombay in Council for the year 1878–79–80* (Bombay, 1882), pp. 3–10.
91. The Kathor distillery was later closed, being replaced by one at Vyara.
92. *Excise Admin. Report, Bombay*, 1888–9, p. 45.
93. BA, R.D. 1883, vol. 6, Comp. 1127 and Comp. 1300.
94. Obituary of Dadabhai Dubash, *Times of India*, 6 November 1896.
95. Loc. cit.
96. Report by C.B. Pritchard, 21 July 1883, BA, R.D. 1883, vol. 6, Comp. 1300.
97. C.B. Pritchard to J.G. Moore, 17 March 1886, BA, R.D. 1886, vol. 328, Comp. 979.
98. BA, R.D. 1894, vol. 310, Comp. 1283.
99. Petition by 390 Parsis of Surat to Governor of Bombay, 22 July 1883, BA, R.D. 1883, vol. 6, Comp. 1300.
100. *Correspondence regarding Abkari arrangements in Baroda and the other Native States in the Bombay Presidency* (Simla, 1889), p. 13.
101. BA, R.D. 1886, vol. 328, Comp. 979.
102. Collector's Report, Surat district, 1894–5, BA, R.D. 1895, vol. 38, Comp. 1305. The district monopolists often broke the law in this manner in order to ensure high profits, and in 1907 the nationalist P.B. Dantra accused Dubash and Co. of being among the worst offenders in this respect; Memorial by P.B. Dantra to Governor of Bombay, 16 December 1907, BA, R.D. 1908, vol. 3, Comp. 99. See also P.B. Dantra's letter in *Times of India*, 13 August 1894, in which he complains about the kid-glove treatment given to Dubash and Co. by Bombay Abkari officials.
103. Dubash himself died in 1896 and the company then came under his two sons, Sorabji and Kavasji, who continued to operate the Surat monopoly.
104. *Excise Admin. Report, Bombay*, 1896–7, p. 20.
105. BA, R.D. 1890, vol. 6, Comp. 526.
106. This was in part because government regulations made it impossible to

use the old methods of distillation by which the renowned *Surti masala daru* had been manufactured; BA, R.D. 1887, vol. 7, Comp. 810.

107. *Valsad Taluka Settlement Report, 1870* (Bombay, 1900), p. 58.
108. *Jalalpor Taluka Settlement Report, 1868*, p. 27.
109. F.S.P. Lely to J.G. Moore, 22 May 1886, BA, R.D. 1887, vol. 7, Com p. 264. The great majority of tree-owners of Thana district refused to pay the tax in protest, which caused a rapid decline in toddy production. This merely played into Pritchard's hands; *Excise Admin. Report, Bombay*, 1879–80, pp. 11–12.
110. BA, R.D. 1879, vol. 6, Comp. 249.
111. *Excise Admin. Report, Bombay*, 1879–80, p. 13; W.R. Pratt to Bombay R.D., 1882, vol. 3, Comp. 191. Mandvi taluka came under the new regulations only in 1892.
112. *Excise Admin. Report, Bombay*, 1879–80, p. 31.
113. F.S.P. Lely to J.G. Moore, 22 May 1886, BA, R.D. 1887, vol. 7, Com p. 264.
114. The petition appears to have been drawn up with the help of a local Parsi called Ratanji Pestonji; petition of 3 October 1885, BA, R.D. 1886, vol. 9, Comp. 842.
115. F.S.P. Lely to C.B. Pritchard, 13 October 1884, BA, R.D. 1884, vol. 9, Comp. 1735.
116. *Excise Admin. Report, Bombay*, 1880–1, p. 18.
117. F.S.P. Lely to J.G. Moore, 22 May 1886, BA, R.D. 1887, vol. 7, Comp. 264.
118. G.L. Whitworth to collector of Surat, 2 July 1883, BA, R.D. 1883, vol. 28, Comp. 1548.
119. The Baroda government imposed the tree-tax only under protest. The dewan of Baroda informed the British Resident in 1880 that he disliked the tax as it would hit the poor particularly hard. However he had no choice but to go along with it, due to strong pressure from the Bombay government; Baroda Records Office, Huzur Political Department, R.D. Section 200, File 23.
120. *Gazetteer of the Baroda State*, vol. II (1923), p. 196.
121. Note by G.F. Shepherd, 26 November 1884, BA, R.D. 1884, vol. 9, Comp. 1735.
122. *Excise Admin. Report, Bombay*, 1882–3, pp. 5–7 and 15.
123. Collector's Report, Surat district, 1883–4, BA, R.D. 1884, vol. 32, Comp. 1548.
124. Resistance was strongest in Jalalpor taluka, but throughout the district there was widespread refusal to tap trees, so that in the district as a whole the revenue from the tree-tax fell from Rs 314,418 in 1883–4 to

Rs 252,852 in 1884–5. Pardi and Valsad were the other two talukas in which resistance was strong; Collector's Report, Surat district 1884–5, BA, R.D. 1885, vol. 33, Comp. 1548.

125. The mixture of ruthless utilitarianism and vulgar Social Darwinism evident in the thought of such officials can be seen in the statement of another Bombay official, E. Maconochie, who wrote in his settlement report of 1896 for some tribal villages of West Khandesh which bordered on South Gujarat: 'That the Bhils and Maochis can by any amount of nursing be brought to the permanent level of wellbeing of the better classes of cultivators I do not believe. Like every other primitive race they are bound to give way before the hardier survivors of a more complex struggle for existence'; *Settlement Report of 148 Villages of Nandurbar Taluka (including Navapur Petha), 17 Villages of Shirpur Taluka, and 11 Villages of Shahada Taluka* (Bombay, 1904), pp. 9–10.
126. The leading lights of this 'new conservative' school of thought were Henry Maine and Raymond West. Their ideas are reviewed in Ravinder Kumar, *Western India in the Nineteenth Century: A Study in the Social History of Maharashtra* (London, 1968), pp. 196–203.
127. Lely made this statement in a book which he wrote on his retirement called *Suggestions for the Better Governing of India. With Special Reference to the Bombay Presidency* (London, 1906), p. 30. In this book Lely made detailed recommendations as to how India should be ruled in a more sensitive, and paternalistic, manner.
128. F.S.P. Lely to C.B. Pritchard, 22 September 1884, BA, R.D. 1884, vol. 9, Comp. 1735.
129. C.B. Pritchard to F.S.P. Lely, 26 September 1884, ibid.
130. F.S.P. Lely to C.B. Pritchard, 13 October 1884, ibid.
131. Note by Sir James Fergusson, 29 November 1884, ibid.
132. Bombay Government Resolution of 15 December 1884, ibid.
133. Report by F.S.P. Lely, 24 February 1885, BA, R.D. 1885, vol. 9, Comp. 1735.
134. Bombay Government Resolution, 5 February 1886, BA, R.D. 1886, vol. 9, Comp. 842.
135. F.S.P. Lely to J.G. Moore, 22 May 1886, BA, R.D. 1887, vol. 7, Comp. 264.
136. Loc. cit.
137. Collector's Report, Surat district, 1886–7, BA, R.D. 1887, vol. 26, Comp. 1548.
138. Collector's Report, Surat district, 1888–9, BA, R.D. 1889, vol. 39, Comp. 1548.

139. Collector's Report, Surat district, 1887–8, BA, R.D. 1888, vol. 21, Comp. 1548.
140. Minute by C.B. Pritchard, 15 July 1889, BA, R.D. 1890, vol. 262, Comp. 179.
141. Collector's Report, Surat district, 1890–1, BA, R.D. 1892, vol. 26, Comp. 1600.
142. Abkari Commissioner to Bombay R.D., 13 May 1907, BA, R.D. 1907, vol. 4, Comp. 99.
143. *Excise Admin. Report, Bombay*, 1924–5, p. 1.
144. Sources for table: *Excise Admin. Reports, Bombay; Land Revenue Administration Reports for the Bombay Presidency; Baroda State Annual Administration Reports; Bansda State Annual Administration Reports.*
145. The Bombay Excise Committee of 1922–3 estimated that 6/7 of the price of country liquor consisted of tax; *Bombay Excise Committee Report*, vol. I, p. 166.
146. *Excise Admin. Report, Bombay*, 1883–4, p. 28.
147. *Excise Admin. Report, Bombay*, 1927–8, p. 18.
148. Memorandum by F.S.P. Lely, 10 January 1904, BA, R.D. 1904, vol. 3A, Comp. 729.
149. *Bombay Excise Committee Report*, vol. I, pp. 105–6.
150. Testimony of Framji Havavala (a liquor and toddy dealer), May 1923, ibid., vol. II, p. 479.
151. Testimony of Haribhai Desai, May 1923, ibid., vol. II, p. 524.
152. The experience of the peasants of South Gujarat in this respect was by no means unique. In Vietnam the French colonial authorities banned the traditional mild spirits made from special delicate varieties of rice and substituted a fiery mass-produced liquor made from cheap rice and various chemicals. In the words of Ho Chi Minh: '. . . the spirits as they are made and sold in Indo-China do not correspond, neither as to the degree nor the taste, to what the natives wish for, and they have to be imposed on them by force'; Ho Chi Minh, 'French Colonialism on Trial', *Selected Works*, vol. II (Hanoi, 1961), p. 35.
153. *Excise Admin. Report, Bombay*, 1930–1, p. 17.
154. Source: *Excise Admin. Reports, Bombay*, 1890–1 to 1939–40
155. *Bombay Excise Committee Report*, vol. I, p. 123 and vol. II, p. 309.
156. Testimony of Jamshedji Karaka, April 1923, ibid., vol. II, p. 400; *Excise Admin. Report, Bombay*, 1936–7, p. 10.
157. Compared to illicit liquor, daru from Parsi shops was as a result notoriously weak; interview with Vadsibhai Chodhri, Bedkuva (Valod taluka).
158. Testimony of Haribhai Desai, May 1923, *Bombay Excise Committee Report*, vol. II, p. 526. Jamshedji Karaka testified to the same committee

that liquor dealers made huge profits from illegal practices, and could afford to bribe well. As a result corruption was rife within the excise department. 'I have seen in the case of many men employed in this Department that they draw Rs 40 as pay, but they have a monthly household expenditure of Rs 100. Despite that they lay by something'; ibid., vol. II, p. 400.

159. *Mahuva Taluka Revision Settlement Report* (Baroda, 1916), p. 7; Khasherao Jadhav, *Opinion on the Revision Settlement Report of Mahuva Taluka* (Baroda, 1914), p. 22.
160. Sumant Mehta, *Samaj Darpan* (Ahmedabad, 1964), p. 340.
161. I.I. Desai, *Raniparajma Jagrati* (Surat, 1971), p. 34.
162. U.L. Desai of Vyara to A.D.C. to Gaikwad of Baroda, 5 December 1923, Baroda Records Office, Confidential Dept., File 301.
163. Collector's Report, Surat district, 1899–1900, BA, R.D. 1901, vol. 55, Comp. 137.
164. This form of illegal tapping was reported from Surat district in the early 1950s; *Report of the Study on the Socio-Economic Effects of Prohibition*, pp. 29–30.
165. J.G. Moore to Nugent, 30 April 1886, BA, R.D. 1886, vol. 328, Com p. 979. The Abkari police were about seventy strong, and Dubash and Co. employed an even larger private force. In 1900–1, the Surat district Abkari police detected 57 Abkari offences, whereas Dubash's men detected 151; *Excise Admin. Report, Bombay*, 1900–1, p. 9.
166. Vadsibhai Chodri of Bedkuva (Valod taluka) informed me that in the 1920s the headman of this adivasi village (himself a tribal) used to beat a drum to warn his fellow-villagers that a police raid was imminent. He had good relations with the police, and they used to warn him when a raid was planned. There was no Parsi in the village.
167. Collector's Report, Surat district, 1890–1, BA, R.D. 1892, vol. 26, Comp. 1600.
168. Collector's Report, Surat district, 1898–9, BA, R.D. 1900, vol. 33, Comp. 137.
169. J. Sladen to Abkari Commissioner, 25 August 1903, BA, R.D. 1904, vol. 4, Comp. 584.
170. *Excise Admin. Report, Bombay*, 1880–1, p. 22.
171. Note by J.L. Jenkins, 28 February 1906, BA, R.D. 1906, vol. 1, Com p. 584.
172. *Excise Admin. Report, Bombay*, 1892–3, p. 7.
173. F.S.P. Lely to R.D. Bombay, 8 July 1903, BA, R.D. 1904, vol. 4, Com p. 584.
174. Between 1896–7 and 1898–9, 66 per cent of the cases of illicit distillation

detected in Surat district were from these three talukas; J.L. Jenkins to Bombay R.D., 31 January 1901, BA, R.D. 1903, vol. 5, Comp. 1014. It is probable that illicit distillation was equally prevalent in the forests of Mandvi taluka, but that it escaped the notice of the authorities. There was little illicit distillation on the other hand in the talukas of Chorasi, Olpad and Jalalpor, and in Surat city; J. Sladen to Abkari Commissioner, 25 August 1903, BA, R.D. 1904, vol. 4, Comp. 584.

175. *Excise Admin. Report, Bombay,* 1905–6, p. 5.
176. The figures provide only a very rough indication of the prevalence of illicit distillation, as the vast majority of cases escaped detection. In 1928 the Abkari commissioner estimated, very impressionistically, that only about one in fifty cases was detected; *Excise Admin. Report, Bombay,* 1927–8, p. 19.
177. This policy of rationing will be discussed in the next section.
178. In the five years 1925–6 to 1929–30, the average number of cases of illicit distillation in Surat district per year was 235; *Excise Admin. Reports, Bombay,* 1925–6 to 1929–30.
179. *Excise Admin. Report, Bombay,* 1926–7, p. 19.
180. The annual average number of cases of illicit distillation in the five years 1930–1 to 1934–5 was ninety-three; *Excise Admin. Reports, Bombay,* 1930–1 to 1934–5.
181. The decline of the Parsis began after 1923, being brought about by a strong movement for adivasi assertion and nationalist opposition to the liquor trade, as will be described below.
182. J.P. Brander to H.O. Quin, 26 June 1914 and W. Plunkett to H.O. Quin, 10 November 1914, BA, R.D. 1914, Comp. 1948.
183. Collector's Report, Surat district, 1892–3, BA, R.D. 1893, vol. 37, Comp. 1305.
184. During the past century temperance movements of this sort have been observed in many parts of the world amongst deprived and exploited groups. An interesting parallel to the South Gujarat case is provided by an example from eastern Bolivia, where the Camba peasantry used to drink with great gusto and abandon. During the twentieth century they have increasingly given up liquor as they have joined Protestant sects and peasant leagues formed to win rights from feudal landowners. Whereas in the past the Camba peasantry had expressed their solidarity in communal drinking-bouts, they now looked upon drinking as socially disruptive. *Not* drinking now became the symbol of solidarity; Dwight B. Heath, 'Comment on David Mandelbaum's "Alcohol and Culture"', *Current Anthropology* 6:3 (June 1965), p. 290. In the gold mines of the Transvaal, opened in the 1880s, black workers opposed the oppressive

liquor regulations by starting temperance movements in the late 1890s; C. van Onselen, 'Landlords and Rotgut', pp. 73–4.

185. Collector's Report, Surat district, 1892–3, BA, R.D. 1893, vol. 37, Comp. 1305.
186. Collector's Report, Surat district, 1894–5, BA, R.D. 1895, vol. 38, Comp. 1305.
187. *Excise Admin. Report, Bombay*, 1905–6, pp. 5–9.
188. District Deputy Collector's Report, Surat district, 1905–6, BA, R.D. 1907, vol. 13, Comp. 511, pt. VI.
189. David Hardiman, 'Adivasi Assertion in South Gujarat: The Devi Movement of 1922–23', in this volume.
190. Bipin Chandra, *The Rise and Growth of Economic Nationalism in India* (New Delhi, 1966), pp. 556–61.
191. J.G. Moore, 24 November 1886, quoted in *Bombay Excise Committee Report*, vol. I, p. 45.
192. Ibid., vol. I, p. 22.
193. *Bombay Chronicle*, 14 May 1914. In his book *Suggestions for the Better Governing of India*, Lely made a scathing attack on the Abkari policy of the Bombay government. On page 22 he wrote: 'There is no other Government in the world that would treat its working classes as the Bombay Abkari Department was allowed to treat the "black races" and similar people between 1879 and 1885.'
194. Memorial by P.B. Dantra, 16 December 1907, BA, R.D. 1908, vol. 3, Comp. 99.
195. David Mandelbaum, 'Alcohol and Culture', *Current Anthropology* 6:3 (June 1965), p. 284.
196. Quoted in *Bombay Excise Committee Report*, vol. I, p. 24.
197. Presidential address to the 2nd All-India Temperance Conference, Banaras, 26 December 1905, BA, R.D. 1906, vol. 4, Comp. 729.
198. Chandra, *The Rise and Growth of Economic Nationalism*, p. 560.
199. Judith Brown, *Gandhi's Rise to Power: Indian Politics 1915–1922* (Cambridge, 1972), pp. 315–16. In Bombay Presidency, liquor consumption fell by 19 per cent as a result of picketing during Non-Cooperation; *Excise Admin. Report, Bombay*, 1921–2, p. 3. Christopher Baker has argued in the context of Madras Presidency that the power behind the anti-liquor campaign of 1921–2 came from on the one hand local liquor barons who had been stung by recent government measures imposing tighter controls over the liquor trade, and on the other from local magnates who wanted to wrest control of the liquor trade from their rivals; 'Non-Cooperation in South India', in C.J. Baker and D.A. Washbrook,

South India: Political Institutions and Political Change 1880–1940 (Madras, 1975), pp. 103–9. The problem with this argument is that it fails to give due weight to the popular dimension of the campaign, seen for instance in the strong caste-based anti-liquor movement of the Gounders of Salem and Coimbatore districts. I would argue that the real dynamics of the movement lay in such popular initiatives. This was certainly the case in Gujarat, where the local liquor magnates were greatly embarrassed by the agitation. They neither encouraged nor provided any leadership for it.

200. *Bombay Excise Committee Report*, vol. I, p. 50.
201. Ibid., vol. I, p. 164. One dram was 1/48 of a gallon.
202. Ibid., vol. I, p. 167.
203. Ibid., vol. I, pp. 59–63.
204. Ibid., vol. II, p. 140. As a counter to this argument, see A.L. Basham, *The Wonder that was India* (London, 1954), pp. 37 and 214. This shows that drinking was common in ancient India. Some authorities believe that the process of fermentation of grain to produce beers and the process of distillation of liquor were both invented in India. See Edwin Loeb, 'Primitive Intoxicants', *Quarterly Journal of Studies on Alcohol* 4:3 (December 1943), p. 388; Horton, 'The Functions of Alcohol in Primitive Societies', p. 210.
205. *Bombay Excise Committee Report*, vol. I, p. 65.
206. *Report of the Prohibition (Finance) Committee, Bombay Presidency* (Bombay, 1927).
207. Rani Dhavan Shankardass, *The First Congress Raj: Provincial Autonomy in Bombay* (New Delhi, 1982), pp. 220–1.
208. Congress Report of 1929, Nehru Memorial Library, New Delhi, All India Congress Committee Papers, file 114 of 1929.
209. Fortnightly Report for the Bombay Presidency, second half of December 1929.
210. Fortnightly Report for Baroda State, first half of October 1928; Fortnightly Report for Baroda State, second half of February 1929; Fortnightly Report for Baroda State, second half of December 1929.
211. Shankardass, *The First Congress Raj*, pp. 223–36.
212. After the merger of the princely states in 1947–8, Surat district included the whole of the old British district, Navsari district of Baroda state, and the princely states of Dharampur, Sachin and Vansda. The Dangs became a separate district, being awarded to Gujarat at the bifurcation of Gujarat and Maharashtra in 1960. Surat district was subsequently divided into two districts in 1964 (Surat and Valsad).
213. *Report of the Study on the Socio-Economic Effects of Prohibition*, p. 6.

214. Tek Chand, *Report of the Study Team on Prohibition*, vol. II, p. 38.
215. Interview with Jatriya Gamit in Nanabandharpada village of Songadh taluka.
216. Interview with Vadsibhai Chodhri in Bedkuva village of Valod taluka.
217. Interview with Jagubhai Chodhri in Balethi village of Mandvi taluka.
218. I.I. Desai, *Raniparajma Jagrati* (Surat, 1971), p. 30.
219. B.H. Mehta, 'Social and Economic Conditions of the Chodhras', p. 178; interview with Becharbhai Chodhri in Makanjher village of Mandvi taluka.
220. Harish Doshi and Vidyut Joshi, 'Benefits of Prohibition (A Study of the Drinkers and the Non-Drinkers—Rural)', unpublished Gujarat Government Report, 1976.
221. Ibid., p. 50.
222. Ibid., pp. 121–2.
223. Ibid., pp. 37–45 and 60–4.
224. Ibid., pp. 45–9.
225. *Pratab* (Surat), 10 March 1981.
226. *Excise Admin. Reports, Bombay*, 1900–1 to 1909–10.
227. This link between drinking and so-called 'crime' is often taken by an intellectual sleight of hand to mean that drinking is a root cause of crime and anti-social behaviour. Thus the *Report of the Study on the Socio-Economic Effects of Prohibition* by the team of sociologists of Bombay University stated (p. 27) that: 'Figures regarding crimes and addiction have been difficult to collect, but it was observed by interviewers that the majority of the crimes of loot and murder are committed by intoxicated persons . . . Thus the whole rural community seems to have undergone a psychological metamorphosis from the calm, quiet and peaceful abode of nature, to one of hatred, distress, and warring criminals. The unwillingness to work, the happy-go-lucky attitude towards life, the indifference and "Don't Bother" way of looking at things, all these have blasted up the most lovely and harmonious atmosphere of villages and turned them into small battlefield of mutual jealousies and avoidable conflicts.' This statement not only reveals certain bizarre attitudes towards drink held by some members of the Indian middle classes, but also shows a blinkered lack of appreciation that in this case it is the law and not drink which creates 'crime'.
228. In certain parts of India, such as Orissa, adivasi families are permitted to distil and keep up to five litres of country liquor for personal consumption; *India Today*, 30 April 1983, p. 71. That it is possible for older, more healthy drinks to regain their position after an epidemic of bad hooch is shown by the history of drink in eighteenth-century London, where

traditional ales were replaced by fiery, ultra-cheap gin during the first half of the century. During the second half of the century high taxes were placed on this gin and ale soon regained its position as the most widely-consumed drink; Hans Medik, 'Plebian Culture in the Transition to Capitalism', pp. 103–5. Doshi and Joshi found that many of the people of South Gujarat who drank illicit daru would have preferred to have been able to drink toddy if it had been available, as they considered it good for the health, unlike the available daru; 'Benefits of Prohibition', p. 34.

CHAPTER 6

Usury, Dearth and Famine in Western India

I

Dearth and famine are among the greatest social crises which a society can face, and the ways in which people have responded to them have been found to provide 'a revealing commentary upon a society's deeper and more enduring difficulties'.[1] In particular, histories of such responses can help us to understand how the poor have attempted to negotiate, resist and challenge the structures of power which have denied them the necessary means of survival.

Societies in which peasant agriculture has been the chief productive force have tended to be particularly vulnerable to dearth and famine. The prime reason for this is that the peasantry have been a subaltern group under the domination of classes which have, as a matter of course, taken such a large proportion of the harvest on such a regular basis that not enough has been left to see them through even rather minor natural or man-made calamities.[2] Each year peasants have had the anxiety of hoping that their inadequate supply of grain will last until the next harvest. Often, the months before the crops ripen have been ones of privation, and if the expected crop has then failed the threat of starvation has loomed. In such a situation peasants are forced to depend on handouts from the classes which have appropriated the bulk of their food supply, who may be landlords, state officials or merchant-usurers.

Very commonly, the relationship of exploitation involved a notion of 'credit', with the dominant classes asserting that the handouts which they gave were 'advances' which had to be repaid with augmented interest at harvest time. If the harvest was inadequate, only a portion of the so-called 'debt' could be repaid, the rest running on enhanced by interest till the next year, and usually beyond that. In practice, most peasants were in a condition of perpetual 'indebtedness' of this sort. In this respect, dearth and usury were for the peasant two sides of the one coin, with dearth creating the need to 'borrow', while high 'debt repayments' ensured that dearth was never far away and famine always a possibility. The majority of peasants were thus trapped in a cycle of dearth and debt.

This predicament gave rise, during periods of shortage, to demands by the poor and counter-arguments by the rich. These have been highlighted in a particularly succinct form in Shakespeare's *Coriolanus.* In 1607, the year before the play was written, there had been a series of riots and other protests by peasants pushed to the margins by enclosing landlords. The outbreaks, in a year of dearth, were strongest in Leicestershire, Northamptonshire and Shakespeare's own native Warwickshire.[3] The conflicting sentiments voiced by the Roman plebeians and patricians of the play reflect, we may assume, altercations heard at the time in England.

The play begins with a crowd of hungry plebeians resolving to take direct action to compel the Roman authorities to bring down the high price of grain. They assert that the dearth has been caused by the greed of the rich, involving usury, hoarding of grain and profiteering, and that in fact there is plenty of grain for all:

> What authority surfeits on would relieve us . . . Our sufferance is a gain to them . . . [The patricians] suffer us to famish, and their store-houses crammed with grain; make edicts for usury, to support usurers; repeal daily any wholesome act established against the rich, and provide more piercing statutes daily to chain up and restrain the poor.

The plebeians thus assert that there are adequate stocks to provide some sort of subsistence if distributed equitably. Hence their demand, backed by force if need be, for the rich to open up the granaries.

The patricians, for their part, counter that the shortage of grain is caused by the will of the gods. In the words of Menenius Agrippa:

> I tell you, friends, most charitable care
> Have the patricians of you. For your wants,
> Your suffering in this dearth, you may as well
> Strike at the heaven with your staves as lift them

Against the Roman state, whose course will on
The way it takes, cracking ten thousand curbs
Of more strong link asunder than can ever
Appear in your impediment. For the dearth,
The gods, not the patricians, make it, and
Your knees to them, not arms, must help. Alack,
You are transported by calamity
Thither where more attends you, and you slander
The helms o'th'state, who care for you like fathers,
When you curse them as enemies.

According to this patrician, the shortage had been caused by the elements, as determined by the gods. Their charitable efforts to provide grain could, in such a circumstance, be only limited. The plebeians were enjoined to resist the temptation to blame the rich. They were, rather, to be patient and not tempt fate by taking any precipitous action, such as rioting. In the play, the arguments of the patricians prevail, the riot is averted, and the hegemony of the ruling class maintained. In reality, we know that the dearth of 1607 gave rise to rioting, suppressed with bloodshed by the Midlands gentry.

What the plays brings out with great clarity is that dominant classes have, characteristically, sought to deny their culpability for dearth and famine, while seeking to legitimize their position by claiming at such times that they would do their best to ensure some sort of subsistence for the poor. They represented this as a sentiment which flowed from the goodness of their hearts, being a matter of paternal generosity or charity. The poor, by contrast, have seen this as a matter of elementary justice. They have, they assert, handed over a large proportion of their surplus to the rich, and the latter have a duty to maintain them. If the rich failed in this respect, they were quite justified in taking direct action to force them to disgorge their ill-gotten gains. James Scott has described this as the popular belief in 'the right to subsistence'. He considers this to have been one of the primary moral expectations of peasants, constituting a central element of 'the moral economy of the peasant'—a concept which he adapted from E.P. Thompson's 'moral economy of the poor'.[4] A failure by members of the dominant classes in this respect caused great resentment, and was often a cause of resistance.

Like Thompson, Scott focuses in his work on a period of transition.

For Thompson, this was the transition to capitalism, with the enforcement, in particular, of free-trade policies. For Scott, whose study is of Southeast Asia, the transition was from pre-colonial to colonial rule. He argues that a moral economy operated in this region without any very severe ruptures until the colonial conquest of the nineteenth century. It was then fractured in a variety of ways, generating tensions which led to widespread peasant revolts. Similarly, studies of South India by David Arnold and of Sri Lanka by John Rogers have shown that after 1860 grain riots were caused by the rigid enforcement of free-trade policies by the British colonial state in a way which violated popular moralities and expectations in years of shortages and high grain prices.[5]

Examples from European history show that even before the period of transition to capitalism, food riots were an ever-present possibility when the dominant classes failed to ensure sustenance to the poor in years of grain shortages and high prices.[6] The same was true in China, with grain riots taking place long before any moves were made to transform the society in a capitalist direction. R. Bin Wong's study of eighteenth- and nineteenth-century China reveals that there was a strong belief among the Chinese poor in a right to subsistence, but in this pre-capitalist context the dominant classes accepted their obligation to try to satisfy this demand. Sometimes, however, they failed to provide in the way expected, and this could lead to popular action to force the opening up of food supplies. These conflicts occurred periodically, but became more prevalent, Wong argues, when imperial authority began to decay in the nineteenth century. Grain rioting fed into major upsurges, notably the Taiping rebellion of the 1850s, which developed into a serious threat to the overall power of the Chinese state.[7]

In a comment on Wong's article, as well as in other writings concerned with the Bengal famine of 1943–4, Paul Greenhough has argued that none of these arguments were true for Bengal. There, patron-client relationships involving reciprocal forms of exchange were sanctioned by an ideology of hierarchy—seen most obviously in the caste system—which legitimized the role of the patron, and by a belief that rank in the hierarchy as well as prosperity flowed from divine indulgence rather than from active endeavour. Because of this, the peasants suffered in fatalistic silence during periods of dearth and famine, and there were no grain riots in Bengal involving a demand for a 'right to subsistence'.[8]

Greenhough's arguments have already been subjected to critical scrutiny by E.P. Thompson and Roger Wells, and I do not intend to repeat their comments here, except to say that I largely agree with them.[9] A valid point he does make, however, is that almost everyone in rural Bengal, whether rich or poor, shared a belief that dearth and famine were caused by supernatural design. What does not follow is his assumption that this necessarily led to passivity on the part of the peasants. As James Scott has shown, shared cultures and systems of belief have never precluded the possibility of resistance. Rather, they have provided a parameter for structured conflicts which have been waged according to rules understood by all the parties involved. Passivity in certain circumstances has to be seen, therefore, as merely a tactic employed by the poor out of temporary necessity.[10]

As I shall try to show in this essay, the poor have time and time again refused to accept that they were helpless victims of fate. They saw very clearly that in times of dearth and famine the rich were the winners and they the losers, and quite logically—given the structure of their beliefs—sought to oppose what they assumed was divine support for the rich by appealing to the gods and spirits of nature using their own prayers and rituals. As these were often designed to counter the rituals of hoarders and profiteers, this could create tension and even cause outright conflict.[11]

Another assumption which informs Greenhough's work is that Indian villages were only marginally integrated into a market economy, and that exchange was to a large extent characterized by reciprocity and redistribution of goods in kind.[12] This view has been contradicted in recent years by several studies of the period between *c.*1650 and 1850 which have shown how strongly commercialized the Indian economy was at all levels in both the pre-colonial and colonial periods.[13]

In this essay I shall take up some of these issues relating to the moral economy of the peasants during periods of dearth and famine in the context of western India. For my purposes, this area will include western Maharashtra, Gujarat and Rajasthan. I shall start by using some of the new writings on the working of the Indian commercial economy to map out the socio-economic and political context of marketing and credit relationships in the late pre-colonial and colonial periods. I shall argue that in this respect the crucial 'moral economy' relationship in western India was that between merchant-usurers and peasants. I shall try to show how the system operated, or failed to operate, during periods of dearth, and the ways in which the peasants responded when the 'protection' of their usurer-patrons failed.

As already suggested, conflicts in these respects were not confined to the sphere of economic exchange alone, but also extended into the realm of the supernatural. By examining the operation of power in this area, it is possible to broaden the concept of 'moral economy' to include what Bob Scribner has called 'the economy of the sacred'—that is, the sphere in which people seek to control the profane and exercise power through access to the supernatural.[14] In the case of western India there was a belief that usurers were able to intervene with gods and spirits so as to alter the weather to their advantage. In examining these beliefs here, I have mostly had to utilize the writings of folklorists. On the whole, works in this genre are vague on details of chronology, date and place, so that it is hard to ascertain how such beliefs and practices have evolved and changed over time. Although the evidence available to me is hardly adequate at this stage to write a history of this sphere of power, some attempts in this direction will be made towards the end of the essay.

II

In seventeenth- and eighteenth-century India, the purchase, storing, trading and transport of grain took place largely in the sphere of commercial capital. Unlike in China, the state exercised only a loose control over this sphere, and did not maintain state granaries or regulate merchants to any great extent. The trade in grain was dominated by members of mercantile castes and communities, the most important of which by far was that of the Baniyas. Members of this and related communities operated their own networks which stretched from village to state capital. Baniya traders-cum-usurers acquired agrarian produce from the peasantry and transported it to the towns, keeping some in private grain-stores (often in the merchants' own houses), and selling some on the market. Artisanal manufacturers—notably the large numbers of handloom weavers who found employment in

India—were advanced loans in cash and kind by dealers, and in return handed over the manufactured product. Foodstuffs and manufactured commodities were transported for sale in large quantities over long distances in packs on the backs of bullocks, horses and camels. These animals, normally owned by members of the Banjara mercantile community, were driven in caravans, often made up of thousands of animals. Merchants in small towns maintained banking and credit arrangements with larger merchants in the cities, with payments being transmitted by bills of exchange.

This allowed for the operation of an elaborate system of credit, in which small merchant-usurers borrowed capital for their own operations at low rates of interest, repaying the loans through the sale of the crops or manufactured goods on which they had a lien. Likewise, the larger town-based merchants and dealers took loans from bigger city-based bankers, again repaying through the sale of exported produce.

State rulers and officials worked in close cooperation with this mercantile structure. The chief form of tax was that on agrarian produce, levied on the peasant family unit according to either the size of its crop or the amount of land which it cultivated. The money to pay this tax was often provided by the village traders-cum-usurers, with a bill of exchange of equivalent value being handed over to an official. This was then treated by the usurer as a debt, to be collected from the peasant family at a later date in cash or kind. The officials took the bills of exchange to a local town, where they presented them to a larger merchant banker, who would normally provide a consolidated bill of exchange which could in turn be presented to a city banker. These top-level bankers acted as the chief financiers to rulers, in effect running their financial affairs. By this means, the tax system operated without the need for the exchange and transport of much actual cash.[15]

The chief feature of this system was the close interlinking of usury, banking, manufacture and the storage and marketing of crops, in particular foodgrain. The occupational term for people engaged in a cluster of such activities was that of sahukar. The sahukars who advanced credit to particular peasant families tended to be clustered in towns and large villages, serving a number of smaller villages round about. They would normally keep a shop, stocked with grain, cloth, vegetable oil, salt, ironware and other necessities, which were advanced to their clients—along with small sums in cash—as and when needed. Larger loans were provided to cover the state demand for land-tax, and to pay for new livestock or agricultural or manufacturing equipment, for the celebration of births and marriages, for mourning at times of death, and for religious rites. In return, clients had to hand over a large proportion of their produce. The normal practice was for a sahukar to come at harvest time with his carts to the threshing-floor used by a client family and demand that they hand over the greater proportion of the harvested crop. To maintain their future credit, the family had little choice but to comply. By this means, the usurers expropriated the fruits of much of their clients' labour.

For the most part, peasants were considered to have a customary right to cultivate an ancestral holding, a right which could not normally be taken from them by the state or other dominant classes. In Rajasthan, for example, there was a popular adage to the effect that the government was entitled to tax, but the peasant was master of the land.[16] In contrast to medieval Europe or early modern Russia, there was no system of serfdom. The peasants were, rather, bound by debt. In return for loans, it was common for them to mortgage the bulk of the crops in advance to their sahukar.

D.D. Kosambi has argued that for over two thousand years usury has played a central role in India in the expropriation of a surplus from subordinate groups, performing the same function there as slavery in ancient Greece and Rome and serfdom in medieval Europe. In his work he demonstrated how forms of usury evolved in ancient India, changing in nature and increasing in importance over time.[17] From around the sixth to the thirteenth centuries, such usury appears to have been closely connected with the priestly classes, notably brahmans, and temple institutions.[18] The occupation of sahukar seems to have emerged around the fourteenth century, being associated with a growth of trade and a greater extension of state authority and state taxation under the Delhi sultanate.[19] The state provided full support for commercial capitalists who advanced loans to peasant and artisan producers, enabling a great expansion of agriculture and manufacturing to take place. In return, the sahukars ensured that a proportion of the surplus found its way into the state coffers.

In India, usury was a specialist occupation which enjoyed strong state support. The state made little effort to regulate the practice, for instance by trying to peg interest rates at a particular level. This was in marked contrast to medieval Europe, where professional usury was considered a marginal and disreputable profession and the taking of any interest over and above *lucrum cessans*—the profit which the commercial capitalist would have made himself if he had kept the money to trade with—was condemned.[20] There the credit system operated in a largely concealed way, with nobles, priests and wealthy peasants providing loans as a side occupation.[21] In early modern Russia, where the commercial structure was poorly developed, landlords provided the bulk of credit for their serfs. There was little provision of credit by professional usurers, and as a class they were despised by gentry and government officials alike.[22] Therefore, although credit was always important in these other peasant societies, professional usury was not institutionalized so as to have been central to the system of surplus appropriation.

In India by contrast, no stigma was attached to the occupation of professional usurer. Being closely connected with ruling authority, usurers had acquired strong cultural validation for their activity. This is reflected in the etymology of the word sahukar itself, which stems from the words *sadhu* ('a good, righteous and holy person') and *kar* ('a doer'). Thus the sahukar was 'a doer of good and righteous deeds', a person who provided 'help' to the needy in the form of loans.[23] In Rajasthan and much of north India, the sahukar is also known as *mahajan* or 'great man', a title with similar connotations. The terminology itself thus provided the occupation with a strong stamp of respectability.

The profession was dominated in western India by members of the Baniya caste. This caste was indigenous to Gujarat and Rajasthan, where commercial capital was particularly strongly developed from the fourteenth century onwards, but was not found very early in Maharashtra, where commerce was relatively undeveloped before the seventeenth century. Baniyas migrated from Gujarat and Rajasthan to Maharashtra from the seventeenth century, and by the end of the eighteenth century were playing a key role in the expansion of business and usury there. In Maharashtra, Baniyas were known as 'Gujars' if they came from Gujarat, or 'Marwaris' if they came from Rajasthan, as most of these Rajasthani Baniyas had migrated from the Marwar area of that region.

The typical Baniya business was a family concern, controlled by a male head of household. Business ethos and skills were inculcated amongst male members of the caste from an early age, with boys being required to sit in the family shop in a subordinate position in order to learn the trade. Baniya women were not expected to play an active role in the business, and were practically all illiterate. Boys were taught to be frugal—and to know how to seize the least chance to turn a situation to financial advantage. This included various forms of swindling and short-changing of clients: a feature common to most bazaar-style markets, in which goods are typically unbranded and sold loose, and where profits tend to be made by adulteration and short measure rather than by price competition.[24]

The dubious nature of these practices was well understood by the peasants, as proverbial lore about Marwari Baniyas bears witness:

> While weighing with scales he shoves them down surreptitiously with his wrist. . . . In capturing his victim he employs all the cunning of a deer-trapper. He overvalues and exaggerates the weight of what he gives, and he undervalues and underweighs what he gives by a quarter. Thus he is none but a Baori [a caste known for petty theft] in the guise of a Baniya.[25]

Therefore, although Baniyas were considered 'respectable', there was also a sharp awareness of the disreputable methods they used to augment their earnings and accumulate capital.

Baniyas maintained a strong corporate organization, with their own systems of self-regulation and self-government through town-based or regional caste councils. These ensured that members of the caste adhered to a high standard of business probity in dealing with other Baniyas, as well as conforming to strict standards of social be-haviour, including marrying only within particular endogamous Baniya subcastes, avoiding dining with members of other castes, and observing rigid dietary rules, including abstinence from meat. Because of this, the Baniyas tended to stand apart from other groups in society. They were also known for their strong adherence to the Jain religion or the Vallabhacharya Vaishnavite sect, both faiths that validated the pursuit of wealth while enjoining charitable behaviour as a means of winning divine merit.[26]

The British conquered western India during the first two decades of the nineteenth century, establishing direct rule in most of western

Maharashtra, the core regions of Gujarat and the enclave of Ajmer-Merwara in Rajasthan. The rest of western India was left under the control of Indian princes, who were permitted some degree of control over the internal management of their principalities while being kept under close watch by the colonial state. The British implemented various policies which had the effect of greatly enhancing the power of local usurers.

Although they dispensed with the services of the large indigenous commercial bankers and established their own treasuries, the British continued to depend on local-level usurers to supply the bulk of credit to the peasants. Until well into the second half of the nineteenth century, colonial tax collectors often took the tax directly from the sahukars, who then took the money along with their own debt-servicing instalments directly from their clients. Although this meant that the usurers were enriching themselves at the peasants' expense, the British did not try to provide any alternative systems of credit such as government loans, which were felt to be cumbersome and expensive to operate.

The British established a new system of civil law which could be used to enforce debt repayments. The existing system of customary enforcement of debt agreements was thus replaced with a system of contract, enforced by law.[27] Courts were established which could be used by creditors to take out cases against debtors, using loan agreements as evidence of contract. The courts were legally obliged to enforce the repayment of a proven and documented debt, if necessary by selling up the property and even the agricultural land of the debtor. Usurers could now extend their power over their clients with the help of the judicial apparatus of the state. Peasants, lacking access to lawyers and hardly understanding the new system of justice, were left in a very weak position.

The British also established a new system of land rights, which involved measuring all agricultural land and providing land-title-deeds to the holders. The peasants were not, however, considered the outright owners, but tenants of the state who could be removed from their holdings if they failed to pay their land-tax, on the grounds that such payments represented a 'rent' to the state. This was a radical departure from the previous system, in which the state was not considered to have any general right of dispossession of peasant proprietors. Under the new regime, eviction could be ordered either by a member of the tax bureaucracy or by the civil court, with the land being auctioned to the highest bidder. The new title-deeds, once granted, provided an excellent security for debt. If usurers so wished, they could, using this security, sell up their clients, turning them into tenants at will.[28]

The colonial state also broke with existing practice by refusing to exercise any check on hoarding and profiteering by sahukars. It was a part of the logic of commercial capital that the greater the scarcity the greater the profit, and sahukars characteristically sought to induce such scarcities by refusing to release produce in their stores into the market. As the sahukars of a place would act in unity in this respect, they were usually able to achieve the desired effect, unless checked either by popular protest or state action. To prevent popular disturbance, pre-colonial rulers had always maintained a right to prevent hoarding and profiteering by merchants and to prevent the export of grain from scarcity-hit areas. These powers were often used.[29]

The British refused to exercise any such controls over markets. They were guided in this by the writings of Adam Smith, who held that high prices in a bad year were beneficial because they fostered frugality and thrift among consumers, thus (as it were) acting to ration scarce resources, as well as providing an incentive to merchants to import grain from elsewhere.[30] In this, there was no appreciation of the corporate power of commercial groups such as the Baniyas, who could control whole regional markets to their advantage with no difficulty at all if not checked by the state. The implementation of the policy of *laissez-faire* in the market—supported if necessary by the deployment of soldiers and police to prevent popular disturbance—provided the sahukars with a strong institutional backing for their profiteering. Not surprisingly, they took full advantage of this situation.

III

The relationship between a sahukar family business and a peasant household was a very personal one, commonly stretching back for generations on both sides. The chief advantages for sahukar families in having such an arrangement were that they had a detailed and long-standing knowledge of the affairs of the peasant family, and that members of the client family were yoked to the arrangement from birth, allowing the business to continue smoothly over the decades. Also, the sahukar concern did not have to worry about competition from other family businesses, so that they were free to impose harsher terms on their own clients. Each sahukar family was considered by others to have a right to business with a particular client family, and sahukars who tried to poach on the territory of others were likely to be censured or even boycotted by their community. Thus members of a peasant family who attempted to change from one usurer to another were likely to receive short shrift.

For a peasant family, the chief advantage was that the members of the sahukar family with which they dealt were familiar with them and their needs and had a certain sense of obligation towards them. To a large extent, this obligation was a matter of hard interest on the part of the sahukars, for if a client family became destitute its debt could no longer be serviced. In the words of one commentator: 'However hard-hearted a Bania may be, he will in most cases try to save his client. He will never try to ruin him . . . [for he] wants to suck him alive . . .'[31]

It was in this respect that a moral economy could be seen to operate in western India. It was based on the transaction which occurred at the peasant's threshing-floor immediately after the harvest, when a member of the Baniya family would come with a cart and demand the bulk of the crop from the client family. The peasant family, with much entreaty, would try to keep as much as possible for themselves. The Baniya would counter: 'What need you care? When yours is done you can have as much as you like from my shop.'[32] In return for taking the produce, the sahukar thus promised to sustain the client family when it ran out of food before the next harvest, and provide seed-grain to sow before the next rains. If the monsoon rains were poor in the following season, the sahukars might provide a trickle of handouts from their hoards of grain while stressing their munificence towards 'their' family. Reports suggest that this indeed happened at times. For example, during a drought in Ajmer-Merwara in Rajasthan in 1848–9 the Baniyas were said to have provided food for their clients at considerable expense to themselves. As a result, the peasants did not migrate out of the area in search of food.[33]

The peasants tried to hold the sahukars to their promises through a language of obligation which stressed the duty of the rich to nurture the poor. There was, for instance, a Rajasthani proverb, whose gist was that as grain sustained life, those who had it had an obligation to supply it to those who did not.[34] Likewise, it was common to hear the refrain in a Baniya's shop: 'You are our sahukar, you look after us.'[35] Using deferential tones which warmed the patriarchal self-esteem of the Baniya male whom they were addressing, peasant-clients sought in this way to remind their 'protector' of his duty.

This 'protection' very frequently broke down during periods of severe famine, for the resources of a sahukar firm had its limits. Its stocks of grain and capital were generally adequate to provide some sort of basic subsistence to clients during one or two years of harvest failure. But if there were a succession of bad years beyond this, or per-haps a year of unusually severe harvest failure or some other calamity, the business might itself be in trouble. Most small sahukars financed their operations by borrowing from indigenous urban bankers, their chief security being the debts which they had built up with peasant-clients, and which allowed them a lien on the crops. A secondary secur-ity was the store of grain held in their house. When peasants were un-able to produce any crop, or when the sahukars' stores of grain began to give out, the urban bankers became unwilling to advance them the capital they required to keep their businesses going. In the words of one district officer, the sahukars:

> have in turn to go for their capital to the big capitalists, and in a bad year they cannot get much advance from them—for not having received any crop from the agriculturists they cannot pay the annual instalment due to these capitalists. So the withdrawal of credit from the agriculturists is often due more to inability than to want of sympathy.[36]

It was because of this that a succession of poor seasons could lead to a gradual drying up of capital for the smaller sahukars, leading to a year of actual famine. In a year of a dramatic and almost complete failure of rain or in the event of some major crisis, the urban bankers normally refused to give advances to the smaller Baniyas immediately. Thus, even if a sahukar wanted to help his clients at such a time, he was often in no position to provide adequate aid, due to the loss of his own credit with bankers who had no personal ties with the peasants.

In such an event, the large majority of usurers were moved more by a sense of self-protection rather than obligation. They might calculate very carefully which of their clients they could afford to support, and which not. A British official who served in Ahmadnagar district during the famine of 1876–7 said later that it 'is a mistake to suppose that in the last famine the rayats were generally supported by their savkars. In one of my talukas I took a census in December 1876 and found that one-third of the population had gone. Whole villages were deserted.' On the whole, he went on to say, only the better-off and more credit-worthy peasants had received help, while the poorer peasants had been left largely to sift for themselves.[37] These poorer peasants flocked to the towns to beg from the wealthy urban sahukars. The fact that it is repeatedly recorded that peasants were forced to leave their villages in this manner reveals the absence of any wide-scale village-based maintenance of peasants by sahukars during severe famines from the pre-colonial to the colonial period.

IV

Despite this, Baniyas took great pride in their 'charity'. In the words of N.N. Vyas, writing on the Baniya mahajans, or sahukars, of south-ern Rajasthan:

> The *mahajan* claimed that with all of his economic strength, he had always stood by the village community in the days of drought, famine and hardship and had proved useful to the members of the village in their social and ritual needs and commitments. Thus the *mahajan* proclaimed that he was the saviour of the people.[38]

To give credence to the claim, they reminded their clients of illustrious deeds performed by members of their caste in past times of famine. In Gujarat, for example, there was a well-known legend about a thirteenth-century Jain Baniya merchant called Jagdusha who, it was said, was forewarned by a sadhu that there would be a great famine in Gujarat, Saurashtra and Kutch lasting for three years. He accordingly had his agents bring huge amounts of corn from distant countries, which he then hoarded. The famine came in 1255–8, and after two years even the royal granary was empty. When the king asked him for a loan of grain, Jagdusha refused, pointing out that a copperplate inscription in his granaries declared that 'these grains of corns are collected only for the poor'. Jagdusha then began distributing the grain he had stored, and thus saved the country from starvation. The famine was subsequently known to the people as 'Jagdusha's famine'.[39]

Perhaps the name was appropriate, seeing that Jagdusha most probably caused it in the first place through his hoarding. This was not, however, how the Baniyas sought to commemorate his achievement. In 1319 a Jain scholar, Sarvananadusuri, composed a long panegyric called *Jagducharit*, which sought to show how Jagdusha had saved the people through his foresight and charity.[40] In Rajkot, Saurashtra, his admirers erected a tower on the banks of the Aji river so as to keep alive the memory of his deeds. Throughout Saurashtra, according to a nineteenth-century source, his name continued to be 'remembered with honour by all classes'.[41] In this respect, Jagdusha was made to epitomize the 'good Baniya', providing an ideal of charity to which all Baniyas were supposed to aspire. It was clearly in the interests of the peasants to remind the usurers of Jagdusha's example, demanding that they also provide sustenance in times of famine. It was for this, above all, that the peasants remembered him and other legendary Baniya philanthropists.

There is no doubt that in both pre-colonial and colonial times, Baniya charity could in certain circumstances play in important role in alleviating suffering during famine. A document of 1593–4 records that Karamchandra of Bikaner opened centres for the distribution of food to the poor during times of dearth.[42] In Gujarat during the same period, the Jain Baniya brothers Rajio and Vajio Parekh of Cambay distributed four thousand maunds of grain and spent nearly two million rupees to help the poor in a single year. In the great famine of 1631–2, Shantidas of Ahmedabad is said to have saved many from death through his charity.[43] In colonial times the sahukars of Sholapur fed thousands of people for several weeks during the drought of 1832–3.[44] When, in 1868–9 there was famine in Bikaner state, 'early in October 1868 the starving had begun to flock into the towns, and the Seths [Baniya sahukars] in Surajgarh and the neighbourhood established small relief funds, which were soon exhausted. But a certain amount of food was daily distributed by many of the well-to-do merchants.'[45] In the famine of 1891-2 in Ajmer-Merwara, the Baniyas of

Nayanagar organized the distribution of cooked food to the hungry, paid for from a charitable fund raised by taxing each transaction in the bazaar at the rate of one pice per rupee. Some wealthy merchants distributed charity on their own initiative.[46] During the famine of 1899–1900 in Gujarat, the Baniyas of Ahmedabad city were generous with relief. Two cheap grain-shops were established and large numbers were provided with cooked food.[47]

These examples all relate to city-dwelling Baniyas, who appear to have fed destitute people after they had been forced through hunger to leave their villages and flock to the city hoping for sustenance. The crowds in the streets were full of suffering and expectation; charity provided the means to defuse some of the tension. It tended to be given fairly randomly, being designed to impress the popular imagination rather than systematically alleviate the problem. There is no evidence that these city-based sahukars attempted to extend their charity to the villages. There, as we have seen, charity by the usurers who dealt directly with the peasants was noticeably lacking.

V

In fact, rather than showing any compassionate concern, most sahukars welcomed the prospect of dearth and turned even the worst famines to their advantage. In the words of a British judge, writing about the Baniyas of Ahmadnagar district in 1846: 'They glory in the prospect of a bad season, as affording to them the opportunity of being able to acquire with greater celerity that which is the object and soul of their pursuit . . .'[48] In a poor year, grain was in short supply and prices were high. Because the peasants had normally pledged much of their crop in advance, they were obliged to hand over whatever meagre amount they had harvested and then take handouts from the sahukars which were debited at highly inflated rates. The sahukars might also force the peasants to hand over jewellery, ornaments and other possessions in return for small amounts of grain. During the famine of 1899–1900 the poor peasants of Surat district handed over their brass and pewter arm- and leg-ornaments to their sahukars in return for handouts of grain. One usurer was subsequently reported to have sold off several tons of such ornaments.[49] The Ahmadnagar judge quoted above went on to say that the Baniyas took 'an iniquitous advantage of the wretched situation of the Ryots to sell them grain of so wretched a quality that cattle would have turned away from it'. They were thus able to offload their oldest grain, which otherwise would have been practically worthless, and in return appropriating the peasants' belonging at minimal cost.

In a situation of shortage, when the peasants had little purchasing-power, sahukars were always tempted to export grain so that they could take advantage of high prices in the cities and neighbouring regions. In the past, such temptations had been checked by the physical difficulty of moving large stocks of grain with any speed, and also by bans on exports imposed by indigenous rulers. But the British refused to impose such bans, and then compounded the problem by developing a far more efficient system of transport. The coming of the railways to India in the second half of the nineteenth century allowed grain to be exported from areas of low purchasing power so quickly and on such a scale as not only to aggravate existing shortages, but even create famines in areas where they might not otherwise have occurred.

For example, a railway line had been built through the Panchmahals district during the 1890s. After the monsoon failed in 1899 the sahukars took advantage of this new facility to export large quantities of grain from the district at a time when the peasants were facing starvation. A deputy collector commented: 'The merchants first cleared large profits by exporting their surplus stocks of grain at the commencement of famine, and, later on by importing maize from Cawnpore and Bombay and rice from Calcutta and Rangoon.'[50] He went on to state that the sahukars had managed to build, or were in the course of building, a large number of new houses for themselves from the profits of this enterprise.

By means such as these the sahukars were able to exhaust the peasants' savings and at the same time mire them deeper in debt. During the famine of 1899–1900 in Rajasthan, the Baniyas only helped their clients on condition that they first accepted new bonds in which their old debts were augmented by the new.[51] During the same famine in Gujarat, some peasants of Kheda district complained to the government that: '. . . moneylenders instead of giving any assistance to the cultivators in these days of scarcity, demand the repayment of their loans and compel the cultivators to assign their lands as security for the loans, the value of such security being far in excess of the money due to them'.[52] In the years after the famine, the sahukars gradually foreclosed on these debts, turning many peasants into their tenants. Figures for land sales and mortgages in Baroda state showed a 91 per cent rise in recorded transactions between the decade before the famine of 1899–1900 and that after it. A large number of these transfers took place in 1902–3, soon after the famine had ended. Whereas during the decade before the famine there had been on average 13,057 such transfers each year, in 1902–3 there were no fewer than 65,060.[53]

In some cases these transfers were made in a very underhand way. For example, in those areas of Baroda situated in South Gujarat, after the famine was over many poor peasants were unable to pay the arrears of land-tax which had accumulated during the years of dearth. Rather than waive these demands, as might have been expected as the peasants were destitute, the local tax officials made arrangements with local sahukars for them to pay for their clients, after which the clients' lands were officially transferred to the sahukars' names.[54]

VI

Dearth was of such obvious advantage to the usurers that it was commonly believed that they used sorcery to prevent rain from falling. In western India, as in many other peasant societies, there was a widespread belief that dearth, famine and other disasters were caused by supernatural design, and that humans had the ability to intercede with spirits or gods to prevent (or indeed to cause) such misfortunes. In medieval and early modern Europe, for example, it was thought that harvest failure was caused in most cases by the will of God, being a divine punishment for sin. It was common to see petitional and penitential processions led by priests, with miraculous images and holy relics being carried while people scourged themselves with whips, carried heavy crosses or wore crowns of thorns. According to David Gentilcore, in early modern southern Italy 'drought was a common threat and procession a common response'.[55] Harvests could also be blighted by evil spirits conjured up by sorcerers or witches. At such times, priests and professional exorcists were called on to intercede with God to chase away the demons.[56]

In such an event, if the priest or exorcist failed to achieve the desired result he might be blamed or even punished by the peasants. In Tsarist

Russia, for example, Orthodox priests were believed to be able to provide ritual protection for the crops, and sometimes when the harvest failed they were beaten by the peasants.[57] Similarly, in pre-colonial central Africa, kings were valued for their ability to intercede with the spirits to bring about rain. A drought was a sign that they had failed in their duties, leading to a loss of their authority.[58]

In India, it was commonly believed gods and spirits could control rainfall. As a result, the peasants were careful always to perform ceremonies at the time of ploughing the fields to ensure good rain.[59] Even when the rain-clouds came, it was believed that they could be persuaded through sorcery to pass overhead without shedding any water, for example by burying a pot full of water, which, it was supposed, trapped the rain.[60] A popular story about the medieval Sufi saint Khwaja Muinuddin Chishti illustrates this. The saint had been insulted by some brahman priests of Ajmer. Using supernatural powers, he drew up all the water from the wells and ponds of Ajmer and put it in a small earthenware pot. After that there was a terrible drought. The king of Ajmer, Raja Pithaura, called the great ascetic Jaypal Jogi to fight the khwaja's power, but to no avail. Eventually, Jaypal Jogi fell at the feet of the saint and implored forgiveness. The khwaja was appeased. He told the jogi to fetch the little earthenware pot in which he had shut up all the water. Jaypal exerted all his strength and magical power, but could not lift the pot; nor did any of Raja Pithaura's warriors prove up to the task. The khwaja then sent his servant, who brought it at once. He opened the mouth of the pot, and immediately all the ponds and wells were refilled.[61]

When rain failed at the expected time, a number of ceremonies could be performed to try to persuade gods and spirits to release it. Brahmans might be required to stand up to their lips in a pond and repeat the name of Indra, the supreme rain-god, for a day or two.[62] A.K. Forbes has described a number of tactics used by nineteenth-century Gujarati peasants to induce rain, ranging from praying and asking local exorcists to intervene with the spirits to quitting their village *en masse*.[63] In Rajasthan, it was common for a party of young girls and women to walk in procession round a village singing songs to Indra, led by a prepubescent girl carrying on her head an earthenware pot filled with water and containing a frog. The pot was constantly filled with water so that it overflowed and drenched the girl beneath.

The pot and the frog were meant to symbolize the drenching rain and the appearance of frogs in a flooded field.[64]

During such times of impending crisis, when the Baniyas began to raise their prices and became less willing to provide advances, the finger of blame was often pointed in their direction. There was a popu-lar belief that Baniyas possessed supernatural powers, which included the ability to stop rain by chanting spells.[65] In the early nineteenth century, according to James Tod, the Jain Baniyas were believed to be *vidyavan*, or people with powerful forms of knowledge. Tod met the chief priest of the temple at Dwarka, who told him that on one occa-sion the Jains of Gujarat had used their supernatural powers to make the moon appear during the dark half of the month. 'Wherever this ancient and numerous sect exists,' 'magical skill is always asserted.'[66]

The Baniyas, in common with everyone else in their society, firmly believed that human fate was influenced by the actions of good and bad spirits. Bad spirits caused illness, but they could be exorcised by people skilled in dealing with the supernatural. Thus, Jain holy men performed ceremonies to confine disease-causing spirits in bottles, which were then buried. During smallpox epidemics, Jain Baniyas often worshipped Sitala Mata, the smallpox goddess. They believed that an evil eye could cause blight and misfortune, and they used various spells to ensure good fortune in business or success in gambling. This was all despite the fact that the Jain religion was in principle opposed to such beliefs and the use of spells.[67]

Baniyas were not infrequently tempted to put their literacy to supernatural use by dabbling with magic diagrams (known as *yantra*) or books of spells (*yantra-mantra*). It was common knowledge in mid-nineteenth-century Gujarat that many Baniyas had a weakness in this direction, often becoming so involved that their businesses suffered.[68] In using such knowledge against their clients they were extending their control over the written word, already seen in their manipulation of account books, into one more domain of power, that of the supernatural.[69]

There were a number of legends about Baniyas who behaved in this way. In one, a Gujarati Jain merchant who had built up a large stock of grain wished to offload it at high prices. He asked his guru to write a spell on a piece of paper which he tied to the horn of a black deer. The effect of this spell was to allow rain only in those places where the deer was at the time. Everywhere else there was drought. This went on for seven years. Eventually a woodcutter noted that wherever the black deer went the earth became green with grass. He went to the raja and informed him about this. The raja caught the deer and retrieved the piece of paper, which was then thrown in a well. After this, it rained heavily.[70] The seventeenth-century chronicler Muhmot Nainsi had a similar story of how the Baniyas' business had suffered in Kutch because of four successive years of good rain and bumper crops. They then approached a person skilled in black magic, who agreed to lock up the rain and cause a famine in the land.[71]

Baniyas supposedly employed a number of techniques to stop the rain. In Rajasthan, according to Beni Gupta, a Baniya engaged a thaumaturgist skilled in black arts to dig a long and deep pit. Seven earthenware pots were then filled with water and various spells were cast, after which the pots were closed with lids and red cloths tied around the brims with untwisted cotton threads and then painted in black with charms. The pots were then placed in the pit side by side. One pot was supposed to stand for the pre-monsoon showers, four for the four months of the monsoon, and two more for the months in which winter rain might fall. The aim was to prevent rainfall during the entire year. The pots were buried, and the place was visited by no one except the thaumaturgist. On each day during the months in which rain was expected he pronounced his spells on the buried pots, and particularly on the pot for that specific month.[72] In an interview in southern Rajasthan, I was told that the Baniyas could stop rain by pouring hot water onto a small image which they kept for the purpose in the Jain temple.[73]

J.C. Oman has recounted similar ploys used by Baniyas, in this case in the Punjab. They sometimes made chapattis which they then mistreated in such a way as to offend the gods, the logic being that the grain from which the chapattis was made came from the bounty of the gods who provided the rain; the angry gods would consequently withhold the rain. He continues:

> At another time I learned that a baniya had recourse to a still more effectual method of keeping off the rain. He had a *charkha*, or spinning-wheel made out of the bones of dead men. Such an article could only be made very secretly and for a large sum of money, but its action was most potent.

> Whenever the clouds were gathering the baniya set his virgin daughter to work the charkha the *reverse way*, and by that means unwound or unwove the clouds, as it were, thus driving away the rain . . .[74]

One variation of the first method was for the Baniyas to expose chapattis in the fields to show the gods that there was no scarcity of food, so that they need not trouble themselves to bring the rain.[75] In Maharashtra, this effect was achieved by placing a leaf-plate loaded with food. Alternatively, a live coal was placed on open ground on a tile, which was then asked to 'swallow the rain'.[76]

Again in the Punjab, Baniyas sometimes filled lamps with liquid ghee, which they lit when rain-clouds gathered overhead. After some time they blew out the light, and this action was thought to drive away the clouds. This was said to have been done with great success in Ambala in August 1883. The use of ghee rather than oil in the lamps was probably intended to show the deity that the people were still well off and did not need rain.[77] In some cases, a Baniya gave an unmarried girl some oil, which she poured on the ground saying:

> If I pour not the oil, mine the sin:
> If thou disperse not the clouds, thine the sin.

Alternatively, he might put some rainwater in a new earthenware pitcher and bury it in the ground at a spot where a roof-spout discharged. This, it was said, would at once cause the rain to stop.[78]

The popular belief that Baniya usurers and grain merchants acted in such ways was extremely widespread, from the Punjab to Rajasthan, to Gujarat and Maharashtra. For example, in 1846 it was reported from the latter region that the Baniyas were generally believed to employ Jain mendicants to prevent rain.[79] We have no means of knowing the extent to which the Baniyas really did practise such black arts. Even if only a few did, their actions would have coloured popular belief; and even when they did not, it could serve their interests to give the impression that they had the necessary skills. In the Bhil regions of Rajasthan it was common before the start of the rain for the Bhils to go to the house of their sahukar and ask him to permit abundant rain. The usurer would come out and make fulsome promises to do so, then distribute raw sugar as a mark of his goodwill.[80] By acting in this manner he stressed his munificence as a patron, but underlying the action was the threat that if the Bhils did not behave as dutiful clients he might punish them by stopping the rain.

VII

Although the peasants were keenly aware of the usurers' duplicity during times of dearth, they also believed that they had a right to be provided with grain. If the sahukars failed them in this respect, they might protest or take direct action. Where it occurred, such resistance normally took place at an early stage of the crisis, most commonly when it was clear that the rain had failed and the usurers had begun to hoard or demand extravagant prices for grain. The peasants, not yet weakened by malnutrition but anticipating imminent starvation, might then take the law into their own hands. As a period of dearth continued, perhaps escalating into famine, their ability to take such action declined. Enfeebled by hunger, using all their energy to search out food, wandering and destitute, they were no longer able to take united action to enforce their demands. In this section I examine a particularly well-documented case of united action which took place in Ajmer and Merwara, the two British-ruled districts of Rajasthan, in 1891.

In this year there was a severe drought after four years of deficient rainfall. Although the Baniyas of the two districts had plenty of grain in their stores, much of it imported on the railway which had opened in 1875, they refused to advance this to their clients, preferring to sell it to merchants in Marwar, who were paying better prices.[81] In the adjoining princely states of Rajasthan the sahukars were required by their governments to provide assistance, but this was not allowed in the British-ruled districts. The assistant commissioner for Merwara district justified this policy by arguing that if the Baniyas were forced to give advances to the peasants the latter's debts would only increase; as it was, they could keep themselves alive by labouring on government relief works, which, in the words of this official, did them 'moral and physical good'.[82] Unfortunately for the peasants, such relief works were opened in Merwara only in October 1891 and in Ajmer in January 1892, whereas the Baniyas had begun to refuse to make any advances at the start of August 1891, when it was becoming apparent that the monsoon was likely to fail. This had become a certainty by the end of the month, and credit dried up entirely. The price of grain rose sharply during September, and the Baniyas refused to hand out anything without cash payment, which the peasants could not give. All the British officials could do was to advise the peasants to migrate elsewhere, as they were unable to provide sufficient aid.[83] It was during this period, when they had no major source of sustenance, that the peasants took matters into their own hands.

The sympathetic assistant commissioner for Ajmer district, A.F. de Laessoe, knew that the sahukars had been harassing the peasants by lodging false cases of grain robbery against them, and on 11 September he issued a circular to the police that they should not arrest any peasants on such a charge without permission from a magistrate. A rumour spread rapidly that the assistant commissioner had ordered that no peasant would be punished for taking grain from the Baniyas by force. On 14 September a series of mass attacks began, continuing for nine days.[84]

These attacks, organized and disciplined, were informed by a belief that so long as grain was taken from Baniyas only, the authorities would not interfere. Peasants who dealt with the Baniyas of a particular place were told to gather in nearby fields, where they arrived armed with sticks, swords, axes, slings and the occasional gun. In some cases they appointed a 'commissioner', 'assistant commissioner' and 'district superintendent of police' from amongst themselves. According to the official report on the rising:

> The three men thus appointed were then sent into the village to explain to the baniahs that it was their duty to give grain on credit, and that proper receipts would be given. On the baniahs refusing, they were told that the grain would be taken forcibly. The three officers then returned to the mob outside the village, and made speeches, explaining the Government could not help them and that the baniahs would not, so they must help themselves. After that they went to the village when the 'Assistant Commissioner' ordered the 'District Superintendent of Police' to have the doors opened. This was done and the grain taken. The baniahs' books and papers were then brought to the 'Commissioner' and 'Assistant Commissioner' who ordered them to be 'dakhil daftered' [placed in the record-room], whereupon they were at once torn up.[85]

In a few cases the Baniyas defused the situation by agreeing from the start to the people's demands, weighing out and distributing the grain in the usual way. But in most cases they refused, leading to an attack on their shops.[86]

The Baniyas of fourteen separate centres were attacked in this way by the peasants of at least forty different villages over a period of nine days. The number of peasants involved in each attack ranged from forty to a thousand, of both sexes and all ages. By caste, they were chiefly Mers and Rawats—leading peasant castes in the area—though peasants from a wide range of other castes were also mentioned as having taken part. In most cases, no resistance was offered either by the Baniyas or by other villagers. Only two Baniyas were reported to have been hurt: they were beaten, but not seriously. In three cases guards who tried to resist were injured. At least two of the attackers were shot dead and about twenty others wounded, in almost all cases by policemen who opened fire on them.

Reinforcements of police and soldiers arrived in the area on 22 September. On the following day peasants who had gathered to attack the Baniyas of three places were themselves forcibly dispersed, with several being shot and others captured. This brought a swift end to the uprising. In the following days nearly seven hundred peasants were arrested and charged with having looted grain.

Those arrested were reported as being able-bodied and by no means starving: the rising was caused by moral outrage against the Baniyas, not by starvation as such. The peasants, however, clearly expected that they *would* be starving if action was not taken soon. The rumour about British support for coerced redistribution of grain tipped the balance against the sahukars, setting off the actual mass attacks. As in many other cases of peasant insurgency in India and elsewhere, the peasants took it upon themselves to set up an alternative system of authority which imitated and paralleled the official one, establishing a 'moral government' which took the action they felt appropriate for a ruling power, and which they hoped would be viewed sympathetically by the authorities.[87] As soon as it became clear that the British were not prepared to tolerate such actions, and would, rather, suppress them using armed force, the rising ended.

VIII

The rising in Ajmer has certain important parallels with the grain riots of eighteenth-century England described by E.P. Thompson. In sixteenth- and seventeenth-century England, there had been paternalistic checks on prices designed to protect the poor. Hoarding had been forbidden. These checks were gradually removed during the eighteenth century as a bourgeoisie committed to a *laissez-faire* ideology gradually increased its power. This 'freeing' of the market was strongly resented by the poor, who continued to believe in a 'moral price' for staple foods. In this, they were often supported by the local gentry, who resented the bourgeois middlemen making such profits from this new state of affairs. Grain riots were triggered by soaring prices during periods of scarcity. When the people attacked the dealers and took away the grain they were hoarding, they sometimes did it to cries of 'God save the king!', so as to stress what they considered to be the legitimacy of their action.[88]

Similarly, the peasants in Ajmer looked to their rulers to intervene on their side against the Baniyas. In the pre-colonial period, and in princely states during the colonial period, rulers commonly forced the sahukars to provide for the peasants during times of dearth, and prevented profiteering by fixing prices. Significantly, the single recorded rising took place in the only British-ruled area of Rajasthan, where the authorities refused to make any such interventions. The rioters in late-nineteenth-century Ajmer, like those in eighteenth-century England, believed that their actions were morally justified, and that by rights the authorities should have been on their side.

One feature of this rising which cannot be compared with English food riots was the seizure and destruction by the peasants of debt-bonds and account books. There were precedents for this in earlier peasant revolts against usury in India, most notably the uprising against Gujarati and Marwari usurers in Pune and Ahmadnagar districts of Maharashtra in 1875. This occurred not during a period of dearth, but after the sahukars had combined to refuse to pay the second instalment of the peasants' land-tax. Over an extensive area, peasants rose up and forced their way into the houses of the usurers, making bonfires of their account books and debt bonds in the streets.[89] Notably, other studies of grain riots in South Asia mention a similar seizure and destruction of such papers.[90] Whereas in eighteenth-century England the relationship between rioter and the merchant was one purely of buyer and seller in the market place, in South Asia the relationship between peasant and sahukar was characterized by long-term clientage and patronage, symbolized, as well as legalized, by the debts recorded in account books and on debt bonds. It was therefore only to be expected that any grain riot directed against sahukars would very easily develop into an attack on this central apparatus of usurer power.

Grain riots along these lines appear to have been closely connected with the rigid imposition of free-trade policies by the colonial state.[91] Almost all the nineteenth-century cases occurred in British-ruled areas, where they were brought about by what was perceived as the failure of the authorities to take action against the Baniyas. In princely states, by contrast, the authorities commonly acted to prevent profiteering by merchants. For example, in Jodhpur in August 1899, when some 'grasping Banias' tried to take advantage of the failure of the rain to drive up prices, officials set up a shop to sell grain at cost price. This move proved popular: 23,566 maunds worth Rs 118,695, were soon sold, forcing the Baniyas to reduce their prices.[92]

In British India, where the government banned any such 'interference' in the market, grain riots became a much more likely possibility during periods of scarcity than they had been in the past. For instance, there were riots in certain towns in Maharashtra in 1832, when there was a rapid rise in prices after a poor monsoon. Although the grain dealers had sufficient stocks to last a year, they combined to force up prices. In September and October the price of grain doubled in Pune and Ahmadnagar districts, and the Baniyas offered for sale only old and damaged grain. They began exporting their good grain to Hydera-bad state, where prices were higher. Though peasants in Ahmadnagar petitioned the collector to ban this trade and to regulate prices, he and other officials took no action. Between 6 and 20 November there were a series of attacks on the merchants, beginning in Pune city, where large crowds gathered and began beating Marwaris and spilling their grain out on the streets. Two days later there were similar riots in Ahmadnagar, then in Mallegaon and Dhule.[93]

As already pointed out, the development of the railways in the later part of the nineteenth century proved disastrous for many peasants. Sahukars and grain merchants were now able to move large stocks of grain during a period of dearth or famine to places where there was a better market for the produce. The sight of grain carts being driven along the roads to the railway stations, and of grain sacks being carried into and heaped up in railway 'godowns' (warehouses) to await export from an area at a moment when the mass of the people desperately needed to replenish their household stores was particularly galling. During the Maharashtrian famine of 1896–7 it was reported that many peasants were forcibly preventing the sahukars taking grain out of their villages, with the sympathetic connivance of some local officials. The government, however, refused to place any checks on the movement of grain or to regulate prices.[94]

This new development caused a marked rise in the incidence of grain riots in the final decade of the century. The rising in Ajmer in 1891 has already been described; there was a very similar rising by Bhils during the famine of 1899–1900 in the Panchmahals district of Gujarat.[95] During the famine of 1896–7 in Maharashtra, as in the famine of 1891 in Ajmer, the people believed that the Baniyas were profiteering by organizing the wide-scale export of grain from areas of scarcity. It was also known that the rulers of adjoining princely states were forbidding such export—a ban which their subjects, apparently, warmly appreciated, and whose absence in the British-ruled areas led to widespread outrage, as it was felt that the authorities there were neglecting their duty by failing to ensure that grain was made available at a 'fair' price.

On 17 October 1896 about a hundred people from the town of Hubli (Dharwar district) took direct action when they saw a convoy of carts taking grain to the railway station for export. A large quantity of grain was being exported to the north, and the people had already made several requests to the Collector to stop this trade. They now snatched bags of grain from the carts and carried them off. Soon after a bigger crowd marched to the station and tried to force its way into the grain-shed there. Confronted by the railway police, they began throwing stones, but were driven away by shots fired over their heads. According to the collector: 'railway stations throughout the district [were] blocked with grain awaiting carriage, and the railway authorities express[ed] some apprehension as to its safety.'[96] There were simi-lar attacks on grain-carts and grain dealers in November in the town of Karad (Satara district) and in Sholapur. At Karad, thirty-seven people were arrested for looting. When the subdivisional magistrate, Clements, visited them in the town lock-up on 13 November he was surrounded by a crowd demanding their release. A passage had to be forced for him by the police, and he left followed by a barrage of stones.[97]

In Yaval (Khandesh district) the Baniyas refused to sell any grain to the townspeople in October, even though they had plenty in their stores. A local Muslim leader, the Kazi, told the authorities that the people were demanding that the price of millet be fixed at a particular level. The local authorities called the Baniyas together on 23 October to try to persuade them to sell at this price. While negotiations were going on a crowd suddenly burst into the house, caught the chief government officer there and beat him unconscious:

> The Banya's houses were then visited. In fear of their lives the banyas opened their storehouses and allowed their grain to be taken away. It was carted to the open space around the Kazi's house. At this moment the Police Jamadar, who had just returned from another village, arrived. He and the Kazi tried to regulate the disposal of the grain. The grain dealers were summoned and told to disperse their grain. They did so and got in nearly every case the market price for it.[98]

Encouraged by this successful outcome, some nearby peasants went to a market being held outside the town and began appropriating grain from the stalls of the traders.

That same week the Baniyas of the town of Jamner, also in Khandesh, refused to open their shops or sell any grain on the day of the weekly market. Asked by the people to intercede with the Baniyas to sell them grain at a reasonable price, the local representative of the government went to the bazaar to negotiate with the shopkeepers. A crowd gathered, a Marwari was hit, the officer lashed out with his horse-whip and the crowd turned on him. He scrambled into a sahukar's shop, where he hid while the crowd plundered the bazaar.[99] There was a similar outbreak in the small town of Shendurni at the same time.

In 1896, unlike in Ajmer in 1891 and the Panchmahals in 1899, those who initiated the action against the Baniyas were townspeople rather than peasants. In common with the peasants, however, they had a notion of a fair price for grain which they sought to impose, at first through peaceful persuasion, but eventually with force. They first sought help from local officials, but when they failed to bring adequate pressure to bear on the Baniyas, they too became a target of attack. Taken together, these outbreaks reveal that by the 1890s the situation had become very tense, with the people being prepared to take action against profiteering Baniyas much more readily. The poor had resented the policy of free trade from the start, as was apparent in the outbreaks of 1832, but it was only when the evils of this policy were compounded by the new developments in grain transport by rail that the outrage burst into the open on a much wider scale.

Even then, the relationship between the peasants and the sahukars was not broken for long. In Ajmer, many of the Baniyas who had been attacked by their clients refused afterwards to name those who had been involved to the police, as they did not want to increase their unpopularity in the the area by acting as informers. Neither did they wish to see their debtors arrested and jailed, and thus be unable to repay their debts. In one village, for example, the Baniyas refused to give the name of a single looter to the police. When the police searched the houses of some peasants and discovered grain, utensils and other property which belonged to the Baniyas, the usurers stated that they had deposited their property with the peasants for safe-keeping during the period of trouble. When the police presented the Baniyas with names of those arrested, they refused to mark their assent by signing the lists.[100] As soon as there was good rainfall, in the following year, they advanced loans to the peasants as freely as they had ever done before the period of dearth.[101]

IX

The evidence for such grain rioting in western India during periods of dearth is sufficient to allow us to construct a history which shows how action of this kind became more common as colonial rule progressed; but a paucity of evidence makes it much harder to construct a similar history of direct action to counter rain-charming by usurers. It appears, however, that forcible action could be taken in this case too.

There is, for example, a ballad current among the Bhils of Masuda, near Beawar in Rajasthan, which tells of a time of terrible famine. The people requested the goddess whom they worshipped to tell them the cause of the failure of the rain. She agreed to help them and led them to the house of their Baniya, where they found huge stocks of grain, which they seized and redistributed. As soon as they did this his spells were broken and there was a cloudburst, with the heaviest fall of rain for a whole century. Seizing the Baniya, the goddess took him to a river, where she held him by his topknot and ducked him in and out until he begged to be killed. She told him that she would agree to this if he sacrificed a buffalo. He said that as he was a Jain who practised non-violence he could not comply; she replied that she would respect his religion and that he could sacrifice a grass buffalo instead. He made the creature and cut its throat with a knife. Torrents of blood flowed out, making all the floodwater red. The goddess then cut off the Baniya's head.[102]

The imagery here is powerful. The link between Baniyas and blood is made in a Marwari proverb: 'A Baniya's logic can never be understood; while he never drinks water without straining it carefully, he drinks blood freely.'[103] In the ballad, the Baniya had killed large numbers of people by using sorcery to prevent the rain from falling. Though professing non-violence as a Jain, his hypocrisy was exposed when he was forced to sacrifice a representation of a buffalo. The blood of his victims flowed out in torrents, and he died polluted and thus damned.

According to Beni Gupta, it was common during droughts for peasants in Rajasthan to force their way into the houses of sahukars and search out their hidden pots or other charms. If found they were destroyed. She concludes: 'Naturally the grain dealer is then beaten but the sorcerer is not molested, because it is feared that he may use his art against those who insult him.'[104] She does not give any specific examples of this practice, or even of where it occurred, so it is impossible to know how widespread it was, or when it took place. Clearly, however, peasants believed that it was in their power to counter the Baniyas' spells.

The only historical material known to me comes from the Sirohi region of Rajasthan, where beliefs about Baniya sorcery were central to a strong anti-Baniya movement which developed in the second decade of the twentieth century. The movement was seen to pose a threat to law and order, and the authorities were forced to take notice of it.

Sirohi was a princely state in the southernmost part of Rajasthan, bordering on Gujarat, with a population consisting mainly of poor Girasia and Bhil peasants. These two communities had strong clan-based organizations, known for their internal solidarities and history of resistance to attempted extensions of power by princely rulers. During the nineteenth century, land-tax had been collected from them according to the number of ploughs owned by each family. During the first two decades of the twentieth century, however, the maharaja of Sirohi brought the area into line with British India by instead assessing the tax according to the area of land held by a family. The land was surveyed, and title-deeds were sold by auction. In most cases, Baniya usurers managed to buy these deeds, with most of the peasants becoming, by law, their 'tenants'.[105] In this way the power of the Baniyas was transformed.

The cause of the Sirohi peasants was eventually taken up by Anup Das, a local artisan who had come into contact with socialist ideas while on active service in Europe during the First World War. On his return home, he published a pamphlet in Hindi, *Jagat Hit Karini*, or 'Acting for the Good of the World', in which he described the Baniyas as rakshasas or 'devils', blaming them for various catastrophes such as famines, diseases, early child deaths, and solar and lunar eclipses.[106] In another publication he called them *Lanka ke Dhed*, or 'untouchables from Sri Lanka'. An associate of his, Harchand Soni, composed anti-Baniya songs, which were sung as bhajans. The aim was to stigmatize the Baniyas as aliens and foreigners to the region.[107]

In 1920 Anup Das founded an association called the Anup Mandal, with the intention of fighting the Baniyas in a more systematic way. He also began to dress as a religious mendicant or sadhu. In May 1920 he held a meeting at the village of Palri attended by nearly a thousand of his followers. The most vocal supporters were members of artisan communities (notably Suthars, or carpenters), who often cultivated small plots of land besides carrying on their trade, but many Girasias also came. After the meeting, they marched to Sirohi town and unsuccessfully demanded an audience with the maharaja. They then left the town and marched around the adjoining region, demanding that the Baniyas accept the teachings of Anup Das. Those who refused were assaulted and forced to hand over supplies of grain. At the village of Padwa they attacked a Jain *dharamshala* (rest-house), beating the Jain sadhus and burning some old manuscripts. After this had gone on for about a week, the state authorities sent police to arrest the ringleaders. About seventy-five followers were tried, of whom forty-six were given prison sentences of between three and nine months. Those tried were a very mixed group, being drawn from the potter, carpenter, oil-presser, drummer, gardener, and transporter castes, but also including Rajputs, Girasias, Dheds (untouchables) and even one brahman. They came from twenty-nine different villages in all. *Jagat Hit Karini* was proscribed and orders were given that all copies should be seized and destroyed.[108]

The movement continued, however, with activists organizing meetings and song sessions in which anti-Baniya sentiments were propagated. Anup Das encouraged a cult of personality, with special Anup Mandal huts being built in villages where his photograph was displayed.[109] The maharaja of Sirohi, who was under the influence of Jain Baniya ministers, ordered that the association be banned. It continued to operate underground, however. In the 1930s the maharaja came into conflict with many of the local Baniyas, who were then leaning towards the Indian nationalist movement and demanding democratic reforms in Sirohi. To counter this, he relaxed the restrictions on the Anup Mandal and passed some anti-Baniya laws, restricting their trade and usury. The Rajputs of the state rallied to his side, declaring that they wanted his rule rather than *Baniya raj*.[110] In 1943–4 he had a law passed which stopped sahukars purchasing any more agricultural land.[111] Although this infuriated the Baniyas, the measures were not implemented in any serious way.

After Indian independence in 1947 the princely states were dissolved and the erstwhile Sirohi state became a district of the new federal state of Rajasthan. The conflict between the peasants and the Baniyas continued under the new order. In 1963 some Jain Baniyas of Sirohi complained in a letter to the chief minister of Rajasthan of the continuing activities of the Anup Mandal: 'Whenever there is any natural calamity—famines, starvation, heavy rains, droughts, small-pox or plague they go round in the name of "Anop Mandal", collect people for Bhajans & "Melas" and preach that calamities are engineered by the Jains and their monks to raise prices and profit thereby.'[112] By the 1960s, the influence of the Anup Mandal had spread to the peasants of the adjoining districts of Jalor, Pali, Barmer, Udaipur and Sabarkantha (which is over the border in Gujarat). Some of the attacks on Baniyas and Jain sadhus have been described in detail.

In 1963, for example, very little rain had fallen in the Sirohi region and the peasants suspected that some Jain sadhus had been instigated by the local Baniya usurers to stop the rain. On 26 August about four hundred people attacked a Jain temple at which five sadhus were passing the four months of the monsoon season. The peasants damaged the temple and beat the sadhus, threatening that if they did not cancel their spells they would return and kill them. Two days later, a crowd of about two hundred attacked another Jain temple nearby. They stoned the doors, shouting 'Kill the Jain sadhus' and 'Throw out the Baniyas', and injured a few Jains, one of whom had to be hospitalized.[113]

Similarly, when the rain failed in Sabarkantha district in Gujarat in 1985 the Bhil peasants went to the Baniya centre at Vijaynagar, where there was a large Jain temple. They believed that the priest of this temple was carrying out rites to stop the rain. The Bhils threatened the Baniyas, telling them that they would be looted if they went to the temple or gave any support to the priest. The Baniyas were so frightened that they kept away from the temple for fifteen days, during which the priest had nothing to eat.[114] In the same year a local newspaper reported that some Bhil peasants of Udaipur district had broken the legs of some Jain sadhus who they believed were casting spells to prevent rain.[115]

In Sabarkantha district around the same time, the Bhils went in procession to the town of Poshina. Standing in front of the houses of the Jain Baniyas, they shouted for them to come out. They did so, fearing that their houses might be sacked otherwise. Each Baniya was ordered to place an earthenware pot full of water on his head. The usurers were taken in procession, and made to stand in a row while the

Bhils shot arrows at the pots, smashing them and drenching the sahukars with water, thus (it was believed) releasing the rain. This was the third time that this ritual had been repeated in eighteen years.[116]

The chief object of all of these attacks was to frighten the Baniyas into rescinding their spells. At most, they were unlikely to receive more than a beating. Even this was a great humiliation, and, smarting from the insult, they were likely to be careful during the next few weeks or months not to bring further attacks on their heads by attempting to profiteer.

All these examples come from areas which are on the border between Gujarat and Rajasthan, a region which in terms of modern capitalist development is very backward. In this region, merchant and usurer capital continues to dominate the local economy, with Baniya usury surviving in a particularly exploitative form to this day.[117] Popular belief in Baniya sorcery would appear to have persisted there because it has provided a focus for the continuing resistance of the peasants to such usury; it is highly unlikely that it would be found today in rural areas in which capitalist agriculture has developed more strongly, and where Baniya usury is now largely a spent force.

Although this history is very area-specific, it is likely, given the ubiquity of the belief in Baniya sorcery in the past, that such actions—in some form or other—were taken far more widely during earlier periods of dearth. There were, however, aspects unique to this particular movement. The Anup Mandal was founded and led by a man who blended local belief with a socialist understanding of exploitation, and who spread his message using the medium of print and what was essentially a modern form of party-political organization. These features ensured that the movement was highly visible, that its activities were recorded in the archives, and that it left its own published record. Such a movement could not have occurred in western India before the twentieth century.

Another striking feature of this movement was the sheer contempt which it voiced for Baniya culture and religion, with attacks being directed against Jain sadhus and priests in particular. In the past, communities such as the Bhils and Girasias had never subscribed to brahmanical Hindu or Jain beliefs, but they had shown a certain respect for the religion of the Baniyas.[118] The consciousness which informed their new opposition to Baniya usury developed in a far more militant direction in the course of the twentieth century; and this despite the fact that the accusations about rain-charming and sorcery were rooted in a much older structure of belief.

X

To conclude, the institution of sahukari had played a crucial role for centuries in the supply and marketing of food grain in the commercial economy of western India. The practice of usury was closely related to the prevalence of dearth, as this led to shortages which were then exploited for the benefit of the usurers. This provided a source of constant tension between usurers and peasants. In the pre-colonial period, the state had tried to prevent such tensions from hardening into resistance through checks on usurers and on markets. The removal of these checks by the colonial state led to more frequent grain riots in the areas under direct British rule.

The form which such riots took can be seen to have conformed to the 'moral economy' model in some striking respects. Popular action involved a demand for a fair price, threats of violence should it not be given, enforcement by a pseudo-authority and occasionally looting. In addition, there was destruction of account-books, a peculiarly South Asian phenomenon relating to the centrality of usury in the power structure of rural India.

There were, however, elements to the 'moral economy' which take us beyond the sphere of commerce into that of the supernatural. In western India this involved the belief that hoarders and profiteers could bring dearth through sorcery. It seems unlikely that such notions were unique to India, for in almost all peasant societies for which we have good evidence, there appear to have been strong beliefs connecting dearth with the supernatural. In this respect, the remedy for dearth was sought, not in the commercial sphere alone, with conflict centred on stocks of grain or usurers' accounts, but also at a supernatural level. Dearth and famine could thus form a base for popular movements with a strong religious content, as was the case in nineteenth-century Italy, where the dearth of the late 1870s helped bring about the messianic movement led by Davide Lazzaretti.[119] Or it could perhaps lead to the persecution of those believed to be responsible for such sorcery, such as Jews in medieval Europe, or witches.[120] These beliefs were found in a wide range of peasant societies, not only the so-called 'pre-modern' ones. If nothing else, therefore, what we have seen of the re-action to dearth in western India shows how much we need to extend our understanding of 'moral economy' to incorporate also such struggles in the realm of supernatural power.

Notes

1. David Arnold, *Famine: Social Crisis and Historical Change* (Oxford, 1988), p. 7.
2. An essential feature of a peasantry, according to Theodore Shanin, is that they are dominated by other classes: T. Shanin, *The Awkward Class: Political Sociology of Peasantry in a Developing Society: Russia 1910–1925* (Oxford, 1972), p. 213.
3. 'Introduction' to William Shakespeare, *Coriolanus*, ed. G.R. Hibbard (Harmondsworth, 1967), p. 12; for the lines quoted from the play, see ibid., p. 61 (I.i).
4. James Scott, *The Moral Economy of the Peasant: Rebellion and Subsistence in Southeast Asia* (New Haven, 1976); E.P. Thompson, 'The Moral Economy of the English Crowd in the Eighteenth Century', *Past and Present*, 50 (February 1971), pp. 76–136.
5. David Arnold, 'Looting, Grain Riots and Government Policy in South India, 1918', *Past and Present*, 84 (August 1979), pp. 111–45; John D. Rogers, 'The 1866 Grain Riots in Sri Lanka', *Comparative Studies in Society and History*, 29 (1987), pp. 495–513.
6. For an example from northern Italy in 1628, see Charles Tilly, 'Food Supply and Public Order in Modern Europe', in Charles Tilly (ed.), *The Formation of National States in Western Europe* (Princeton, 1975), pp. 380–2.
7. R. Bin Wong, 'Food Riots in the Qing Dynasty', *Journal of Asian Studies*, 41 (1982), pp. 767–88.
8. Paul Greenhough, 'Comments from a South Asian Perspective: Food, Famine, and the Chinese State', ibid., pp. 793–4; Paul Greenhough, 'Indulgence and Abundance as Asian Peasant Values: A Bengali Case in Point', ibid., 42 (1983), pp. 831–50; Paul Greenhough, *Prosperity and Misery in Modern Bengal: The Famine of 1943–4* (New York, 1982).
9. E.P. Thompson, 'The Moral Economy Reviewed', in his *Customs in Common* (London, 1991), pp. 344–7; Roger Wells argues that the evidence presented in Greenhough's work shows that there were many food riots in Bengal during the famine of 1943–4, and the reactions of merchants

and officials were very clearly determined by a desire to prevent more wide-scale outbreaks: R. Wells, 'E.P. Thompson, *Customs in Common* and Moral Economy', *Journal of Peasant Studies*, 21, pt 2 (1994), pp. 286–8. I might add that Greenhough's argument appears to be coloured by the notion popular in British colonial times that Indian peasants have accepted extreme forms of hierarchy—and exploitation—in a passive and fatalistic manner, as they believed that their social position in life was determined by fate. This is flatly contradicted by a massive amount of evidence for peasant insurgency in the pre-colonial and colonial periods, from Mughal to British times, on a scale wide enough to challenge the power of the state: see, for example, Irfan Habib, *The Agrarian System of Mughal India, 1556–1707* (Bombay, 1963), pp. 330–51; Ranajit Guha, *Elementary Aspects of Peasant Insurgency in Colonial India* (Delhi, 1983); Eric Stokes, *The Peasant Armed: The Indian Rebellion of 1857* (Oxford, 1986).

10. James Scott, *Domination and the Arts of Resistance: Hidden Transcripts* (New Haven, 1990).
11. James Scott has noted how some religious practices may provide 'a critique of the existing order and an alternative symbolic universe that is so potentially explosive' that they may be banned by those in power: Scott, *Moral Economy of the Peasant*, p. 237.
12. For a statement of this view, quoted by Greenhough with approval, see Walter Neale, 'Reciprocity and Redistribution in the Indian Village: Sequel to Some Notable Discussions', in Karl Polanyi, Conrad Arensberg and Henry Preston (eds), *Trade and Markets in the Early Empires: Economies in History and Theory* (New York, 1957), pp. 221–34. In this analysis of Indian rural economy not a single reference is made to the role of merchants, traders and usurers.
13. Notable in this respect have been studies by Frank Perlin, 'Of White Whale and Countrymen in the Eighteenth-Century Maratha Deccan: Extended Class Relations, Rights and the Problem of Rural Autonomy under the Old Regime', *Journal of Peasant Studies*, 5 (1977–8), pp. 172–237; Frank Perlin. 'Concepts of Order and Comparison with a Diversion on Counter Ideologies and Corporate Institutions in Late Pre-Colonial India', *Journal of Peasant Studies*, 12, pt 2 (1984–5), pp. 87–165; Jairus Banaji, 'Capitalist Domination and the Small Peasantry: Deccan Districts in the Late Nineteenth Century', *Economic and Political Weekly*, 12 (1977), pp. 1375–1404; C.A. Bayly, *Rulers, Townsmen and Bazaars: North Indian Society in the Age of British Expansion, 1770–1870* (Cambridge, 1983); S.P. Gupta, *The Agrarian System of Eastern Rajasthan* (Delhi, 1986); Dilbagh Singh, *The State, Landlords and Peasants: Rajasthan in the 18th Century* (Delhi, 1990).

14. R.W. Scribner, *Popular Culture and Popular Movements in Reformation Germany* (London, 1987), pp. 1–2.
15. Irfan Habib, 'Usury in Medieval India', *Comparative Studies in Society and History*, 6 (1963–4), pp. 393–419; G.D. Sharma, 'Indigenous Banking and the State in Eastern Rajasthan during the Seventeenth Century,' in *Indian History Congress: Proceedings of the Fortieth Session, Andhra Pradesh University, Waltair, 1979* (Delhi, [1980?]), pp. 431–41; Gupta, *Agrarian System of Eastern Rajasthan*, pp. 92–100.
16. James Tod, *Annals and Antiquities of Rajasthan*, ed. William Crooke, 3 vols (London, 1920; repr. Delhi, 1971), 1, p. 573
17. D.D. Kosambi, *An Introduction to the Study of Indian History* (Bombay, 1956), p. 240 and *passim.*
18. This argument is largely conjectural, based on what we know for other regions, and needs further research. For South India, see David Ludden, *Peasant History in South India* (Princeton, 1985), pp. 33–4.
19. The word sahukar is first recorded around this time, suggesting that a term was needed to describe a function that had become important in society. I owe this information to the linguist Harivallabh Bhayani.
20. Peter Spufford, *Money and its Use in Medieval Europe* (Cambridge, 1988), p. 260. I am grateful to Bob Moore for this and the following reference.
21. Jacques Heers, *L'Occident aux XIVe et XVe siecles* (Paris, 1973), pp. 254–5.
22. P. Dukes, *The Making of Russian Absolutism 1613–1801* (London, 1982), p. 48; Anne Lincoln Fitzpatrick, *The Great Russian Fair: Nizhnii Novgorod, 1840–90* (Basingstoke, 1990), p. 125. In a private communication, Yanni Kotsonis has told me that professional usury was 'extremely stigmatised' in Russia. In the Russian Pale, many usurers were in addition Jews, which added to the stigma. See Prince Serge Dmitriyevich Urussov, *Memoirs of a Russian Governor*, ed. and trans. Herman Rosenthal (New York, 1908), p. 164. I am grateful to David Moon and David Saunders for references to the works cited here.
23. For the etymology of *sahu*, see S.W. Fallon, *A New Hindustani-English Dictionary* (Banaras, 1879), p. 743.
24. This may be contrasted with the shops of modern capitalist society, in which most goods are sealed, branded, and of marked weight and quality, leading to competition primarily by price: Frank S. Fanselow, 'The Bazaar Economy; or, How Bizarre is the Bazaar Really?', *Man*, new series, 25 (1990), p. 253.
25. Pandit Sukhdeo Prasad, *The Final Report of the Famine Operations in Marwar during 1899 and 1900* (Jodhpur, 1900), p. 185.

26. For Jain Baniyas, see Michael Carrithers and Caroline Humphrey (eds), *The Assembly of Listeners: Jains in Society* (Cambridge, 1991), especially the articles by Carrithers, Humphrey, Josephine Reynell, Christine M. Cottam Ellis, J. Howard M. Jones, N.K. Singhi and Vilas Sangave; for Vaishnavite Baniyas, see A.M. Shah, 'Division and Hierarchy: An Overview of Caste in Gujarat', *Contributions to Indian Sociology*, new series, 16 (1982), pp. 1–33.
27. S. Ambirajan, *Classical Political Economy and British Policy in India* (Cambridge, 1978), p. 109.
28. For a variety of reasons examined by Sumit Guha, this did not happen on a significant scale in the British-ruled areas of western India until the 1860s: S. Guha, 'Commodity and Credit in Upland Maharashtra, 1800–1950', *Economic and Political Weekly*, 22 (1987), A-126–40.
29. G.N. Sharma, *Social Life in Medieval Rajasthan, 1500–1800* (Agra, 1968), p. 318.
30. S. Ambirajan, *Classical Political Economy and British Policy in India*, pp. 60–1. For Adam Smith's original argument, see *An Inquiry into the Nature and Causes of the Wealth of Nations*, ed. Edwin Cannan, 2 vols (Oxford, 1976), i, pp. 533–4.
31. Manilal Nanavati, *Report on the Agricultural Indebtedness in the Baroda State* (Baroda, 1913), p. 59.
32. The example is from Gujarat in the 1850s, A.K. Forbes, *Ras Mala;* or, *Hindoo Annals of the Province of Goozerat in Western India*, new edn (London, 1878), p. 548.
33. C.G. Dixon, commissioner, Ajmer and Merwara, 22 October 1849, in his *Report on Ajmeer and Mairwara, Illustrating the Settlement of the Land Revenue and the Revenue Administration of those Districts to 1853* (Agra, 1853), pp. 19–20.
34. Sardar Singh, *The Lessons I Received and my Pali Tour Diary* (Jodhpur, 1896), p. 147.
35. Interview with Chhotaji Bhatt, Tilonia, Ajmer district, Rajasthan, April 1987.
36. Maharashtra State Archives, Bombay, Revenue Dept. (hereafter B.A., R.D.), 1913, 511, pt iv, J. Ghosal, Panchmahals district collector, 5 September 1912.
37. B.A., Judicial Dept. (hereafter B.A., J.D.), 1889, 81, A.F. Woodburn, 'Report on Working of Deccan Agriculturists' Relief Act', 27 April 1889.
38. N.N. Vyas, *Bondage and Exploitation in Tribal India* (Jaipur, 1980), p. 7.
39. M.R. Majmudar, *Cultural History of Gujarat* (Bombay, 1965), pp. 54–5;

N.A. Thoothi, *The Vaishnavas of Gujarat* (London, 1935), p. 186; C.M. Doshi, 'The Dasha Shrimali Jain Baniyas of Kathiawad', MA thesis, University of Bombay, 1933, p. 409.

40. *Shri Jagducharit*, ed. Maganlal Dalpatram Khakkhar (Bombay, 1896), cited in Makrand and Shirin Mehta, 'The Gujarat and the Arab Merchants, A.D. 942–1500: Some Observations Based on Contemporary Sources', *Al Watheekah*, 18 (January 1991), pp. 204–5.
41. *Gazetteer of the Bombay Presidency*, 26 vols (Bombay, 1880–1901), 8, pp. 190–1.
42. Sharma, *Social Life in Medieval Rajasthan*, p. 345.
43. Ibid., pp. 375–6 and 409. In this region, one maund is taken to be about twenty kilograms.
44. Sumit Guha, *The Agrarian Economy of the Bombay Deccan 1818–1941* (Delhi, 1985), pp. 185–6.
45. P.W. Powlett, *Gazetteer of the Bikaner State* (Bikaner, 1932), pp. 107–8.
46. C.H. Pritchard, assistant commissioner, Merwara, 'Reports on Famine Relief in Merwara, 28 February 1893', in C.H. Pritchard and J.A. Devenish (eds), *Reports on Famine Relief in Ajmere-Merwara during 1891–92* (Calcutta, 1893), pp. 87–8. The report notes that on the other hand village-level sahukars provided no charity at all.
47. *Times of India*, 7 September 1899.
48. India Office Library, London, Board's Collection, 1852, F4 2472, no. 46, Mr Forgett, Principle Sudr Amin (sic), Ahmadnagar, 'Memorandum on the Rural Police in Poona District', 1846.
49. *Report on the Famine in the Bombay Presidency 1899–1902*, 2 vols (Bombay, 1903), 1, p. 90.
50. B.A, R.D., 1901, 52/137, pt iii, Panchmahals district deputy collector's report, 1899–1900.
51. Prasad, *The Final Report of the Famine Operations in Marwar during 1899 and 1900*, p. 186.
52. B.A., Famine Dept., 1899, 47/59, anonymous petition from several villages of Kheda district, 1 October 1899.
53. Nanavati, *Report on the Agricultural Indebtedness in the Baroda State*, app. vii (pp. 20–1).
54. C.N. Seddon, *Vyara Taluka Settlement Report 1906–07* (Baroda, 1907), p. 9.
55. David Gentilcore, *From Bishop to Witch: The Symbol of the Sacred in Early Modern Terra d'Otranto* (Manchester, 1992), pp.116–17; for similar beliefs and rituals in Spain, see William Christian, *Local Religion in Sixteenth-Century Spain* (Princeton, 1981), pp. 46–7, 63–4, 119–20 and 128–9; for nineteenth-century Brazil, see Arnold, *Famine*, pp. 77–8.

56. Martin of Arles mentions such beliefs in sixteenth-century Spain in *Tractatus de superstitinibus* (1517), in *Tracatatus universi iuris*, 18 vols in 25 (Venice and Lyons, 1584), xi, pt 2, fos. 405[b], 407[a]; see pp. 48 and 64–9 of Euan Cameron's unpublished translation from the Latin, which he has kindly allowed me to consult. Cameron has also shown me an illustration of witches brewing up a hailstorm in a reproduction of the title-page of Ulrich Molitor, *De laniis et phitonicis mulierbus* (Cologne, 1989).
57. James Scott, *Weapons of the Weak: Everyday Forms of Peasant Resistance* (New Haven, 1985), p. 340, n. 79.
58. Randall M. Packard, *Chiefship and Cosmology: An Historical Study of Political Competition* (Bloomington, 1981), p. 6, cited in Jan Vansina, *Oral Tradition as History* (London, 1988), p. 198.
59. For Rajasthan, see Beni Gupta, 'Magical Beliefs and Superstitions in Rajasthan', *Journal of the Rajasthan Institute of Historical Research*, 10, pt 2 (1973), p. 22.
60. W. Cockburn, 'Nazar—Clouds', *Panjab Notes and Queries*, ii (1884–5), p. 6.
61. Pandit Ram Gharib Chaube, 'The Saint Khwaja Muinuddin Chisti', *North Indian Notes and Queries*, 4 (1894–5), p. 146.
62. Pandit Janardan Dat Joshi, 'Notes from Kumaon—Games, Superstitions, &c.—(c) Rajan Spells', *North Indian Notes and Queries*, 3 (1893–4), p. 134.
63. Forbes, *Ras Mala*, pp. 605–6.
64. Gupta, 'Magical Beliefs and Superstitions in Rajasthan', pp. 22–3.
65. N.K. Singhi, 'A Study of Jains in a Rajasthan Town', in Carrithers and Humphrey (eds), *Assembly of Listeners*, p. 157.
66. Tod, *Annals and Antiquities of Rajasthan*, ed. Crooke, ii, pp. 602–3, 621–2 and 813.
67. R.E. Enthhoven, *Folk Lore Notes*, 2 vols (Bombay, 1914–15), i, p. 88; Vilas Sangavi, *Jaina Community:* A Social Survey (Bombay, 1980), pp. 239–43; Beni Gupta, 'A Historical Study of Magical Beliefs and Superstitions in Rajasthan during Medieval Period', D.Litt. thesis, University of Rajasthan, 1975, pp. 51, 87, 93 and 291.
68. Dalpatram Daya, *Bhut Nibandh* [An Essay on Spirits], trans. A.K. Forbes (Bombay, 1849; repr. Delhi, 1990), p. 87.
69. A similar connection between literacy, sorcery and power was found in medieval Europe, where it was common knowledge that all sorts of 'clerics'—that is, literate people of middling social status—dabbled in necromancy in order to enhance their power over others: Richard Kieckhefer, *Magic in the Middle Ages* (Cambridge, 1990), pp. 153–5.
70. Gupta, 'Historical Study of Magical Beliefs and Superstitions in Rajasthan',

p. 111. The story has strong similarities with one from Jaipur, collected in 1899, but without the Baniya element. In this, the brahmans of Merta tied up the rain to the horns of a musk deer, causing a seven-year-long drought. When the king was eventually informed, he hunted and killed the deer, releasing the rain. G.A. Grierson, *Linguistic Survey of India*, 11 vols in 19 (Calcutta, 1903–28; repr. Delhi, 1968), ix, pt 2, pp. 176–7.

71. Kalika Ranjan Qanungo, *Studies in Rajput History* (Delhi, 1960), p. 58.
72. Gupta, 'Historical Study of Magical Beliefs and Superstitions in Rajasthan', pp. 322–3.
73. Interview with Bhanabhai Meghaji Kharali, Adivali, Kherwada Tehsil, Udaipur district, February 1987.
74. J.C. Oman, *Cults, Customs and Superstitions of India* (London, 1908), pp. 309–10.
75. Denzil Ibbetson, 'Keeping Off Rain—Baniyas', *Panjab Notes and Queries*, 1 (1883–4), p. 109.
76. K. Raghumathji, 'Keeping Off Rain—Bombay', *Panjab Notes and Queries*, p. 126.
77. R.C. Temple, 'Rain—Keeping Off', *Panjab Notes and Queries*, p. 65; Ibbetson, 'Keeping Off Rain—Baniyas', p. 109.
78. Chaina Mall, 'Rain Spells', *Panjab Notes and Queries*, 3 (1885–6), p. 115.
79. India Office Library, Board's Collection, 1852, F4 2472, no. 46, Mr Forgett, Principle Sudr Amin (sic), Ahmadnagar, 'Memorandum on the Rural Police in Poona District', 1846.
80. Interview with Komal Kothari, Jodhpur, July 1987.
81. Report by C.H. Pritchard, assistant commissioner, Merwara district, 28 February 1893: Pritchard and Devenish (eds), *Reports on Famine Relief in Ajmere-Merwara during 1891–92*, p. 9.
82. Ibid., p. 109.
83. Report by A. Martindale, commissioner Ajmer-Merwara, 6 June 1893, ibid., pp. 23–6; report by G.H. Trevor, chief commissioner, Ajmer-Merwara, 22 July 1893, ibid., p. 10.
84. Report by G.H. Trevor, ibid., p. 11; *Civil and Military Gazette*, 7 November 1891.
85. Rajasthan State Archives, Bikaner (hereafter R.S.A.), Ajmer Commissioner's Office Records, English Office Z (12) 20, basta 132, J. Biddulph, commissioner, Ajmer-Merwara, 23 January 1892.
86. Ibid., H.C. Clogstoun, district superintendent of police, Ajmer, 'Statement B, Details of Cases', 27–28 October 1981.
87. For further examples from India, see Ranajit Guha, *Elementary Aspects of Peasant Insurgency*, p. 10; for western Europe, see Tilly, 'Food Supply and

Public Order in Modern Europe', pp. 388–9; for the Pugachev rebellion in Russia, see Paul Avrich, *Russian Rebels 1600–1800* (New York, 1976), pp. 203–5.

88. Thompson, 'Moral Economy of the English Crowd in the Eighteenth Century', pp. 78–9, 89, 95 and 108–12.
89. Details of this rising are to be found in B.A, J.D., 1875, 82/730.
90. Arnold, 'Looting, Grain Riots and Government Policy in South India, 1918', p. 127; Rogers, '1866 Grain Riots in Sri Lanka', p. 502. In both cases this feature of the riots is mentioned in passing.
91. This is not to say that there were no outbreaks of looting of sahukars in pre-colonial India, only that the structure and causes of such attacks are likely to have been different from those recorded later. Unfortunately, there are no good studies of these outbreaks for the pre-colonial period. For passing references, see Bayly, *Rulers, Townsmen and Bazaars*, pp. 295–6 and 330–3. For a grain riot in Ahmedabad city in 1681–2 caused by the high price of grain, see *Gazetteer of the Bombay Presidency*, viii, p. 191. This riot led to the duty on grain being remitted.
92. Prasad, *Final Report of the Famine Operations in Marwar during 1899 and 1900*, p. 186.
93. B.A, J.D., 1832, 8; 1833, 11/276.
94. B.A., Famine Dept., 1896, 9/63, memorial by Deccan Sabha to J. Monteith, 14 December 1896.
95. I have described this latter rising in detail elsewhere: David Hardiman, 'The Bhils and Shahukars of Eastern Gujarat', *Subaltern Studies*, v (New Delhi, 1987), pp. 37–54.
96. B.A., Famine Dept., 1896, 21/43, E.L. Cappel, Dharwar district collector, 19 October 1896.
97. Ibid., district superintendent of police, Satara (unnamed), 15 November 1896.
98. Ibid., A. Cumine, Khandesh district collector, 23 November 1896.
99. Ibid., *Khandesh Vaibhav*, 30 October 1896, in 'Reports on Native Papers for Bombay Presidency for the Week Ending 7 November 1896'; B.A., Famine Dept., 1897, 150/247, A. Cumine, Khandesh district collector, 4 February 1897.
100. R.S.A., Ajmer Commissioner's Office Records, English Office Z (12) 30, basta 132, H.C. Clogstoun, district superintendent of police, Ajmer, 'Statement B, Details of Cases', 27–28 October 1891.
101. National Archives of India, Delhi, F.D., October 1892, Intl-B, 87–8, report by A. Martindale, commissioner, Ajmer-Merwara, 9 September 1892.

102. Ballad recorded by Komal Kothari, and kept in the tape archives of the Rupayan Sansthan, Borunda, Bilada tehsil, Jodhpur district, Rajasthan.
103. Jains, who consider it sinful to kill any living being, are supposed to strain water before drinking it, lest they swallow and thus kill any insects or microbes. The proverb is cited in *Report on the Census of Marwar and Mallani Taken on the 26th of February 1891*, 2 vols (Jodhpur, 1891–4), ii, p. 130; the translation is mine.
104. Gupta, 'Historical Study of Magical Beliefs and Superstitions in Rajasthan', p. 323.
105. K.D. Erskine, *A Gazetteer of the Sirohi State* (Ajmer, 1910), pp. 276–7; *The Sirohi State Administration Report, 1940–41* (Ajmer, 1942), p. 35.
106. Notification by Durga Prasad, deputy secretary, Home Dept., Government of Rajasthan, 5 August 1957, *Rajasthani Gazette*, ix (1957), p. 270; Sirohi Jila Jain Sangh [the Sirohi District Jain Association] to chief minister of Rajasthan, 10 October 1963. I am grateful to Denis Vidal for providing me with copies of the latter document, and of those cited in nn. 108, 109, 112 and 113 below, all of which are from the registry of the Home Department, Government of Rajasthan, Jaipur.
107. Singhi, 'Study of Jains in a Rajasthan Town', p. 156.
108. Home Dept., Government of Rajasthan, Jaipur, summary of criminal case no. 339 of 1919–20, Sirohi state (Panch Mahajans of Jawal, Barloot, Bhav, Arathwara and Sanwara *v.* Jesa Suthar and seventy-four others), by Maganlal Mehta, judicial officer, Sirohi state, 30 June 1920, reproduced as 'Appendix A', Sirohi Jila Jain Sangh to chief minister of Rajasthan, 10 October 1963.
109. Home Dept., Government of Rajasthan, Jaipur, Sirohi Jila Jain Sangh to chief minister of Rajasthan, 10 October 1963.
110. This information comes from files of clippings from Rajasthani newspapers in R.S.A., Bikaner State, Foreign and Political Dept., Newspaper Cutting Branch, file 53 of 1936; *Administration Reports of the Sirohi State for the Year Ending 31st October 1936* (n.p., 1939), p. 3; *Times of India*, 6 February 1939.
111. *The Sirohi State Administration Reports, 1943–44* (Sirohi, 1945), p. 14.
112. Home Dept., Government of Rajasthan, Jaipur, Sirohi Jila Jain Sangh to chief minister of Rajasthan, 10 October 1963.
113. Ibid.; Home Dept., Government of Rajasthan, A.R. Surana, general secretary All India Jain Conference, to home minister of Rajasthan [1963].
114. Interview with Bhanabhai Meghaji Kharadi, Adivali, Kherwada tehsil, Udaipur district, Rajasthan, February 1987.
115. *Rajasthan Patrika* [Udaipur edn], 15, 16 and 19 July 1985.

116. Information from Dr Harbans Patel, who interviewed both Bhils and Baniyas in the area in 1985.
117. For a report on usury in this region, see Shreekant Khandekar, 'Money-Lenders: Their Pound of Flesh', *India Today*, 31 January 1986, pp. 140–3.
118. The interaction between Jain and Bhil belief, expressed in a number of legends as well as in religious practice, is examined in detail by Caroline Humphrey, 'Fairs and Miracles: At the Boundaries of the Jain Community in Rajasthan', in Carrithers and Humphrey (eds), *Assembly of Listeners*, pp. 201–25.
119. E.J. Hobsbawm, *Primitive Rebels: Studies in Archaic Forms of Social Movement in the 19th and 20th Centuries* (Manchester, 1974), pp. 65–73.
120. In medieval Europe, Jews, as well as lepers, were believed to be able to cause evil by means of sorcery; they were, for example, blamed for the Black Death: Carlo Ginzburg, 'The Witches' Sabbat: Popular Cult or Inquisitorial Stereotype?', in Steven L. Kaplan (ed.), *Understanding Popular Culture: Europe from the Middle Ages to the Nineteenth Century* (Berlin, 1984), pp. 43–4. For scapegoats during periods of dearth in twentieth-century Africa, see Arnold, *Famine*, p. 77.

CHAPTER 7

Small-Dam Systems of the Sahyadris

One of the criticisms made today of large-dam projects in India is that irrigation needs are served better and more equitably by a large number of small dams rather than by a few big dams. Small dams, it is argued , change the environment less drastically and encourage more sustainable and environmentally friendly forms of agriculture. The systems are more under the control of local people, are used more efficiently, and serve local needs better.[1] However, although it is clear that systems of irrigation based on small dams were important for agriculture in many parts of India in the past, very little is known about the extent of such systems, the manner in which they were organized, or the reasons why they often declined. Were they found only in a few limited areas where the terrain was suitable? Were they organized by autocratic rulers, who deprived the cultivators of most of the fruits of their labour? Did they die out because they had become an anachronism? Answers to questions such as these could help us to evolve better strategies for the sustenance or revival of such systems today.

The existing literature provides no clear answers. Irfan Habib, in his comprehensive study of the agrarian system of Mughal India, has a lot to say about the major state-sponsored canal systems of the plains regions, and about tanks and wells, but very little about small-dam systems. He has, however, one short paragraph which is of relevance.

> In the Dakhin the practice of leading small canals from rivers and streams was, like that of storage, an ancient one. We are told, for example, that in Baglana 'they have brought into every town and village thousands of canals, cut from the river for the benefit of cultivation', and these were managed, probably, according to the co-operative *phad* system, which still survives in that area.[2]

Baglan was a region in the Sahyadri mountains, with fertile river valleys. Although dams are not mentioned in this source, evidence which will be set out later in this essay shows that small dams were central to the irrigation system of Baglan. Such locations seem to have been particularly suited to small-dam based agriculture. In South Bihar, where many small rivers run off the central Indian plateau towards the basin of the Ganges, there was similarly widespread irrigation using small dams. Water was diverted by the dams to the fields by channels. Rice could thus be grown in an area without very high rainfall. Nirmal Sengupta, who has studied these systems, believes that they date back to 700 BC and that they provided a surplus sufficient to allow major civilizations to flourish in the region.[3] Similar small dams feeding water via channels to rice fields were found in the southern tip of India, in what is now Tamilnadu. Again, the dams were on rivers running from mountain ranges, and they allowed rice to be grown in areas where otherwise the rainfall was inadequate. These systems date back about a thousand years.[4] In many Himalayan valleys agriculture depended on the use of irrigation channels. Small dams were not needed, however, as water could be merely diverted from the rapid-flowing and perennial rivers. Small dams would not have withstood the constant pounding of these torrents.[5] It seems, therefore, that small-dam systems flourished mainly in piedmont areas where rainfall was less and the rivers often dried up or dwindled to a trickle during the dry season. The dams not only fed canals but also created reservoirs in which water could be stored during the dry months of the year.

How was all this organized? There are conflicting schools of thought in this respect. According to one school, irrigation systems of all sorts have in the past required highly centralized forms of organization. According to Wittfogel, they have provided the chief basis for despotism.[6] This has been disputed by Robert and Eva Hunt, who, in a comparative study of traditional systems of irrigation throughout the world, have argued that while such systems have normally been created by a ruling class, which has then exercised an overall responsibility for their continuation, organization and maintenance have been carried out at the local level most commonly by local collectivities.[7] This has been borne out in studies by Edmund Leach (Sri Lanka),[8] Clifford Geertz (Bali),[9] and others.[10] For India there appear to be no studies of similar quality on the organisation of such systems, and it is hard to

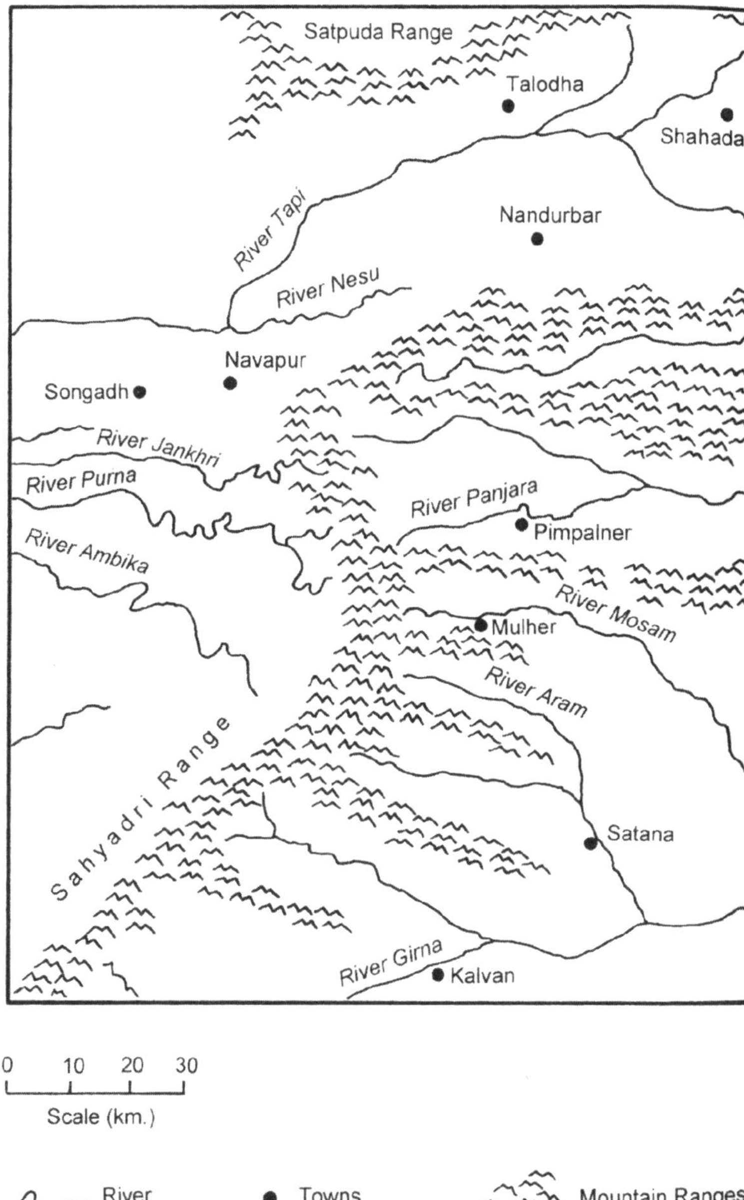

Map 3: The Baglan Region

come to any definite conclusions. Nirmal Sengupta admits that little is known about the organisation of the small-dam systems of South Bihar in earlier times, but during the colonial period they were maintained largely by zamindars. Peasants were required to carry out maintenance work—if they refused they were likely to be coerced by the zamindars. Gyan Prakash, in his study of agrarian labour in this region, has used oral tradition to argue that the dams were built and canals dug by low caste labourers under the supervision of members of the gentry.[11] The small-dam system of South Bihar seems therefore to have involved highly exploitative relationships of production, but not a highly centralized autocratic state. The small-dam systems of southern Tamilnadu, on the other hand, appear to have been built by kings but managed subsequently by others. David Ludden argues that the maintenance was carried out initially by local chiefs, later, in some cases, by temples, and then by powerful peasants, and never by the peasant community as a whole.[12] M.S.S. Pandian, on the other hand, shows that during the early nineteenth century the rulers—in this case the kings of Travancore—made it a legal requirement that the peasants carry out community labour to maintain the central canal in the Nanchilnadu region. Smaller channels were the responsibility of local communities. At the village level the dominant peasantry—as a corporate group—employed workers to maintain the channels and open and close the sluices. The workers were paid with a share of the crops—which helped to ensure that they were diligent in their work.[13] Pandian's evidence shows that community-based systems of irrigation did exist in India, as in Sri Lanka, Bali and elsewhere.

These systems all seem to have declined badly over the past two centuries. Why did this happen? Sengupta argues that the decline set in after the British took over the management of the systems of South Bihar from the zamindars in the 1930s.[14] Ludden believes that the British were interested only in large-scale irrigation works which could be controlled by the government and which would provide a high revenue. The state therefore neglected the small systems of southern Tamilnadu. High taxes on irrigated land and the loss of power by the local gentry also played a role.[15] Pandian likewise holds that the state—in this case Travancore—ruined the indigenous system of irrigation. The state asserted its control more tightly in the late nineteenth century and then neglected the infrastructure. In the 1920s it superseded the existing managing collectivities by Irrigation Boards. These proved inappropriate and they were moribund from the start. Without proper attention, the canal systems disintegrated quickly.[16] Over-centralization of management, introduced during the colonial period, is therefore blamed for the decline of these small-dam systems.

In this essay I want to explore some of these points taking as my focus the area mentioned by Irfan Habib—the Baglan region. While travelling in the valleys of this part of the Sahyadri range in the 1980s I came across the remnants of ancient dams on small rivers running off the mountains. The dams were mostly broken and out of use. However, in the valley of the Mosam river I found the dams still in use. The peasants had dug small channels to carry water from these dams to their fields. This was organized by the people—there were no landlords or dominant peasant castes in the valley controlling these systems. I shall examine the small-dam systems of Baglan using what written sources are available to me. I have not carried out any systematic mapping of the old dams or sought other archaeological evidence, or explored oral traditions in this respect. This would be a highly worthwhile task for the future.

II

The kingdom of Baglan was situated in the northern reach of the Sahyadri range of the Western Ghats, in the area running from north of Nasik to the Tapi river. The kings, who were of the Rathod clan, at times controlled parts of the adjoining plains regions of Khandesh, the Deccan and South Gujarat. Their base was at Mulher—a strongly fortified hill commanding the valley of the Mosam. This river rises at Salher, the second highest mountain of the entire Sahyadri range. Salher and other mountains were also fortified. These strongholds were extremely hard to reduce. They helped to ensure that the kingdom maintained its independence until the mid-seventeenth century. The Baglan kings normally accepted the overall paramountcy of more powerful rulers—paying tribute to them. Between 1317 and 1347 they were under the paramountcy of the rulers of Daulatabad. After a period of independence, in 1370 they were again obliged to pay tribute—this time to the Rajas of Khandesh. In the fifteenth century they were tributaries of the Sultans of Gujarat. When Akbar conquered Gujarat in 1573, they transferred their allegiance to the Mughals.[17] At that time Abul Fazl described Baglan as being a country one hundred kos long and thirty kos broad (one kos was equivalent to about two kilometres). The ruler commanded 16,000 infantry and 2,000 horse and the revenue was six and a half crores of *dams* (at that time a *dam* was worth between Rs 35 and Rs 40[18]).[19] The kingdom therefore represented a rich prize, and in 1599 Akbar attacked it. Akbar failed, however, to reduce the hill forts, and the two rulers eventually came to an agreement in which certain territory was ceded to Baglan.[20] In 1638 the future emperor, Aurangzeb, finally conquered the kingdom for the Mughals. The king of Baglan appears to have been allowed to continue to rule under the paramountcy of the Mughals for a time, but around 1658 the kingdom was merged into the province of Khandesh.[21]

Accounts of the mid-seventeenth century talk of the great agricultural prosperity of the region. Jean Baptiste Tavernier travelled through this area on more than one occasion between 1640 and 1667. Writing of Navapur, which was in the Baglan kingdom, he said:

> Nawapura is a large village full of weavers, but rice constitutes the principal article of commerce in the place. A river passes by it, which makes the soil excellent, and irrigates the rice, which requires water. All the rice which grows in this country possesses a particular quality, causing it to be much esteemed. Its grain is half as small again as that of common rice, and, when it is cooked, snow is not whiter than it is, besides which, it smells like musk, and all the nobles of India eat no other. When you wish to make an acceptable present to any one in Persia, you take him a sack of rice.[22]

This description was echoed by Jean de Thevenot, who passed through the Baglan region in 1666 and wrote later: 'The rice (wherewith the fields are covered) is the best in all the *Indies*, especially towards Naopura, where it has an odiferous taste, which that of other countries has not.'[23]

According to Irfan Habib, this famous variety of rice was known as *kamod*.[24] Other agrarian products for which the region was famous were sugarcane, grapes, pineapples, pomegranates and citrus fruits.[25] Pineapples had been introduced to India by the Portuguese only in the sixteenth century, which shows that the farmers of Baglan had been quick to cultivate the new crop.[26]

Unfortunately, little is said as to how these crops were grown. Irrigation from the rivers running off the hills was clearly very important—going by the account of Tavernier. Sadiq Khan's statement—quoted earlier—that 'they have brought into every town and village thousands of canals cut from the river for the benefit of cultivation' bears this out.[27] Nothing is said, however, about small dams.

The Baglan region was conquered by the Marathas in 1670. Between 1723 and 1795 the area around the old capital of Mulher was controlled by the Nizam of Hyderabad. Between 1750 and 1753 there was a fierce battle for control of the region between the Nizam, the Peshwa, and the Maratha families of the Bandes and Gaikwads. The latter two families, who were allied, looted the villages to prevent the Nizam or Peshwa from realizing taxes. The Bhils of the adjoining forest tracts took advantage of the disorder to carry out their own looting. In the process, many dams were destroyed and the region became depopulated. The Peshwa's army gained control over the area in 1753, and in 1754 the Peshwa ordered that Rs 5,000 be paid annually for five years to repair the dams which had been broken.[28] The tract remained under the rule of the Peshwas to 1818, when it came under the British. A subdivision of Khandesh was formed which was called Baglan. In 1869 this taluka was transferred to Nasik district, with the headquarters at Satana. This arrangement continues to this day.

The British found a whole network of dams in the area. They were known locally as *bandharas*. In 1857 an anonymous officer of the Bombay government wrote a detailed description of them.[29] They were, where still erect, solidly constructed of blocks of black basalt stone bound together with coarse concrete mixed with small pieces of brick and pointed up with high quality cement. They were thick at the base, tapering to the top. They were kept in place by foundation stones which were set in holes cut in the bedrock of the rivers. If a firm rock base could be found stretching straight across a river, the dams were straight, otherwise they were bent in an irregular manner, following the line of available rock. In this respect they were built to be practical, not to look good. The dams raised the height of the water in the river (making it resemble a weir). Channels were constructed on one side, taking water to subsidiary channels, and thence to the fields. These channels were excavated from the earth, with earth banks.[30] They followed the contours of the land so as to avoid a fast flow of water which would have eroded or broken the banks. The channels needed constant maintenance, with silt having to be cleared from their bed and heaped on their banks or adjoining fields. Many of the dams were still in use in 1857, though some were abandoned—due to lack of water or because they had become silted up—and others were dilapidated or in ruins. In some places the only evidence revealing the existence of a former dam was a row of foundation holes cut in the bedrock of the river. The official who wrote the description believed that 'the dams of this Province must have been very numerous in former times; for one scarcely crosses a nullah of any size, on which remains of them are not distinctly visible.'[31]

The largest number of dams were found closest to the western border of Khandesh. The border ran south to north along the high escarpment of the Sahyadri range, with, on the west, a precipitous drop towards Gujarat. To the east, running into Khandesh, there were a series of subsidiary ranges running parallel to each other. In the valleys between these ranges there were rivers running east. These were the rivers on which most of the dams had been constructed. Most important was the Mosam river, which rose on the northern flank of Salher mountain and flowed down a valley past Mulher. For the first ten miles of this river there were a series of dams still intact with reservoirs stretching upriver from them.[32] Other such rivers were the Aram, rising on the southern flank of Salher and flowing down a valley towards Satana; and the Panjara, which rose west of Pimpalner. These river valleys formed the heartland of the old Baglan kingdom. In 1857, of all the talukas of Khandesh, Baglan had the most dams which were still intact—97 in all. Of the other areas which had been a part of the kingdom, Nandurbar had 60 dams and Pimpalner (which then included Navapur) 56 dams. As one went east into the flatter plains of Khandesh (an area outside the sway of the Baglan kings), the number of dams became fewer and fewer. Dhulia taluka had 18, Malegaon 12 and Amalner 10. North of the Tapi river, where there was a plain bordered on the north by the dramatic escarpment of the Satpuda mountains, there was only one dam—near Sultanpur. Here, it seems that the fall of the rivers off the mountains was so steep as to make dam construction impractical.

The report of 1857 covered only Khandesh district. Parts of the Baglan kingdom had however lain outside the boundaries of the British district. For instance, the upper valley of the Jankhri river, which ran west towards Surat from near Pimpalner, had once been a part of Baglan. There, the anthropologist B.H.Mehta, who carried out field work in the area in 1929–30, found the remains of 187 substantial masonry dams.[33] In Kalvan taluka, to the south of Baglan taluka and also once a part of the old kingdom, there were 59 dams on the Girna and other rivers.[34] In all of these areas the landscape was well suited to dam building, with rivers running off the mountains down long valleys. The gradient was such as to allow a good flow of water in the monsoon, but not a torrent. The mountains attracted high rainfall, which was then carried by the rivers to areas with less rain.

The report of 1857 said that according to local tradition the bandharas were built by 'the Mohamedans' and that it was not unlikely that this vast system of irrigation had been constructed when Khandesh was ruled by the Mughal minister Malik Amber (1610–30).[35] This was felt to be likely because 'the Mohamedans' were great builders of canal systems, while Hindu kings were better at constructing vast tanks. This argument seems wide off the mark, for the Mughals did not at the time of Malik Amber control the Hindu-ruled kingdom of Baglan, where most of the dams were located. The *Khandesh Gazetteer*, on the other hand, felt that it was probable that many of the dams 'date from the time of the late Faruki kings.'[36] The Faruki kings ruled Khandesh from 1295 to 1600. Again, they were not rulers of Baglan, so it is hard to see what connection there could be between them and the majority of the dams. Local people to whom I spoke in the 1980s told me that the bandharas had been built at the time of 'Gaoli Raj'. This is the name commonly given in the region for the Yadav dynasty of Devgiri (later Daulatabad, near Aurangabad), which controlled Khandesh in the thirteenth century. Many old temples, ponds and wells of Khandesh are said to have been built by an officer called Hemadpant, who was in charge of the region during the reign of Mahadev Yadav (1260–71).[37] At that time Baglan came under the overall paramountcy of the Solankis of Gujarat, rather than the Yadav kingdom,[38] so it is unlikely that Hemadpant and the Yadav kings were responsible for the bandharas. The popular tradition about the Gaoli Raj might, if nothing else, be a means of indicating that the dams are extremely old. It is possible, however, that the idea reflects a fairly accurate understanding of the antiquity of the dams.

This is possible because at the end of the thirteenth century there was a period of great social disruption in the region, brought about by the terrible Durga Devi famine, which continued from 1396 to 1408. This devastated the area, wiping out much of the population.[39] The chief peasant community of Baglan—the Konkanas—have a tradition that they came to the area at that time, themselves escaping from the effects of the famine.[40] They came from the Konkan region.[41] It is probable that they brought with them certain skills of agricultural engineering. The Konkan consists of a series of valleys running down to the Arabian Sea. The peasants had made fields by terracing the sides of the valleys. Water from the many small rivers and streams flowing off the mountains was diverted to the fields by dams and channels. A lot of land had, moreover, been reclaimed from the sea with the help of long embankments.[42] The Konkanas who migrated north to Baglan are likely to have brought with them the skill of building strong embankments, a skill used now to dam rivers rather than keep out the sea, and knowledge on how to construct systems of channels to convey water to terraced fields. If this was so, then it suggests that a peasant community was responsible for the construction and maintenance of the bandhara system of Baglan, rather than some centralized authority—such as a king or minister—as the British assumed (with a characteristic bias) must have been the case.

It is in fact difficult to know who was responsible for building and maintaining these dams. The Maratha evidence for the mid-eighteenth century shows that the state played an active role in encouraging the rebuilding of dams after they were broken during disturbances by providing grants. We do not however know whether the state took such work in hand itself or provided the means for the peasants to carry out the work themselves. The official who wrote the report of 1857 felt that the dams had been built by the state, for they were large and solid and would have required much labour and organization to construct. The report also says that the state appointed certain people to maintain the dams and remunerated them with grants of tax-free land. The villagers were then required to dig and maintain the channels themselves. Because of this, the channels were less substantial in construction.[43] The *Khandesh Gazetteer* said that the channels were maintained by channel-keepers called patkaris, who were endowed with considerable grants of land.[44] A report of 1928 stated, however, that maintenance of the dams and water channels, and access to the water, was controlled by the peasant community as a whole—a system known as phad. This was defined as: 'A system of irrigation under which a number of small holders join together for the economic use of the water supply available, for the growing of irrigated crops on a regular plan.'[45] When I visited the upper reaches of the Mosam valley in 1982, I was told that the system was organized on a co-operative basis, with the fields being distributed so that each household had a share of the irrigated land. Maintenance of the channels was carried out by the people themselves.

There is no technical reason why the people themselves could not have organized the construction of a large majority of the dams. The stone was available locally, and in the dry weather the rivers declined to a trickle, making construction work possible without the need for any diversion of the water. The dams were built in a rough and ready manner—not with the style associated with state-built dams, designed to enhance the prestige of the ruler. The only outside material used was the high quality cement with which the work was finished off. This could have been obtained outside and carried in the peasants' own bullock-carts to the site of the dam. It is however likely that the state took an active interest in the construction of the dams. The wealth of the kings of Baglan—and thus their power in the region—seems to have rested largely on the agriculture made possible by these dams. The Peshwas, likewise, understood the importance of these dams for the prosperity—and thus the revenue—of the area, and provided grants for their reconstruction. It needs also to be noted that these dams needed the military protection of the state, for they could be broken fairly easily by enemies, as happened during the disturbances of 1750–3.

It seems unlikely that these systems were operated at the village level by a dominant class, such as the gentry of South Bihar. The inhabitants of the villages of these valleys tended to be overwhelmingly of one community, without any very great internal stratification and without any class of dominant peasants or gentry. There is no evidence that any such classes ever dominated these villages in the past. With each dam serving only a fairly limited area, extra-local organization was not in any case required. The state may well have appointed people to look after some of the bigger dams and their channels, while leaving the maintenance of the large majority of smaller dams to the people themselves. Such a division of responsibility has been found to exist generally in small-dam irrigation systems in pre-capitalist societies all over the world.[46]

In all, it seems probable that these small-dam systems were constructed as a result of cooperation between the state and peasant cultivators skilled in the use of such systems. The peasants were probably involved in the building of the actual dams, with some aid from the state. They are likely to have taken the initiative in constructing the water channels and terraced fields. A village council representing the cultivating households appears to have been responsible for the maintenance of the systems.

Little is said in the land settlement reports for Nasik district or Khandesh district about the manner in which crops were cultivated in these villages. The settlement report for Songadh taluka (under Baroda state) describes rice cultivation using the method known as *rab*. This involved selecting a piece of ground for a seedbed and then fertilizing it by burning tree-loppings and other vegetation before the seeds were planted. Once the rains had set in, the seedlings were transplanted in the fields. This was considered by many officials of the day to be a 'primitive' form of agriculture. The settlement report in question described the peasants as 'slothful and averse to hard work', and thus inefficient. This ignored the fact that a lot of labour would have been required to transplant the seedlings and then irrigate and weed the fields.[47]

A report for the Dangs of 1902 provides a more detailed account of rab. The Dangs was the region lying due west of Baglan. In the past it had been under the overall paramountcy of the kings of Baglan, though local Bhil chiefs had considerable independence. The population was in the nineteenth century divided almost equally between Bhils and Konkanas. According to the report of 1902, during the wintertime branches were lopped from trees and bamboos were cut and arranged in a square on the ground. This was burnt in the summer, after the wood had dried out. Seeds were sown in the ashes. The adjoining land was ploughed with a bullock-drawn plough, and when the seedlings were large enough they were transplanted. This form of agriculture was practised in river valleys on more level ground, largely by peasants of the Konkana community rather than by people of other communities—such as the Bhils.[48]

Although we are not told in the reports whether rab was used for cultivation in the valleys which formed the core of the old Baglan kingdom, it seems probable that it was. Rab is a method practised all over Maharashtra, both in the Deccan and Konkan.[49] There are good accounts of the method for the latter region, and as the Konkanas came from there originally, it is worth describing them here. During the dry weather each year, bits of wood and other vegetation were gathered from the hills above the terraced rice fields. Layers of cow-dung, tree-loppings, shrubs, leaves and grass were piled up on a field selected as a seedbed. Earth was piled on top to keep it all in place until it was set on fire just before the monsoon. Once the rain came, rice was sown and allowed to grow a few inches high. The seedbeds were always on ground slightly higher than the main body of the fields, as rice seedlings rotted if allowed to become too wet. Once they had grown sufficiently, they were transplanted onto land which had been ploughed up in the previous weeks. Transplanted rice gave a far higher yield than broadcast rice. Rab provided a particularly good medium for rice seeds. Cowdung manure retained too much water, whereas rab allowed for a drier and more porous soil. Burning also destroyed any weeds in the soil before the rice-seeds were sown. It was calculated that for every acre of rice grown in this way, about three acres of forested upland were required to provide the rab. Valleys with such uplands were therefore ideal for such agriculture.[50]

It is therefore likely that rab cultivation was used in Baglan to grow its famous rice and other commercial crops such as sugarcane. These crops did not however cover most of the cultivated area. In 1880–1 only 0.95 per cent of the cultivated land of Baglan taluka was under sugarcane, and 0.71 per cent under rice. The chief crops were the millets *bajra* (56.47 per cent), and *juvar* (10.38 per cent).[51] In Pimpalner taluka in 1878–9, bajra was grown on 37.29 per cent of the cultivated land; rice on 12.76 per cent. Sugarcane took up only 0.35 per cent of the land.[52] Even though it is likely that the area under rice and sugarcane had declined considerably since the seventeenth century,[53] it is likely also that bajra, and to a lesser extent juvar, had even then been the staple food crop of the peasants. These crops required far less water than rice or sugarcane, and they were likely to have been grown higher up the sides of the valleys, beyond the reach of the water channels. In the villages of Baglan as a whole, only a small area was irrigated by water channels. In 1868 only 2,908 acres fell in this category, out of a total cultivated acreage of 91,132 acres. Although the system of bandhara irrigation was by then in a state of decay, it is unlikely that the extent of land irrigated by water channels had ever been anything more than a fairly small fraction of the total land which was cultivated. What this meant was that the fine varieties for which this region was so famed in the seventeenth century were grown on only a limited irrigated part of the land, with many other crops being grown on unirrigated land on the sides of the valleys.

It is probable, going by evidence from a part of the Sahyadri range lying to the south of Baglan, that the peasants sold the crops which had a high marketable value, retaining the crops with a lower value for their own consumption. A report on the Mahadev Kolis, the chief inhabitants of this southerly region, written in the 1830s, mentions ten varieties of rice grown by methods very similar to those found in Baglan. These varieties ranged from very fine to very coarse. The best were much prized by the Brahmans and other moneyed people of Maharashtra. Most of the better rice was sold to local traders, who in turn sold it in the towns and cities. The villagers kept only a small amount for themselves, to be eaten when festivals were celebrated. They also sold the coarser varieties of rice. They grew the local staple foodgrain, *nagli*, on their poorer, unirrigated land. Besides this, they grew some wheat, maize, pulses, vegetables and sugarcane of a low quality, mostly for their own consumption.[54] It is likely that the peasants of Baglan did the same, selling much of their high quality rice and sugarcane to earn money to pay taxes to the state, while keeping the less marketable produce for their own consumption.

III

The heyday of this system of agriculture was from the sixteenth to eighteenth centuries, with the decline coming in the early nineteenth century. A report written in 1839, mentioning this development, said that the dams were not so far gone as to be unrepairable, and that timely maintenance would allow large areas to be irrigated once more.[55] The 1857 report revealed a system in a state of collapse, with dams and water channels being allowed to silt up, and peasants carelessly damaging the sides of channels by driving their carts or cattle over them.[56] Figures for the number of working dams in Baglan taluka show a continuing decline in subsequent years. In 1857 there were in Baglan 97 bandharas, in 1881–2 49, in 1902–3 31.[57] In west Khandesh as a whole (excluding Baglan, which came under Nasik district in 1869), there were in 1857 157 working bandharas, in 1911–12 80, in 1922–3 only 3.[58] The system therefore disintegrated under British rule.

Why was this allowed to happen? At the advent of British rule, the system was not in a healthy state, as a result of a profound social crisis which occurred in the region towards the end of the Maratha period. In 1802–3, civil war amongst the Marathas led to ruthless looting of the peasants to pay and feed the warring troops. This led to a devastating famine, with large numbers of peasants either dying of starvation or having to desert their villages, never to return.[59] Many villages were left with no population, and the land soon became covered in scrub, then trees.

There had however been earlier crises, as in 1750–3, and the systems had been repaired with state support. Why did this not happen again after the crisis of 1802–4? The Peshwas were still the rulers in the region, but now they lacked the resources, power and will to organize such work. The British, who replaced them in 1818, could however have done this. Briggs, the first Collector of Khandesh, commented on the subject:

> In many instances I met with the most importunate petitions for repairs of the numerous fine dams in Candeish which will at some future period so naturally tend to the increase of the land revenue, but I invariably told them it must depend on the expected increase of revenue, desirable from those repairs whether or not Govt would undertake to sink so much money . . .[60]

As a result he turned down all such requests for grants. The reaction was short-sighted in the extreme, for without the restoration of the systems, the prosperity of the region could not be restored. As Stewart

Gordon remarks, his attitude contrasted strongly with that of the Peshwas in 1754, who were quick to provide immediate aid for such rebuilding. Because of this, resettlement in the region was patchy and slow.

Although the British claimed frequently that they wished to preserve these irrigation systems, in practice they did little to encourage them. Generally, they placed a low value on any irrigation system which the peasantry themselves were responsible for. Even the otherwise sympathetic report on the bandharas of 1857 was very critical about the way in which the water channels meandered around the contours of the slopes without any masonry lining to prevent the water from being absorbed by the soil. It was argued that the channels needed to be improved by the Public Works Department (PWD), with cuttings to straighten the line of the channels, and the use of more masonry.[61] This was never done, due to lack of funds for a department which was responsible also for road construction and official buildings. Whatever little money was available for irrigation works tended to be spent on new projects, laid out according to plans drawn up by the Civil Engineer, and which were subsequently under the complete control of the department. It was considered that the peasants were incapable of maintaining sustainable systems of irrigation by themselves. Maintenance of existing bandharas was hampered furthermore by the fact that permission for all PWD projects had to be obtained from Bombay. In some cases this meant that the file had to pass through the hands of nine different officials (not including the Civil Engineer himself) before work on a bandhara could go ahead.[62] This hampered any attempts at regular maintenance of the bandharas.

Official neglect is not however the only reason for the decay of the small-dam systems. In many cases the peasants themselves contributed to the decay. This was most obviously the case in the areas which were resettled after the crisis of the early years of the nineteenth century by members of the Bhil and Maochi communities, who practised slash and burn agriculture in an area which had reverted to forest.[63] A field was cut from the forest, the cut vegetation was burnt, and seeds were planted in the ashes. After two or three years of cultivation, the peasants selected a fresh plot in the forest. One such area was Navapur—formerly famed for its fine agriculture and prized rice—which was described in 1864 by the Collector of Khandesh as a 'vast jungle tract . . . The present inhabitants are mostly Bhils, with a few Konkanis, almost as wild as their country . . .'[64] Shifting cultivation did not require dams, water channels and terraced fields, and without maintenance the systems quickly disintegrated. They have never been revived to this day.

In some areas small-dam-based agriculture seems to have survived the crisis of the early years of the nineteenth century, only to have decayed later on. The report of 1857 found that many peasants who should have been capable of running such systems were failing to do so. One reason—advanced in a report on Nandurbar taluka of 1862—was that many of the rivers were no longer supplying adequate amount of water to fill the dams and feed the channels. Because of this, of the 69 dams found in the taluka, only nine were still in use by 1862. The local people attributed the drying up of the rivers to British rule—though they could not explain why this was so beyond advancing what the official called 'superstitious reasons'. This official provided his own scientific explanation, arguing that the felling of trees in the adjacent hills during the early nineteenth century now caused the monsoon rain to run off the slopes so fast that very little water was absorbed by the ground. In the process much soil was washed down, leading to the rapid silting up of the dams and water channels, making them almost useless. On top of that, lack of trees had led to a decline in rainfall.[65] The people of the area said that the hills had been well wooded not long ago.[66] Deforestation therefore appears to have been an important cause of the decay of the bandharas and their channels in many parts of Nandurbar.

This does not explain the decay of the small-dam systems in the valleys in which there was no radical change of population or deforestation during the nineteenth century. Baglan and Pimpalner talukas came into this category. There the cause appears to have been a combination of high taxes and growing indebtedness which made irrigated agriculture uneconomic.

When the British conquered the region, they found a system of taxation in the channel-watered villages in which the rate of tax depended on the value of a crop grown in a field. Sugarcane paid the highest rate—normally over Rs 30 per bigha (in that area, one bigha was 3/4 of an acre). Rice paid Rs 15 or more per bigha. Other crops paid less.[67] Rates in different channel-irrigated villages ranged from Rs 2 1/2 to Rs 70 per bigha, according to crop grown.[68] The rates reflected the amount of water needed for each type of crop, and they helped to ensure that crops which used most water were grown in only a limited way, so that no excessive strain was placed on the irrigation systems. After 1818, the British imposed a uniform tax per unit of irrigated land. The rate was fixed high—the aim being to encourage the peasants to concentrate on growing the most valuable crops, so as to maximize the tax revenue.[69] The average rate per bigha in Baglan taluka was fixed at about Rs 12.[70] Although lower than the rates levied previously on rice and sugarcane, it was much higher than the rates paid for the less valuable crops which covered much of the land. As a considerable amount of capital was required to grow the more valuable crops, many peasants had to borrow money to grow crops of sufficient value to pay their taxes. By manipulating the books, the moneylenders soon had the peasants deep in debt. Using the civil courts established by the British, they could threaten to have the peasants' property and even land confiscated unless they handed over a larger and larger proportion of their crops at each harvest. By the 1860s it was being reported of Baglan that: 'Even the best channel-watered villages had few signs of wealth. Most of the people were forced to seek the moneylender's help and were in debt.'[71]

Increasingly, peasants found that the only way they could survive was to abandon the high-taxed irrigated fields and concentrate on low-taxed unirrigated cultivation. In this way they ceased to have any interest in maintaining the bandharas and water channels. They allowed the sides of the channel to disintegrate, so that the fields below became swamped. Once such decay set in, a whole system could become useless in very little time.[72] In the end, bandhara-based irrigation survived in only a few pockets, such as the more remote reaches of the mountain valleys, where tax was paid according to the number of ploughs used rather than area cultivated.

The decay of the small-dam systems of the Baglan region was therefore brought about by a combination of causes, the most important of which were colonial disinterest, resettlement of certain regions by shifting cultivators who had no interest in the dams, deforestation, and the decay in the old system of community-based control. The forest policy pursued by the British at the end of the nineteenth century made the situation still worse. The hilltops were demarcated as reserved forests under government control and the peasants were prevented from gathering material for rab for their seedbeds. This caused great resentment, with protests against the forest laws culminating in forest satyagrahas in the 1930s.[73]

Nowadays this region is considered to be a backward one, inhabited by 'primitives', classified now as 'scheduled tribes'. Development projects in the area concentrate on building large dams—such as the Haranbari dam on the Mosam river—which flood a huge area of what were once fertile fields irrigated by small bandharas and their channels. Revival of small-dam systems is not a programme high on the agenda of the Irrigation Department—though a few small steps have been taken in this direction.

IV

The evidence in this essay shows that small-dam systems of irrigation existed in the past which were sustained over long periods of time. Although they depended on state support, at village level they were controlled and managed by village communities. Although the precolonial state derived a substantial surplus from this agriculture, there does not appear to have been severe exploitation of one class by another within the villages, as was the case with many small-dam systems studied in other parts of India.

Whether or not such a form of agriculture can be revived or extended today on a large scale in areas with a suitable terrain is problematic. The problem is not merely a technical one, depending on the policy of the Irrigation Department, but also a social one. Rural society has become so polarized over the past two centuries that it is hard to see how a genuinely cooperative system of management and resource allocation could be established. Nowadays access to any system of irrigation reflects the inequalities of society.

If nothing else, however, a general policy in favour of small-dam systems would be far less damaging to the environment. Also, with small-dam systems in operation the conditions for more cooperative and environmentally friendly forms of agriculture would at least exist. With a certain amount of state support, the struggle to achieve this could be carried through. With large-dam systems, these conditions do not exist.

Notes

1. E.g. see Claude Alvares and Ramesh Billorey, *Damming the Narmada: India's Greatest Planned Environmental Disaster* (Penang, 1988), pp. 56 and 157–61.
2. Irfan Habib, *The Agrarian System of Mughal India (1556–1707)* (London, 1963), p. 31. The quote within the quote is from Sadiq Khan, *Shahjahan-nama* (mid-seventeenth century).
3. Nirmal Sengupta, 'The Indigenous Irrigation Organization in South Bihar', *Indian Economic and Social History Review*, 17:2 (1980), pp. 157–89.
4. M.S.S. Pandian, *The Political Economy of Agrarian Change: Nanchilnadu 1880–1939* (New Delhi, 1990), pp. 27–8 and 33–6; David Ludden, *Peasant History in South India* (Princeton, 1985), pp. 21–2.
5. Jogishwar Singh, *Banks, Gods and Government: Institutional and Informal Credit Structure in a Remote and Tribal Indian District (Kinnaur, Himachal Pradesh) 1960–1985* (Stuttgart, 1989), p. 80.
6. Karl Wittfogel, *Oriental Despotism: A Comparative Study of Total Power* (New Haven, 1957).
7. Robert C. Hunt and Eva Hunt, 'Canal Irrigation and Local Social Organisation', *Current Anthropology*, 17:3 (1976), p. 395.
8. Edmund Leach, *Pul Eliya: A Village in Ceylon* (Cambridge, 1961), pp. 28–47.
9. Clifford Geertz, 'Organisation of the Balinese *Subak*', in Walter Coward (ed.), *Irrigation and Agricultural Development in Asia* (Ithaca, 1980), pp. 72–84.
10. See chapters by Beardsley, Hall, Ward, Lewis, Bacdayan, Roberts and Coward in ibid.
11. Gyan Prakash, *Bonded Histories: Genealogies of Labour Servitude in Colonial India* (Cambridge, 1990), pp. 50 and 73–8.
12. Ludden, *Peasant History*, pp. 30 and 90.
13. Pandian, *Political Economy of Agrarian Change*, pp. 33–41.
14. Sengupta, 'Indigenous Irrigation', pp. 171–2.
15. Ludden, *Peasant History*, p. 145.
16. Pandian, *Political Economy of Agrarian Change*, pp. 105–13.
17. *Gazetteer of the Bombay Presidency*, vol. XVI, *Nasik* (Bombay, 1883), pp. 187–8 (hereafter *Nasik Gazetteer*); Abul Fazl, *The Akbar Nama* (repr., Delhi, 1973), p. 41.
18. Habib, *Agrarian System*, p. 388.

19. *Akbar Nama*, p. 43. The revenue was surely exaggerated; what is important is that the Mughals believed it was very high.
20. William Finch, in W. Foster (ed.), *Early Travels in India* (Oxford, 1921), pp. 136–7.
21. Habib, *Agrarian System*, p. 9; *Nasik Gazetteer*, pp. 403–4.
22. Jean Baptiste Tavernier, *Travels in India*, vol. I (London, 1889), pp. 49–50.
23. S. Sen (ed.), *Indian Travels of Thevenot and Careri* (New Delhi, 1949), p. 102.
24. Irfan Habib, *An Atlas of the Mughal Empire* (New Delhi, 1982), p. 26.
25. Ibid.
26. Habib, *Agrarian Systems*, p. 50.
27. Ibid., p. 31.
28. Stewart Gordon, 'Recovery from Adversity in Eighteenth-Century India: Rethinking Villages, Peasants, and Politics in Pre-Modern Kingdoms', *Peasant Studies*, 8:4 (1979), pp. 67–71. I am grateful to Mahesh Rangarajan for this reference.
29. 'The Dams and Rivers of Khandesh', *The Bombay Quarterly Review*, vol. V (January–April 1857), pp. 48–73.
30. In the Mosam valley I have myself observed that the channels are carried over small gulleys in hollowed-out tree-trunks. Otherwise, they are all dug from the earth, meandering around the sides of the hills.
31. 'Dams and Rivers of Khandesh', p. 50.
32. *Nasik Gazetteer*, p. 400.
33. B.H. Mehta, 'Social and Economic Condition of the Chodhras, an Aboriginal Tribe of Gujarat', unpublished M.A. thesis, University of Bombay, 1933, p. 576.
34. *Nasik Gazetteer*, p. 396.
35. 'Dams and Rivers of Khandesh', pp. 50–1.
36. *Gazetteer of the Bombay Presidency, Khandesh*, vol. XII (Bombay, 1880), p. 139 (hereafter *Khandesh Gazetteer*).
37. *Khandesh Gazetteer*, p. 242.
38. *Nasik Gazetteer*, p. 401.
39. *Khandesh Gazetteer*, p. 40.
40. R.E. Enthoven, *Tribes and Castes of the Bombay Presidency*, vol. 2 (Bombay, 1922), p. 265.
41. In his linguistic survey of India, Grierson reported that this tradition is supported by the fact that the Konkanas' language continued to have in it many elements of northern Konkani. G.A. Grierson, *Linguistic Survey of India*, vol. IX (Calcutta, 1907), p. 130.
42. *Gazetteer of the Bombay Presidency*, vol. XII, pt I, *Thana* (Bombay, 1882), pp. 281–4 (hereafter *Thana Gazetteer*).
43. 'Dams and Rivers of Khandesh', p. 57.

44. *Khandesh Gazetteer*, p. 140.
45. *Report of the Royal Commission on Agriculture in India* (London, 1928), pp. 325 and 755.
46. R. and E. Hunt, 'Canal Irrigation and Local Social Organisation', p. 395.
47. *Jamabandi Settlement Report of the Songadh Taluka of the Navsari Division 1902–3* (Baroda, 1902), p. 14.
48. Report by E.M. Hodgson, 29 August 1902, Maharashtra State Archives, Bombay (hereafter BA), Revenue Department (hereafter R.D.), 1902, 107/949, pt II.
49. D.D. Kosambi, *The Culture and Civilization of Ancient India in Historical Outline* (London, 1965), pp. 44–5.
50. *Thana Gazetteer*, p. 284; J.A. Voelcker, *Report on the Improvement of Indian Agriculture* (London, 1893), pp. 109–10. See also Indra Munshi Saldanha, 'The Political Ecology of Traditional Farming Practices in Thana District, Maharashtra (India)', *Journal of Peasant Studies*, 17:3 (1990).
51. *Nasik Gazetteer*, p. 406.
52. *Khandesh Gazetteer*, p. 400.
53. The reason for this will be discussed later.
54. A. Mackintosh, 'An Account of the Tribe of Mhadeo Kolis', *Transactions of the Bombay Geographical Society*, vol. I, 1836–8, pp. 211–16.
55. Dallas to Blane, 23 March 1839, BA, Political Department 1839, 15/1011.
56. 'Dams and Rivers of Khandesh', p. 55.
57. Ibid., p. 51; *Nasik Gazetteer*, p. 401; *Nasik Gazetteer*, B vol. (Bombay, 1903), p. 12.
58. 'Dams and Rivers of Khandesh', pp. 51–3; *Khandesh Gazetteer*, B vol. (Bombay, 1926), p. 70. In the latter reference the figures are for sources of irrigation other than wells or tanks—which meant in that region bandharas.
59. *Khandesh Gazetteer*, pp. 182–3.
60. Quoted in S. Gordon, 'Recovery from Adversity in Eighteenth-Century India', p. 76.
61. 'Dams and Rivers of Khandesh', pp. 49–50.
62. Ibid., pp. 60 and 65–6.
63. *Papers Relating to the Original Survey Settlement of 148 Villages of Nandurbar Taluka (including Navapur Petha), 17 Government Villages of the Shirpur Taluka, and 11 Government Villages of the Shahada Taluka of the Khandesh Collectorate. Selections from the Records of the Bombay Government,* no. CCCCXXIV—New Series (Bombay, 1904), pp. 2 and 5. This report says that many of the Bhils and Maochis who practised slash and burn cultivation in Navapur taluka had been in the area only since the last years of Maratha rule.

64. Quoted in *Papers Relating to the Revision Survey Settlement of the Nandurbar Taluka of the Khandesh Collectorate, Selections from the Records of the Bombay Government,* no. CCCXLIX—New Series (Bombay, 1896), p. 4.
65. 'Report on Nandurbar Taluka, 25 January 1865', in *Papers Relating to the Introduction of Revised Rates of Assessment into Eight Talookas and Two Pethas of the Khandeish Collectorate, Selections from the Records of the Bombay Government,* no. XCIII—New Series (Bombay, 1865), p. 471.
66. Ibid., p. 469.
67. 'Dams and Rivers of Khandesh', p. 62.
68. *Khandesh Gazetteer,* p. 279.
69. 'Dams and Rivers of Khandesh', pp. 59–60.
70. *Nasik Gazetteer,* p. 253.
71. Ibid., p. 251.
72. 'Dams and Rivers of Khandesh', pp. 55–6.
73. Interview with Madav Joshi, Mulher, 6 January 1982.

CHAPTER 8

Well Irrigation in Gujarat

Systems of Use, Hierarchies of Control

Introduction

The history of well irrigation during the colonial period is a somewhat neglected one. This is in contrast to the study of canal systems, which dominates the literature for that period.[1] Wells, however, provided the chief form of irrigation in many parts of India in the pre-colonial era,[2] as they do again today.[3] It was only during the colonial period and early postcolonial period that they suffered a temporary, and only partial, eclipse. It was estimated at the beginning of the twentieth century that whereas government-owned canals provided water for about 41 per cent of the irrigated land of British India, wells provided for about 30 per cent of the whole.[4] In 1949–50, figures for the irrigated area of the rather different landmass covered by the new state of India showed government canals covering 34.01 per cent of the total, wells 27.49 per cent. Well-irrigated land exceeded government-canal-irrigated land from 1971–2 onwards.[5]

Elizabeth Whitcombe, in her study of the effects of British canal on agriculture in UP, shows that once the canals were built and canal-water became available, irrigation wells were neglected and soon collapsed.[6] But what of the many areas in which wells continued to provide the chief source of irrigation throughout the colonial period? One of the few historians to examine such areas in any detail is Christopher Baker, in his history of rural Tamilnad between 1880 and 1955. He argues that the British, in seeking to turn agriculture into an instrument of accumulation, concentrated their resources on canal irrigation in the deltaic regions of South India, neglecting irrigation in the uplands, which was predominantly from tanks and wells. The only area in which there was any marked expansion in well irrigation during the nineteenth century was Coimbatore, where the dominant Gounder peasantry had the resources to finance their own construction. During the first half of the twentieth century, the advent of new pumping technology saw considerable growth in this sector over a wider area; in 1900 wells provided water for about a fifth of the total irrigated land of Tamilnadu, by the Second World War a quarter. The expansion was however almost entirely financed by the farmers themselves; the government provided very little help.[7]

In such a perspective, the resurgence of well irrigation during the twentieth century might seem like a victory of the small-scale and local over the large-scale, monolithic and centralized forms of water provision favoured by the colonial state. Any celebration of this would appear, however, to be premature. This is because over the past thirty years extraction of groundwater from wells has in many areas far surpassed any natural replenishment in the subsoil. Many wells have as a result gone dry. Each year farmers have to bore wells deeper and deeper at greater and greater expense to obtain any supply at all. To recoup the investment, the well-owner needs to sell as much of this water as possible to other farmers—frequently carried over long distances in pipes—so long as the well remains productive. Furthermore, in many coastal regions, the depletion of groundwater has led to ingress by seawater, so that wells become filled with salty water. When used for irrigation, crop yields decline sharply. The vicious circles thus created are having devastating environmental consequences in many prime agricultural areas of India.[8]

Bela Bhatia, in an excellent article on this problem as it exists in Gujarat today, has argued that modern technology is the chief culprit. In the past, wells hardly ever dried up entirely, even in years of severe famine. Only during the twentieth century has it become possible to bore deep tube-wells, and to pump the water out using submersible pumps. At the same time, an insatiable demand for water has been created by Green Revolution agrarian technology, involving high-yielding hybrid crop varieties which need a massive amount of watering. The demand is satisfied by those who have sufficient resources to construct tube-wells and pump out and sell water to their neighbours. This has led to a gross over-exploitation of this natural resource, and, very quickly, a collapse of the whole ecosystem. The phenomenon appears to provide striking evidence to justify Garett Hardin's well-known 'tragedy of the commons' thesis—namely that uncontrolled access to a common resource leads inexorably to its degradation.[9]

Others argue that this has been brought about at a more fundamental level through the decay of village institutions which before colonial times ensured that natural resources were conserved. Anil Agarwal and Sunita Narain believe that traditional water-harvesting systems disintegrated and disappeared in large parts of India during the early colonial period. High rates of land-tax left no surplus for the effective maintenance of irrigation systems, and much land went out of use. They cite the example of the ryotwari areas of Madras Presidency, where by the 1850s one-third of the irrigated land lay unused as it was unable to produce crops of sufficient value to cover land-tax demands. Land-tax began to be taken in cash rather than kind, so the economy became commercialized, with parasitic merchants gaining a hold over the peasants, causing further exploitation and regression. All of this hastened the 'destruction of the institutions that managed and maintained, through community participation, a series of traditional water harvesting structures'.

> Indian society imploded under this colossal impact. Local people, having lost the control of their environment, became increasingly alienated and finally joined in the plunder, and what were once 'community managed commons' steadily turned into 'free access resources'.[10]

In a variation on this sort of argument, Uma Shankari and Esha Shah hold that in the pre-colonial period the state left villages free to manage their own affairs. All that the state required was that the land-tax be paid collectively. The British made individuals responsible for paying taxes, which undermined the corporate character of the village community. At the same time, common properties were annexed by the government, so that 'village communities lost control over them and gradually interest in maintaining them'. Village communities were also deprived of the power to raise taxes to finance the building and maintenance of water resource systems, and neither were they able any longer to compel villagers to labour on such works. This led to a situation in which farmers developed private sources of irrigation, particularly wells and tube-wells. The end result has been that: 'Every farmer dreams of having his own well and "doing his own thing". He then does not have to co-operate, adjust or accommodate with the other farmers.'[11]

Others have seen the basic problem as one of the commodification of water. Chhatrapati Singh has argued that before the colonial period water was controlled according to customary law which, in its great variety, was in tune with local need. Customary law recognized community, rather than individual, rights over water. Generally, there was no notion of selling titles to land and its water resources. Under the colonial rule of property, land, and the water on it, was held to be a commodity which the individual title-holder could sell without needing to take into consideration the wider community. In effect, this meant that only those who owned land had a right to the water on it. In this way, all those who did not hold colonial land-deeds were excluded from access to water. This, he argues, caused the collapse of traditional water management structures and led to the irresponsible use of the resource for personal gain.[12]

There is another possible argument which is not advanced specifically by any of these authors, but which is implicit in the approach taken by ecologists such as Agarwal and Narain, who emphasize in their work the importance of general watershed management. Earlier methods of harvesting rainfall could involve building check-dams on rivers or channelling rainwater into reservoirs, so that water had time to soak into the ground and thus fill the wells. Allowing a river to flood could ensure the same result. It can be argued that it was the decay of arrangements of these sorts which caused a decline in groundwater levels in many areas, and thus a drop in water levels in wells, and even their drying up.

In this essay I shall examine these various arguments in the context of Gujarat. In this part of India there were no important colonial canal projects, and well irrigation did not suffer any comparative eclipse. During the 1930s wells accounted for over 78 per cent of the irrigated area of British Gujarat, canals only 10 per cent.[13] Irrigation was, however, extremely limited in the region as a whole at that time, covering only 2.6 per cent of the total cropped area.[14] It is likely that irrigation had in fact declined since the pre-colonial period. The general picture is one of decay and stagnation. New structures of land use and control had however already been forged which would determine the structure of a much enlarged irrigated sector of the postcolonial period. Despite the building of many large dams feeding extensive canal networks, wells accounted for 74 per cent of the total irrigated area of Gujarat in 1986–7, as against 17 per cent covered by government canals.[15] The irrigation history of Gujarat over the past two centuries must therefore, of necessity, focus on wells.

Pre-colonial Systems of Water-harvesting and Conservation in Gujarat

Gujarat depends for almost all of its water on the south-west monsoon which falls between June and October. Rainfall varies considerably between different areas. It is strongest in the south, where the average annual fall is often over 1,000 mm. Central Gujarat and the coastal regions of Saurashtra receive between 800 and 1,000 mm on average, while north Gujarat and the rest of Saurashtra receive between 400 and 800 mm. Kutch frequently has less than 400 mm.[16] Rainfall records, which date back in a systematic fashion to only the mid-nineteenth century, do not suggest that there has been any significant change in rainfall over the past century and a half.[17] The current crisis has not been caused by less rain so much as by over-extraction and a failure to conserve the rain that does fall.[18]

In the pre-colonial period, wells provided probably the single most important means for tapping this water for irrigation on a year-round basis.[19] Extensive tracts of fertile land in Gujarat were found in areas of deep alluvial soils which acted as a giant sponge, soaking up the monsoon rains. In most of such areas, water could be tapped at no great depth. The British, when they established their rates of taxation for wells in the nineteenth century, did not levy any tax on wells with subsoil water 40 feet (12.19 metres) or more below ground level. As this tax brought in substantial returns, this indicates that the sub-soil level was in most cases less than this.[20] Two British reports for Ahmedabad district of 1825 and 1827, written less than ten years after the colonial annexation of the area, provides details of the wells found in the area at that time. When water was found close to the surface, a rough, temporary well could be dug which lasted only for a season. When a deeper well had to be constructed, some sort of masonry had to be used, either of rock or brick. If the water was not so deep down, unhewn stones could be used without any cement to bind them together. This sort of well could be built by peasants without the need for professional help. Brick wells built by professional well constructors could be sunk to greater depths. When such a well was built, an excavation was made up to a depth of thirty *haaths* (about 12 metres).[21] A large wooden wheel of the circumference of the intended well was then taken to the bottom of the pit to serve as a base for the bricks. The bricks were built up, using only some clay to bind them together. They were then covered with *chuno*—a lime plaster—to provide a very substantial construction which could last for many years.[22]

Hove, travelling near Amod in central Gujarat in 1787, described a well built using stone slabs rather than bricks. These slabs had been brought at great expense from Bhavnagar in Saurashtra, which lies on the opposite side of the Gulf of Cambay to Amod. Presumably, they had been carried by boat. Hove dropped a 17-yard (15.54 metre) line into the water, but was unable to touch bottom. The well was 46 feet (14.02 metres) in diameter.[23] This might seem large, but wells of this size appear to have been common, allowing for the erection of several water-extracting devices around the edge.

In many parts of Gujarat, such as in the north and the east, as well as in much of Saurashtra, there was only a thin layer of soil covering a rocky substratum. Shallow wells, reaching down to the rock, could not provide a year-round supply of water. Here, it was necessary to dig through the rock to tap deep-down springs. Sites were chosen with care and great skill by water diviners—*panikals*—who were paid for the service. According to a British observer: 'Their judgement is unerring, and many instances are on record of their practical ability. They can also generally tell at what depth the spring will be tapped.'[24] In some cases the villagers themselves undertook such work as a long-term project, hewing out the rock with a chisel. It could take up to ten years to complete the work. In some cases, blazing logs were used to split the rock.[25] In the area around Damnagar in Saurashtra wells such as these were blasted through rock with gunpowder and lined with stone. F.A.H. Elliot, who saw these wells in the 1880s, believed many to be a hundred and fifty or two hundred years old or more. The local people told him that they lasted hundreds of years. They were always full of water which was sweet and good for irrigation. Although such wells were relatively few in number, water was carried from them in channels over often long distances. Every farmer tried to gain a right to use some land irrigated by them.[26] Similarly, in the area around Champaner in north-eastern Gujarat, N.H. Beyt reported in 1880 that in previous centuries—but no longer—the area had been well known for its fruit produce: 'Its magnificent wells were stone built, square and round sunk deep into the solid rock, tapping inexhaustible springs, serving the purpose of irrigation . . .'[27]

Water was lifted from a well chiefly by means of a large leather bag—*kos*. This was raised by bullocks, pulling a rope attached to the bag over a pulley erected above the well. At the top, the bag was emptied into a trough, and from there the water flowed into channels to the fields. There were two types of bag. One, the *sundhiyun*, had a trunk at one end so contrived that when it reached the well-head, the water poured by itself into the trough. This could be worked by one peasant with a pair of bullocks, and it tended to be used in wells of not more than about ten metres depth. Small bullocks were adequate for this kos. The other, *ramaiyo*, was a larger bag without a trunk, made up from a whole bullock hide, which could hold about 0.8 to 1.4 cubic metres of water. The well-head was built up above the surrounding land, allowing for a ramp to be built down which the pair of bullocks could run to make it easier for them to draw up this heavy weight. Two or three peasants were needed to operate this form of kos, one or two to encourage and guide the bullocks, the other to drain the water into the trough. As a rule, this method was used in deeper wells. The bullocks had to be large and strong. The depth of the well determined the amount of land which could be irrigated in a day, though about half an acre for one kos of either type was a rough rule. If a second pair of bullocks was available, the work could be carried out at greater speed, and more land could be irrigated.[28]

It was common to work more than one kos from a single well. Wells were in fact known by the number of kos they could accommodate at one time. In Ahmedabad district in 1827 it was reported that almost all wells were for two or more kos and that four-kos wells were common.[29] In Kheda district, some wells were able to take up to eight kos at one time.[30] In the majority of cases, four kos could be operated together.[31] In what would appear to be an exceptional case, a well near the south coast of Saurashtra was said to be capable of holding 32 kos.[32]

Hove also described a manually operated water-raising machine which consisted of a wheel five metres in diameter which was suspended vertically on four poles, with a rope ladder around the rim on which were tied earthen pots. The wheel was turned by human power; men sat on the cross-beams and turned the wheel with their hands and feet. Hove tried it himself, and found that it was not hard to move the apparatus. The pots emptied into a trough, and the water flowed from there to the fields.[33] This device appears to be similar to the ancient water-lifting apparatus known in Sanskrit as *araghatta*.[34] Irfan Habib has argued that whereas it was more efficient to lift water from relatively shallow wells using the leather bag technique, the device which used a wheel, rope and pots came into its own when the well was very deep.[35] In Gujarat, kos was almost certainly used more widely than the latter machine, which suggests that most wells were not so deep.[36]

These devices were used not only in wells, but were also found frequently on the banks of rivers. In Gujarat, the rivers had generally scoured out deep channels below the level of the surrounding plain, so that water had to be lifted to the level of the adjoining fields. The kos and araghatta-type device which Hove described were in both cases being worked on the banks of the Dhadhar river, in what is now Bharuch district. There had to be a vertical, or near-vertical, drop from the bank to the river if the apparatus was to be operable. In some cases, channels were dug in the river bed to bring water beneath a suitable vertical bank.[37] Or, alternatively, a pit—known as *dhekudi* or *oria*—was dug in the river bed below a suitable bank, into which water percolated. As the banks were not very stable, and also as the rivers shifted in their beds considerably from year to year, the devices were erected as a rule only temporarily.

Reservoirs—*talav*—were important not only for direct irrigation, but also because they allowed water to percolate into the soil and top up surrounding wells. The Solanki dynasty, which ruled from Anilwada Patan in north Gujarat from 941 to 1215, developed an extensive system of reservoirs in that area. V.K. Jain, using contemporary Sanskrit manuscripts, has provided a long list of them. To take one example, the Rupen river was diverted at Modhera to take water to the Karna Sagara reservoir at Karnavati (near present-day Ahmedabad)—a distance of about seventy kilometres.[38] An early-twentieth-century report on the Visnagar area recorded the evidence of a huge irrigation tank at Khandoran, by then in ruins, once fed by the Rupen river. The line of the canal taking water from this reservoir to Anilwada Patan could still be traced with ease.[39]

Khasherao Jadhav, a Baroda state official, argued in a report of 1916 that the country of north Gujarat was best suited for irrigation through reservoirs rather than through wells. The water was at a great depth, making well-digging difficult. As the area was prone to flooding during the monsoon, the reservoirs constructed in the past were able to both check and store the water for later use. He felt that they should be restored.[40] Evidence from the Solanki period suggests, however, that wells employing the araghatta lifting device were in common use in the area at that time.[41] It is likely that the large reservoirs helped maintain the water level in these wells. Once these systems had disintegrated after the collapse of the Anilwada Patan kingdom in the thirteenth century, the water table is likely to have fallen considerably, so that well irrigation became impractical using existing water-lifting devices. Only with the coming of modern pumps could this situation be reversed. The reservoirs, unfortunately, have never been reconstructed, and today the tube-wells of the area stretch to prodigious depths.[42]

Similar systems of irrigation were found in the kingdom of Champaner in eastern Gujarat, ruled by the Chohans in the fourteenth and fifteenth centuries. Reservoirs of all sizes were constructed, allowing extensive irrigation in this region. After the fall of the dynasty in 1484 the works began to decay. By the nineteenth century only traces remained.[43]

During the Mughal period, the construction and maintenance of reservoirs appears to have been encouraged by rulers, but without any systematic planning of the sort seen earlier. Many very impressive ornamental reservoirs were built under state patronage, but they tended to serve the water needs of the cities which they adjoined, not being designed for irrigation-use.[44] James Forbes, who resided at Dabhoi near Baroda in 1777–8, stated that there was generally a tank in each large village. They were enclosed with strong masonry, and their banks were adorned by banyan, mango and tamarind trees.[45] In Dholka Pargana, near Ahmedabad, reservoirs were used on a large scale for irrigation. The countryside sloped gradually from north to south, and the reservoirs were constructed to take advantage of this natural feature. Their northern sides were hardly built up at all, while on the south there were large, strong embankments. The overflow from one reservoir thus filled the one below it.[46]

Reservoirs could be filled either by rain or by flood inundation. Hove, while travelling in central Gujarat, saw many large reservoirs close to rivers which were filled from floods in the rivers. A few were formed utilizing river creeks, with a bank being built to close them off from the river, but most had been dug out with great labour. Their banks were built up above the level of the river bank, being planted with trees to strengthen them. A sliding sluice was constructed in the bank adjoining the river which was left open when the river was in spate. Once the reservoir was full of water—and in some years this would be to a level higher than the river banks—the sluice was closed. Sluices in other parts of the reservoir were then opened, allowing the water to flow into channels which took the water to the fields. Strips of land were left between the fields, in which temporary channels could be dug to allow water to be carried throughout the village lands. In many cases it was taken over considerable distances, being used not only for direct irrigation but also to fill wells. When the level of the water in the reservoir fell below the level of the sluices, lifting devices were used to raise the water into the channels. As the water did not have to be raised to any great height, a considerable area could be irrigated in this way. Hove calculated that a twelve-acre farm could be watered using an araghatta-type device in five hours.[47]

Hove noticed that 'interceptions' were constructed on the river beds during the dry season to encourage a rapid build-up of water during the monsoon, causing a maximum flood potential.[48] Cruikshank, writing in 1825, mentions similar dams, of mud, built across the Khari river in Ahmedabad district, designed to encourage the flooding of the surrounding countryside.[49] The floods served both to fill the reservoirs, and also to give the ground a soaking, providing sufficient moisture in the soil to allow a monsoon crop to be raised with no further irrigation. The check-dams and flooding also raised the water-table and filled the wells. This deliberate encouragement and guidance of floods appears to have gone out of use in many areas during the nineteenth century. However, as one colonial officer observed, inundation—if carefully controlled—could raise crop yields considerably.[50]

Political Economy of Wells in Pre-colonial Gujarat

Wells were constructed either by labour from within a village, or by hired professionals. In the case of shallow, unlined wells, the villagers themselves would do the work. Masonry or rock-cut wells were much harder to build, and farmers who constructed such wells on their land had either to carry it through as a very long-term project, as in the case of chiselling laboriously through rock, or they had to hire skilled well constructors to perform the task for them. The latter were normally from a specialist caste—the Ods. Ods were professional reservoir and well-diggers, and brick and stonemasons who have been found in Gujarat for at least a thousand years. An eleventh-century text refers to them as 'uddo'.[51]

As the building of a masonry or stone-lined well, with its elaborate water-lifting apparatus, was extremely expensive, the work had invariably to be financed with a loan from a merchant-usurer (sahukar). In the 1820s in Ahmedabad district, brick wells were said to cost between Rs 150 and Rs 1,000 to build, depending on depth and width. It was reported that peasants never managed to find this sum from their own capital, they always had to borrow from a moneylender and pay at least 12 per cent in interest.[52] In effect, this meant mortgaging the future produce of the land, and perhaps even the well itself, to the usurer. As this arrangement was of great profit to usurers, they were always keen to encourage well-digging by their clients. In many cases they made arrangements with the Ods to come to do the work, paid them direct, and entered the sum as a debt in the account of a peasant family.[53] Because of this, the usurer could dictate the crop that was grown, invariably a high-value irrigated crop. Peasant well-owners were not in this respect free agents.

The financing of well building by merchant capital would appear to have a long history in Gujarat. An inscription on a stepwell (*vapi*) at Mangrol states that it was built in 1319 by Sodhala of the Modh caste of merchants. A member of the merchant community called Vastupal who was also a minister to the Solanki rulers is known similarly to have built wells, stepwells, reservoirs, tanks, and watering troughs at a number of places in Gujarat. According to one contemporary text he constructed 700 wells and 465 vapis. Jain considers these figures to be 'highly exaggerated'.[54] It is known, however, that merchants such as these provided loans on a large scale to cultivators, and it is most likely that Vastupal provided finance for these wells in the form of loans, rather than constructed them personally.[55]

This tendency was reinforced in the sixteenth, seventeenth and eighteenth centuries, as large parts of rural Gujarat became firmly embedded in an expanding all-India and international trade. Merchant capital helped to finance a large extension of agriculture throughout Gujarat to take advantage of this trade. Central Gujarat, rather than north Gujarat, became the core agricultural zone. Irrigated cash crops, such as cotton, rice, fruits and sugarcane were produced on a large scale for export to other parts of India and abroad.[56]

Wells were also built and owned by landlords to provide water for the tenants who cultivated their lands. A text as early as AD 906 mentions an irrigation well with araghatta maintained by a landlord, with skilled supervisors, four cultivators and female labourers.[57] In later years, landlords often financed the construction of such wells with loans from sahukars. In areas under the control of local Rajput thakors (landlords), there was a practice in which a sahukar agreed to finance the construction of a well on condition that the thakor agreed to grant them a share of the crop for a stated number of years. The idea was that the share would both pay back their capital as well as interest on the capital. The advantage to the sahukar, quite apart from earning a good interest, was that the arrangement would raise the productivity of the land, and thus enhance profits from their usury business over a long period. As the thakors themselves were invariably deep in debt to the same usurer, this arrangement strengthened the financial hold of the latter over the village.[58] Thakors could encourage castes known to be skilled in agriculture to settle in a village of their estate by gifting them a well so built.[59]

Although the building and maintenance of reservoirs required organization on a more cooperative basis, this work seems also to have been organized largely at the village level, being funded, if necessary, by sahukars, and with some encouragement being given in certain cases by rulers in the form of tax relief. As land-tax was generally paid by a village as a corporate group through a sahukar, this would have meant that the usurer would have administered the fund, with the village élites organizing labour on the reservoir by subordinate villagers. For example, in Parantij Pargana, controlled before the colonial conquest by the Gaikwads of Baroda, two grants of Rs 50 were given by the state and 'the Murwary' (presumably a Marwari sahukar) towards the cost of Rs 300 needed for repairing the Sujra tank.[60] An early colonial report on Dholka mentions a talav watering 150 to 200 bighas of land which was kept in repair by an annual allowance deducted for the purpose from the village land-tax.[61] In most cases, however, the day-to-day maintenance was held to be the responsibility of villagers; according to another British source, there was 'a traditional and customary obligation upon the irrigators to do petty repairs'.[62]

All of this points to a problem with one aspect of the argument employed by Anil Agarwal and Sunita Narain to explain the deterioration of small-scale irrigation works under colonial rule; namely that merchant capital gained a hold over the peasants only during the colonial period, and that this undermined the capacity of land-controlling farmers to finance such works. In fact, merchant capital was already embedded deeply within rural society, and it was this capital which was often crucial in funding irrigation works which raised agricultural yields and allowed for the expansion of cash-crop production. This continued to be the case during colonial times. Also, it would be wrong to believe that commercialization, in itself, brought about any decay in well irrigation, for there was a considerable degree of commercialization in the pre-colonial period. The reverse is almost certainly the case.

In addition to the landlords and sahukars, the state had a strong interest in irrigation, as higher taxes could be collected from irrigated lands. This was the case as far back as the Solanki period. According to an inscription of 1287 for an area under the rule of this dynasty, a field irrigated by *dhimada* (probably a device for scooping water from a stream) paid an extra two seers of produce, one watered by araghatta paid an extra eight seers.[63] Under the Mughals, there was no tax on irrigation as such; varying taxes were however levied on fields according to the crops grown. Fields with valuable cash crops, raised as a rule through irrigation, were assessed at higher rates.[64] In the eighteenth century, land-tax varied according to the crop grown on the land. In the Chikhli region of south Gujarat, for example, the Marathas demanded Rs 8 to 9 per bigha for best rice land, and Rs 5 to 6 per bigha for inferior rice land.[65] In Dholka pargana, the Gaikwads levied a tax of Rs 10 per bigha on irrigated land, but only Rs 3 to 4 per bigha on unirrigated land.[66] Unlike in Saurashtra, these taxes were paid in cash. Local officials had considerable discretion over tax assessment, and it seems to have been their practice to encourage well construction by granting tax concessions. In the Ahmedabad region, for example, it was common to waive the tax on a *rabi* crop raised through irrigation from a recently constructed well. The concession continued until the tax exemptions were held to have equalled the cost of construction.[67]

Owners of Well Water

Sahukars and Bhagdars

How was the water from wells distributed? Was it considered to be 'owned' by the farmer or landlord on whose land it stood? Was it sold in any way to other cultivators? Or was it shared between those whose lands lay around the well?

I have not been able to find any very adequate evidence on this matter. There is however a report of 1885 relating to the Siyanagar peta of Amreli district of Saurashtra, which was under the rule of the Gaikwads of Baroda:

> The custom of the country is that every man who wants water should take it from the wells of his neighbour if he requires it and this is freely done, thanks to their inordinately long water channels. As I have said, Mewasa fetches its water for irrigation right through its neighbouring village of Shahpur.[68]

There is no indication whether the water had to be paid for in some way, either in cash, kind or labour. However, the tone of the report, with its reference to 'the custom of the country' and its statement that the water was supplied 'freely', suggests that no payment as such passed hands. In fact, it would have been highly unlikely to have been a commercial transaction. The village economy of the peninsula region was at that time only slightly monetized (in marked contrast to the heartland of Gujarat, which had been monetized since pre-colonial times). Land-tax was paid in kind. The villages in the Siyanagar area were controlled by *garasiyas* (feudal lords). According to Elliot's report, the government collected half of the non-irrigated crop and two-ninths of the irrigated crop from the peasants, sold it, and then, after deducting various state charges, paid a proportion of what remained to the garasiya in cash (the shares of garasiyas differed from village to village—a quarter of the land-tax was however a common amount). As the garasiyas were normally deep in debt to usurers, much of this cash went directly to pay off their debts. The whole rural economy of Saurashtra was in fact controlled by usurers, either of the Baniya or Luhana communities. They were the ones who 'purchased' the produce from the government, which in practice meant that they normally collected the produce from the villages with the support of state officials, debited the state's and the garasiya's respective shares in their books, and handed over a *hundi* (bill of exchange) to the government which could be cashed with a banker in the district headquarters town.[69] The peasants of this region would therefore appear to have lacked the means to pay for water in cash.

In this area, the cultivators were mainly Kanbis who had been encouraged to settle villages by garasiyas in the preceding centuries (mainly the eighteenth and early nineteenth centuries). The Kanbis were not considered the owners of the land, and they were taxed very highly, and there was relatively little differentiation amongst landholding peasants. In Siyanagar, as in many other villages of Saurashtra, the village community was largely synonymous with one cultivating caste. This would have facilitated a culture of sharing amongst the majority of the peasants of the village as a whole.

A similar lack of internal differentiation was found in Bhil villages on the northern and eastern borders of Gujarat. There, the villages were controlled by Rajput thakors, with the large majority of the peasants being Bhils. According to Morris Carstairs, who carried out anthropological research in the Rajasthan–Gujarat border region in the early 1950s:

> Bhils seem to like to work together. It is a common practice for five or six households (some related, some merely neighbours) to co-operate at the time of ploughing and sowing, or dig a well, or dam a river for fishing. Each village near Khajuria had one or more wells which watered a large area under wheat and other winter crops, and each such well was run by a syndicate of several families. They took turns to bring their yokes of oxen and work the well, and they cultivated the field as one unit. At the time of harvest, the crop would be shared out among them all, as follows: one part to the owner of the well, an equal part for each yoke of oxen which had contributed to the common work, and a half share to the family (usually one with no oxen of their own) which performed the service of tending all the others' oxen when they were put out to graze.[70]

The well was not a communal one, but owned by a particular Bhil family, which received one extra share of the harvest in recognition of this fact. Otherwise, the crop was distributed equitably to each plough-team. Nothing is said of the role of merchant capital. However, the winter crops—in this area mainly wheat and gram—were grown largely for market, and it is likely that a sahukar had a lien on these crops.[71]

In both of these cases, there was a general level of poverty, with no very profound class differences amongst landholding peasants of the village. This appears to have promoted a culture of sharing of resources. Unfortunately, I have not found any reports which shed light on the matter for the highly stratified villages of central Gujarat. There are however some details in Hove's report of 1787 which are suggestive in the light of what we know about the rural society of that area, though they relate to the organization of irrigation through river-inundation rather than well irrigation.

It appears from Hove's description that the peasants themselves had hollowed out the reservoirs which were filled by river floods, and that they also constructed sluice gates and channels. He was in the area when the monsoon broke out on 20 July 1788, and two days later he went to Kerwan village. The rain continued to pour down: '. . . the exultation that every person and child expressed on this occasion may be easier conceived than described.'[72] As soon as the rain stopped, every cultivator set out for the fields, ploughed the land and planted seeds. By 24 July, with the river swelling rapidly, they opened up the entrances to the reservoirs to allow the water to flow in. They watched while they were rapidly filled, then closed them up. In the following days they cut narrow channels, about a metre broad, from the reservoirs to the fields. According to Hove: 'They performed it with such correctness that, in justice to them, their industry in culture does them great honour.'[73] In late August, Hove saw peasants draining water from the higher fields into the reservoirs, using narrow temporary channels. By the beginning of September, once the wells in the area were everywhere full, the channels were levelled and planted over with *bhaji* (spinach) and *methi* (fenugreek).[74]

Hove tells us nothing about the social organization of the villages or ownership of land, or how it was decided to share the water out. We know however from other sources that this area north of Bharuch was one in which the villages were controlled by strong corporate groups known as *bhagdars* (shareholders). In almost every case, the bhagdars were of a lineage of a particular caste or community (mainly Kanbi or Sunni Bohra). The village land was divided amongst the bhagdars, with a share incorporating land of differing qualities. They saw themselves as the owners of the land, with full right to alienate it according to how they, as a group, decided. Below them were a number of subordinate classes, such as peasants who were not shareholders but who had occupancy rights so long as they paid their taxes, and tenants who worked the lands of bhagdars who could be ejected at will. The area was considered to be one of the richest in Gujarat, paying the highest rates of land-tax. When the British took control in 1805 they found that 88 per cent of the land was cultivated, much of it under high-quality cotton.[75]

It is likely that the agrarian wealth of this region was due in no small part to the great efficiency with which the bhagdars organized its irrigation. They would have been able to direct subordinate villagers to carry out maintenance and other work, deploying a knowledge of the landscape and water flow gained through experience. It is likely also that they would have ensured that their fields were best situated to take advantage of the system, and that water was made to reach their fields and their wells first of all. They are likely to have reaped the major benefits.

All of this endorses the idea of strong village-based control over irrigation-resources in the past. Although sahukars provided the finance to build wells and other irrigation works in the first place, they were maintained and operated by the peasants themselves. The water was distributed according to arrangements made within the village, and rights over the harvest were determined by the villagers. This may be described as control by the 'village community', but it is important to emphasize that such 'communities' were internally differentiated to a greater or lesser degree, and that in the more stratified villages it was a relatively small élite which took the responsibility for organizing irrigation, which owned the wells, and which accordingly reaped the most benefit. In the less stratified villages, the peasants shared the produce more equitably, but the bulk of it was then appropriated by landlords and sahukars. It was a system which provided a subsistence for the poor, but did not alleviate their poverty.

Advent of the Britishers

Revamping the Irrigation Systems

After the 1780s there was a marked decline in irrigation in Gujarat. Whereas Hove had found that crops were regularly irrigated in the parts of the province which he visited in 1787–8, in the nineteenth century it became a commonplace of colonial knowledge that agriculture in Gujarat was primarily rain-fed. Raising water from wells using human and animal power was considered to be a primitive method, requiring so much labour and time that it was undertaken on a large scale only in years in which low rainfall threatened the survival of the crops. Cotton, the single most important cash crop of Gujarat, was considered by the British to be almost universally a non-irrigated crop. British officials even claimed that irrigation weakened the fibre of the cotton and reduced its value.[76] In fact, cotton yields are raised considerably by irrigation, and Hove's report reveals that in the 1780s most cotton grown in the region received regular watering throughout the growing season. This practice ceased between then and the early colonial period. Colonial records give us no clues as to the causes.[77]

The decline appears to have taken place for the most part in the late eighteenth and early nineteenth centuries. This was a time of continuing warfare in the region, with the British, the Peshwas, the Gaikwads, other Maratha aristocrats, as well as local chiefs, struggling for ascendancy. A campaigning army could shatter the economy of a village in a matter of hours. James Forbes marched with a Maratha force through central Gujarat and observed how it exhausted all the wells and reservoirs of a locality in which it camped in one night. He remarked also of the Cambay area: 'In this city and its surrounding domain are fifty thousand wells, and some very fine tanks; but the nabob, to prevent the Mahratta armies from encamping near his capital, drained most of the lakes, and cut off their resources.'[78] Hove mentions how in Saurashtra members of the warlike Kathi community would hinder attacks by the Gaikwad's army by burning villages and crops and poisoning wells and reservoirs.[79] The military campaigns were financed by selling tax-collection rights to tax-farmers for ever-escalating sums; the latter repaid their expenses through ruthless enhancements of the land-tax, collected often with the use of torture. The political turmoil created a situation in which Gujarat became particularly vulnerable to famine, with that of 1812–13 being particularly severe. Many sharehold villages could not bear such strains, leading to the collapse of bhagdari-style arrangements in many places. The cohesion provided by village élites—essential in the organization of effective reservoir and inundation irrigation—was thus undermined. Once these irrigation systems were allowed to decay they were soon washed away by succeeding monsoons. Many wells also went out of use. A. Gibson, who travelled in northern Gujarat in the 1830s, came across large numbers of derelict wells of substantial construction on land now overgrown with grass and scrub. He dated this 'desolation' back to 'the great famine of 1803'.[80]

The British, when they took power (which in many areas of Gujarat was in 1817), seem to have assumed that irrigation systems had always been poorly developed in the region. Melvill's report on Ahmedabad district for 1827 claimed that the rivers of the area were almost worthless for irrigation, the reservoirs in the sandy-soiled parts of the district were few and of no consequence, and even in the areas where there were many of them, they could only be 'sometimes used advantageously'.[81] R. Boyd, the collector of Bharuch, stated similarly that river water could not 'be usefully applied to agricultural improvement' in that district.[82] In Melvill's view, irrigation could only be carried out to any extent through wells, using kos. Such devices were however considered to be primitive and ineffective. J. Cruikshank stated in 1825 that: 'the rudeness of these contrivances exhibits in a striking point of view the want of European machinery . . .'[83] All of these observations were in striking contrast to those of Hove, made forty years earlier, who had been full of enthusiasm for the ingenuity used by the people of Gujarat in irrigating their fields, and who had provided detailed descriptions of the extensive use of river water north of Bharuch.[84]

The new rulers did not value what had been achieved in previous centuries, and failed to restore some excellent irrigation systems which had broken down in the previous decades, even though the expense would not have been great. For example, the large reservoir near Ahmedabad, the Karna Sagar—which had existed since the time of the Solankis—was fed from a dam on the Rupen river. This was washed away in the monsoon of 1814. The British, who took control of Ahmedabad in 1817, never made any effort to reconstruct this dam and the reservoir ceased to exist.[85] As R.G. Gordon later wrote: 'The repair of tanks was not attempted by Government in the early years of our rule.' The responsibility was left entirely in the hands of the cultivators.[86]

Believing that irrigation could only be carried out effectively in Gujarat from wells, the British tried to encourage well construction through tax exemption. In many parts of Ahmedabad district, for example, when a new well was built to a depth of twenty haath (about eight metres) or more, the land thus irrigated was exempted from tax on the *rabi* (spring) and *unalo* (summer) crops for either a specified period of between two and eight years or for as long as it took to repay the cost of construction. The general rule was that the deeper the well, the longer the exemption.[87] A similar arrangement was in place in Kheda district, where according to a rule of 1819 no extra tax was levied on land irrigated by a new well until its cost had been repaid. In some cases, the rabi tax was exempted. A deed was handed over, specifying the terms of the exemption and the number of years for which it was to run. When the time was up, a panchayat was assembled from the village and a new tax rate was agreed for the land in question. This system did not operate in villages held by wealthy shareholders (known as *narva* villages in that district), where the government left it up to the shareholders to allocate tax demands amongst themselves.[88] In Bharuch and Surat districts no such exemptions were granted.[89]

The system only really helped the wealthier cultivators who could afford to dig a well in the first place. Most peasants were too poor to benefit, one of the chief reasons being that land-tax rates were far too high.[90] In general, the peasantry were severely over-taxed by the British during the first three decades of their rule. After 1820 there was a catastrophic fall in agrarian prices, which continued until the end of the 1840s. Cotton prices, for example, fell in Bharuch district from up to Rs 80 per *bhar* in 1819–20 to Rs 39 per bhar in 1821–2. Between 1820–1 and 1852–3 the highest price was Rs 56 (1833–4), the lowest Rs 26 (1841–2).[91] As the British insisted on tax collections in cash, with no remissions to take into account the fall in prices, the peasants were hard-put to sustain their payments. The village élites, to save themselves, turned the pressure on the subordinate peasantry. The British backed the élites, hoping thereby to maintain their revenue. In Bharuch district this led to a rising by the subordinate peasants against the bhagdars in 1847.[92] This all put severe strains on village cohesion and the organization of village-based irrigation works. The large majority of the peasantry became mired deep in debt, lacking the means to maintain even their own wells. Many farmers sought to eke out a living by concentrating on rain-fed subsistence crops. Much land went out of cultivation during this period.[93] Only from the mid-nineteenth century onwards did cotton become more popular again, and by then it had become entirely an unirrigated crop. The irrigation knowledge of previous generations appears by then to have been lost irretrievably.

Expansion of Well Irrigation and Policy of Water Taxation

Initially, the British had assessed taxes on irrigated land according to existing practice in each locality, with rates being determined in some cases according to the crop grown, in others according to the irrigation carried out. The tax settlements made in Gujarat from the mid-nineteenth century onwards introduced a more uniform system of taxing land on the basis of its irrigated status. The village lands were everywhere surveyed and assessed for tax. A dry-crop rate was assigned to each field, with extra charges being levied over and above this amount according to its capacity for irrigation. Distinctions were made between *bagayat*—land irrigated by a well *himayat*—land watered from channels from a reservoir or by inundation, *dhekudiat*—land irrigated by water lifted from an adjoining river, and *akasia* (from *akash*, or 'sky')—terraced rice-lands which were irrigated by rainwater draining from higher ground.[94] Once a field was classified, the extra tax had to be paid regardless of whether or not the land was actually irrigated in a particular year (this did not apply in the case of 'dhekudiat' land if a river changed its course, making irrigation of that land thenceforth impossible). Every masonry or stone well had to pay an additional charge according to its kos capacity, and each temporary well a similar charge on the number of kos actually used to work it.[95] A concession was granted in 1846 to encourage well construction: any peasant building a well was exempt from any irrigation-tax for thirty years from the date on which the work was started. During this period only the dry-crop rate was levied.[96]

On their conquest of India, the British had asserted themselves to be the ultimate owners of the land and all of its natural resources. In this light, land-tax was supposed to be a 'rent' paid by cultivators for the use of state land. This rent was augmented with further rents on the use of other natural resources 'owned' by the state. In this way, the British sought to appropriate the water resources of India from those who had a customary right of use, and then charge a rent for the privilege of extracting the resource. In the words of the Superintendent of Survey for Gujarat:

> Water in the soil, and very close to the surface, is a gift of nature almost peculiar to the province of Gujarat. It ought, therefore, to be considered as one of the fertilizing elements of the soil and its value incorporated and included in the soil assessment whenever it is practicable.[97]

No obligation was placed on the British to ensure that there was a flow of water; this responsibility lay primarily with the cultivators, and they were obliged to pay their water rent whether or not water was available.

The village élites of Gujarat—in particular those of the fertile Charotar tract of Kheda district—were not prepared to allow such a presumption to go unchallenged. The implementation of this system in the Charotar in the mid-1860s generated a heated debate between the Bombay bureaucracy and some influential Patidars of Kheda district who were village shareholders (*narvadars*). In October 1868 one such narvadar of Nadiad wrote to the *Times of India* complaining about the heavy tax on wells. In a rejoinder, the Collector of Kheda stated that as all land was imperial property, the narvadars of Nadiad had no rights on it as such. In the following month, an article appeared in *Native Opinion* which supported the Nadiad narvadars. The government was doing nothing to develop irrigation resources in Gujarat, and yet it was levying a heavy tax on those who tried to do so out of their own pockets. In a further article in the same paper it was calculated that each well had to pay a tax of about Rs 95—hardly a 'moderate charge' as the government claimed. In December there was another official rejoinder in the *Times of India* challenging this figure—Rs 45 was the actual charge. In any case, it was argued, the narvadars of Nadiad were landlords who were able to rent out their irrigated lands for between Rs 40 and Rs 50 per acre. They therefore dug the wells as an investment, enabling higher rents to be collected from their land.[98]

This all fed into a wider debate about water-taxation policy in Bombay Presidency which continued over the next two decades. As a so-called 'concession'—which was in fact a major turnabout in principle—the Bombay government agreed in a ruling of 1881 that it was unfair to tax the efforts made by peasants to improve their land. Wells dug at the expense of the landholder or occupier of the soil would not henceforth be subject to any enhanced charge. An additional resolution of 1884 stated that occupants of land were entitled to enjoy the entire profits of improvements made at their own cost.[99] What this meant, in effect, was that landholders had the right to exploit water resources beneath their land to whatever extent they liked and not be liable to any extra taxation. By implication, this meant that rights in groundwater belonged to the owner of the land and not to the state, as the British had tried to assert initially. An attempted appropriation of this natural resource had thus been reversed, to the advantage of landowning families with a well and the means to extract water. The case of groundwater thus stands in marked contrast to that of forests and common lands, where the appropriation was carried through with unswerving rigour.[100]

The British also sought to favour well-owners by spreading the burden of the existing bagayat tax amongst the landholding community as a whole. An objection to bagayat rates, from the tax official's point of view, was that they taxed only well-owners, and not adjoining cultivators who might purchase water from the well-owner. By the late nineteenth century, a water market of this sort had begun to emerge in the Charotar tract, part of which was in Kheda district and part under Baroda state rule.[101] The answer, it was argued, would be to tax the water potential of all such land, regardless of whether or not there was an actual well on it. This, it was held, would provide an incentive to landholders to build wells. This principle was applied in the thirty-year revision settlements of the 1890s. All land was made liable to an extra 'subsoil rate' imposed on top of the regular tax-rate. The rate was calculated on a sliding scale, depending on the depth of the groundwater in a particular place. The top category was that of sweet water available throughout the year at ten feet or less, which paid an extra six annas in the rupee (e.g. an extra 37.5 per cent of the land-tax). Land with water-tables lower than this, or with water of poor quality, paid lower rates. No extra tax was paid if the water was 40 feet (12.19 metres) or more below ground. During the survey, the depth of water in all wells was ascertained, and other evidence compiled relating to each place. Tracts were delineated on village maps, showing where water was available at different depths, and whether it was sweet or brackish.[102] In this way the bagayat tax on land watered by wells was replaced by a tax on the water-bearing quality of the land, the tax being paid whether or not water was actually extracted.

These two measures—the agreement not to tax 'improvements' and the new subsoil rates—gave 'an immense impetus to the construction of wells' in Gujarat.[103] They also gave an 'immense impetus' to the development of a market in well-water. After the great famine of 1899–1900, and succeeding years of poor rainfall, the water-table dropped considerably in many parts of Gujarat. This made irrigation by existing wells using traditional lifting devices at least difficult, often impossible. To overcome this, the government began to encourage the boring of tube-wells at the bottom of existing wells. To extract water from such wells, a steam or oil-driven pump was required. From 1908 onwards, the Department of Agriculture began hiring out well-boring equipment to farmers in Gujarat. In Matar taluka of Kheda district successful borings were an average depth of fifteen metres below the bottom of the existing well, whereas in Borsad taluka of the same district successful borings were on average twenty-four metres. By 1911, fourteen boring machines were in operation in Kheda district. This was a year of poor rainfall, and, in the words of the District Collector,

'Applications began to pour in by hundreds for boring sets from well-owners'.[104] The Collector stated that every single well in the district—11,188 in a total of 789 villages—needed such attention. It was confidently believed by the Bombay Department of Agriculture that a large part of Gujarat could be made famine-proof by such means.[105]

Well boring of this sort was expensive for the farmers. The full cost of hire of the apparatus had to be paid, as well as the labour to work it (well-borers were at that time hand-driven). On average, this came to Rs 142 per well. This sum had to be paid even if the boring failed—between 1912 and 1915 almost a quarter undertaken failed to strike water in Kheda.[106] Once water was found, at an average depth in the district of 23 metres below the existing well bottom, a pump had to be purchased and installed. In the case of a six and a half horsepower pump fuelled by kerosene the cost was Rs 1,395, for a twenty-six horsepower pump Rs 3,493. Over and above this, it was calculated that the annual cost of operation (including cost of kerosene, deprecations, repairs, and interest on capital borrowed for the investment) came to Rs 1,284 for the smaller pump, Rs 3,573 for the larger.[107] During the First World War these costs all escalated considerably. The authorities encouraged such work by providing government loans (*takavi*), but in many cases the money had to be borrowed from sahukars at high rates of interest.

Because the installation of a tube-well and pump was such an expense, involving debts which had to be paid off, the owners had to sell as much water as they could to their neighbours. Increased extraction rates made this possible on a greatly enhanced scale. It was calculated in 1918 that an average bullock-powered kos, working at a rate of one load of 18 gallons per minute, could lift 1080 gallons in an hour. Such a kos could irrigate one acre of land in 54 hours—which given a working day of eight hours meant about a week. Pumps, on average, could draw 4,803 gallons per hour, irrigating an acre in twelve hours.[108] It was calculated for one Charotar village in 1920 that two pumps had replaced 35 pairs of bullocks—that is, 70 bullocks in all—and the area in the village which was irrigated as a result had risen by a quarter. The main snag was that when a pump was in use, the water level in the well fell rapidly.[109]

In Borsad taluka in 1924 there were 2,326 masonry or stone wells in 91 villages. At that time 39 pumps were in operation in the taluka.[110] A decade later, the number of pumps had increased to 143. Almost all of them were in the richer Patidar villages, controlled by narvadars. In fact, ten such villages accounted for 59 of the pumps, or, to put it another way, 11 per cent of the villages accounted for 41 per cent of the pumps. The pumps belonged to wealthy farmers who sold the water at the rate of one and a half to two rupees an hour of pumping-time. Some of these pump-owners were reported to have made losses, as the pumping had rapidly exhausted their wells.[111] At the same time, the well-owners laid down a network of underground pipes to take the water to different parts of the village land. For example, in Navli in the Charotar, one installation completed before 1920 had pipes stretching for one and a half kilometres.[112]

Before independence, the commodification of water was seen in its most developed form in the Charotar tract, where there were some particularly powerful village élites who were able to mobilize capital to dig wells, buy pumps, and lay out pipe networks. This was however to become the model to be followed by other emerging rich peasants throughout Gujarat in the years after independence, and particularly after about 1970. Problems of over-extraction caused by such selling of water, already seen on a very minor and localized scale from the 1920s onwards in the Charotar, became gradually more widespread.

Crisis of Popular Access to Water Resources

In Gujarat, British policy thus encouraged a form of irrigation controlled by the individual landholding family. This fact might appear to justify the argument that the current water crisis has been caused by the decline of the 'village community' and a corresponding growth of economic individualism. This argument is problematic. As I have already argued, the 'village community' was in many cases internally differentiated along lines of caste and class, being bound together by an authoritarian and exploitative village élite. The so-called 'village community' was often, in reality, synonymous with this corporate élite. These corporate groups did not decay during the colonial period; they were, rather, fostered and strengthened by the colonial state. In Bharuch district, the bhagdars were supported against the non-bhagdars; in Kheda the narvadars and Patidars against other peasants.[113]

What we thus see was a twofold process. On the one hand the colonial state removed powers of allocating land rights within villages from dominant corporate groups, giving each landholding family an individual title-deed to the land which could be bought and sold freely.[114] Although the British claimed to be the ultimate owners of the land and the water under it, they encouraged these individual families to dig wells and exploit the water beneath the soil to their own advantage, granting concessions to well-owners which were made more and more generous over time. This all helped foster a climate of economic individualism. Yet, on the other hand, the British strengthened the political position of dominant communities within rural society. This twofold process created a situation in which dominant communities exchanged water amongst themselves on strictly controlled terms, and supplied water to subordinate groups in highly exploitative ways, normally involving sharecropping arrangements.

I observed this process in operation when I carried out fieldwork in 1976 in Virsad, a village in the Charotar tract of Kheda district. In the past this had been a sharehold village controlled by narvadars of the Patidar caste. In Virsad, the ex-narvadars had the surname 'Amin', whereas non-narvadar Patidars had the surname 'Patel'. Previously, these subordinate Patidars had owned no land of their own, but rented what they cultivated from the Amins. Most of the Amins had lived during the colonial period by renting out their land; hardly any had worked it with their own family labour. After independence, the sharehold system was abolished and tenants were allowed to claim ownership of rented land. In fact, only the tenants of castes considered by the Amins to be 'respectable'—such as the Patels and the Kachhia gardeners—took advantage of this provision on any scale. Very few low-caste tenants dared to cross the Amins by asserting this right; their position in the village—I was told repeatedly by those I spoke to—would have been untenable. As a result, the Amin landlords retained ownership of their fields, being recorded in the village records now as owner-cultivators.

The chief cash crop in the village was tobacco, irrigated in 1976 by tube-wells with pumps. There were 132 wells in the village as a whole, but many were no longer productive. I was told that this had not been the such a problem in 1950s when the water-table was 9 to 12 metres below ground. By 1976, as a result of over-pumping, the water-table had fallen to about 45 metres below ground. By then, the only effective wells were ones with a bore of 60 to 90 metres and with a submersible pump at 45 metres. There were 37 such wells in the village, mostly owned by rich Amins.

In 1976, of the two hundred or so Amin families in the village, I found that only two laboured on the land with their own hands. The large majority continued to rent their lands to sharecroppers. The terms of the sharecropping arrangements reflected the amount of input each of the parties provided. Water was one such—very important—input. If the landlord provided all of the inputs, the tenant generally received only a quarter of the crop.

As pump-owners, the Amins exercised a decisive control over agricultural production in the village, determining exactly which non-pump-owners would be supplied with water, and the time they would receive it. I spoke to Ravjibhai Amin, one of the few Amins who laboured on his land. He told me that although his family did not own a well and pump, they always received water whenever they needed it from the pump of their neighbour, Ambalal Amin. They paid in cash regularly and Ravjibhai considered his family to be Ambalal's favoured customers.[115] This seemed to be the general pattern for the Patels as well. Members of lower castes whom I talked to had a very different experience. Bhikabhai Parmar told me how his family took land on a sharecropping basis. They did not own a well or pump. There were two pumps owned by Amins nearby, but the water was not always made available to them at the right time. They relied on the monsoon for the most part, cultivating mainly subsistence crops. Because of this uncertainty, they did not try to grow tobacco, the most profitable crop.[116] Other low-caste sharecroppers backed this up—the Patels, they complained, always had priority of access to water from wells owned by the Amins. As a result, their cash crops were always inferior to those grown by the Patels. Although it might appear to have been in the interest of Amin landlords to supply water freely to their tenants whatever their caste, their desire to maintain their political dominance outweighed economic rationality in this respect.

These politics were brought home to me most starkly when I visited a small settlement of Christians of the Vankar community—considered an 'untouchable' group. They had sunk their own tube-well and purchased a pump. In part, they used this to water their own land, but they had a surplus which they had tried to sell to some adjoining Patels who needed water for their fields. Despite their need, the Patels had refused to buy the water, considering it to be 'polluted'. The general impression I received was that the Patels considered the Christians to be acting above their station, and that they had boycotted them in this respect so as to teach them a lesson.

What I saw in Virsad calls into doubt the argument advanced by Tushaar Shah that the market in groundwater in Gujarat is highly competitive, efficient and individualized, bearing all the marks of what economists define as 'economic rationality'. He cites cases of pump-owners failing to establish price-fixing water unions due to a climate of fierce economic competition.[117] Issues of caste and community are however entirely absent from his analysis. Water-controlling cartels do not require a formal union or constitution; they operate according to a precise local knowledge in which each family is only too aware of its standing within the hierarchy, its corresponding entitlements, and the bounds beyond which it cannot step.

In the past, the dominant classes controlled subordinate groups within a village with an iron hand, often involving violence. Today, their political control is challenged, with members of lower castes voting for politicians of their own community and attempting to assert themselves in a whole number of different ways. Increasingly, therefore, dominant groups have to rely on their economic power both to control subaltern classes and prevent them from gaining any economic power themselves. This is the real 'rationality' of the system.

What might therefore appear superficially to be a 'tragedy of the commons'—in Garrett Hardin's terms—is in fact nothing of the sort. It is a crisis of popular access to natural resources. There is no 'tragedy' for the dominant rural classes; they can afford to bore deep tube-wells, buy submersible pumps, provide water for their own fields and sell the surplus to whoever they choose.

Conclusion

This history in part endorses and in part questions the arguments which I set out at the beginning. It is true that there was a profound decay in water-harvesting systems during the early nineteenth century, caused initially by political disturbance and warfare, but reinforced by colonial disinterest and ruinous rates of land-tax. Knowledge of earlier techniques was lost and never recovered. Whereas in the past there were multiple forms of water conservation, using check-dams, channels, controlled flooding, reservoirs and wells, in the colonial period the major emphasis was on wells. The existing water-lifting technology used in these wells, which was an appropriate technology given the water-bearing capacity of the subsoil, could not provide irrigation on a large scale. It was only in the early twentieth century that the British began to encourage the use of mechanized pumps to expand irrigation in Gujarat, and this in an extremely limited area. This new technology, moreover, had potential dangers, as it could lead to the extraction of groundwater in unsustainable ways. The British system of property in land also gave rise to a situation in which it became possible to market water as a commodity, as Chhatrapati Singh has argued.

It is not true, however, that commercialization and indebtedness contributed to this process. In fact, these two forces had in the past been responsible for the expansion of well irrigation on a large scale. Also, and most important, the current water crisis has not been caused by what is held to be the irresistible rise of economic individualism under the rule of colonial modernity and the concomitant sweeping of the 'village community' into the dustbin of history. There were many forms of 'community' in the past, whether of the dominant caste, subordinate castes, or of the village as a whole organized by its élites. Colonial rule did not destroy such communities, rather it forced them to reconstitute themselves on new footings. In particular, by granting property in land and rights to water beneath that land to families which belonged to dominant rural groups, the colonial state both modified the basis of their power, as well as strengthened it. These families, acting together in concert, could now assert their control not so much through the threat of physical coercion, as they had done in the past, but through the logic of economic compulsion.

Such a system survives today because the rural poor continue to lack access to resources, particularly land and water. In the case of water, this gives rise to a situation in which the élites exert their power by controlling and manipulating its supply. It is in their interest for there to be shortages. So long as this nexus prevails, it is hardly possible for more equitable systems of water harvesting and distribution to evolve.

One legalistic solution to the problem is to attempt to apply stricter state controls over extraction of groundwater. Only very feeble attempts have been made in this direction so far. In 1970, a Bill was introduced in the Gujarat legislative assembly which sought to license ownership of tube-wells and regulate and limit their depth. Repeatedly stalled, it was made law by ordinance in 1976, but the ordinance lapsed before it had been ratified by the legislative assembly. Repeated attempts were made during the 1980s to revive the measure, but they came to nothing due to opposition from rich peasants and their political allies.[118]

Even if such a law is passed, it is unlikely to have much effect unless combined with a strong movement for self-assertion by the poor. Already, there have been a number of hopeful developments in this respect, in which lower-caste peasants have organized a challenge to the monopolization of resources by the higher castes.[119] Ultimately what has to be sought is the forging of a variety of local systems of water harvesting which are determined by the varying topography of each particular area and which are controlled by communities of those who need, rather than by communities of those who already have.

Notes

1. Most notably, Elizabeth Whitcombe, *Agrarian Conditions in Northern India: The United Provinces under British Rule, 1860–1900* (Berkeley, 1971); Ian Stone, *Canal Irrigation in British India: Perspectives on Technological Change in a Peasant Economy* (Cambridge, 1984); Imran Ali, *The Punjab under Imperialism, 1885–1947* (Princeton, 1988); David Gilmartin, 'Scientific Empire and Colonial Science: Colonialism and Irrigation Technology in the Indus Basin', *Journal of Asian Studies*, 53:4 (1994); David Gilmartin, 'Models of the Hydraulic Environment: Colonial Irrigation, State Power and Community in the Indus Basin', in David Arnold and Ramachandra Guha (eds), *Nature, Culture, Imperialism* (New Delhi, 1995).
2. Irfan Habib states that 'wells were probably the major source of artificial irrigation in most areas' of northern India during Sultanate times. See

'Northern India under the Sultanate', Irfan Habib and Tapan Raychaudhuri, *The Cambridge History of India*, vol. 1 (Cambridge, 1982), p. 49.

3. In 1989–90, 50.6 per cent of the total irrigated area in India was irrigated by wells. Government canals irrigated 35 per cent of the area, tanks only 7.1 per cent. *Statistical Outline of India 1994–95* (Bombay, 1994), p. 63.
4. *Report of the Indian Irrigation Commission 1901–1903, British Parliamentary Papers, 1904*, vol. 66 (London, 1903), p. 44.
5. Figures for the period 1949–50 to 1986–7 are given in Anil Agarwal and Sunita Narain, *Dying Wisdom: Rise, Fall and Potential of India's Traditional Water Harvesting Systems* (New Delhi, 1997), pp. 378–9.
6. Whitcombe, *Agrarian Conditions in Northern India*, p. 70.
7. Christopher John Baker, *An Indian Rural Economy 1880–1955: The Tamilnad Countryside* (Oxford, 1984), pp. 14, 94–5, 201–3 and 477–8.
8. For an example of this latter process, see S. Shukla, 'Salinity Ingress in the Coastal Areas of Kutch and Saurashtra', *Gujarat*, 26:8 (21–27 June 1985).
9. Bela Bhatia, 'Lush Fields and Parched Throats: Political Economy of Groundwater in Gujarat', *Economic and Political Weekly*, 19–26 December 1992, p. A-143. For Hardin's formulation, see Garrett Hardin, 'The Tragedy of the Commons', in G. Hardin and J. Baden (eds), *Managing the Commons* (San Francisco, 1977) (first published in *Science*, 162, 1968).
10. Agarwal and Narain, pp. 308–11.
11. Uma Shankari and Esha Shah, *Water Management Traditions in India* (Madras, 1993), pp. 22–3.
12. Chhatrapati Singh, *Water Rights and Principles of Water Resources Management* (New Delhi, 1991), pp. 55–7.
13. M.B. Desai, *The Rural Economy of Gujarat* (Bombay, 1948), p. 68.
14. Ibid., p. 66.
15. Agarwal and Narain, *Dying Wisdom*, p. 380.
16. K.R. Dikshit, *Geography of Gujarat* (New Delhi, 1970), pp. 31–3.
17. I have compiled rainfall figures for Kheda district in central Gujarat from 1860–1 to 1969–70 (110 years) from the district gazetteer and its supplementary volumes, district census handbooks, and land revenue administration reports for Bombay. I managed to find figures for 93 of these years in all. The average annual rainfall for the entire period was 808 mm. By decade, the averages, in millimetres, were: 1860s—712; 1870s—745; 1880s—861; 1890s—834; 1900s—681; 1910s—759; 1920s—842; 1930s—815; 1940s—951; 1950s—964; 1960s—863 (for decades in which I did not have all the figures, the average was for the years available).

Certainly, there does not appear to have been any consistent change in the amount of rain which has fallen. Anecdotal evidence, however, suggests that the distribution of the rainfall over the season has altered, with stronger rain for shorter periods, and longer periods when there is no rain, causing the crops to suffer. Also, deforestation of the hills during this period will have led to a much faster run-off of water, more erosion and less storage of water in the subsoil.

18. Bhatia, 'Lush Fields and Parched Throats', pp. A-144–5.
19. According to Irfan Habib, this was the case also in sixteenth- and seventeenth-century Punjab, where widespread well construction since the fifteenth century had turned formerly arid regions into rich agricultural areas. 'Presidential Address (Medieval India)', *Indian History Congress: Proceedings of the Thirty-First Session Varanasi 1969* (Patna, 1970), pp. 153–4.
20. R.G. Gordon, *The Bombay Survey and Settlement Manual*, vol. 2 (Nagpur, 1960), p. 231.
21. At that time a haat or haath—meaning 'hand'—was a commonly used measure of length from the elbow to the tip of the middle finger. See *A Dictionary of Goojratee and English* (Bombay, 1846), p. 400. The measure can be considered to be roughly 40 centimetres.
22. J. Cruikshank, 30 September 1825, 'Report on the Portion of the Duskroee Purgunna situated in the Ahmedabad and Kaira Collectorate', and P.M. Melville, January 1827, 'Report on the Purgunnas of Puranteej, Hursol, Morassa, Bayur, and Veerumgam, of the Ahmedabad Collectorate', *Selections from the Records of the Bombay Government*, no. 10 (Bombay, 1853), pp. 13 and 90. Cruikshank noted that most of the wells in the area were built at least fifty years ago, p. 93.
23. Hove, 'Tours for Scientific and Economical Research, made in Guzerat, Kattiawar, and the Conkuns, in 1787–88', *Selections from the Records of the Bombay Government*, no. 16—New Series (Bombay, 1855), p. 42.
24. *Gazetteer of the Bombay Presidency*, vol. 8, *Kathiawad* (Bombay, 1884), p. 179. A study of the 'science and art of finding water' through divination both in classical texts and in popular tradition in Saurashtra has been carried out by Dhirajlal Amritlal Vohra, *Shri Dakargala [Bhugarbha]* (Bhavnagar, 1987).
25. Melville, January 1827, 'Report', p. 13.
26. F.A.H. Elliot, March 1884, 'Proposed Settlement of 13 Khalsa Villages in the Old Damnagar Tuppa of the Damnagar Taluka', Baroda Records Office (hereafter BRO), Huzur Political Office (hereafter HPO), Sec. 263, 36a.
27. N.B. Beyt, 15 March 1880, 'Papers Relating to the Revision of the Rates

of Assessment on the Expiration of the First Settlement of 73 Villages of the Halol Taluka of the Panchmahals Collectorate', *Selections from the Records of the Bombay Government*, no. 170—New Series (Bombay, 1885), pp. 19–20.

28. Hove described kos being used in the Jambusar and Amod region of central Gujarat in 1787. Hove, 'Tours', p. 37. More details are provided by J.Cruikshank, 30 September 1825, 'Report on Duskroee Purgunna', p. 92; J. Mollison, *A Text-Book on Indian Agriculture*, vol. 1 (Bombay 1901), pp. 65–6; *Gazetteer of the Baroda State*, vol. 1 (Bombay, 1923), p. 270.
29. Melville, January 1827, 'Report', pp. 13, 23.
30. Annual Collector's Reports for Kheda District 1851–2 and 1852–3, Maharashtra State Archives, Bombay (hereafter BA), Revenue Department (hereafter R.D.), 1858, vol. 29.
31. *Gazetteer of the Bombay Presidency*, vol. 3, *Kaira and Panchmahals* (Bombay 1879), p. 43.
32. *Gazetteer of the Bombay Presidency*, vol. 8, Kathiawar, p. 178.
33. Hove, 'Tours', pp. 36–7.
34. There has been some controversy over the araghatta. Habib distinguishes it very clearly from the saquiya, or 'Persian wheel', which he claims was brought to India from West Asia at the time of the Delhi Sultanate. He states that in Mughal times the saquiya was found only in areas of Jat settlement in north India and the Punjab. 'Presidential Address' (Varanasi, 1969), pp. 149–51. L. Gopal has argued that the araghatta was less distinct from the saquiya than Habib contends. L. Gopal, *Aspects of History of Agriculture in Ancient India* (Varanasi, 1980), pp. 114–68.
35. Habib, 'Presidential Adress' (Varanasi, 1969), p. 151.
36. Figures for the 1930s show that 89 per cent of wells in British Gujarat were worked by kos, only 7 per cent by 'Persian wheels'. M.B. Desai, *The Rural Economy of Gujarat*, p. 69.
37. Cruikshank, 30 September 1825, 'Report', p. 89.
38. V.K. Jain, *Trade and Traders in Western India (AD 1000–1300)* (New Delhi, 1990), pp. 30–2.
39. Using a modern map, I would estimate the length of this canal to have been about twenty kilometres. Khasherao Jadhava, 30 June 1916, *Jamabandi Revision Settlement Report of the Visnagar Taluka of the Kadi Division 1916–17* (Baroda, 1918), p. 14.
40. K. Jadhav, 6 May 1916, *Jamabandi Revision Settlement Report of the Dehegam Taluka of the Kadi Division, 1916–17* (Baroda, 1918), p. 18.
41. Jain, *Trade and Traders in Western India*, pp. 27–30.
42. By the early 1990s, the water-table in this region was between 60 and 100 metres below ground level. Tushaar Shah, *Groundwater Markets and*

Irrigation Development: Political Economy and Practical Policy (Bombay, 1993), pp. 81–2.

43. J.L. Jenkins, 7 March 1889, 'Jarod Taluka Settlement Report', BRO, HPO 263/26, pp. 6–7.
44. Hove, 'Travels', p. 65; Cruikshank, 30 September 1825, 'Report on Duskroee', p. 90.
45. J. Forbes, *Oriental Memoirs: A Narrative of Seventeen Years Residence in India*, vol. 2 (London, 1834), p. 40. J. Cruikshank described a reservoir near Sanand (Ahmedabad district) which was kept in repair by an annual allowance deducted from the land-tax. 31 December 1825, 'Report on Dholka', p. 6.
46. Cruikshank, 31 December 1825, 'Report on Dholka', p. 6.
47. Hove, 'Travels', pp. 109–10, 147 and 183.
48. Hove, 'Tours', p. 183.
49. Cruikshank, 30 September 1825, 'Report on Duskroee', p. 89.
50. J.W. Barnes witnessed such an inundation in Bahawalpur (now in Pakistan) in 1871. He concluded that 'for every acre of summer crop destroyed, there are fifty which survive because of the flooding'. Quoted in R.B. Barnett, 'The Greening of Bahawalpur: Ecological Pragmatism and State Formation in Pre-British Western India, 1730–1870', *Indo-British Review*, 15:2 (December 1988), p. 7.
51. Jain, *Trade and Traders in Western India*, p. 28. According to R.E. Enthoven, Ods were earth and stone workers who might have come from Karnataka, for *oddu* means the occupation of joining stones in buildings in Kanarese. The Gujarati Ods have exogamous clans with Rajput clan-names, which Enthoven believes indicates past attachments of different sections of the community to Rajput overlords. *The Tribes and Castes of Bombay*, vol. 3 (Bombay, 1922), pp. 138–9 and 146. Being a mobile community, they were by colonial times found all over India. In Tamilnadu, where they were known as Oddar, they were known for their skill in building deep wells. Baker, *Indian Rural Economy*, p. 468. In northern India, the labour required to build the intricate masonry headwater system for the Ganges canal during the 1840s and 1850s was provided 'by the nomadic Oade tribe, members of which had by tradition wandered the area between the Sutlej and the Jumna with their cattle and other livestock undertaking excavation of tanks and water courses'. Stone, *Canal Irrigation in British India*, p. 57. Further research on this community would be highly worthwhile.
52. Melville, January 1827, 'Report on Puranteej etc.', pp. 23–5.
53. This allowed for numerous swindles. A case from nineteenth-century Maharashtra tells how a Baniya usurer paid the well-diggers and masons direct, and then deducted Rs 3,000 from his client's books. Later, the

client, a Maratha peasant, discovered that the work had in fact cost only Rs 1,000. *Report of the Committee on the Riots in Poona and Ahmednagar 1875* (Bombay 1876), Appendix B, pp. 5–6. It is worth noting that in north India, when the British were constructing canals using Ods as labourers, they dealt with them through Baniya usurers who negotiated contract terms, advances, and the distribution of payments to the Ods. Stone, *Canal Irrigation in British India*, p. 58.

54. Jain, *Trade and Traders in Western India*, fn. 133, p. 33. Vapis were at that time often used for irrigation, with lifting devices being erected above them. Ibid., pp. 27–8.
55. For a discussion of rural credit systems at that time, see David Hardiman, *Feeding the Baniya: Peasants and Usurers in Western India* (New Delhi, 1996), pp. 18–20.
56. Hardiman, *Feeding the Baniya*, pp. 21–2. As Hove reveals, in the pre-colonial period the highly prized cotton of Gujarat was to a large extent an irrigated crop. 'Tours', pp. 42, 147 and 181–3. During the colonial period cotton came to be considered largely as a non-irrigated crop.
57. Jain, *Trade and Traders in Western India*, p. 30.
58. Denis Vidal, *Violence and Truth: A Rajasthani Kingdom Confronts Colonial Authority* (New Delhi, 1997), p. 164. This evidence relates to the thakors of Sirohi state, which lies on the border between Gujarat and Rajasthan.
59. I came across such a case in the small estate of Pal, formerly under the maharaja of Idar, in which the thakor made a gift of a well in a village settled by Dangi and Modh Patel cultivators. Interview with Galjibhai Badaji Solanki, Dadhvav, Vijaynagar taluka, Sabarkantha district, December 1997.
60. J.H. Cherry, Collector of Ahmedabad, to Commissioner in the Deccan, 31 March 1824, *Compilation of Papers Selected from the Records of the Governmnet of Bombay Revenue Department Relating to Artificial Irrigation* (Bombay, 1838), pp. 10–11.
61. Cruikshank, 31 December 1825, 'Dholka', p. 6.
62. R.G. Gordon, *The Bombay Survey and Settlement Manual*, vol. 2 (Nagpur, 1960), p. 462.
63. Jain, *Trade and Traders in Western India*, p. 28.
64. Irfan Habib, *The Agrarian System of Mughal India (1556–1707)* (Aligarh, 1963), pp. 207–12. This was in theory; in practice local tax officials determined the land-tax in a whole variety of ways.
65. C.J. Prescott, 11 September 1865, 'Papers Relating to the Revision Survey Settlement of the Chikhli Taluka of the Surat Collectorate', *Selections from the Records of the Bombay Government*, no. 381—New Series (Bombay, 1899), p. 53.

66. A. Walker, 18 June 1804, 'Reports on the Resources, &c. of the Districts of Neriad, Matur, Mondeh, Beejapoor, Dholka, Dundooka, and Gogo, the Tuppa of Napar, and the Kusba of Ranpoor, in Guzerat', *Selections from the Records of the Bombay Government*, no. 39—New Series (Bombay 1856), p. 15.
67. Cruikshank, 30 September 1825, 'Report on Duskroee', p. 93.
68. F.A.H. Elliot,, 22 February 1885, 'Settlement Report of the Damnagar Taluka, Part II, Siyanagar Peta', BRO, HPO 263/36b.
69. This system is examined at a general level in my book, *Feeding the Baniya*, pp. 23–4 and 137–40. For indebtedness in this region of Saurashtra, see F.A.A. Elliot, March 1884, 'Proposed Settlement of 13 Khalsa Villages in the Old Damnagar Tuppa of the Damnagar Taluka', BRO, HPO 263/36a.
70. Morris, 'The Bhils of Kotra Bhomat', *The Eastern Anthropologist*, 7:3 and 4 (March–April 1954), pp. 176–7.
71. For details about the role of merchant capital in these Bhil areas, see David Hardiman, 'The Bhils and Shahukars of Eastern Gujarat', in Ranajit Guha (ed.), *Subaltern Studies IV* (New Delhi, 1987).
72. Hove, 'Tours', p. 155.
73. Ibid., p. 160.
74. Ibid., pp. 168–70.
75. Raj Kumar Hans, 'Agrarian Economy of Broach District (Gujarat) during the First Half of the Nineteenth Century', unpublished Ph.D. thesis, M.S. University (Baroda), 1987, pp. 45–51 and 77.
76. Such an assertion was made by the collector of Bharuch, Inverarity, in 1855. *Gazetteer of the Bombay Presidency*, vol. 2, *Surat and Broach* (Bombay, 1877), p. 393.
77. Alexander Gibson raises this issue in his preface to Hove's 'Tours', pp. vii–viii, but reports it as an oddity and fails to suggest any reasons. The official gazetteer for Bharuch district, published in 1877, likewise raised the matter, but is similarly baffled. *Gazetteer*, p. 393. A later Bombay government publication stated merely that: 'Cotton is entirely an unirrigated crop'. P.R. Mehta, *The Elements of the Agriculture of the Bombay Presidency* (Bombay, 1905), p. 225.
78. Forbes, *Oriental Memoirs*, pp. 323, 363.
79. Hove, 'Tours', p. 138.
80. A. Gibson, 'A General Sketch of the Province of Guzerat from Deesa to Damaun', *Transactions of the Medical and Physical Society of Bombay*, vol. 1 (Bombay, 1838), p. 13. No famine is recorded for 1803—was he in fact referring to the great famine of 1812–13?
81. Melville, January 1827, 'Report', p. 13.

82. Boyd to Commissioner in the Deccan, 20 September 1824, *Compilation of Papers Selected from the Records of the Government of Bombay Revenue Department Relating to Artificial Irrigation* (Bombay, 1838), pp. 12–13.
83. Cruikshank, 'Report on Duskroee', p. 89.
84. Hove was a Polish scholar employed by a British aristocrat to investigate the agricultural wealth of Gujarat, and seems to have lacked the arrogance of the colonial conquerors. Also, of course, European technology did not appear so comparatively 'advanced' in the 1780s as it did by the 1820s. For details about Hove, see A. Gibson, 'Preface', to Hove, 'Tours', pp. vii–viii.
85. Jain, *Trade and Traders in Western India*, fn.116, p. 30.
86. Gordon, *Bombay Survey and Settlement Manual*, vol. 2, p. 462.
87. J.H. Cherry, Collector of Ahmedabad, to Commissioner in the Deccan, 31 March 1824, *Compilation of Papers Selected from the Records of the Government of Bombay Revenue Department Relating to Artificial Irrigation* (Bombay, 1838), pp. 10–12; A. Crawford, Collector of Ahmedabad, to Norris, 28 March 1825, p. 31.
88. E.B. Mills, Assistant Collector of Kheda, to Commissioner in the Deccan, 24 May 1824, ibid., p. 14.; Williamson, Collector of Kheda to Norris, 13 April 1825, ibid., pp. 27–8.
89. R. Boyd, Collector of Broach, to Commissioner in the Deccan, 20 September 1824, ibid., p. 12; Lumsden, Collector of Surat, to Norris, 12 May 1825, ibid., p. 32.
90. A. Crawford, Collector of Ahmedabad, to Norris, 28 March 1825, ibid., pp. 29 and 31.
91. Hans, 'Agrarian Economy of Broach District', p. 121.
92. Ibid., p. 175.
93. Ibid., p. 115.
94. Note by F.G.H. Anderson, 1918, in Gordon, *Bombay Survey and Settlement Manual*, vol. 2, pp. 461–7.
95. R.G. Gordon, *The Bombay Survey and Settlement Manual*, vol. 1 (Bombay, 1917), pp. 101–4 and 156.
96. E.G. Fawcett, 20 February 1849, 'Report on the Collectorate of Ahmedabad', *Selections from the Records of the Bombay Government*, no. 5—New Series (Bombay, 1854), p. 32.
97. C.J. Prescott, 1865, *Bombay Survey and Settlement Manual*, vol. 1, p. 157.
98. This correspondence is reprinted in full in Javerilal Yajnik, *Notes on Kaira, a District in Fertile Gujarat* (Bombay, 1871), pp. 82–108.
99. Gordon, *Bombay Survey and Settlement Manual*, vol. 1, p. 150.
100. For this history, see Madhav Gadgil and Ramachandra Guha, *This Fissured Land: An Ecological History of India* (New Delhi, 1992), pp. 123–34.

101. C.N. Seddon, 27 February 1905, *A Jamabandi Settlement Report of the Petlad Taluka and Sisva Mahal* (Baroda, 1905), pp. 5–6.
102. Gordon, *Bombay Survey and Settlement Manual*, vol. 2, pp. 231–2.
103. Ibid., vol. 1, p. 168.
104. Report of 16 March 1912, BA, General Department 1913, 95/77.
105. *Annual Report of the Department of Agriculture, Bombay Presidency 1910–11* (Bombay, 1912), p. 13.
106. Calculated from *Annual Report of the Department of Agriculture, Bombay Presidency 1912–13, 1913–14, 1914–15* (Bombay, 1913), 1915, 1916.
107. *Annual Report of the Department of Agriculture, Bombay Presidency 1910–11* (Bombay, 1912), p. 72.
108. *Annual Report of the Department of Agriculture, Bombay Presidency 1917–18* (Bombay, 1919), p. 87.
109. Khasherao Jadhav, 20 June 1920, *Jamabandi Revision Settlement Report of the Bhadran Peta Mahal of the Petlad Taluka of the Baroda Division* (Baroda, 1921), p. 68.
110. A. Master, 28 January and 31 March 1924, BA, R.D. 5714/24 (a), p. 20.
111. A.D. Patel, 'Agrarian Economics of Borsad Taluka (Kaira District)', unpublished M.A. thesis, University of Bombay, 1936, pp. 48–51, 70–1 and 79. Selling water according to the amount of time it is pumped has been the norm in Gujarat to this day. Shah, *Groundwater Markets and Irrigation Development*, pp. 52–3.
112. Ibid., p. 59.
113. This process is examined by Alice Clark, 'Central Gujarat in the Nineteenth Century: The Integration of an Agrarian System', unpublished Ph.D. thesis, University of Wisconsin, 1979.
114. This was not the case in the *talukdari* villages (located mostly in western Ahmedabad district) and in the states ruled by princes in Saurashtra. There, ruling clans continued to be considered the owners of the villages. These areas were brought into line with British Gujarat with the land reforms of the 1950s.
115. Interview with Ravjibhai Chhotabhai Amin, Virsad, 23 March 1976.
116. Interview with Bhikabhai Pochabhai Parmar, Virsad, 28 March 1976.
117. Shah, *Groundwater Markets and Irrigation Development*, p. 65.
118. Bhatia, 'Lush Fields and Parched Throats', pp. A-160–1.
119. For example, in the Bhal tract of Ahmedabad district the poor Koli peasants have been trying to develop their own water supplies against fierce opposition from the dominant Rajput *darbars*. See 'Some Comments on the "Special" Development Plan for the Bhal Region being Proposed by the Government of Gujarat', cyclostyled report by Utthan Mahiti (Ahmedabad, 1983), and 'Women the Power of the Bhal', cyclostyled report by Utthan Mahiti (Ahmedabad, 1991).

CHAPTER 9

Farming in the Forest

The Dangs 1830–1992

In early 1990, a group of *adivasis* who lived in the Dangs district of Gujarat entered an area of reserved forest and began clearing it for cultivation. They claimed that the area was *juni gaothan*, meaning the site of an old village in which they had an ancient right of cultivation. The forest department of the Gujarat government did not accept this claim and arrested about ninety people for violating the forest laws. Rather than crush the movement, as anticipated, the authorities met with an unexpected resistance. The people, they found, had a fervent belief in the righteousness of their act.[1]

In this struggle, which grew in strength in the following two years, two systems of belief came into sharp conflict. On the one hand there were the adivasis, who believed that through ancient custom they had the right to cultivate in their homeland when and where they pleased; on the other hand there were the forest officials who asserted their full right under the law to determine exactly how all tracts of reserved forest should be utilized. It is this conflict, which has continued in the Dangs for well over a century, that forms the subject of this chapter.

Background

The Dangs is a predominantly adivasi region, which lies between the fertile plains of south Gujarat and the rugged plateau of western Maharashtra. (see Map on p. 363). It is a land of mountain ranges, covered in forest and intersected by deep river valleys. During the medieval period, it was under the control of Bhil chiefs, who ruled over other Bhils as well as various subordinate communities, the chief of which were the Konkanas (sometimes also known as Kunbis), the Varlis, and

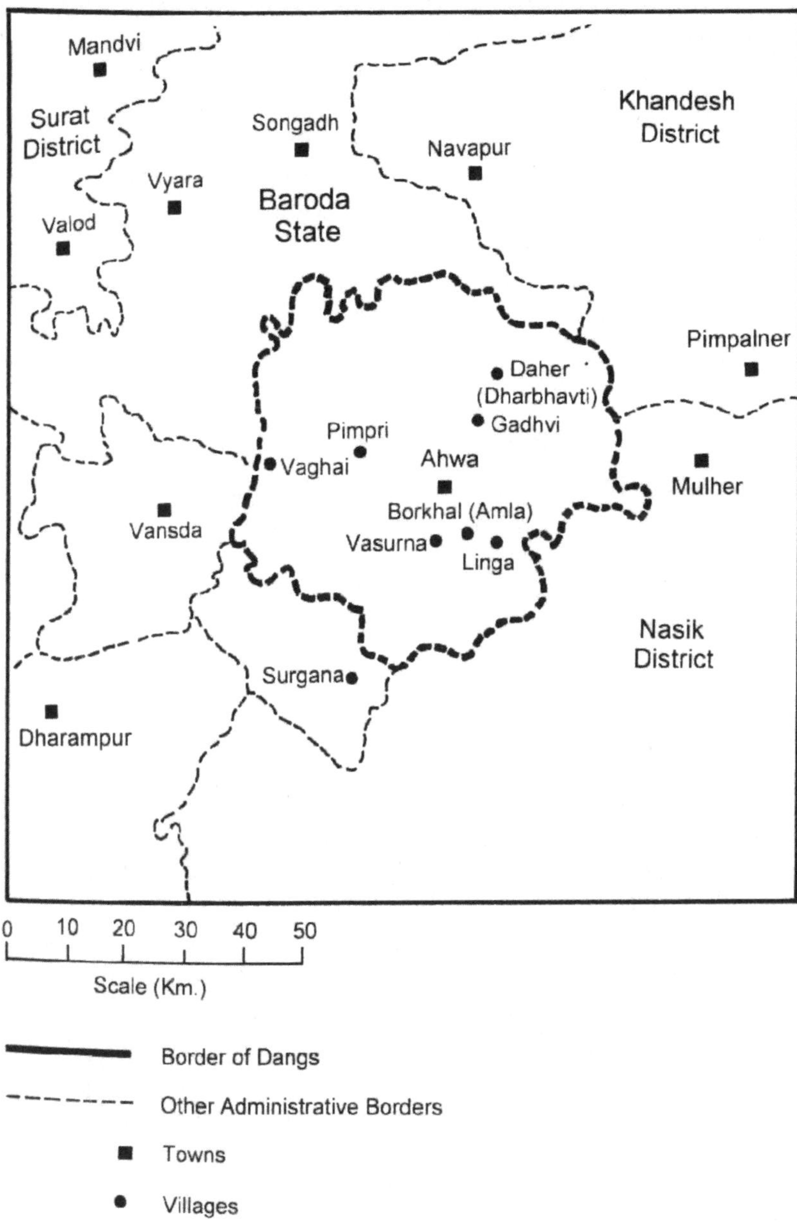

Map 4: The Dangs and Adjoining Regions

Gamits. The 1872 census of the Dangs counted 7426 Bhils, 6,517 Konkanas, 2,491 Varlis and 302 Gamits.[2]

Bhil chiefs were established in this region at least four hundred years ago, for the British traveller Sir John Hawkins referred in 1608 to the Dangs chief of 'Cruly'—most probably the Bhil chief of Kirli. The Konkanas migrated into the region from the coastal areas of Maharashtra to the south-west—the Konkan. This is borne out not only by their community name, but also their language, which is a dialect of Marathi with certain North Konkani elements. According to an oral tradition, the community migrated north as a result of the terrible Durgadev famine of 1396–1408 that devastated the Konkan region.[3]

Early Resource Use Systems

The Bhil chiefs appear to have been ranked according to the power exercised by any one of them at a particular time. Almost all Bhils were related in some way or the other to a chief. The hierarchy among the Bhils was based on power and status rather than material wealth. Their simple dwellings were built of a wooden frame with bamboo walls smeared with a mixture of cowdung and mud, and the roof thatched with leaves. The chiefs themselves did no field labour, expecting their non-Bhil subjects to grow crops for them. The non-Bhil cultivators were required to pay an annual land-tax, the amount of which varied according to whether cultivation was by plough or hand. It was normally paid in grain.

The Konkanas were associated with *rab* cultivation, which was confined to the flatter areas of the valleys. Debris from the forest was piled on a small plot of land and burnt. Seeds, normally of *nagli* (a grain) or rice, were sown. Once the monsoon rains came, the area around this plot was either ploughed or worked with hoes. It seems to have been common for Konkanas to use bullock-drawn ploughs.[4] When the seeds had sprouted, they were transplanted to the prepared land. Weeding had to be carried out periodically, and the crop was harvested soon after the monsoon. The rab of burnt forest waste is a particularly good medium for seed growth, and yields are high. The Dangs, with its abundant supply of such waste, was well suited for such agriculture. As a rule, an area was cultivated only for two or three years. After this the soil was left to fallow and a fresh patch of land was sought.

The Bhils and the Varlis opted for *kumri* or *dalhi* cultivation, which required no ploughing or weeding.[5] A portion of the forest was selected—often on the top of a plateau or the higher side of a valley—and the forest was cleared of scrub. Once it had dried, it was burnt. Seeds—normally of nagli—were sown in the ashes. The seeds sprouted and grew once the rains came, and harvesting was possible by the end of the monsoon. Crop yields were low, as the quality of soil on these plateaus and slopes was poor. It appears to have been a common practice to select a fresh patch of forest each year.[6]

The Bhils and the Konkanas used different techniques and terrains for their agriculture and the two methods complemented each other. Both required plenty of forest and space. Villages were very small, and few and far between. According to an official, writing in 1877: 'The Dangs may be termed a sea of forest and trees, with small and isolated patches of cultivation scattered over it.'[7] A 'village' represented a broad area in which two or three families might reside for a few years before moving on. A record of such a 'village' called Khapadya exists for the period 1830–70, which gives an idea of the way in which a locality was occupied and later deserted. In 1830 the area was being cultivated by a Konkana called Jana Patel. After the Dangs was conquered by the British in 1830, he deserted the place. It remained uninhabited for many years. Eventually Jana returned with his son Eru, now aged thirty-five. However, as they were forced to provide labour for touring officials and others from outside the Dangs, they soon left and went elsewhere. In 1867, Janu, Eru and three other Konkanas returned to settle the site once more. In 1868 cholera broke out and Janu and some others died. The rest, including Eru, deserted the village. It was still uninhabited in 1871.[8]

Despite the fact that they had to pay taxes to the chiefs and satisfy other demands from the Bhils, the Konkanas were normally able to eke out a living without having to rely on hunting and gathering. The kumri cultivation of the Bhils and Varlis, on the other hand, provided grain for only two or three months after harvest; during the rest of the year they depended on other sources of subsistence. They ate forest fruits, *mahua* flowers, grain from wild grasses, and various roots. The Bhils were also keen hunters with the bow and arrow and, in a few cases, guns. They would set fire to the tall grass to drive the animals out so that they could sight them and kill them. Hares were smoked out of their holes or trapped in nets. They also caught and ate fish and birds.

The Forest Economy of the Dangs

The Dangs was well integrated into the economic life of the outside world. Forest produce was in demand, and the people of the tract could earn both money and payment in kind by providing it. They did not cut and sell timber, for they were not able—or indeed prepared—to transport huge tree trunks up the Ghats to Khandesh or down to the richer markets of south Gujarat. Large teams of bullocks to drag the timber through the forests, and sturdy bullock-carts, often drawn by four bullocks, were required to transport the wood across the plains to the market. This trade, which thrived before the coming of the British, was organized by merchants who lived in towns surrounding the Dangs. The normal pattern was for a trader to contact a Bhil chief in whose area he wished to operate. Once permission had been obtained, peasants with bullock teams and carts were hired from the plains. These peasants were free from their own agricultural work between February and May, and during this period they went to the Dangs. The wood was cut by them, and the local chief was paid a sum for each cartload exported. The payment was made both in cash and kind (e.g. grain, cloth and other products not obtainable in the Dangs). The levy on timber provided a major source of income for the chiefs—greater than other sources, such as the tax on subordinate peasantry or the protection money they levied on the surrounding plains. For instance, in 1825, Silpat had an annual income of about Rs 5,000. Of this, less than Rs 1,000 came from protection money,[9] and still less from land-tax.

The Dangis sold and bartered other forest produce to merchants who lived on the borders of the Dangs or to Banjara pack-bullock carriers who came to the forest to graze their cattle during the summer. In 1843 the trade in mahua flowers was reported to be second only to that of teak from the Dangs.[10] On 10 April 1856, a forest official travelling in the Dangs reported that the flowers of mahua were seen in full bloom and that the entire population was out gathering them for sale.[11] Some of the crop was carried by the Banjaras to the plains; the rest was taken to the borders of the Dangs and sold to liquor dealers who used it for making country liquor to be marketed in the villages and towns. For many Dangis, the mahua trade provided the chief means for earning cash, which they used for buying clothes and other essentials. The Dangis also made bamboo products—such as baskets, bamboo matting, and winnowing mats—which they then took to the borders of the Dangs. Traders purchased these products and sold them in the plains. Other forest products sold in this manner were honey and lac.

Dangis kept livestock, though they were not important for providing food directly. The Konkanas used bullocks mainly for ploughing and cows for breeding. The cattle were of small stature, and the cows did not provide adequate milk for the people. Very few buffaloes or goats were kept. The cattle were let out to graze in the forest. In addition, Banjaras came into the Dangs during the hot weather to graze their herds, which could consist of up to five hundred animals. They paid the Bhil chiefs for the right to graze—usually a charge fixed per a hundred cattle. They often brought with them a little coarse cloth, cheap jewellery, beads, earthen pots, and salt, which they sold or bartered to the Dangis.

The relationship between the Dangis and the outside world had its more violent side. The Bhils levied protection money from the rulers of the surrounding plains, on threat of looting if the money was not paid. In the early 1820s, for instance, they began raiding villages in the territory of the Gaikwad of Baroda lying to the north of the Dangs, claiming that the Gaikwad's officials were refusing to hand over their customary tribute. Silpat claimed that protection money worth Rs 1,520 a year was due to the Bhil chiefs, whereas the Gaikwad was prepared to concede only Rs 940.[12] This dispute led the Gaikwad to send some troops into the Dangs in 1825 to crush the Bhils. Th Gaikwad suffered a humiliating defeat, being driven from the Dangs with casualties.

The evidence brings out the complexities of the forest economy of the pre-colonial period in the Dangs. It is difficult to argue that forest dwellers such as the Dangis were in any way 'natural conservators' of their environment. For the people of the Dangs the forest was eternal; there was no consciousness that human beings could destroy this massive expanse of vegetation. They used the forest to maintain their way of life, and the Bhil chiefs profited by allowing outsiders to exploit it on their own terms. Clearly, however, they had a strong affinity with these woods and hills—their home as well as place of refuge—and any destruction that they carried out was small scale and made very little difference to the environment as a whole. With the coming of the British, a great change was initiated in which the forests—and the people who lived there—were to become managed as a resource within a wider system of production.

The Erosion of Tribal Forest Control in the Early Colonial Period

The British conquered the Peshwas and occupied the region to the east of the Dangs in 1818. The district of Khandesh was established, with its collector being made responsible for the Dangs. However, it was only in 1830 that British troops were sent into the Dangs to subjugate the Bhil chiefs who had from time to time raided villages in Khandesh. The chiefs were recognized as independent rulers under overall British paramountcy, with their protection monies being paid regularly by the colonial state. No attempts were then made to rule the Dangs in any direct way. Many British soldiers had died of malaria after the 1830 expedition, a mortality that revealed the dangers of living in those hills, even in the 'healthy' season of the year from March to May. Instead, the British relied on a system of informal control, using an official known as the 'Bhil Agent'. The chief role of the Bhil Agent was to keep the Bhils quiet and out of trouble.

The Bhil Agents sought to encourage the Bhils to settle down and learn to subsist settled agriculture rather than raiding, hunting, gathering, and shifting cultivation. In the words of one Bhil Agent: 'I have always made it a rule when visiting Bhil settlements to personally go and see for myself how the Bhil is getting on with his cultivation, and have endeavoured with kindness and quiet persuasion to encourage him in the steady and peaceful occupation of agriculture.'[13] As early as 1834 the Khandesh authorities tried to encourage merchants to enter the Dangs and provide loans to Bhils to enable them to carry on settled agriculture. They also sought to encourage peasants to migrate into the tract from outside to settle and cultivate the land. The emphasis here was on clearing rather than preserving the forest.

Left to themselves, the Bhil Agents and authorities in Khandesh would have been happy to have continued this loose relationship with the Dangi Bhils, not forcing the pace of change in the tract in any dramatic manner. The thrust for a more active intervention within the Dangs came from the British navy which needed high-quality teak for the construction of warships. During the early years of the nineteenth century, the navy had obtained such wood from the forests of the Malabar coast, but overcutting led to a dwindling of supplies in the 1830s. Increasingly, they looked to the forests of south Gujarat. Initially they purchased wood from local timber merchants who had made agreements with the chiefs to cut the wood. It was felt, however, that prices were too high, and in 1843 the Bombay Government decided to start extracting timber directly. The chiefs were forced to sign leases handing over their right to all timber from the Dangs. They were compensated with a relatively small annual payment.

The chiefs did not initially understand what they had signed. There is a strong oral tradition in the Dangs that the British tricked the chiefs into taking money, not knowing that this entailed the loss of their rights to use the forests. When the full significance became clear, they tried to repudiate the leases and returned the first payments. In the words of Anandrao, chief of Vasurna: 'No interruption [to our control of the forest] was ever experienced by us during the Mughal and Peshwa's Government, nor under the British till now.'[14] The chiefs forced the first woodcutters, whom the British sent into the Dangs, to stop their work. To forestall further trouble, the Bhil Agent agreed to raise the annual payments slightly but insisted that the British be given full and sole power to cut, conserve and plant timber in the Dangs. The chiefs were allowed to cut timber for their own use only. The government would establish customs posts and levy taxes on timber and other articles that might be taken from the tract. The government was allowed to clear land in the Dangs and provide for its cultivation, though the tax on cultivation was to go to the chiefs. The government was permitted to improve roads to facilitate the export of timber. The leases could be relinquished by the government at a six-month notice, but not by the chiefs. After sixteen years the government would be allowed to take out new leases on terms they might judge as equitable.

The chiefs were required to give full assistance to the government timber agents. If local people were asked to cut timber, they were to be paid the prevailing rate by the timber agents.

The leases that the different chiefs were forced to sign were very one-sided. The sums granted in compensation were meagre when compared to the value of the wood. As an official later gloated: '. . . such leases [were] . . . obtained at a marvellously cheap rate from the rude and uncivilized owners by means of persuasion.'[15] The new leases allowed the chiefs to take wood from the forests for their personal use; there was no provision for the rights of the inhabitants of the Dangs as a whole. The chiefs were allowed to collect land-tax, but this was because the amount was small and the British would have found it troublesome to collect it themselves. Although the leases were limited to sixteen years, the limit had no substance as the British insisted on having the sole right to renew the leases on whatever terms they pleased. The Bhils had no power to revoke the leases at any future date; this privilege lay entirely with the government.

From this time onwards the power of the forest officials gradually began to eclipse that of the Bhil Agents in the Dangs. In contrast to the latter, the forest officials placed much emphasis on the utilitarian virtues of hard work and careful husbandry. They viewed the forest as a resource with two dimensions to it. First, the forest officials considered it as a property they were holding in trust for the chiefs and from which they were entitled to take an income. Their periodic statements of accounts showed the cost of administering the forest (including the amounts of lease money paid to the chiefs), which was set against the amount derived from the sale of wood and sale of permits to cut wood. When this balance showed a loss (which was rare), noises were made that the Dangs were 'not worth keeping'.[16] On the whole, however, the 'capital' invested by the British earned large dividends. It was the duty of forest officials to 'protect' this resource from the ravages of the indigenous inhabitants. According to one official, the forests of the Dangs were 'a sort of national wealth, and it behoves the state to devise means whereby its future supply may not diminish by injurious treatment of the trees at the hands of an improvident class of people'.[17] Another official likened the forest to a form of capital from which society drew interest and which was being threatened by its inhabitants:

> It is the destructive attacks made upon the capital, dissipating the latter, and rendering the continuance of interest impossible, which the Forest Officer, from his professional education, perceives when it is not apparent to the uninitiated, and which he finds so sore a burden on his conscience.[18]

Such a view was wholly alien to the people of the Dangs; for them the forests were a way of life and a spiritual home, not mere timber with a capital value. Second, the officials viewed the forest as a 'natural resource' that the government had a duty to protect. Naturalists had for long realized that forests occupied a key place in the natural cycle. Since classical times, writers had observed that whenever there was a loss of forest cover, rivers dried up during droughts and flooded badly when there was heavy rain, carrying away topsoil. This knowledge was given a scientific base in the late eighteenth and early nineteenth centuries. Forests were seen to encourage rainfall, check run-off, prevent floods, and help water to percolate into the ground and be available from perennial springs. During droughts, they provided succour to the people who could come to the forest to search out wild roots and fruits, while hungry livestock could be brought to eat dry grass and leaves. The voice of conservation was always weak as opposed to the much stronger imperial need for wood and arable land which could grow foodgrain and provide a higher income to the state from land-tax. The official argument was, however, important and valid, and the government paid attention to it by creating forest reserves during the second half of the nineteenth century.

The colonial officials' view of conservation was, however, gravely flawed. They believed strongly that forests could be saved only if managed in an authoritarian manner by foresters. They also believed that left to itself, nature degenerated. According to Donald Worster: 'That impulse became a defining theme among Victorians, much as it had been for their reforming Protestant forebears. While they went on loving their gardens and city parks, where *they* were in control, they were determined to dispel any foolish notions about the innate goodness of natural forces at work on earth.'[19] It was the duty of the colonial official to tame and control the natural world.

Human beings who lived close to nature were also seen as a threat. It was believed that civilization could advance only with constant application, effort, and exertion. Otherwise, humans remained in a slough of savagery, using resources wastefully, and causing greater and greater degradation to their environment. For the Victorians such savagery was thus 'an offence that ought to be crushed out wherever it was found.'[20] Forest officers believed that they had to police the forest to protect it from the 'primitives' who lived there. Their relationship with the forest dwellers was thus one of antagonism rather than co-operation. This attitude prevented them from learning how to work with them to protect the forests. If they had done this, their task of conservation could have been carried on with much less friction, and with a far greater chance of success.

A further problem with forest conservation, as it developed into a profession in Europe in the nineteenth century, was that foresters were connected closely to hunting. According to Jack Westoby, 'There has always been an association between landed property, forest estates, foresters and hunting . . . At one time many young men chose the forest profession precisely for this reason.'[21] Foresters saw their role as not only protecting timber but also as maintaining hunting grounds for the recreation of the rich. Most foresters in India were also keen *shikaris*. This also brought them into conflict with the people. For example, hunting of tigers caused much distress in the Dangs, as the animal was revered there as Vagh Dev (forest spirit/god). The Dangis did their best to avoid being involved in such slaughter. The forest dwellers also disliked performing the dangerous task of beating the drums to drive wild animals towards the guns of the hunters. In some cases, tribals fled their homelands when the local rajas forced the villagers to perform these tasks.

In the Dangs these contradictions in attitudes came into sharp conflict only towards the end of the nineteenth century, when the forest officials took active steps to 'save' the forests from the people who lived there. For the first fifty years of the forest leases, control over the day-to-day life of the Dangis was slack, for no officials lived permanently in the Dangs and there were hardly any roads to allow easy movement into the tract. There was, however, a consistent and rising exploitation of the forest.

During this period the demand for teak for shipbuilding was superseded by a much larger demand for teak for railway sleepers. Initially this new demand was met from the thinner and more accessible forests of Thane and Surat districts, and the princely states of Dharampur and Vansda. By the late 1850s these forests were showing signs of exhaustion, and timber dealers were demanding that they be given access to the Dangs. Since the signing of the leases, the British had taken direct control of cutting, hauling, and selling timber from the tract, using peasant labour hired from the plains. During the 1860s they tried out a system of giving a timber contract to supply sleepers for the Great Indian Peninsula Railway from the Dangs to a private dealer. The contractor invested his own capital in building roads to carry wood from the tract. But, in 1869 the British changed to a system in which the right to cut and transport timber from a stated forest area was auctioned to timber contractors for a particular period. The variety and the amount of wood to be cut was mentioned in the contract. The idea was that the forest officials would single out trees ready for cutting and mark them. The contractor then hired cutters to go into the forest to fell the trees. The cut timber was taken to checkposts on the borders or to depots outside the Dangs, where it was measured, its value determined, a stamp put on it, after which it could be removed. The contractor had to pay the government the sum agreed for each variety of wood thus extracted. To help the contractors, the British constructed a new road into the heart of the Dangs, which provided access to fresh tracts of uncut timber. As a result, the volume of timber exported rose considerably during the 1870s.

Thereafter, forest officials became more and more strident in their demand for better 'protection' of the forest from the people who lived there. Without much logic, the onus for its destruction was placed on the Dangis rather than on the system of timber extraction operated by the government. One practice considered particularly harmful was the annual burning of the forest floor to clear the tall grass which harboured wild animals and made hunting and travel through the forest difficult. Large numbers of saplings were supposedly destroyed in these fires so that regeneration of the forest was prevented; existing trees were damaged, so that they grew crooked and became 'valueless' as timber. Slash and burn cultivation was also blamed. The lopping of branches for rab and kumri cultivation was considered to damage trees. The Bhils were accused of cutting and then burning large tracts of choice forest. The scanty crop that they raised was not, according to forest officials, worth the value of the smallest tree cut.

Consolidating Government Forest Controls in the Dangs

From the 1870s onwards, officials of the Bombay Forest Department began to demand that the forests of the Dangs be managed along the same lines as prevailed in the Bombay Presidency. The Forest Act of 1865 created tracts of 'reserved' forest in India in which the government could ban all cultivation. The government held full rights of ownership over these reserves.[22] The rules were tightened up by the Forest Act of 1878, which held that peasants who lived in the reserved areas had no 'right' to the forests. At best their use of it was a 'privilege' granted by the state.[23] During this period the forests of Bombay Presidency were surveyed, the 'privileges' of the existing inhabitants listed—in a way depriving them of most of their customary rights—and boundary posts were erected to demarcate the extent of the area reserved under the terms of the Forest Acts. Forests which had not yet been surveyed, but which, it was hoped, would be reserved in the future, were classified as 'protected'. The forest officials in charge of the Dangs demanded that the tract be similarly surveyed and divided into reserved and protected zones. The difficulty was that the Dangs were legally under the Bhil chiefs, and the laws of the Bombay government did not apply there. They could not therefore be brought automatically under the operation of the two Forest Acts.

In 1878, the Bombay government decided to look into the problem by appointing a commission of enquiry consisting of political as well as forest officials. The final report of the forest officer stated:

> For years past, the wasteful system of cultivation carried on by the inhabitants of the Dangs, and their consequent migration from one place to another, on the appearance of cattle disease, or of a reputed witch, or in consequence of the death of a member of their community, or for any other absurd reason, have undoubtedly tended to the destruction of the forests. We are, therefore, of opinion that efforts should now be made, at any rate,

> to restrict such destruction, in order to ensure a fair supply of valuable timber for the future. This can only be done by demarcating forest tracts and, as far as possible, separating these from the area actually required by the people for cultivation.[24]

It was recommended that agriculture be concentrated only on land suitable for perennial cultivation, with a constant supply of water nearby. Settled colonies needed to be established on this land. The rest of the Dangs would then be designated as reserved forest in which grazing would be allowed, but no cultivation. The recommendations were accepted by the Bombay government in 1879. It was ruled that about half of the land area of the Dangs should be demarcated as reserved forest in which cultivation would not be permitted.[25]

Although the principle of forest reservation for the Dangs was thus accepted, more than a decade passed before reserved areas were actually demarcated. This was partly due to technical difficulties; the Dangs had never been surveyed thoroughly; more importantly, the Bhil chiefs opposed the entire idea vociferously. They argued that the British had no right under the terms of the leases to limit cultivation to particular areas of the Dangs. The authority of the chiefs over other Dangis was connected closely with their right to determine who cultivated any particular part of the area under their rule. They also valued their own right to move about in, live in, and use their forests as they pleased. The idea of being confined to particular areas angered the Bhil chiefs. For many years they had faced growing harassment from lower-grade forest officials, and they knew that once the forests were reserved this problem would become worse.

The British countered by promising to increase payments to the chiefs under the terms of the leases. After much forceful persuasion by the British, the chiefs agreed to the principle of reservation and signed the following agreement in 1889:

> I understand that Government wish to reserve for forests a portion of my Dang, not exceeding one half, and that if this is done in the portion reserved, no one would be allowed to enter without permission from the forest officer. I am willing to agree to this arrangement on the understanding that sufficient land for cultivation will be excluded from reserved forest. I and my people will be allowed to use the trees outside reserved forests for agricultural and domestic purposes, but not for sale or barter.[26]

The demarcation surveys were carried out in 1891 and 1892. The chiefs did their best to keep as much land as possible outside the reserved area. In the end, after many compromises, 34 per cent of the land area was designated as reserved forest.[27]

The chiefs resented the loss of even this amount of their forest, and they actively encouraged the peasants of the Dangs to cultivate in the reserved rather than in the unreserved areas. They also connived at the wanton destruction of the forest. Damaging fires were started and many trees were cut and destroyed. In 1901 one official reported that he saw large numbers of stumps of recently cut trees. Forest, which eight or nine years before had been covered with thick, fine teak and bamboo, was now scarcely worth the trouble of conservation; 'the deterioration has been going on at a terrible pace since the demarcation was made and particularly since 1896.'[28] Forest officers who tried to prevent this destruction were threatened and even beaten by the Dangis. During the period of famine and death between 1899 and 1902, this discontent and the starvation distress triggered off a wave of looting of the subordinate peasantry by the Dangi Bhils. Particularly notorious was a gang of some relatives of the Raja of Amla who carried on their raids from a base on the Atalya hill. A force of more than two hundred men was sent eventually to suppress them, and only after most had been captured or driven underground did peace return to the Dangs in 1903.[29]

On 1 January 1903, responsibility for the administration of the Dangs was transferred from the authorities in Khandesh to the forest department of the Bombay Presidency. Thereafter, the Bhil Agents ceased to have any power in the tract. The divisional forest officer for Surat circle, in which the Dangs were the chief forests, became the assistant political agent responsible for the day-to-day administration of the Dangs. He was accountable to the political agent, who was also the collector of Surat. The assistant political agent was given judicial powers to try all but the most serious criminal cases in the Dangs. E.M. Hodgson was appointed to this post, serving in it from 1903 to 1910.

Hodgson started by constructing the headquarters at Ahwa, a village on a plateau in the heart of the tract. Besides building a forest rest house for white officials, houses were built for other officers, police officers, and servants. A small dispensary, a jail, a post office, and a storeroom were constructed. Hodgson also reorganized the administration. He drew up a code of administrative standing orders, which conformed as far as possible with the laws in force in the Bombay Presidency, modified to the particular circumstances of the Dangs. He organized a police force with fourteen constables based at Ahwa. Roads were improved, allowing better communication with Ahwa. Forest rest houses were constructed at various strategic points, and wells were dug to provide clean drinking water.

Hodgson reclassified certain tracts in which cultivation could not be prevented as 'protected forest'. There were therefore three categories of land in the Dangs: reserved, protected and open. He banned all cutting of live trees in the reserved forests and of immature trees in the protected forests for ten years, to allow the forest to regenerate after the devastation of the previous decade.[30] Due to the greater efficiency of the administration and the opening up of the Dangs through better communication, the revenue from the forest did not suffer from these restrictions. In fact, it increased.

Hodgson also tried to stop the annual burning of the forest floor. In the 1890s, officials had despaired of ever being able to prevent these fires. Hodgson began by trying to persuade the chiefs to dissuade their followers and subjects from starting fires. He promised to give rewards and turbans to minor chiefs and village headpeople who managed to prevent fires. He burnt strips of forests to create firebreaks to prevent fires from spreading all over the Dangs. Vigorous efforts were made to catch and punish anyone causing fires. In 1907 a complete ban was imposed on the burning of grass under mahua trees, the smoking out of rats and other animals, and the use of fire torches to provide illumination at night. Liberal payments of rewards and distribution of turbans were made to those who cooperated. As a result, whereas in 1905–6, 93 per cent of the Dangs had been burnt, one year later only 17 per cent had been burnt.[31] This proved to be the turning point; thereafter, the incidence of fires remained low.

The seeming success of this policy masked a continuing resentment amongst the Bhils against Hodgson's policy. They continued to regard the entire forest as their preserve, to be used as they pleased. They disliked settled agriculture and resisted being made to live in the valleys and cultivate fixed plots of land. Many continued to cultivate where they wished, which led to inevitable conflicts with the forest guards and police. Deprived of their livelihood, some of them took to extracting food and other goods from the subordinate peasantry on a more regular and exploitative basis. The subordinate peasantry then looked to the police for protection, which led to further conflicts. These tensions gave rise to three uprisings by the Bhils between 1907 and 1914.

In the first of these, in September 1907, some Bhils attacked Ahwa, smashing all government property they could lay their hands on. Files and books were torn up and furniture was broken to pieces. Trees in the compound were uprooted. They forced their way into the dispensary and broke the surgical and medical instruments and smashed the bottles of medicine. In 1911, some Bhils of Kadmal village protested against the forest department by setting fire to large tracts of forest. Forest guards sent to Kadmal to inspect the damage were threatened by the Bhils; to save themselves, they handed over a large number of licences to cut wood free of cost. The defiance spread, and the forest was burnt elsewhere. In Ahwa there was a mood of alarm, and a feeling that the events of 1907 were about to be repeated. Police reinforcements were sent from outside, and the ringleaders arrested. In this outbreak, the leaders against the forest regulations were not the top chiefs but some of the lesser chiefs. They received firm support from the majority of the Bhils. Their object was to reassert the authority they had lost—demanding that the forest guards stop interfering with their use of the forests. The Bhils did not receive support from the subordinate peasantry. The latter helped the authorities when they could and lay low when the Bhils went on the rampage. The Bhils clearly resented that many Konkana village headmen were assisting the British, and they were also often singled out for attack.[32]

A further outbreak occurred in December 1914. This was set off by rumours that the British were facing imminent defeat in the European war. The Bhils saw this as an opportunity to reassert their authority. Large bands of Bhils armed with bows and arrows assembled under the leadership of the Naik of Pimpri and rajas of Gadhvi and Amla. They set about burning the forest and cutting down trees. Forest officials who tried to stop them were threatened with violence, though none was actually harmed. The British took quick action, sending a large body of armed police to the Dangs, who soon restored order. Those who had taken part were fined or imprisoned. Four chiefs who had remained aloof and many Konkana Patels who had helped to restore order were given rewards of bangles and money.

Increasingly, the peasants were being made to settle down to cultivate the land demarcated for agriculture. They were encouraged to stay on fixed sites, construct permanent fields, and even make terraces for paddy cultivation. They were helped—through government loans—to buy carts and bullocks to make up a plough team. They were ordered to use a mixture of cowdung, grass and forest debris for their rab, rather than tree cuttings, as before. A few small dams were constructed by the government to store water throughout the year and to carry out irrigation. The peasants were told that they should grow 'better' (i.e. more marketable) foodgrains such as *juvar* (sorghum) or rice, and to keep stocks of grain as well as fodder. Fruit trees, such as mango and tamarind, were planted near villages to encourage the peasants to stay in one place. The money spent on these activities was not, however, great, and the impact was limited. Although the peasants were forced to keep out of the reserved forests, they refused to radically change their methods of farming.

The final years of the colonial rule were ones of great hardship for the people of the Dangs. The forest department ruled the tract with a heavy hand, forcing the people to carry out paid labour for the forest department and much unpaid labour for the touring officials. Although the paid labour provided some source of income to replace that lost from selling forest produce, the Dangis continued to resent having to do such work. Forest guards were free in their use of punishments to keep the people from using the forest reserves.

During the First World War there was an urgent demand for timber, which led to its large-scale cutting and extraction. In 1914–15 the timber income from the Dangs was Rs 154,133; by 1918–19 it was Rs 460,021. The chiefs themselves continued to be paid their lease money. In 1924 the payments were raised by 50 per cent to a total of Rs 26,921. This increase however, did not adequately reflect the amounts being earned from the Dangs: during the 1920s the average annual profit to the British was Rs 154,917 per year. By the 1930s the chiefs were demanding that their payments be increased, considering the profits being made. The Bombay government turned down this request, arguing that if they received more money they would merely squander it on drink.

After the failure of the 1914 revolt, the Bhils did not dare to risk any further confrontations with the colonial state, but resisted only surreptitiously. They maintained their self-respect in a period of adversity by taking pride in their claims of royal lineage and by keeping alive the memory of the times when they had once ruled the forests.[33] They tried to deny the legitimacy of the loss of their forests by repeating stories of the devious deceptions by which—it was said—the British had swindled them of their inheritance. Likewise, they continued to celebrate their revolts against the British during the early years of the twentieth century. In 1949, encouraged by the news that the British had left India, they staged a further revolt, burning large areas of forest. The revolt, however, was suppressed quickly by the police of independent India.[34]

Forest Management after Independence

When India won independence in 1947, the Dangs district was opened to political activists and social reformers who had until then been excluded from the tract. The ground had already been prepared for them by a few Konkanas who had started Gandhian-style activities—such as spinning, weaving, anti-liquor and anti-meat activities—on their own initiative in the years preceding independence. In 1948 the brothers Chhotubhai and Ghelubhai Nayak came to the Dangs and established a Gandhian *ashram* at Ahwa. A large number of Dangis flocked to the ashram with complaints against the forest department, many of which related to sexual harassment by the forest guards against adivasi women. The two Gandhians accepted these grievances but advised the people that in the long run they could only improve their position through education and social reform. They started primary schools, taught people to spin and weave cotton, and persuaded many to give up drinking liquor. In 1949 they started a multi-purpose co-operative that, among other things, distributed grain to members. The Bombay government agreed to give this cooperative the right to cut wood in certain forest coupes, the aim being to undercut some of the power of the forest department in favour of the people.[35] This was the start of a development that was to have a profound impact on the Dangs.

The first forest labour cooperatives in Bombay state were started in Thana district in 1947 as part of a strategy to counter the strong communist agitation there against landlords, moneylenders and forest contractors. The Gandhian, Jugatram Dave, started similar forest labour cooperatives in Surat district 1948, the intention being to break the hold of powerful forest contractors who had always been allied closely with the British. The cooperatives proved a success: those who cut wood through them soon found their work conditions much improved. No longer were they exploited and humiliated by powerful contractors, and their earnings were also higher. The cooperatives provided a strong political base for the Gandhian activists who headed them, and they used the cooperatives to propagate their ideas.

In 1950, six new forest labour cooperatives were established in the Dangs. They soon, however, became embroiled in a political controversy revolving around the issue of whether the Dangs should form a part of Gujarat or Maharashtra. Being a border region, with local dialects consisting of Gujarati as well as Marathi elements, and a tradition of rule by both Maharashtra (Khandesh) and Gujarat (Surat), the status of the tract was ambiguous. During the twentieth century, the ruling authority had been based in Surat, and the Gandhian activists who became the first new-style political leaders in the area were Gujaratis. Education in their schools was in Gujarati. Maharashtrians were not, however, prepared to accept this. Two Gandhians of Nasik founded a new institution, the Dang Seva Mandal, which opened schools in which Marathi was the medium of instruction. They persuaded the Bombay government to give some forest coupes to the forest labour cooperatives they had started. However, in 1954 the Bombay government discovered certain financial irregularities of the Gujarati societies, which led to their liquidation.

In 1956, as a result of a strong agitation in Maharashtra, the Government of India announced that Bombay state would be divided into two separate linguistic states. The actual division did not, however, take place for another four years, and the status of the Dangs continued to be uncertain. In the Dangs, the two rival Gandhian groups fought for the Dangs to be included in either one or the other state. By this time there were twenty forest cooperatives working in the Dangs, all loyal to the Gandhians from Maharashtra. They made large profits, and much money was reinvested into organizing the agitation for demanding that the Dangs go to Maharashtra. There were frequent meetings and demonstrations. Leading nationalist politicians of Gujarat came to the Dangs to counter this propaganda. Chhotubhai and Ghelubhai Nayak founded 179 primary schools to propagate Gujarati education. In 1958 the first elections was held for the new Dangs district panchayat. The election was contested fiercely by the two groups. The Gujaratis won twenty-six out of thirty seats, and Chhotubhai Nayak became the president of the district panchayat. It was largely because of this result that when Gujarat and Maharashtra were divided in 1960, the Dangs was awarded to Gujarat.

The Maharashtrian forest labour cooperatives were abolished in 1962 by the new government of Gujarat, and until 1967 all cutting was carried out by either the forest department or contractors. The cooperatives were revived in 1967. However, as soon as Chhotubhai Nayak won the award of forest coupes for the two societies he had started, his political rivals from other parts of South Gujarat countered him by establishing other societies under their control. As his rivals did not reside in the Dangs, they encouraged some young Konkanas to take over the day-to-day management of their cooperatives. The leading figure among this rival group was Ramu Thakare, a Konkana of Sarva village who had served for a time in the Indian army before returning home to the Dangs in 1967. He consolidated his position rapidly, and in 1970, using the cooperatives as a political base, managed to oust Chhotubhai Nayak from the presidentship of the district panchayat. He has remained president to this day. The young Konkanas quickly captured control over Chhotubhai's cooperatives and founded some new ones, bringing the total to thirty-two.

Between 1967 and 1986 forest cutting throughout the Dangs was controlled by these highly politicized labour cooperatives. They built a network of power, which revolved around forest employment. With continuing growth in population, it became increasingly hard for most Dangis to make an adequate living from cultivation. Between 1931 and 1991, the population of the Dangs grew from 33,750 to 143,500. The only other major source of livelihood was forest work. The power to award such work lay with the leaders of the cooperatives and their agents in the villages. This power allowed them to build up vote-banks and win seats for themselves on the district panchayat. This, in turn, gave them control over the allocation of government development funds—power that was often used corruptly. Many of these managers and agents of the cooperatives were suddenly seen to acquire new farmlands, large houses and personal jeeps. Ordinary adivasis found that they had to bribe these new leaders to obtain forest work or to have any government policy implemented in their villages (e.g. to obtain government loans for land improvement). Very little of the government money earmarked for developing the Dangs actually reached the poor, although income from the forests of the Dangs increased from Rs 1,250,000 in 1970 to Rs 9,860,000 in 1985.[36]

The increase in forest income reflected to some extent an increase in the exploitation of the forests. Both the Gujarat government and the leaders of the cooperatives were interested in maximizing earnings from the forest. The latter had little interest in conservation; their main concern was to earn as much as possible while they held power. The rise in income was compounded by the soaring price of wood. But just as important, it reflected an increase in the area under reserved and protected forest. For many years the forest department had been gradually encroaching on areas in which cultivation was permitted, which included a good deal of protected forest, and reclassifying them as reserved forest. They were able to do this because most Dangis were still cultivating on a shifting basis in an area around their, by now, fixed village sites. Land, which was not being cultivated in a particular year, could be planted with saplings by forest employees and reclassified as forest.

In the late nineteenth century, about 66 per cent of the Dangs was classed as available for cultivation. By 1956–7 the figure had fallen to about 54 per cent. During the 1960s, the Gujarat government conducted a survey of the Dangs, aiming to give land-occupancy deeds to the cultivators. As a result of this survey, 79,913 hectares were classified as farmland, which represented 45 per cent of the total area.[37] Much of the cultivated land was omitted from this figure, as it was not being farmed at the time of the survey. Land deeds were distributed in 1970, on condition that the forest department would continue to own trees on the land and that the occupants could only lop branches for rab and not fell trees. No forest produce could be taken from the reserved forests, which by now occupied about 50 per cent of the Dangs. During the next decade, the forest department continued to encroach on farmland, often by planting trees against the wishes of the occupants. In 1981 only 51,186 hectares were recorded as cultivated land, or 36 per cent of the Dangs.[38] It was claimed that the land had been surrendered voluntarily, which was hardly credible in view of the rapid growth in population, creating a severe land hunger throughout the tract. These developments benefited chiefly the Gujarat government and the leaders of the labour cooperatives. Both had a vested interest in increasing their income by extending the forest and enforcing forest laws. As the farmlands of the Dangis were interspersed with tracts of reserved forest, it was all too easy for a peasant to break these laws by, say, allowing cattle to wander into the reserve. Anyone suspected of taking wood or other produce from the reserves was arrested and fined. Often, the only way of escaping such punishment was to bribe the forest guards who were nicknamed *kam-da chor* (chicken thief) for habitually demanding free chickens to look the other way.[39]

Contemporary Community Forest Control Movements

From the late 1970s, the people of the Dangs began to assert themselves against the forest officials and corrupt politicians. The chief demands—as recorded in a 1977 meeting—were that they be given a right to fell any tree on their land, that they be allowed to take bamboo from the forests, that land taken by the forest department for tree plantation be returned, and that a new survey of the Dangs be conducted to correct the shortcomings of the 1960s' survey. A new organization, the Gram Vikas Mandali, was started to voice these demands. The founder of this body was an Australian social worker, Barry Underwood, who was based in Ramu Thakare's village of Sarva. He enjoyed the support of some educated adivasi youths who felt that the forest officials and the leaders of the forest cooperatives were stifling the social and economic development of the Dangs. One of their chief demands was for more employment for educated adivasis. Barry Underwood, in contrast to the Gandhians, ran the organization democratically, encouraging the youths to be directly involved in decision making. Because of this, the organization not only continued to flourish after he left the Dangs in 1983, but extended its activities to adivasi women.

In 1986, alarmed at the rapid destruction of forests throughout India, the government imposed a moratorium on all cutting of trees in forest reserves. Thus, the forest labour cooperatives in the Dangs lost their chief reason for existence. The only work left involved conservation activities, and there was comparatively little employment in this sphere. Large numbers of Dangis were forced to migrate outside the Dangs to obtain seasonal agricultural employment in the plains of south Gujarat. Within four years of the moratorium, at least one-third of the entire population left the tract as soon as the monsoon was over, returning only in summer, before the next monsoon. Working conditions in the plains were extremely bad; the pay was very poor, and although the migrants could obtain a bare subsistence by such means, they could send back home very little money and often returned at the end of the season almost empty-handed. On the whole, the younger and fitter people migrated, leaving the elderly behind in a state of almost complete destitution.

Active resistance by the people of the Dangs began in 1989, when a dozen forest guards went to Gira-Dabdar village to confiscate wood that the villagers had allegedly taken from the reserves. Village women surrounded the guards and told them forcefully that the forest department had no right to the wood. They argued that the forest had been taken from the Dangi people by the government through trickery and that they had a moral right to earn their livelihood by using forest produce. The guards were forced to retreat. These women had been involved in the activities of the Gram Vikas Mandali, for which Gira-Dabdar was a stronghold. The event led on to a more organized and planned resistance. The leaders who now emerged were two outsiders—Irfan Engineer, a Naxalite from Bombay and Virsinhbhai Patel, a Chodhri adivasi of Songadh, in Surat district. In November 1989 they started an organization called the Adivasi Bhumihin Kisan Hak Rakshak Samiti (Association for the Protection of the Cultivation Rights of Adivasis). This built up a strong base in twenty-one villages in the western Dangs where the Gram Vikas Mandali had already been most active. There were members in an additional forty or so villages. Their chief demands were that a new survey of agricultural land in the Dangs be conducted and that land be made available in the forest reserves for agriculture.

The Bhils had, since the creation of the forest reserves in the late nineteenth century, refused to accept that the state had a right to prevent cultivation in what they maintained were their forests. This consciousness was preserved through stories describing how the gora sahebs (white men) had tricked them and taken the forests. Although by the 1980s the people were mainly cultivating fields outside the reserves, they still knew the location and names of the village sites which had been 'swallowed' by the reserves. They were known as the *juni gaothan* (old villages). Although in the past the Bhils had mainly asserted the right to cultivate these lands, the movement that emerged in 1989 included the Bhils, Konkanas, and other adivasi groups, such as the Varlis. It was informed by a strong belief that whatever their community, subaltern groups in the Dangs had common interests.

In early 1991, members of the Adivasi Bhumihin Kisan Hak Rakshak Samiti went into a thickly forested part of the reserve, which they said was a juni gaothan, and began clearing it. They demanded that their right to the spot be recognized. The forest department responded by sending in the police, and about ninety people were arrested and beaten. To intimidate others, raids were carried out on their original villages. In one case, the villagers fought back, surrounding a police party and forcing the subdivisional forest officer, to eat grass. They told him, 'You often call us cattle. Now see how it feels to be like that yourself.'[40] The police returned soon after armed with guns. They were met by a large group of Dangis armed with bows and arrows and slings. When the police acted high-handedly, they advanced menacingly, waving their weapons. A stone was hurled from a sling, and, panicking, the police retreated in confusion, abandoning two rifles.

The official in overall charge of South Gujarat, R.S. Pathan, felt that a more imaginative approach was needed to counter what he saw as the 'Naxalite threat'. By now the conflict was generating publicity for the forest administration outside the Dangs. Pathan had already been experimenting in parts of Surat district with new approaches to forest management, notably the formation of forest protection committees

(FPCs) in which local people were encouraged to be responsible for forest protection and were given, in return, certain rights to forest produce.[41] He had achieved some success in this, and felt that the strategy could be extended to the Dangs. Ironically, the Adivasi Bhumihin Kisan Hak Rakshak Samiti had, as part of its work, already begun organizing forest protection along such lines in two villages, with guards being posted at night to prevent illicit cutting by people from outside the Dangs. Pathan did not, however, try to build on this base.

Another problem with the FPC idea was that it ran against the interests of the leaders of the forest labour cooperatives. For them, the major problem was not that of forest protection but of labour employment—preferably under their control. Through their political influence they ensured that the scheme, which was eventually unveiled in October 1991, favoured their interests rather than those of forestry. Funds were to be made available to finance a new initiative, known as *van sathe vikas* (development with the forest). Local committees were to be established to organize road-building, small-dam construction, well digging, land levelling, soil conservation, gully-plugging, and to raise teak and fruit tree saplings. People were to be given bamboo at reduced rates to make bamboo items, which were to be marketed through a cooperative. The committees were to be under the village panchayats.[42] This meant that they would be dominated by the leaders of the forest labour cooperatives and their allies in the villages, and that by handing out employment they would be able to restore the hold they had lost after the moratorium on forest cutting. The whole exercise—as established in practice—had almost nothing in common with the FPCs established by R.S. Pathan elsewhere in south Gujarat.

The forest officials based in the Dangs, as well as the civil authorities, saw this as merely a distraction from the chief need, which was to restore their lost authority. They were troubled in particular that one of the leaders had Naxalite connections, for this was the first time that any militant communist had managed to establish a firm rural base among a subaltern group in Gujarat state. The officials therefore called in more than a thousand special reserve police to attack the villages in which resistance had been the greatest.

The reign of terror began in November 1991, when police officers went to Kosimda village and fired on a group of adivasis, killing a twenty-four-year-old Bhil woman named Taraben Pawar. Soon after, the authorities arrested and imprisoned the two leaders, Irfan Engineer and Virsinhbhai Patel. Local adivasi activists were seized and beaten severely. Villages were raided, people were thrashed, women molested, household utensils and grain-holders smashed, and property seized. The police threatened that if people did not leave the 'Naxalite group' they would suffer more of the same, and that Taraben would not be the only one killed. The terror continued until March 1992, effectively shattering the movement.[43]

The power of the forest department was thus reasserted. The grievances of the Dangs people remained, however, largely unredressed. Although certain forest officers, notably R.S. Pathan, wanted to evolve new strategies, they were unlikely to succeed in the prevailing antagonistic climate against the forest department. As we have seen, this antagonism has had a long history, and is likely to continue so long as no attempt is made to work with the organizations in which the people of the Dangs themselves have confidence. Although the Adivasi Bhumihin Kisan Hak Rakshak Samiti has been disbanded, the Gram Vikas Mandali is still active. Its members could be receptive to a more conciliatory approach at this juncture. What has to be worked out is a system in which farmers and foresters agree to allow use of forest produce and to maintain the forest in a sustainable manner. Besides building on the past methods of cultivation, new techniques would have to be evolved to allow for a more intensive use of resources, for the population pressure is far greater today. Ideally, such a system would be extended to the current reserved areas. This might, in fact, provide the best means for the preserving such tracts, which are now threatened by illegal cutting by people from outside the Dangs.

Even if the forest department radically rethinks its basic approach, which seems unlikely, there would still be the problem of alternative employment; unless this is provided, the pressures on the forest from farming will continue to grow. However, the whole issue of alternative employment is highly politicized. Dangi politicians want to control jobs, as this is a critical element in building a support base. Until 1986 this was done through control over the forest labour cooperatives, which had become little fiefdoms. Now, they hope to use the van sathe vikas initiative to this effect. Much of the money generated by such activities, whether cooperative or committee based, will almost certainly be misappropriated by the politicians. The benefits for the majority of the people will be minimal. Such abuses of power can be fought only politically, and, again, bodies such as the Gram Vikas Mandali provide most hope in this respect. Assistance and funds need to be provided to bodies with a record of working in an egalitarian way, to establish more equitable forms of development.

The history of the Dangs over the past two centuries has been one of defeat and loss of land and livelihood. However, it has also been a history of resistance by the people of the Dangs to the idea that farming in any way represents a threat to the forest. Despite often harsh repression, this belief prevails to this day. As yet, the Gujarat government has refused to accept that the people might have a case. Until it does, the contradiction between forest use and forestry will remain, the forests of the Dangs will dwindle year by year, and the people will continue to live in poverty and need.

Notes

Some parts of this essay have appeared in my contribution, in David Arnold and David Hardiman (eds), *Subaltern Studies VIII: Essays in Honour of Ranajit Guha* (New Delhi, 1993). Abbreviations used in the notes are as follows: BA: Bombay Archives (Maharashtra State Archives, Bombay); BRO: Baroda Records Office; F.D.: Foreign Department; NAI: National Archives of India, New Delhi; P.D.: Political Department; P. & S.: Political and Secret; Pol.: Poli-tical; R.D.: Revenue Department.

1. Shiney Varghese, 'Women, Resistance, and Development: A Case Study from Dangs, India', *Development in Practice*, 3(1), 1993, p. 11.
2. *Census of the Bombay Presidency*, 1872, pt 3 (Bombay, 1875), p. 632.
3. R.E. Enthoven, *The Tribes and Castes of Bombay*, vol. 2 (Bombay, 1875), p. 632.
4. A. Lucas to Collector of Khandesh, 1 September 1891, BA, R.D. 1892, 144/948. This report says that plough cultivation was confined almost entirely to Konkanas—hardly any Bhils or Varlis had ploughs. An account of a raid by Bhils on a village in the plains of Gujarat in 1809 mentions that nineteen iron ploughs were part of the booty carried away. It is possible that the Bhil chiefs encouraged such cultivation by the Konkanas by providing them with implements in this way. A. Skaria, 'A Forest Polity in Western

India: The Dangs 1800s–1920s' Ph.D. dissertation, University of Cambridge, 1992, p. 66.

5. Some Konkanas also carried on this form of agriculture. Kumri and dalhi were generic terms for it: the Dangi term was *khandad.* Skaria, 'A Forest Polity in Western India.
6. This form of cultivation is described by A.T. Shuttleworth, 6 April 1871, BA, R.D. 1871, 18/552; report on Dangs by E.M. Hodgson, 29 August 1902, BA, R.D. 1902, 107/949 II; Shuttleworth to E.W. Ravenscroft, 27 August 1877, BA, R.D. 1877, 69/1566.
7. Shuttleworth to Ravenscroft, 27 August 1877, BA, R.D. 1877, 69/1566.
8. Inquiry by J. Campbell, 5 July 1871, BRO, Rajdaftar office, serial no. 710, *daftar* V/426, file 113, Residency file nos. 167A and 316, pp. 126–38.
9. In 1828 the Gaikwad paid Rs 910 in protection money to Silpat. Silpat received almost no other such payments. G. Giberne to J. Williams, 20 January 1828, BA, P.& S. Dept. 1828, 29/320.
10. W.J. Morris to H.W. Reeves, 22 May 1843, NAI, F.D. Pol., 24 February 1844, pp. 1–10.
11. Report by W.J. Fenner on a tour of the Dangs in April 1856, in A. Gibson, *Forest Reports of the Bombay Presidency for the Years 1849–50 to 1855–56* (Bombay, 1857), p. 80.
12. Memo by the Gaikwad of Baroda, August 1864, BRO, Rajdaftar office, serial no. 719, daftar V/479, file GRS/7, Residency file no. I-73, p. 177.
13. Digby Davis, 14 September 1888, *Annual Reports on Western Bhil Agency, Khandesh,* British Library, I.S. BO 1/2.
14. Petition by Anandrao Virsingh, Raja of Vasurna, to Government of Bombay, 15 March 1843, BA, P.D. 1843, 20/1441.
15. W.H. Propert to E.P. Robertson, 26 March 1878, BA, R.D. 1878, 58/127.
16. For such a calculation, see Bombay Forest Report 1863–4, in *Forest Reports of the Bombay Presidency for the Years 1860–61 to 1867–68* (Bombay, 1869), pp. 115–16.
17. R.H. Madan to A.T. Shuttleworth, 28 October 1891, BA, R.D. 1892, 144/948.
18. *Administration Report of the Forest Department in the Bombay Presidency, including Sind, for the Year 1888–89* (Bombay, 1890), p. 13.
19. D. Worster, *Nature's Economy: A History of Ecological Ideas* (New York, 1985), p. 127.
20. Ibid., p. 171.
21. Jack Westoby, *Introduction to World Forestry: People and Their Trees* (Oxford, 1989), p. 80.
22. Richard Tucker, 'Forest Management and Imperial Politics: Thana District, Bombay 1823–1887', *Indian Economic and Social History Review* 16(3), July–September 1979, p. 281.

23. Ramachandra Guha, 'Forestry in British and Post-British India: A Historical Analysis', *Economic and Political Weekly* 18(44), 29 October 1983, p. 1884.
24. Report of the Commission on Dang Forests, September 1878, BA, R.D. 1879, 90/947.
25. Minute by Sir Richard Temple, 7 July 1879, ibid.
26. Agreement with Dang chiefs at Pimplaidevi, 2 May 1889, BA, R.D. 1889, 164/948.
27. Bombay Government Resolution, 15 December 1893, BA, R.D. 1893, 133/948; report by A. Cumine, 26 December 1894, BA, R.D. 1895, 314/948.
28. Report by J.A. McIver, 12 July 1899, BA, R.D. 1901, 151/949 I.
29. Report on Dangs by E.M. Hodgson, 29 August 1902, BA, R.D. 1902, 107/949 II; Annual Administration Report on Dangs, 1902–3, BA, Education Department 1903, 64/739; report by G.E. Marjoribanks, 3 July 1911, BA, R.D. 1911, 120/1113.
30. *Administration Report of the Forest Department in the Bombay Presidency, including Sind, for the Year 1903–4* (Bombay, 1905), p. 7.
31. Annual Administration Report on Dangs, 1906–7, BA, Education Department 1908, 63/739.
32. This account of the 1911 outbreak is based on reports by G.E. Marjoribanks of 16 May, 2 June, and 3 July 1911, and a report by F.G.H. Anderson of 3 August 1911, BA, R.D. 1911, 120/1113.
33. Ghanshyam Shah, 'Growth of Group Identity among the Adivasis of Dangs, Gujarat', *Journal of the Gujarat Research Society* 34:1, April 1972.
34. Ajay Skaria, 'A Forest Polity in Western India', p. 311. Although princely states were abolished in India after independence and the Bhil chiefs ceased to be considered rulers, they continued to receive their annual handout, which in 1954 was reclassified as a 'political pension'. They are given this at an annual function held at the time of Holi at Ahwa.
35. Satyakam Joshi, 'Dakshin Gujaratni Jangal Kamdar Sakhari Mandalio; Ek Abhyas', Ph.D. thesis, South Gujarat University, 1992, pp. 413–22.
36. Shiney Varghese, 'Women, Resistance, and Development', p. 5.
37. I have made these calculations using figures in *District Gazetteer: Dangs*, p. 211 and 'Dangna Adivasioni Ladat: Ek Tapas', *Arthat* 10(2), April–June 1991, p. 24.
38. S.P. Punalekar, 'Agricultural Profile of Dangs District', mimeographed report (Surat: Centre for Social Studies, 1989), p. 1.
39. See Shiney Varghese in *Development in Practice*, p. 7.
40. Ibid., pp.11 (footnote 16) and 14.
41. R.S. Pathan, N.J. Aral and M. Poffenberger, *Forest Protection Committees in Gujarat: Joint Management Initiative* (New Delhi, 1990).

42. Interview with N.K. Sinha, district forest officer, Dangs, December 1992.
43. Irfan Engineer, 'Dang: Report of Struggle and Repression of the Tribals', *Mainstream*, June 1992. Irfan Engineer and Virsinhbhai Patel were released at the end of March but have been banned from entering the Dangs.

David Hardiman

List of Publications

1. Books

Peasant Nationalists of Gujarat: Kheda District 1917–1934, Oxford University Press, New Delhi 1981.

The Coming of the Devi: Adivasi Assertion in Western India, Oxford University Press, New Delhi 1987. Gujarati version published as *Devi Andolan*, Centre for Social Studies, Surat 1986.

Peasant Resistance in India (edited collection with introductory essay by David Hardiman), Oxford University Press, New Delhi 1992.

Subaltern Studies VIII: Essays in Honour of Ranajit Guha (coedited with David Arnold), Oxford University Press, New Delhi 1994.

Feeding the Baniya: Peasants and Usurers in Western India, Oxford University Press, New Delhi 1996.

Gandhi: In His Time and Ours, Permanent Black, New Delhi 2003; Hurst, London 2004; Columbia University Press, New York 2004; University of Natal, Pietersmaritzberg 2004.

2. Articles

'Politicization and Agitation among Dominant Peasants in Early Twentieth Century India', *Economic and Political Weekly*, Bombay, vol. XI, no. 9, February 1976.

'The Crisis of the Lesser Patidars', in D.A.Low (ed.), *Congress and the Raj: Facets of the Indian Struggle 1917–1947*, Heinemann, London 1977.

'Baroda: The Structure of a "Progressive" State', in Robin Jeffrey (ed.), *People, Princes and Paramount Power*, Oxford University Press, New Delhi 1978.

'The Roots of Rural Agitation in India 1914–47: A Rejoinder to Charlesworth', *The Journal of Peasant Studies*, vol. 8, no. 3, 1981.

' "The Indian 'Faction": A Political Theory Examined', in R. Guha (ed.), *Subaltern Studies I*, Oxford University Press, New Delhi 1982.

'The Roots of Rural Agitation in India 1914-47: A Comment on Charlesworth's Reply', *The Journal of Peasant Studies*, vol.11, no. 3, 1984.

'Adivasi Assertion in South Gujarat: The Devi Movement of 1922–23', in R. Guha (ed.), *Subaltern Studies III*, Oxford University Press, New Delhi 1984. Translated into Gujarati as 'Devi Andolan', in *Arthart*, 1985. Translated into Hindi as 'Dakshin Gujarat mein Adivasi Atmagraha: 1922–23 ka Devi Andolan', in Shahid Amin and Gyanendra Pandey (ed.), *Nimnvargiya Prasang, Bhag 1*, Rajkamal Prakashan, New Delhi 1994. Translated into Bengali as 'Debir Abirbhab', in Gautam Bhadra and Partha Chattopadhyaya, *Ninmabarger Itihas*, Ananda Publishers, Calcutta 1998.

'Congress Organisation in Gujarat During the Nineteen-Twenties and Thirties', in D.N. Panigrahi (ed.), *Aspects of Indian Economy, Society and History*, Vikas, New Delhi 1985.

'From Custom to Crime: The Politics of Drinking in Colonial South Gujarat', in R. Guha (ed.), *Subaltern Studies IV*, Oxford University Press, New Delhi 1985.

'Subaltern Studies at the Crossroads', *Economic and Political Weekly*, 15 February 1986.

'The Bhils and Shahukars of Eastern Gujarat', in R. Guha (ed.), *Subaltern Studies V*, Oxford University Press, New Delhi 1987.

'The Quit India Movement in Gujarat', in Gyanendra Pandey (ed.), *The Indian Nation in 1942*, K.P. Bagchi, Calcutta 1988.

'Class Base of the Swaminarayan Sect', *Economic and Political Weekly*, Bombay, vol. XXIII, no. 37, September 1988.

'Towns of an Adivasi Tract', in M.J. Mehta (ed.), *Urban History of Western India*, Gujarat University Press, Ahmedabad 1989.

'Penetration of Merchant Capital in Pre-Colonial Gujarat', in Ghanshyam Shah (ed.), *Capitalist Development: Critical Essays*, Popular Prakashan, Bombay 1990.

'Power in the Forest: The Dangs 1820–1920', in David Arnold and David Hardiman (ed.), *Subaltern Studies VIII*, Oxford University Press, New Delhi 1994. Translated into Gujarati as *Jangal Vistarma Sattana Sambandho: 1820thi 1940nu Dang* (Relationships of Power in the Jungle Tracts: The Dangs 1820–1940), and published as a short monograph by the Centre for Social Studies, Surat 1994.

'Community, Patriarchy, Honour: Raghu Bhangare's Revolt', *The Journal of Peasant Studies*, vol. 23, no. 1, October 1995.

'Small-Dam Systems of the Sahyadris', in David Arnold and Ramachandra Guha (ed.), *Nature, Culture, Imperialism: Essays on the Environmental History of South Asia*, Oxford University Press, New Delhi 1995.

'Usury, Dearth and Famine in Western India', *Past and Present*, no. 152, August 1996.

'Farming in the Forest: The Dangs 1830–1992', in Mark Poffenberger and Betsy McGean (eds), *Village Voices, Forest Choices: Joint Forest Management in India*, Oxford University Press, New Delhi 1996. Reprinted in Vandana Madan (ed.), *The Village in India*, in the series 'Oxford Readings in Sociology and Social Anthropology', Oxford University Press, New Delhi 2002.

'The Alternative Economics of Liberation', *Asian Age*, 10 March 1997.

'Usury in Western India: State Policy and Peasant Resistance 1876–1947', in Ghanshyam Shah (ed.), *Social Transformation in India: Essays in Honour of Professor I.P. Desai*, vol. I, Rawat Publications, Jaipur 1997.

'Origins and Transformations of the Devi', in Ranajit Guha (ed.), *A Subaltern Studies Reader*, University of Minnesota Press, Minneapolis 1997.

'Well Irrigation in Gujarat: Systems of Use, Hierarchies of Control', *Economic and Political Weekly* (Bombay), vol. 33, no. 25, 20 June 1998.

(With Parita Mukta), 'The Political Ecology of Nostalgia', *Capitalism, Nature, Socialism*, vol. 11, no. 1, March 2000.

'Passing Blame on Godhra Muslims', *Economic and Political Weekly*, Bombay, 11 May 2002.

'Christianity and the Adivasis of Gujarat', in *Labour, Marginalisation and Migration: Studies on Gujarat, India*, in Ghanshyam Shah, Mario Rutten and Hein Streefkerk (eds), Sage Publications, New Delhi 2002.

'The Politics of Water in Colonial India,' in *South Asia: Journal of South Asian Studies*, vol. 25, no. 2, August 2002.

'Assertion, Conversion and Indian Nationalism: Govind's Movement amongst the Bhils', in Rowena Robinson and Sathianathan Clarke (eds), *Religious Conversion in India: Modes, Motivations, and Meanings*, Oxford University Press, New Delhi 2003.

Entry on 'Famine Relief' in Joel Mokyr (ed.), *The Oxford Encyclopaedia of Economic History*, vol. 2, Oxford University Press, New York 2003.

Entries on Richard Couch, J.B. Peile, C.B. Pritchard and Vithalbhai Patel for *New Dictionary of National Biography*, Oxford University Press, Oxford 2004.

'The Politics of Water Scarcity in Gujarat,' in Amita Baviskar (ed.), *Waterscapes: The Cultural Politics of a Natural Resource*, Permanent Black, New Delhi 2007.